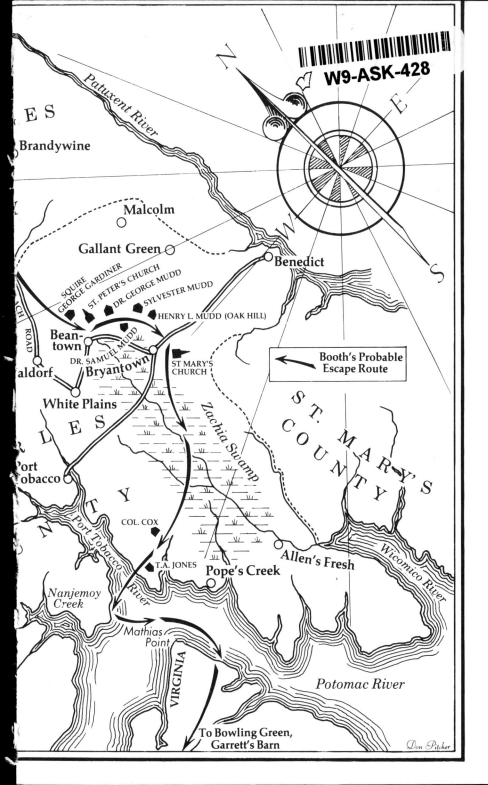

Ethel K. Smith Library

Wingate University
Wingate, North Carolina 28174

The unlikely figure of Dr. Samuel Alexander Mudd has long been the center of one of the major controversies of American history. Born into the tobacco aristocracy of Maryland's patrician Charles County, he could easily have lived and died without creating more than a regional ripple. Instead he found himself catapulted onto the front page of every newspaper in the country in the weeks, months and years following the assassination of Abraham Lincoln, and even today scholars and amateur historians still debate what role he may or may not have played in the murder of America's sixteenth President.

In THE RIDDLE OF DR. MUDD, Samuel Carter presents the first full-scale biography of this enigmatic man, a major feat of research in view of the number of the doctor's private papers that were destroyed by fire or confiscated by the government in the period surrounding his trial. What he stood accused of was conspiring to assassinate Lincoln.

(Continued on back flap)

THE RIDDLE
OF
DR. MUDD

By Samuel Carter III

G. P. PUTNAM'S SONS
NEW YORK

To B. N. N.
— or Tuesday in Paris, if she prefers

Copyright © 1974 by Samuel Carter III

SBN: 399-11370-3
Library of Congress Catalog
Card Number: 74-79641

PRINTED IN THE UNITED STATES OF AMERICA

Contents

*Illustrations will be found
following page 192.*

FOREWORD AND ACKNOWLEDGMENTS

ON a quiet country road in southern Maryland, on the northern fringes of Zachia Swamp, stands the modest frame home built in 1857 by Samuel Alexander Mudd. A small porch has been added since the doctor's time; the fields are well tended; there is an air of sunny peacefulness about the place. Except for a small historical marker at the entrance, there is little to distinguish this unobtrusive dwelling as the site of one of the fateful encounters of history, an encounter that holds so much of the mystery still surrounding Lincoln's assassination at the hand of John Wilkes Booth.

Yet comparing the stories of the two men, Samuel Mudd and John Wilkes Booth, one cannot avoid the feeling that their meeting here in April, 1865, had a certain predestined quality about it—as if their lives had been on a collision course from the beginning. Considering Mudd's position as a Maryland country doctor and Booth's plans for escape through Maryland, it was inevitable, in the light of attending circumstances, that their paths should cross and that the hour should mark a point of no return for both of them.

In a grim way Booth came out perhaps the better of the two. He had achieved a lunatic goal and did not live to see the consequences. But Samuel Mudd was forced to live through those consequences and bear the burden of them, to become one of the more controversial figures of his time. Though the Mudds of Maryland are today, as they have been through the centuries, one of America's distinguished families, the controversy remains.

To the explorer of history, Samuel Mudd emerges as a challenging personality not so much because of what is known about him as what can never be known about him. Those who follow his story are obliged, as often as not, to do their own editing, draw their own conclusions. Mudd's biographer confronts the same dilemma. Even where abundant records are available, they are so often contradictory that one can only accept those facts and versions that seem to fit the picture best and be aware that others may not agree with the selection or interpretation.

Except for the letters he wrote in prison, there is little autobiographical material about the doctor. All Mudd's personal papers, his farm and medical records, any journals or diaries he may have kept, were confiscated by the federal authorities at the time of his arrest. What little might have remained, especially records and papers relative to his childhood, family life, and education, were destroyed when his parental home, Oak Hill manor, burned to the ground in 1881.

So one is reduced to seeing Mudd largely through the eyes of his contemporaries, his friends and relatives and to some extent, after 1865, his enemies. Three sources above all have been relied on in preparing this account. Foremost is the two-volume genealogy, *The Mudd Family of the United States,* compiled and published by Samuel Mudd's grandson, Dr. Richard D. Mudd of Saginaw, Michigan. My sincerest thanks go to the author for his patient answers to my queries and for his help in tracking down material not included in his eminently thorough study of the family.

Dr. Mudd's two-volume genealogy combined with Nettie Mudd's biography of her father, *The Life of Samuel A. Mudd,* recently reprinted by Dr. Richard Mudd and including most of the doctor's earlier letters to his wife from prison, give a fairly comprehensive picture of the doctor's life. To cover the circumstances of his trial and its day-to-day proceedings, a third book, Benn Pitman's *Assassination of President Lincoln and the Trial of the Conspirators,* rounds out the story in its particulars.

With these three major points of reference I have followed my own, sometimes hit-or-miss, procedure in tracking down the more personal, intimate facts of the life of Samuel Mudd. This led me to Washington and Baltimore and to a pilgrimage through the country of the Mudds of Maryland, Charles County especially; there it was possible to trace the probable route of Booth's flight through the county to Virginia. Though somewhat like following the blind leads of a paper chase, the end was gratifying.

For background material on mid-nineteenth-century Maryland, much guidance was received from Mrs. Nancy G. Boles, Curator of Manuscripts at the Maryland Historical Society in Baltimore, and from Mary Boccaccio, Archivist at the McKeldin Library at the University of Maryland. Additional material was obtained from the manuscript division of the Enoch Pratt Library in Baltimore, and the excellent, locally oriented files of the Charles County Library at La Plata, Maryland.

Records of Dr. Mudd's pursuits at college and medical school are scant, beyond the basic facts of registration and curriculum, but helpful suggestions were received from Judge Edward S. Delaplaine of Frederick, Maryland, where young Sam began his education, and from Miss Miriam Strange, Archivist at St. John's College in Annapolis. For the research assistance of Miss Anne Blair of Baltimore I am much indebted, especially for her patient, time-consuming search for those small but important details that add flesh-and-blood reality to any story.

Unless one knows something about tobacco, the life of the Maryland planter is far less familiar than that of the cotton barons of the deep South. While early copies of the Port Tobacco *Times* were a source of much contemporary market information, I owe special thanks to Dr. Claude G. McKee of the Maryland University Extension Service, who was kind enough to outline the probable routine and procedure followed at Samuel Mudd's Rock Hill Farm near Bryantown.

Concerning the key year of 1865 and the trial of the Lincoln conspirators, the city of Washington is of course a gold mine. Contemporary newspaper accounts of events in that year, including the *National Intelligencer's* verbatim report of the trial (to supplement Benn Pitman's records), were obtained at the Library of Congress, along with additional published material and many of the illustrations appearing in this volume.

My special thanks, however, go to Mr. Elmer O. Parker of the National Archives and Records Service, who gave the matter of Dr. Mudd's trial and material pertaining thereto his personal attention. Many documents referred to in the text, not included in Pitman's work, came from this source as well as from the National Archives, Legislative, Judicial and Fiscal Branch, headed by Mark G. Eckhoff.

For information on Dr. Mudd's days at Fort Jefferson in the Dry Tortugas there is no more knowledgeable source than Miss Betty Bruce of the Dade County Library in Key West. From the library's files came biographical data on D. W. Whitehurst and J. Sim Smith, along with background material on Fort Jefferson before and during Dr. Mudd's imprisonment. Miss Kathy Kirby, National Park Service historian, supplied additional research data on the fort. I owe special thanks to Jack Kirkland, manager of Fort Jefferson National Monument, for a directed tour of the premises—surely one of the more impressive and authentic historical sites in our national history.

Valuable aid came often from distant sources. Only a few pages of the Fort Jefferson "Prison Book," or daily report on the guards and prisoners, remain available at Garden Key. But missing pages were acquired through the kindness of Larry E. Burgess, Curator of the Lincoln Shrine at Redlands, California. Further information on Fort Jefferson, its garrison, and its prison personnel were obtained from Mrs. Mary Jane Kuh, Executive Secretary of the Florida Historical Society in Tampa, from David T. Alexander, Museum Director of the Historical Association of Southern Florida, and from Samuel Proctor, editor of the Florida Historical Quarterly in Gainesville.

A more personal note of thanks is owed to Mr. and Mrs. Joseph Mudd of Bryantown for their gracious hospitality at Dr. Mudd's old home in Maryland, still well groomed in their care; to Mrs. Jessie Porter Newton of Key West who may not remember, years ago, arousing my interest in Samuel Mudd by showing me samples of his prison handicraft; and to Mrs. Rita Ann Lofink for her expert typing of these pages.

1

FROM STRANGEWAYS BY THE ARK AND DOVE

ZACHIA Swamp in southern Maryland stretches in an undulating arc from a little north of Bryantown to Allen's Fresh at the mouth of the Wicomico River. Fifteen miles long and five to ten miles wide, it is not so much a single everglade as a chain of sumps and marshes, interspersed with spongy hills. Rusty streams crisscross the area, creeping into Wicomico Creek, the marsh's spine, or ending in deep ponds wearing the dyed scum of decaying vegetation. Dense growths of black gum, water ash, and juniper are nesting grounds for owls and turkey vultures. The creeks are alive with snakes, lizards, muskrats and occasional otters.

Until its partial reclamation, Zachia Swamp, in the early nineteenth century, was no fit place for human habitation. A few trails sneaked through the wilderness, passable to those who knew them well. Some trappers, hunters, and swamp guides lived in huts on Wicomico Creek. Smugglers and fugitives found a transient refuge in the jungle vegetation. But it was only at the swamp's extremities—at Allen's Fresh, for instance—that the land was sufficiently drained to cultivate and communities could develop.

To the north, near Bryantown, the swamp surrendered, though reluctantly and only here and there, to rising ground and arable land: rich loamy soil of red clay, perfect for tobacco. Around what could be called a ridge, by contrast to the tidal swampland, stretched the plantation of Henry Lowe Mudd, named Oak Hill for the grove of trees in which the great plantation manor stood.

Oak Hill dominated the landscape as the Mudds themselves

had dominated Zachia Swamp for nearly two hundred years. Compared with the homesteads of Virginia planters or the Greek Revival mansions of the Georgia piedmont, the house lacked elegance and grandeur. Its gaunt frame structure, tall and gabled, reflected some of the dark foreboding of the swamp itself. Only its whitewashed clapboards made it stand out on the hillside with appropriate authority. For authority was what it symbolized, along with spartan discipline and rectitude. Cheerless perhaps, but as solid and enduring as the Mudds themselves.

Henry Lowe Mudd, born in 1798 and named for Maryland's Governor Low, to whom he was distantly related, was a sixth-generation member of the Mudds of Maryland who had settled and named Charles County in the seventeenth century. Since his only brother had died before the age of eighteen, Henry inherited most of his father Alexis' property on the east side of Zachia Swamp, known as "The Devil's Nest." He was also bequeathed a horse, saddle and bridle, three slaves, and presumably an ample sum of money. The latter enabled him to add to the plantation several sections of arable bottomland—which he christened "Mudd's Double Trouble," "Little Philadelphia," "Jordan," and "St. Catherines" —bringing his total holdings up to 850 acres.

Like his forebears, Henry Lowe was born to be a tobacco planter, which, short of the professions and often combined with the professions, was the appropriate calling for a country gentleman in lower Maryland. In 1826 he married Sarah Ann Reeves, the only daughter of Dr. James Reeves, whose mother was a Dyer. This, too, was according to acceptable pattern. Within the limits of Charles County there were perhaps a half-dozen families that measured up in stature to the Mudds, and two of them were the Reeves and Dyers. They had already intermarried and would go on doing so.[1]

Daguerreotypes of Henry Lowe and Sarah Ann, taken shortly after marriage, suggest the portraits of Thomas Hart Benton. Both have a sort of determined, pioneer look about them, as if they had been caught staring out across the Great Plains. Henry has the proverbial high forehead of the family, amplified by receding hair, a long dominating nose, thin

lips above a firm chin, and eyes with the gleam of judgment
in them. The sunbonneted Sarah has a softer look, appropriate to womanhood, with conventional features disturbed
by widespread eyes. Her mouth, too, is firm and lean. They
must have been a no-nonsense couple; similarities of features
and expression suggest that they were made for one another.

Simultaneously with his marriage to Sarah, Henry Lowe
began the construction of Oak Hill Manor. That it should
dominate all he surveyed was not the reason for its location;
it had to rest on dry land firm enough to hold it. For by
the standards of the county, which belittled ostentation, it
was a large, impressive home, containing, downstairs, a
parlor, dining room, study, and library—the latter harboring
one of the finest book collections in the area. Upstairs the
chambers were equally spacious, for the Mudds were a prolific
clan, and Henry Lowe intended that his branch of the family
would be no exception. A classroom and dormitory for his
children were constructed before the children were conceived.

A feature of the manor was the Catholic chapel on the
second floor, following the home chapel tradition started
by the early generation Mudds. Here Mass was said every
Sunday for the family and neighbors who cared to attend;
the officiating priest came from St. Mary's Church in Bryantown, of which Henry Lowe and his neighbor Dr. William
Queen were trustees.

The couple's first son, James Anthony, was born in the
summer of 1829. A second son, also named James, died prematurely. Four days before Christmas, 1833, their third child
arrived. He was christened Samuel Alexander for six earlier
Samuels and two preceding Alexanders. Yet to come was
a string of six daughters and another son—a large brood
that was typical of family tradition, starting with the patriarchal Thomas Mudd two centuries before.

Trying to track down the ancestral source of the Mudds
of Maryland is like trying to trace the original star in the
Milky Way. Somewhere in England, presumably in Yorkshire,
they seemed to explode into existence and spread prolifically
throughout the fifteenth century. Their names were spelled

variously Mode, Moody, Mudge, etc., but seemed to derive from the Anglo-Saxon Mod or Modh, signifying "courage, vigor, and spirit." One record indicates that "the Mudds in England for many generations had been doctors and lawyers and were distinctly Saxon in type, being tall, blue eyed and sandy haired." Which particular branch of the family produced the Mudds of Maryland is difficult to say. There are abundant documents—all contradictory.

Legend suggests that the earliest Mudds to arrive in America sailed from England in 1633 aboard the venturous vessels *Ark* and *Dove* with Leonard Calvert, second Lord Baltimore, seeking the freedom to worship as Catholics, which the British Crown denied them. Legend further indicates that they originated from the small Lancashire town of Strangeways, no longer on the English map, said to have been located between Bryn and Wigam. This vagueness as to name and place suggest that the town was a rainbow figment of imagination, especially since one of the brothers traveled under the pseudonym of "Strangeways Mudd," possibly to avoid identification by his religious persecutors.[2]

Legend aside, the first authenticated name of an early Mudd arriving in America appears in *A Record of the First Settlers in the Colonies of North America, 1654 to 1685*. Here it is stated that "Thomas Mudd departed from Bristol, England on Aug. 14, 1665, bound to Anthony Noakes for three years in Va." The fact that Thomas sailed from Bristol tells nothing of his birthplace, since Bristol was the point of departure for emigrants to the New World from all over England. So one might as well settle for the possibly mythical town of Strangeways. Likewise, the fact that Thomas was bound to Anthony Noakes for three years, thus starting life in the colonies as an indentured servant, is no indication of poverty. In 1665 Thomas would have been only eighteen years old. To secure passage across the Atlantic he would have to have bound himself to someone, since he was not yet entitled to his inheritance.

From this starting point the story of Mudds in America becomes well documented, if extremely complicated. Thomas served out his indenture in Virginia, and then, assembling eight pioneer colonists like himself, crossed the Potomac into

Maryland. The enlistment of eight recruits entitled him to 450 acres of the vast land granted by King Charles I to the first Lord Baltimore. Thomas named his section "Mudd's Rest," but he did not settle for this tiny territorial beginning. Through a judicious marriage to Sarah Boarman, widow and heiress of Major William Boarman, he acquired a vast 2,000-acre tract known as "Boarman's Reserve" and annexed to "Mudd's Rest" such picturesquely named marshlands as "Mudd's Confusion," "Mudd's Confession" and "The Devil's Nest." Near "The Devil's Nest" the couple built the Old Homestead, a white-frame, gable-roofed manor, which became the cradle of Charles County Mudds.

Thomas' son Henry inherited Boarman's Reserve along with the Old Homestead and passed it on to his offspring Thomas, who married into the prestigious Gardiner family of Charles County. Thomas, in his will, divided the property among his three sons—Henry, or "Harry," receiving the property that embraced the Homestead. Known as "Priest Harry" or "Henry of Devil's Nest," he was the first of the Mudds to add, at some personal risk, a chapel to the manor. Here, with priests brought clandestinely from the surrounding parish, Henry conducted regular Catholic services, which were forbidden at the time.[3]

The restriction on religious worship caused many later-generation Mudds to migrate to the West, floated by flatboat down the Ohio River to Missouri. Others trekked by wagon train across the Appalachians to Kentucky. In this first state to be settled in the west, they made Washington County their particular domain, just as they had named and populated Maryland's Charles County.

In Kentucky at the turn of the century, Mary Mudd, granddaughter of the patriarchal Thomas, married Mordecai Lincoln, brother of Thomas Lincoln of nearby Hardin County. At different intervals Mordecai and Thomas and their respective wives gave birth to sons they christened Abraham. Fifty-five years later Abraham Lincoln of Hardin County, sixteenth President of the United States, would lie dead of an assassin's bullet, while Mary Mudd's Abraham Lincoln would hang his head in bewilderment and shame.[4]

Priest Harry died in 1810 and "The Devil's Nest" and the

Homestead passed on to his second son, Alexius (or Alexis or simply "Alec"), father of Henry Lowe and grandfather of Samuel Alexander Mudd. The Homestead subsequently went to the elder of Alec's two sons, Thomas Alexander, while Henry settled for the horse and bridle and the land on which he built Oak Hill Plantation. For reasons not traceable, the Old Homestead, considered the ancestral birthplace, drops out of mention in the story of the Mudds; and Henry Lowe's Oak Hill becomes the center of the clan.

If it could be said to have had a center. For by that time, in the second quarter of the nineteenth century, there were Mudds all over southern Maryland. There were Mudds in Port Tobacco and Prince George's and St. Mary's counties. There were Nanjemoy Mudds on the peninsula east of the Nanjemoy River. There were younger-generation Mudds in Washington and Baltimore, but not many of them, for even the restless young were bred to the rural planter's life. How much land they owned collectively is impossible to calculate.

Using tobacco in hundred-pound quantities for currency, they traded in land among themselves to the point that it was uncertain just which Mudd owned what. Boundaries were hazy, and property was identified principally by such descriptive names as "Mudd's Confusion," "Hickory Thicket," "Mudd's Hard Bargain," "Freedom," "Strife," and "Prickly." With respect to a different form of property, that of slaves, the same vagueness about ownership prevailed. Slaves seemed to move like shifting sand among the different households and plantations, and the fact that they often assumed the names of their masters and mistresses must have driven the early census takers to distraction.

For all practical purposes, however, Zachia Swamp in Charles County was the home of the sixth-generation Mudds, and Bryantown might be held to be the family seat, allowing that Oak Hill was the official or at least outstanding homestead of the clan. The political seat of Charles County, however, was Port Tobacco, a bustling, prosperous, undisciplined seaport at the head of the Port Tobacco River. It was a logical choice, for waterways took the place of roads in southern Maryland—only a single highway, often impassable, led for sixty miles down from Washington through Surrattsville and Bryantown to the lower Potomac and Port Tobacco.

The harbor town reflected the obsessive tobacco interests of lower Maryland, where the wealthy planters formed the ruling aristocracy. A good half of the tobacco grown, generally the better grades, was exported to Europe, especially to France. Port Tobacco's jerry-built wharves were picket-fenced with the masts of French sloops and schooners, along with the spars of the coastwise vessels bound for Baltimore and Charleston and Savannah. Sold at home and abroad, tobacco was a handsome-paying crop, and the lives of the planters came close to matching those of the Georgia and Louisiana cotton barons.[5]

Something of a tradition for tobacco planters as a class was established at an early day by Franklin Weems at Mount Republican, of whom a local historian recorded:

> Weems was one of the great "bon vivants" of Southern Maryland in his day and is said to have kept his cellar filled with fifty barrels of brandy and the best wines, of which he partook freely himself and freely dispensed to his friends to whom he was host in a life-long celebration. It is told in perfect seriousness in Charles County that Franklin Weems kept a poker game going in Mount Republican continuously for forty years. Three times a week he entertained a party of young people and many mornings he set out upon a fox hunt without having been to bed at all for more than twenty-four hours. A pack of one hundred fox hounds were maintained at Mount Republican and many of the best hunting dogs in Maryland have the blood of these hounds in their veins.[6]

A similar social life seems to have prevailed on the plantation of Daniel Jenifer on the banks of the Wicomico River. As a Maryland congressman, Jenifer entertained his congressional cronies, including such illustrious guests as Henry Clay and Daniel Webster, at hard-drinking, card-playing house-parties commonly spoken of as "fishing trips." The fishing began in the morning following an all-night card game, the guests being given poles with the lines already submerged by the time they reached the riverbanks. Reeling in on signal, the uniform catch turned out to be a bottle of champagne for every angler.[7]

But one can dismiss Weems and Jenifer as typical only of the abuse of wealth and privilege in the slaveholding classes, not typical of members of those classes. Such luxurious living from the profits on tobacco could not, of course, have existed without slavery. And in Charles County at about this time, a single, seemingly insignificant incident sounded the death knell of that institution. A slave named Josiah Henson suffered such abuses at the hand of his Charles County master that he fled to Canada in 1830, leaving behind a life story that Harriet Beecher Stowe immortalized in *Uncle Tom's Cabin*.

Samuel Alexander Mudd was born twelve years before that epochal novel started circulating. And although life at Oak Hill was far removed from that exemplified by Weems and Jenifer, self-denial was practiced only as an exercise in discipline. His father, Henry Lowe, was above average in means; his portion of Devil's Nest had grown by steady accretion to more than 850 acres; his three inherited slaves had, by birth and purchase, grown to eleven. His family had expanded, too. After the two Jims and Sam came, in close order, Mary, Anna, Sarah, Henry Lowe, Jr., Frances and Elizabeth.

Unlike their counterparts on plantations farther south, in Virginia, Georgia and the Carolinas, none of the Mudds was a prolific correspondent, diarist, or record keeper. But Henry Lowe's granddaughter Nettie left her impressions of mid-century Oak Hill, writing of the estate, which,

> for more than a mile, extended along the "Old Mill Swamp," gradually rising on the east side of a stream known as the Zachia. The surface of the land increased in elevation from the Swamp until, with a steep upward sweep, it ascends to a high hill, sloping toward the north and south, the summit crowned with locusts and wide-spreading oaks; from these it derived the name it bears, "Oak Hill."
>
> On the top of the hill was built the old homestead. In architecture it was not different from other houses in the vicinity. Wide, old-fashioned halls and spacious rooms, sub-

stantially furnished, formed a comfortable abode and place of entertainment for the family and visiting guests. At the north wing of the house was the schoolroom, where many childish tears were shed, and many airy castles were built never to be realized. Above this was the home chapel. Bed chambers occupied the remainder of the second floor.

Viewed from the nearest point in the valley it presented in appearance a large structure without any architecturally definite shape. Outside it looked well enough. It seemed to the eye roomy and hospitable. A large lawn, sloping to the public road, was dotted with shrubbery, which contrasted prettily with the white background formed by the painted weatherboarding of the house.[8]

That Nettie looked through rose-colored glasses at this background of her youth is suggested by her description of life on Henry Lowe's plantation, "where may have been seen more than a hundred slaves, who made the evenings merry with song, and with banjo and violin accompaniment. Scattered over various sections of the farm may also have been seen the 'quarters' of these humble colored folk, who were always treated with the kindest consideration by their master and mistress, and who would say of these white friends, after they had passed from earth, 'God bless my old Marse and Miss; I hope dey is in heaven.' "

A practical view of the plantation would have been less idyllic. For tobacco was the most arduous of all crops, and its cultivation more demanding than the cotton of the deep South. Except for the horsedrawn plows, it was essentially a hand operation, from the tender planting of seedbeds in the early spring to the husking, stripping and hanging of the leaves in autumn. Though the plantations were often huge, running to thousands of acres, only a small percentage could be planted to tobacco since one man, working full time, was required for each two to three acres.

Though modern (for the time) methods of farming, including crop rotation, had already reached lower Maryland, the risks were great for the tobacco planter. Droughts caused the crop to fail, heavy rains caused excessive growth of coarse, unacceptable leaves. And for all practical purposes, tobacco was the single crop of southern Maryland, the coin of the realm, determining the fate and fortune of the people.[9]

Maryland farmers had little good to say about tobacco, but they planted it with compulsion, often themselves working in the field, with their slaves and indentured servants, till their hands were stained brown with nicotine.

But stained hands or no, tobacco raised them above the common level to the hazy stature of the Southern cavalier. Certainly tobacco made them what they were and gave them the qualities one Maryland historian lists as openhanded sociability, conviviality, a high sense of honor and chivalry, along with "arrogant and empty pride, a musty conservatism, and the various forms of ancestor worship peculiar to the region."

Those traits might well have applied to Henry Lowe Mudd, and to some extent been passed on to his son Sam. Not much, however, is precisely known about Sam's father, beyond the recollection of one descendant, who noted of Henry Lowe that "He was kind and charitable but exacted strict obedience from those around him." The plantation was run like clockwork, with horns summoning the hands and family to meals, bells sending the children off to school, and Henry Lowe's sharp commands keeping his slaves at work with military discipline. It may be that strictness that caused his first son, James, to leave home at an early age, without attending college, and go in for farming on his own. He did not quit Bryantown, but to all appearances he kept his distance from Oak Hill.

That left young Sam to grow up with one older sister and a growing succession of younger sisters as his playmates; his only other brother, Henry, born in 1844 and therefore eleven years his junior, could hardly qualify as a companion in the early years. In this matriarchal atmosphere he must have been a lonely youngster, and perhaps his father was aware of it. The children of well-to-do planters were generally taught by tutors in the home, but when Sam was eight, he went experimentally to public school in Bryantown.

The interval lasted only fourteen months, but it introduced him to two people who, as much as any other two that one could name, would drastically affect his life. Young Daniel Thomas, of about Mudd's age, found Sam pleasant company and "full of fun and jokes"; and there were other school- mates who remembered Sam as a quiet, fun-loving youngster. But Sam found Daniel Thomas a sneak, a liar, and a vicious prankster; he did not put his opinion in words, but others of Daniel's class and generation would put theirs in stronger words. Sam would live to regret the day he ever met young Thomas.

At the pinnacle of his preference among his Bryantown schoolmates was petite, brunette Sarah Frances Dyer, of a stalwart Maryland family that had emigrated from England in the seventeenth century. Two years younger than Sam, Frances had an elfin, poutish charm, and a tomboyish vivacity uncommon to restricted young ladies of her generation, a spirit that totally captivated the twelve-year-old Mudd. She lived with her parents and brother Jeremiah on a farm con- tiguous to Oak Hill, so their classroom acquaintance had opportunity to ripen into an enduring friendship.

It was a blow when father Henry Lowe Mudd decided to take Sam out of public school to be tutored at home with his sisters by an English-born spinster known only as Miss Peterson. It did not end his attachment to Frances, but imposed some limitations on it. There was little social contact between the sexes even at that early age, no country dances, no formal athletic events, no county fairs, or parish picnics. Though Charles County families were convivial, they were convivial with the family clan, and as yet the Dyers had not married Mudds—a situation Sam intended to correct.

The principal social activity of the county, peculiar to lower Maryland, were the summer "tournaments" held at Bryan- town and Brandywine. They had a certain medieval flavor to them, being primarily tests of riding skill, in which the local and invited "knights" tilted with lances at targets hung from the branches of trees or raised by props above the ground. Each knight sparred for the lady whose colors he wore around his sleeve, and the contest followed a lordly tradition until, when all was over, the kegs of beer were opened, the oysters shucked, and a music band from

Washington struck up the raucous verses of *Hey, Betty Martin* and *Old Zip Coon*.[10]

Sam Mudd would have been too young to participate in these events. While he certainly knew how to ride, he seems rarely to have hunted, fished, or explored the marshy wilderness around him. He reportedly did well with his studies under Miss Peterson and began taking an interest in music, practicing on the organ in the chapel and the pianoforte in the parlor, which Henry Lowe Mudd considered as much the mark of a gentleman planter as the rare books lining his library from floor to ceiling, most of them never read or opened.

So one sees Samuel Alexander Mudd at age fourteen a somewhat lonely, moody, sensitive youngster, restricted for the most part to Oak Hill Plantation and the company of younger sisters; disciplined to rectitude and proper manners by a strict and somewhat dour pair of parents; surrounded by an awesome colony of highly respected Mudds—aunts and uncles, great aunts and uncles, first and second cousins —which must have given him at least a sense of identity and stable background.

As much time as possible was spent with Frances, whom he started calling "Frank"—a nickname suggested perhaps by her gamin qualities, perhaps by Sam's feeling of need for male companionship. Even at this early age she became the pivot around which his life revolved. If he thought of marriage, he thought of Frank—the difference in his case being that an adolescent dream was destined to become reality.

Seventy miles north of Oak Hill Farm, on the family estate at Bel Air, John Wilkes Booth was growing up in a precisely opposite atmosphere, to a way of life that would have been incredible to Mudds. Spoiled by a drunken genius of a father and a weak, indulgent mother, Wilkes was born into a heavenly mayhem—living solely for himself, by standards he created from an overripe imagination. Perhaps Ned Spangler, carpenter on the Booth estate, came close to understanding him; for Spangler, too, was a rootless character riding on the winds of whim. But no one really understood

John Wilkes—not his elder brother, Edwin, nor his sister, Asia, who adored him, nor his drunken genius of a father, Junius Booth.

Junius laid down only one rule to his four acknowledged sons, namely that no living thing should be hunted or killed on the plantation. "A robber of life can never give back what he has taken," he advised his boys. And he quoted Pythagoras to the effect that, "Every death its own avenger breeds." John Wilkes paid little heed to this advice. He shot everything in sight, from the slaves' hounds around the farm to a neighbor's sow who strayed upon the property. One biographer suggests that this compulsion to kill animals derived from "no other reason than that this was the most sacred of the family taboos."[11]

Though Junius hoped to give his sons a better education than he himself had had, which was virtually none at all, young Wilkes protested against home tutoring on the grounds that he preferred to roam the woods on horseback—an argument to which his father yielded. His older brother, Edwin, who preferred to play the banjo and was studying to be an actor, considered Wilkes relatively harmless, but "a wild brained" youngster "who would charge on horseback through the woods on the Maryland farm, spouting heroic speeches, holding in his hand a lance, a relic of the Mexican War." The role of a Don Quixote sparring at imaginary windmills would appeal to him more greatly with advancing years.

When fall came, the Booth family moved from Tudor Hall —the grandiose name for the decaying, ill-kept mansion at Bel Air—to their winter home on Exeter Street in the better part of Baltimore. Here young Wilkes ran with his own rat pack of juveniles, sharing its leadership with Michael O'Laughlin, a dark-haired lad of lonesome eyes who lived across the street. John Wilkes and his companions roamed the alleyways of Baltimore as Wilkes had roamed the woods of Bel Air, climbing over backyard fences, hitching rides on street cars to the waterfront where the forest of ships' masts from around the world matched the forest of masts at Port Tobacco farther south.

In Baltimore John Wilkes first attended public school.

Municipal funds allowed no more than a single teacher to a grade, and chance placed before him, at the desk beneath the classroom blackboard, the most unlikely candidate one could have chosen. Sarah Ann Mudd, Sam's only paternal aunt, had followed one of the few channels open to the females of the Mudd clan, that of sisterhood or teaching, separately or combined.

Marriage had brought Sarah to Baltimore, and teaching afforded the independence that the Mudds, as a family, respected. The subjects she taught are not recorded. More important, what manner of communication passed between this fifty-year-old teacher, reared on conservative traditions, and the undisciplined Booth, who was already shutting out society and defying all authority, is impossible to say. Quite possibly Sarah found something appealing in the large, dark, hungry eyes of the Latin-looking youth; most women did. But even so, they must have seen one another as creatures from a different world, across a wide gap that yet another strange coincidence would some day bridge.[12]

"In no portion of the hospitable state of Maryland can be found a more high-toned and cultivated society than that of Charles County," wrote a mid-nineteenth-century journalist, defining the family of Henry Lowe Mudd and descendants as "one of the oldest and most honored" of that county.[13]

It was indeed a proud and close-knit society that Samuel Mudd was growing up in, a community composed almost entirely (if one counted only those who mattered) of intermarrying Mudds, Gardiners, Dyers, Reeves and their relations, who together created a somewhat ingrown and provincial Catholic dynasty in southern Maryland.

"Not that there was a monotonous uniformity among them," wrote Richard D. Mudd, family genealogist. "No characteristic seems to have been cultivated more sedulously than individuality." Dr. Mudd goes on to give a picture of his Maryland ancestors:

> The average home of the early Mudds was not out on the highway but hidden among a cluster of leafy elms;

roses garland the ample porch, and honeysuckles strive
at a hundred points to break through the windows to enjoy
the warmth within. Children's laughter and the bark of
the watch dog and the cackling of the guinea hen are the
only noises, unless the pea fowl scent a coming storm and
cry out their shrill warnings. Within all is labor, labor of
love. The wife is proud of the table she has prepared for
the return of the husband and son from the toil in the
fields, and the daughter emulates the mother, who watches
with satisfaction the young arms equalling in dexterity her
best culinary art. The tired workmen sit at their meal, after
grace is said, and rarely in words but always in looks, render
thanks and sweetest praises to the earthly as well as the
heavenly Bestower.[14]

One cannot quarrel with that picture. For as a family, the
Mudds of Maryland were devout, high-principled, and
dedicated to the land, blessed or cursed by a certain naïveté
born of limited horizons. They were oriented to the clannish
Southern way of life, more deeply steeped in tradition and
ancestor worship than was general in America.

Oak Hill, three miles northeast of Bryantown, was the
center of the family constellation, around which spun the
satellite plantations: the mansions and fields of Grandfather
Alexis Mudd, Uncle Thomas and Great Aunt Sarah, and
Cousin Jeremiah Theodore Mudd, who in later life so closely
resembled Abraham Lincoln that he was often mistaken for
the President. As the circle widened, one came, at the rim,
to the plantations of the cousins, second cousins, in-
laws—Boarmans, Edelens, Gardiners, Poseys, Clarkes (the
names were endless)—all linked as by the spokes of one tight-
structured wheel.

Except for some with individual leanings toward medicine
(the most acceptable of the professions), all were tobacco
planters. They took their hogsheads of tobacco to the river
port of Benedict on the Patuxent River; frequented Port
Tobacco only for supplies; rarely visited, in these late years,
the tawdry, crime-ridden capital of Washington, with its
struggling pretensions. When they went anywhere, it was
to one another's houses, often to stay for days or weeks.
Mudds lived with Gardiners, aunts stayed with cousins. It

was almost communal living, on, however, an exalted scale.

There was little social or intellectual life except that to be found at Port Tobacco, the county seat and rather shabby social center of the district. The weekly Port Tobacco *Times*, besides carrying price quotations for Maryland tobacco and other crops, filled its pages with sentimental novelettes by "Emmie Emerald," but it could hardly compete with the Washington or Richmond papers or with *Godey's Lady's Book*, obtained by mail from Philadelphia. Occasional dramatic troupes came down from Washington to perform in tents outside the village; and the Port Tobacco Literary Debating Club met every Wednesday afternoon at three—a time that allowed for the horseback or buggy journey into town—to consider such topics for discussion as: *Does Caloric emanate directly from the Sun, or is it latent in the atmosphere or earth, and produced by light?*

A circumscribed existence, surely, and one that imposed an inescapable, predestined pattern on the life of Samuel Mudd. He would become a planter or a doctor, marry Frances, bring an appropriate number of young Mudds into the world. He would prosper modestly, worship devoutly, and pass away with honor, to be buried in the family plot behind St. Mary's Church. If no great tragic or ecstatic happening were apt to overtake him, nothing wrong was apt to happen either. Life for Sam in 1847 appeared uncomplicated, simple and secure.

To young John Wilkes Booth, spending that summer on the family plantation at Bel Air, life was not similarly patterned and secure. No family ties or parental guidance lay across his path. Ignoring his father's insistence on the Fifth Commandment, he amused himself by taking potshots at his mother's cats. For one so young, he handled the .54 Mississippi rifle well.

2

GENTLEMAN PLANTER, M.D.

THE Charles County gentleman planter, though he might have nicotine-stained hands and calluses, put a high premium on education. The first Lord Baltimore had written that "tobacco is our all, and indeed leaves no room for anything Else." Tobacco growing had not changed a great deal since the Calverts' time, but culture had gained a toehold in Charles County. Mudd daughters, after tutoring at home, attended Catholic academies and convents; Mudd sons learned Greek and Latin, studied for the ministry or won degrees in medicine or law. Then, and only then, did they usually chuck the whole thing over and return to their predestined calling—the exacting, exasperating, generally prosperous role of the tobacco planter.[1]

Though Sam Mudd's education was destined to follow the pattern of most well-born youths in lower Maryland, there was a slight departure from the norm when he reached the age of fifteen. Young love may have been an explanation. Most youngsters living south of Washington attended Charlotte Hall in St. Mary's County, a school of strong religious leanings. But in the fall of 1849 Frances Dyer, to whom young Sam was still devoted, entered the Visitation Academy in Frederick, Maryland, and simultaneously Sam Mudd's name appeared on the student roster of Frederick College in that city.[2]

It may not have been solely the pursuit of Frances that took him seventy miles from Bryantown, a goodly distance in those days before the Baltimore and Ohio was completed.

The Reverend Charles H. Stonestreet, president of Frederick College, came from a Maryland family only slightly less distinguished than the Mudds, and there had been some ties between them. Land deeded by Nicholas Stonestreet to Theodore Mudd in 1836 composed part of the Mudd family holdings, and Sam's devout father, Henry, was undoubtedly impressed with the clerical standing of the Frederick College president. Sam's cousin, Sylvester, Uncle Theodore's son, had also entered Frederick College three years earlier.

There could have been little or no contact between Sam and Frances in the two years he spent at Frederick College. Discipline was the essence of education; discipline and education were, in fact, synonymous. Latin, Greek and mathematics were the principal studies taught by the old-fashioned rule of the hickory stick. There were no athletic or social diversions, though one can assume Sam had a chance to pursue his interest in music in what little extra time he had. Summer vacations lasted through July and August, but otherwise holidays were few. Several days' recess at Christmas was allowed to students who lived near enough to Frederick to go home; otherwise Stonestreet discouraged leaving the school grounds at any time, and never without express permission of the president.

In the fall of 1850 Stonestreet himself moved on to a post at Georgetown College in the District of Columbia, and Sam followed him there the next year. The only other undergraduate college he might have attended was that of the University of Maryland in Baltimore, which was having its feverish ups and downs in trying to achieve the status of its Georgetown rival. Though the forty-year-old Georgetown College remained principally a training school for the Catholic priesthood, it had a high scholastic rating in the classical and foreign languages, and, oddly enough, in astronomy and seismology.

He was enrolled in the school as a boarder in mid-September, 1851. Here, at a less gawky eighteen years of age, he began to acquire many of the social graces and moral standards common to the Maryland gentry. He was moving up the ladder into an elite circle, for less than one in a thousand Maryland youths attended college. Though the entrance requirements were strict, demanding a command of Greek and Latin, ability to pay the tuition was more of a deciding factor. Sam's older brother, Jim, had turned his back on higher education and was already looking for a bride with whom to settle down to farm life. As a consequence the boys' father was more than ever willing to splurge on Sam.

Georgetown took up where Frederick College had left off. Just to get into the college Sam was obliged to pass written and oral examinations in Caesar, Ovid, Virgil, and Xenophon, plus tests of his ability to translate English dictation into Latin. Colleges, observed one Maryland professor, were "not so much places for acquiring general information, as intellectual gymnasia, where the mental and moral faculties were trained and strengthened, and the student instructed how to use his powers to best advantage."

The life was spartan; schoolrooms were large and bare; students sat on straightback chairs, using their knees as desks to write on. Classes were two hours long, with time given to inculcating "principles of virtue, moral character, and purity and refinement of taste." For, as noted in the prospectus, it was the express duty of the faculty "to impress notions of order, decency, and good manners, to form the habits of industry and attention by which youth are secured from idleness and consequent depravity."[3]

Notwithstanding this severe, restrictive regimen, young Sam managed to pursue and develop his interest in music, acquiring a high degree of proficiency on the piano, flute and violin. His keen ear for tone and harmony enabled him to pick up almost any instrument and master it in little time. Music, though recommended for young ladies, was not considered an average gentleman's pursuit in Maryland, and Mudd's dedication to the art is the unique feature of his early education.

After graduating in the spring of' 1854, Sam spent the summer with his family at Oak Hill. None of his sisters was of marriageable age as yet, and only Jim had left the homestead. But he still sought companionship away from Oak Hill.

He spent as much time as possible at the Dyers', renewing his pursuit of Frances, who had graduated from the Visitation Academy with high honors. It was time for this courtship to reach a conclusion, but Sam's future was still unsettled. He seemed at this point to have no inclination to become a farmer, but just when his interest turned to medicine is impossible to say. He had an inviting example in his older cousin George, now a well-established doctor whose practice extended over all three southern counties of the state.

Henry Lowe and his family were dedicated readers of the Port Tobacco *Times*, a source of both political and social gossip and a guide to market prices for farm products and tobacco. In midsummer an uncustomary advertising card appeared on the front page of the paper:

> The 47th Annual session of the School of Medicine will commence on Oct. 9, 1854, and end March 1, 1856. The Baltimore Infirmary, which belongs to the school, offers abundant means for the Clinical illustration of the principles of Medicine and Surgery.
>
> G. W. MILTENBERGER, M.D., DEAN

In educational circles in Maryland, Dean Miltenberger's was a legendary name. As a student at the university, he had promoted the first "sit-in" in America's scholastic history, helping to force the transfer of authority from state to faculty in 1839. Now, as dean of the school of medicine, he headed one of the six top schools of its kind in the nation, with a monopoly of medical education in the state of Maryland.

The original College of Medicine of Maryland, established in 1807, had for the past half-century, with a change of name, been the center and *raison d'être* of the university. Schools of law, divinity, and arts and sciences had been added to justify the larger name; but the medical school was unique in its superior rating. Though it had gone through periods of "gloomy dilapidation and despondency," it had survived with high professional standards.

Attendance did not commit one to practicing medicine. A third of the school's graduates went on to become planters, politicians, merchants, clergymen, or journalists; and some practiced medicine as a sideline. But the medical diploma was the hallmark of an educated and well-rounded individual, somewhat as a law degree would later become an open-sesame to politics, government service, and certain forms of business. Perhaps that in itself appealed to Sam who had not, unlike his cousin George, had any premedical training to test his aptitude in this direction.

George himself had graduated from the university's school of medicine, as had two other Mudds, Jerome and John, back in the 1820's. Sam's cousin, James Marcellus Mudd, Uncle Theodore's son, was to enter the school that fall. But it was doubtless George's influence that prompted Sam to apply to Dean Miltenberger for admission; and George most likely assured him of an apprenticeship in his Bryantown office after graduation.

The fact that he had a college degree made acceptance in the university almost certain. Few of those applying for the two-year course in medicine had been to college; in fact, the school, despite its outstanding reputation, was having difficulty finding qualified applicants with sufficient money for tuition. It found about thirty percent of them among the well-to-do planters' families of southern Maryland.

There was yet Frances to consider. Sam was twenty now; too old, he thought, for the waiting game. In late summer, with the determination of one with a visible, imminent career, he proposed to her.

Frances' response revealed a certain impish quality in her nature, an untypical reluctance to let go of independence. It was not the reply of a meek submissive maiden, nor that of a sentimental Southern belle. As she told her daughter, Nettie, some years later:

"There was nothing romantic in our love affair, and it was impossible to think of getting married just then. When Sam asked me, 'Frank, are you going to marry me?' I answered, 'Yes, when you have graduated in medicine, established a practice for yourself, and I have had my fun out, then I'll marry you.'"

When Sam questioned what she meant by "having her fun out," she reassured him, "You need not be jealous; I promise I won't have anybody else."[4]

Apparently satisfied, Sam wrapped his bible in the conservative black clothing he wore, packed his sheet music, flute, and violin, and headed by coach to Baltimore. From all indications he never unpacked, or at any rate never touched, the flute and violin, or seriously resumed his music. A new era was dawning; he was about to acquire an exclusive skill that would be his ultimate undoing—one that would, like a fatal magnet, draw into his life the malignant, crippled form of John Wilkes Booth.

To natives of that shady quarter of Baltimore the college was something like a medieval castle, silent and secret behind its high stone walls. The walls had been a necessity during the time, not long before, when medical students were regarded as fiendish grave robbers who bought their cadavers from assassins, with no questions asked. A mob had stormed the school when it was rumored that the body of a woman's missing husband was being dissected in a second-floor chamber, "reached only by a winding stairway," in the so-called practice building.

The walls had gone up; but the school of medicine, despite popular disapproval, had made dissection compulsory in 1848—the first but one of the medical colleges in the country to overcome squeamishness and prejudice. As a result, Baltimore became known as "the Paris of America," not for light-hearted gaiety, but because of its surfeit of "morbid and healthy cadavers." Even the distinguished Nathan Ryno Smith, professor of surgery, established a sort of business monopoly for the college, reaping a tidy profit from the sale of cadavers to other schools.

In a confidential letter to a surgeon at Bowdoin College in Maine, Smith described the operation:

> It will give me pleasure to render you any assistance in regard to subjects. I think you may rely upon having them. I shall immediately invoke Frank, our body-snatcher (a better man never lifted a spade), and confer with him on the matter. We can get them here without any difficulty at present but I would not have the world know that I have winked at their being sent out of the state.
>
> I will cause about three to be put up in barrels of whiskey.

I suppose they will require about half a barrel each, of whisky. This at 35 cents a gallon will be $16.80. The barrels a dollar each; the subjects, the putting up, etc. $10 each, making in all $50.00.[5]

Sam Mudd was fortunate in attending the school when such medical giants as Professor Smith, Samuel Chew, George Miltenberger, and William Aiken were on the faculty. They were of a new, dynamic generation, replacing the archaic hierarchy previously led by Granville Sharp Pattison—a playboy surgeon so supercharged with mercury, which he swallowed as a cure for syphilis, that he was reluctant to open doors for fear of the electric shock the doorknobs gave him. Pattison, however, made one giant contribution by promoting the construction of the college's infirmary, providing for 150 patients who paid three dollars a day for bed and board, nursing care and doctor's fees. Apart from its benefit to the public, the infirmary offered practical intern experience to the undergraduates, and Sam Mudd spent his second year assisting at the hospital.

The infirmary, the three-story practice hall, and the main building, built to look like the Pantheon of Rome, were the nucleus of the tiny university on Greene and Lombard Streets. In Sam Mudd's time and up to the Civil War, the medical school faculty numbered only seven, all so versatile they could stand in for each other as occasion warranted; the student body fluctuated between 200 and 300, with 63 graduating in an average year.

The curriculum consisted of two six-month terms extended over two years. Tuition amounted to $20 for each course, or $140 for the seven courses taught by the seven professors; the students made their own arrangements for boarding in the city. A list of expenditures compiled by one undergraduate came to $271.23 for the year, including such diverse items as tobacco, and "lost at whist."[6]

Possibly it was at medical school that Sam developed his fondness for tobacco and for any form of cards. They were the only vices in his temperate and cautious nature. He did not smoke, but kept a wad of Maryland Light concealed between his upper lip and jaw, so carefully concealed, in fact, that few knew he used tobacco. His devotion to whist and poker constituted his only form of relaxation, both in college and in later life. Even during vacations at Oak Hill he hardly ever fished or hunted or rode for pleasure; he did not read novels, even those of the popular Washington Irving or Charles Dickens; never attended the theater, and confined his social activities to church on Sundays.

Though medical students of mid-nineteenth-century America were classically regarded as a rowdy lot, the discipline at the college offered little opportunity for high jinks. Lectures started at nine—late on the assumption that the students had been burning midnight oil in preparation—and continued until seven in the evening, Saturdays not excepted. There were no vacations beyond a day at Christmas, and rooming houses sanctioned by the university closed and locked their doors at ten. As a consequence, student deportment was exemplary, and membership in the college was accompanied by acceptance into the better homes of Baltimore.[7]

Unfortunately the better homes were in another part of town. The university's location in the southeast corner of the city was a neighborhood of slums and poverty, far removed from the residential section around Exeter Street where such better-class, if individualistic, families as that of actor Junius Booth resided.

Though Sam Mudd took all the obligatory courses at the university, ranging from anatomy and surgery to the brand-new microscopy, his idol and mentor among the faculty was Samuel Chew, professor of principles and practice of medicine. A forty-eight-year-old Marylander, Chew was described as "dignified and reserved in manner, but genial with his friends," characteristics that washed off on Mudd himself. When it came time to graduate in the spring of 1856, Sam dedicated his forty-page thesis on dysentery to Dr. Samuel Chew.

He won none of the gold and silver medals that were awarded to outstanding students upon graduation but did return home with his diploma and some practical experience gained by side work at the college's infirmary—part of this experience being treatment of the strange disease of yellow fever, which briefly struck nearby Norfolk in 1855. Frances had stipulated that they would be married "when you've established a practice for yourself." It was easier said than done. Though generally underpaid and unappreciated, medicine was an overcrowded profession in Maryland, with one doctor to every six hundred people in the southern counties, one of the highest ratios in the nation.

Sam, however, had Cousin George to help him get started. The earlier practice of learning medicine by apprenticeship to an established doctor had evolved to postgraduate apprenticeship as a means of developing a practice of one's own. For the next two years Sam worked as George Mudd's assistant, accompanying him on house calls, assisting him in the setting of broken limbs, the cleansing and bandaging of wounds and sores, the treatment of diseases. Though medicine was still in an elementary stage, with purging and bleeding a cure for nine-tenths of human ills, it had developed a code of ethics and responsibility well above the rum-and-laudanum quackery of the first half of the century.

By the fall of 1857 Sam felt qualified to start out on his own and Frances agreed. On Thanksgiving Day, November 26, they were married at the Dyer home in Bryantown. It was not a double wedding, although Sam's older brother Jim was married on the same day to Emily Mary Boarman of the landed Boarmans, who had deeded so much property to Mudds.

As a wedding present, Sam's father gave him two hundred acres of farmland north of Oak Hill, on Gallant Green Road between Malcolm and Beantown. The term "gave" is loosely used. Henry Lowe doled out land to his children right and left, but whether or not they actually owned that land or were simply living on it through Henry's good graces was not clear. Sam's property was known as "Dr. Mudd's farm," just as the adjacent acreage was known as his cousin Sylvester's farm, but matters of boundary and legal ownership were always hazy.

Until Sam could build a house of his own, the couple lived with Frank's bachelor brother Jeremiah at the Dyer home, rather than in the more ample but forbidding mansion on Oak Hill. Sam conducted his practice out of George's office in Bryantown, making house calls on horseback and carrying his medicine kit on the pommel of his saddle, in the manner of the frontier doctors of the West. He performed "kitchen surgery" on straight-legged tables, boiled water and sterilized his instruments in dishpans, delivered babies, mended broken limbs with boxwood splints, and compounded his own pills and nostrums from supplies obtained from the Apothecaries' Hall in Port Tobacco.

Despite dedication, long hours, and hard work, his practice did not flourish, notwithstanding referral patients from his cousin George. One might surmise that George had already garnered the cream of the not-prolific crop. Home remedies and mail-order nostrums from the country almanacs were relied on by poorer families in the county, and it was from the poorer families that young Dr. Sam got many of his patients. Pay was often slow in coming, if it came at all, and like many country doctors, he often found himself performing the role of veterinarian, prescribing for an ailing mule or treating the sores on a horse's leg.

By the summer of 1857, however, he and Frances were able to move into their own two-story home, erected on the land provided by Sam's father. It was a pleasant enough location, four miles north of Bryantown on slightly rising land that he had cleared of trees. The house itself was a nearly square, conventional frame building with a gabled roof. On the ground floor a small hall led to a large high-ceilinged parlor on the left; behind that the dining room with an adjoining kitchen; and off the dining room a small chamber that Mudd used first as an office, later as a bedroom for himself and Frances when the children came along.

A steep, narrow staircase, facing the front entrance, led from the small front hall to the second story. A sizable guest room, with twin beds, occupied the right front corner of the upper floor; to the rear of that, a master's bedroom; and across the hall a bedroom-dormitory for the children yet to come. Behind the house were the outhouses, barns and cabins for the slaves he would have to have if the farm were to prosper—for it was apparent by now that he would have to supplement his income with some paying crops, a not uncommon practice for a country doctor.

Nonetheless, his heart was still in medicine; the pursuits of a tobacco planter would, he believed, constitute no more than a profitable sideline. That fall, even before he and Frances moved into their new home, which they christened Rock Hill Farm, Sam leased or borrowed slaves from his father and Cousin Sylvester and began plowing the fields that sloped south and east for his first crop to be planted in the spring. He would henceforth have two professions, those of gentleman farmer-planter and respected country doctor. The future for him and Frances, at this youthful point in their lives, was bright with promise.

On the Kennedy Farm, just seventy miles northwest of Dr. Mudd's, there was a similar bustle of activity and preparation. The farm had been rented to one Isaac Smith, and since midsummer wagonloads of heavy boxes labeled "Picks" and "Axes" had been arriving at the place, to be unloaded and stacked in the barns by a growing band of laborers, black and white. Mr. Smith and his two sons had several times made the five-mile trip across the river to Harper's Ferry, where the bearded New Englander was known to be interested in farming and mining in the neighborhood.

On October 16 the "picks" and "axes" from the opened crates became pistols, rifles, pikes and ammunition, and John Brown, alias Isaac Smith, alias "Old Osawatomie," made his celebrated raid on Harper's Ferry. Though southern Maryland breathed easier when Colonel Robert E. Lee and his marines arrived to repossess Harper's Ferry after the holocaust, the incident marked a turning point in the life of Samuel Mudd—one that would prove more drastic to him than to many other Marylanders caught between the two sides of a growing conflict.

It marked a turning point in the life of John Wilkes Booth as well, as Booth watched John Brown's body swinging on the scaffold. Despite his profession of a passionate love for the South, he would never enlist to fight for her survival. But on this occasion he had briefly joined the Richmond Grays, a stylish volunteer militia, for the express purpose of attending John Brown's hanging. As he stood with the honor guard beneath the gallows, he felt a twinge of admiration for "the brave old man" who "had been deserted." A lonely martyrdom was a good, dramatic exit from life's stage.[8]

From that moment on, the Maryland-born Booth considered himself a champion of Southern causes, deserving of the South's applause. He would forever after tell his listeners that he had helped to capture and hang Old Osawatomie, the archabolitionist. But meanwhile he lost no time in shedding the uniform of the Richmond Grays to return to the theatrical costumes that became him better. Though physically fit and adroit with foil and firearms, he would never risk having his features scarred in battle—having made that promise, he said, "for mother's sake." He would seek his fame in other ways—on a stage, behind the footlights, and before an audience.

In the wake of John Brown's body, time moved a little faster in America. It had been gathering speed since the beginning of the decade. "The first undercurrents of the Civil War were already being felt in the county by the early 1850's," wrote Calvert Posey, Charles County historian, distantly related to the Mudds of Maryland. Continued Posey:

> The county was on the route much traveled between the North and South, which made it the target for the propaganda of both sides. Being slave owners themselves, the Charles Countians felt the pressures that were being brought for the abolishment of slavery. The slaves themselves were becoming restless because of this pressure and their closeness to freedom. It had become so general that by 1856, nightly patrols were maintained in the county to prevent their escape.[9]

Samuel Mudd in 1859, the last year of relative normalcy in southern Maryland, continued to double as country doctor and tobacco planter; but there was a sense of urgency throughout the county quite uncommon to its usual tidewater calm. The barrage of abolition propaganda from the North bred fears and rumors of slave uprisings on plantations bordering Zachia Swamp. "Incidents which seemed to verify rumours merely increased the prevailing tension," wrote Dr.

Richard Duncan in his study of Maryland conditions at the time. He added:

> In one such incident six negroes attacked their owner's house in Charles County during his absence but were repulsed with a gun by the owner's wife. The local neighbors threatened to hang the attackers and only through the intervention of the master's wife were the slaves saved and merely whipped as their punishment.[10]

Perhaps the nightly patrols—which continued up to, and more or less secretly through, the Civil War—were warranted. The officers were appointed by the Justice of the Peace, who more often than not was a Mudd relation. Sam's cousin and neighbor, Sylvester Mudd, joined one of these units, and Dr. George Mudd took time off to serve as needed. It was not so much a partisan, anti-abolition action, as a civic duty and responsibility. Sam did not participate simply because he had his hands full with his double duties, and Frances, already tied down with their first child, Andrew, was expecting another child in June.

By that time, the spring of 1860, he was doing comfortably well. His medical practice was slow, but he was getting the top price of $12 a hogshead for his light tobacco. He had seven slaves, worth $2500 each on the Washington or Richmond markets, along with an indentured English handyman, John Best. The slaves seemed loyal, although he was having trouble with young Elzee Eglent, who was becoming intractable. Other slaves, at Oak Hill, on Sylvester's farm, at Squire Gardiner's neighboring plantation, had grown restless, too. Many were simply taking off, perhaps into Zachia Swamp for refuge or perhaps up North, however they could get there. On the shores of the Potomac and the Eastern Branch, on both sides of Washington, vast black communities, like the casbahs of North Africa, were mushrooming up, providing a faceless and inpenetrable ghetto jungle for the fugitives.

To the Maryland tobacco planter, as it was to the cotton growers farther south, slave labor was essential to survival. Measured by the acre, it took from thirty to forty man-hours simply to prepare a field or plant a seedbed. Mudd's projected twenty-five acres of tobacco, which he planned for 1860, would require at least four hands devoted to that crop alone. On top of that would be the job of cultivating other fields for necessary crop rotation, not to mention the need for human labor to tend the horses, livestock, drainage ditches, and the other countless chores around the farm.

Which made this abolition propaganda from the North such total folly. It was not only idiotic in his mind, it was *unpatriotic*—threatening the structure of American society at its best, for the Southern way of life was surely superior to the godless existence of the North. If only the Yankees could be made to understand.

"A majority of the people of the North," he wrote, in one of his rare outbursts on the subject, "believe Slavery to be Sinful, thereby they attempt to force down our throats their religious Convictions, which is Anti Catholic and uncharitable. . . .Christ, our Saviour, found slavery at his coming yet he made no command against its practices. Therefore I think it is a great presumption in man to supply the omissions which God in his infinity thought proper to make."[11]

Plainly, in the doctor's eyes from now on, God was with the South, no matter what course the nation followed in the wake of John Brown's body. Plainly, too, the Mudds of Maryland were on the side of God.

Sam and Frances, little more than two years married, would never see another spring of peace again. The war would come and go for others but for them, the scars resulting from the war would never heal. An abyss was opening before the entire nation; they were doomed—though mercifully they did not know it—to live in its depths for the remainder of their lives.

3

THE DESPOT'S HEEL

"IT is the longing of my heart that the same old Star Spangled should continue to wave over the land of the free and the home of the Brave," wrote Dr. Sam Mudd, at a time when such a possibility began to seem beyond hope. He was not solitary in that longing. In the early months of 1860 such was the sentiment of many, if not most, of the Charles County planters. Let the Union be maintained, but let the North keep hands off when it came to sacred institutions of the South.[1]

But as 1860 moved toward the fall elections, apprehension rose and hope waned. With the Democrats divided between Breckinridge and Douglas, a Republican administration seemed assured. And with Abraham Lincoln in the White House, who could tell what dire consequences would result? This was the worst time in the world to have a Northerner as President. One of the planter-doctor's few surviving letters on the subject provides a small key to his thinking and character:

> The people of the South are differently constituted from those of the North—attributable to education and climate. As an example they are more sensitive—their sense of honor is much more keen and they would sooner run the risk of death, than live with an injured reputation. It is seldom you hear of a duel in the North, where parties are challenged to mortal combat to settle their grievances, but you find instead a recourse to law—a few dollars satisfying the dishonored.[2]

41

Recourse to law, respect for the courts, was not too common in the family. True, Francis Scott Key, the author of *The Star-Spangled Banner* had been an attorney for Thomas James Mudd, Dr. Sam's cousin; but after the case was settled Thomas turned around and sued Key, presumably for faulty representation. In general, however, the Mudds stayed away from court. When Sam Mudd needed an attorney to certificate a will or represent him in a realty transaction, he went to Port Tobacco, to a rising young lawyer named Frederick Stone, who would one day defend the doctor's right to live.

On November 6, 1860, Charles County voted almost solidly for Breckinridge and was dismayed to learn when the count was in that, though the popular vote went to the two combined Democratic candidates, Lincoln had won by 180 electoral votes over 72 for Breckinridge.

The reaction in Mudd country was immediate. The call went out for a citizens' meeting to be held near Bryantown in mid-December to censure those of the county who had cast their votes for Lincoln. A committee of three, which included Sam's cousin William Mudd and two distant Mudd relations, was appointed to take "appropriate action" toward seeing that the miscreants left Charles County before January 1.[3]

No more drastic act of repudiation occurred in America before South Carolina, five days later, declared that "the union now subsisting between South Carolina and . . . the United States of America is hereby dissolved." Over Fort Moultrie, South Carolina, the state's Palmetto flag was raised. The die was cast, and throughout Maryland crowds rallied to pro-Union meetings in the northern sections of the state, to secessionist meetings in the southern counties. North of Baltimore, only in John Wilkes Booth's hometown of Bel Air did the local *Aegis* declare that "Maryland's loyalty should be tied with Southern institutions and honor."[4]

The federal government moved quickly to fortify and later seize Fort Taylor in Key West and Fort Jefferson in the Dry Tortugas in the Gulf of Mexico. Few people saw Fort Jefferson as more than a monument to folly. Its construction had begun in 1846 in anticipation of the war with Mexico and had never been completed. Its lichened, crumbling walls already sinking in the sand, its dank cells and cracking casemates would be of little use in defending the Gulf or fulfilling its projected role as the Gibraltar of America. But it would prove useful as a dungeon for army deserters, captured spies, and intractable Southern prisoners of war. To Samuel Mudd it was a pinpoint on the map. For now.

That Christmas in Maryland, as in the rest of America, was shadowed by the growing crisis of partition. Frances had borne a second child, Lillian Augusta, a few months before, and lost no time in becoming pregnant once again. Their third child, Thomas Dyer, would be born on July 6, 1861. The slaves on the farm were becoming restless, and, with the family expanding, Sam Mudd was worried. A large part of Maryland's tobacco trade was with the South. If Maryland stayed with the Union and Virginia followed South Carolina's secession, the Potomac would become a barrier that would make Charles County an isolated island.

Like Kentucky and Missouri, Maryland was a border state, a slaveholding state but with its interests divided between North and South. The Baltimore *Sun* advised a posture of neutrality, an unrealistic attitude impossible to maintain. During January, as Mississippi, Florida, Alabama, and Georgia left the Union, Governor Thomas H. Hicks cautioned the people of Maryland, in a strongly worded message, against the folly of secession; at the same time, in a somewhat contradictory reaction to the crisis, Hicks called for new recruits to strengthen the Maryland militia.

Charles County Marylanders laughed up their sleeves at the prankish reports that Abraham Lincoln, on the way to Washington for his inauguration, had passed through their state disguised as a woman in skirts, veil, and shawl. It was true that precautions had been taken to protect the President's arrival—Baltimore was a hotbed of secessionist conspiracy—but the false report was seen as an insult to Maryland's sense of Southern hospitality and honor. A few days later Lincoln was sworn into office by Maryland's Chief Justice

Roger Taney, who had already expressed the sentiments of Maryland by declaring that Congress had no authority to limit the extent of slavery.

The firing on Fort Sumter, April 12, impelled Virginia into the newly formed Confederate States and split troubled Maryland into northwestern and southeastern halves. From Port Tobacco to Anne Arundel County, public meetings, many attended wholeheartedly by Mudds, declared that "Maryland's destiny was intertwined with that of the South, and Virginia." Yet further north, in Sam Mudd's old college town of Frederick, a Union flag with a streamer bearing a portrait of Governor Hicks was raised above the courthouse to the strains of *Hail Columbia*.

One week after Sumter, however, Maryland showed its militant Southern leanings. The Sixth Massachusetts Regiment, summoned to Washington, was hooted and stoned by a mob as it passed through the streets of Baltimore. The stoning turned into a riot in which a dozen were killed and many more were wounded—the first bloodshed of the Civil War. Soon afterward, Brigadier General Benjamin F. Butler—variously known as "Butcher," "Beast" and "Cockeyed Ben"—occupied the city, seized the Federal Hall, and took command of the Department of Annapolis, which included Baltimore.

Before Maryland was occupied, the legislature met in Frederick on April 29 and voted 53 to 13 to stay with the Union. It was a heavy blow to secessionist-minded Charles County and to lower Maryland in general. On the same day the newly elected Southern President, Jefferson Davis, addressed the Confederate Congress in Montgomery, making his celebrated claim, "All we want is to be left alone." Basically that was all Charles County wanted, all that any of the Mudds desired. They had their established community, their customs and traditions, their religion, and their personal ideas of honor. All they asked was to be left alone.

But when the war broke out in earnest, such a wish was obviously futile. No state was more vulnerable than Maryland, especially its southern counties. Situated between the Union and Confederate capitals, it was the logical route of invasion for either side, the obvious pathway for troops moving north and south to other areas of battle. The Potomac, from its mouth to Harper's Ferry, was the war's frontier. Charles County, caught between the Union and Confederate flanges of a vise, waited for the jaws to close.

"THE ENEMY APPROACHES," read the headline in the Port Tobacco *Times*. Having caught the reader's eye, the editor went on to elaborate his theme:

> The Bed Bug Season is now at hand and every family and owner of a bed should at once provide themselves with a bottle of "Bed Bug Poison." It never fails as prepared wholesale and retail by Apothecaries' Hall, Port Tobacco, Md., Corner fronting the court house.[5]

In point of fact, the enemy was indeed approaching, and in a sense, from two directions. Militant Virginia had called on its neighboring state of Maryland to join in a march on the Union capital. It was more of a prod than a serious invitation. Who was there in Maryland to enlist in such an expedition? Almost all the able-bodied males in the southern counties had crossed the Potomac to join Lee's forces in Virginia; others, from counties farther north, had enlisted in the Union army.

But the belligerent gesture made Washington uneasy. Lincoln had already warned the Maryland legislature that "military use or occupation of Maryland was dependent upon circumstances"—provocation would mean occupation. The legislature responded with a practical solution: namely, that the President should end the war. With General Butler transferred to Fort Monroe in Virginia, Secretary of War Simon Cameron reacted to this suggestion by naming General John A. Dix, a well-meaning martinet, commander of the District of Maryland. Military occupation had become a fact.

Dix tried to smother rebellion at one source by muzzling Southern-slanted newspapers; but he could not squelch Charles County's voice-of-the-people, the Port Tobacco *Times*. While the *Times* at first avoided inflammatory anti-Union statements, it took sly digs at Washington by printing "unsolicited contributions" from its Southern readers, boxing on its front page a bit of poesy by a semianonymous author named "Mariann":

> Jeffdavis rides on a white horse,
> Lincoln rides a mule.
> Jeffdavis is a gentleman,
> And Lincoln is a fule.[6]

Things remained at an impasse in southern Maryland throughout that first hot summer of the war until, in September, 1861, Lincoln sanctioned the wholesale arrest, without formal charges, of Maryland citizens suspected of disloyalty. This was followed by the arrest of "disloyal" legislators just before the state assembly was scheduled to meet on September 17. The legislature, what was left of it, did not disband; it simply did not assemble. The state government of Maryland had surrendered to the federals.

Then came the unkindest cut of all. By order of the retiring General Winfield Scott, federal troops started pouring into Maryland. Originally the occupation took the form of pickets or outposts along the Potomac, designed allegedly to check Maryland's invasion from Virginia. A hundred of these sliced through Zachia Swamp, entered the home of Samuel Cox, former captain of militia, and demanded the state-owned arms that Cox had stored there. Cox had no alternative but to submit; but he vowed revenge for this invasion of his home, and he would get it.

In September the blue troops came in earnest, with Charles County as their goal; their aim, the weeding out of pockets of secessionism in the area. Colonel Daniel Edgar Sickles and his New York Excelsior Brigade, five thousand strong, with another brigade of equal size from Hooker's Washington division, swarmed over Charles County, following every vengeful pointed finger, every spiteful hearsay, to the doors of unsuspecting citizens. People were hauled from their beds and homes and arrested on the flimsiest of rumors. Those branded as serious offenders were shipped to the Old Capitol Prison in Washington to wait for trials that never came.

The Mudds were a taciturn family, and they generally kept

their feelings to themselves. Few were heard to make anti-Union or "disloyal" statements; it would have been unwise to do so, for there were informers in the land, some of them spies of the federal government or free-lance spies seeking government favor. One such was Daniel Thomas, Mudd's schoolboy classmate of earlier days, who professed to be a government agent assigned to hunting out subversives. Whether he was or not, no one in Charles County could be sure. It was a period when any one man could play many roles.

Merely keeping silent did not guarantee immunity from jail or persecution. In the midst of the epidemic of arrests, Jeremiah Dyer, Frances' brother, appeared on Sam Mudd's doorstep seeking sanctuary. He was one jump ahead of Sickles' men, who he learned were looking for him.

Sam, of course, never hesitated to provide what help he could. He owed much to his brother-in-law; he and Frank had spent the first years of their marriage under the same roof with Jeremiah. And no Mudd would ever turn away another member of the family, no matter what the situation was.

Dyer refused to stay in the farmhouse. If caught, he would bring disaster down on Sam and Frances. He did not know what he was wanted for; he had been too old to qualify for either army. But Sickles, a zealous rebel-hater, would think of something and would make it apply to anyone who sheltered rebels or suspected rebels. All Jeremiah asked was to hide out somewhere on the property. His own home was no longer safe.

Sam took him to a pine grove near a spring, two hundred yards from the main house. He brought bedding and blankets from the farmhouse and they fixed up a lean-to type of shelter. The place seemed secure, and that night Dyer brought two other fugitives to the hideout, Bennett and Andrew Gwynn, both friends of the Dyers and the Mudds.

All three stayed for a week, until the epidemic of arrests was to have passed. Not trusting the slaves to keep their mouths shut, Sam himself brought them baskets of bread, biscuits, and ham, although he allowed the slave girl, Mary

Simms, to carry them pots of coffee in the morning. Andrew Gwynn also left his horse in Mudd's barn, to be fed and watered by John Best.

It was risky, and the doctor knew it. Jeremiah Dyer and the Gwynns had both been members of a semi-guerrilla military company before the war, a group planned as the nucleus of a Maryland militia if the state should find itself attacked by federal forces. The company disbanded after Maryland had voted to stay loyal to the Union. But their reputations, along with those of others who were hiding at the farms of friends and neighbors, were well known to Colonel Sickles.

When Sickles' brigade moved farther south to Port Tobacco, Dyer and the Gwynns found it safe to leave the refuge and sneak through Zachia Swamp to the Potomac and Virginia. Sam Mudd breathed easier.

The federal troops were still around, however, and in nearby Port Tobacco there were serious clashes between citizens and soldiers. Hooker's brigade had encamped northwest of Port Tobacco River; Sickles' troops settled at Mulberry Grove near the plantation of Thomas Jones, a brother-in-law of Samuel Cox. From Sickles' standpoint it was a bad choice of location. Jones' house, on a high bluff overlooking the Potomac, provided a perfect place for a signal station from which to spy on federal operations and keep track of traffic on the river. Under the unseeing eyes of the Excelsior Brigade, rebel fugitives and Maryland volunteers continued to cross the Potomac to Virginia on directions from the signal station.

As occupying armies have been throughout history, the federal troops were regarded as at worst a band of brigands, at best an unmitigated nuisance. And at all times an insult to Charles County pride. In mid-December of 1861 the editor of the Port Tobacco *Times* summarized what he headlined as "OUR SITUATION." Declaring that the county could not be *proven* disloyal, the writer added that the "twenty thousand Federal troops" stationed in Charles County

> are here "*For our protection*," we are told, "to protect us from the Rebels," and yet, in fact, we are exposed to more danger or at least as much as if these very Rebels were here. Our farmers are deprived of their provender to such

an extent that their cattle must die. Our citizens are deprived of homes almost; and fences, farms, and fields fall prey to the ruthless hands of those very friends who come here to protect us.

Our negroes—ah, this is the point—our negroes—are taken from us time and again, with no remuneration and the threats of violence if we seek to recover them.[7]

Protests were useless, however. The fact that the Mudds were generally wealthy, well bred and highly respected in the community, some of them being "professional men" as well as planters, probably spared them much of this indignity. Sam Mudd's farm was not disturbed in the first years of the war, nor were Oak Hill or the neighboring Mudd plantations. But "runaway" slaves became a problem. These were often stolen outright as "contraband of war," taken to Washington in protective custody, then sold back to their owners at outrageous prices by unconscionable military officers.

In November one of the real villains in the background of Mudd's later life appeared on the darkening scene. Lafayette C. Baker, described by a contemporary as a "man of little culture, dark, taciturn, square-shouldered, and of powerful frame" (and later in a Congressional report as "a miserable wretch"), had gained some notoriety as one of the San Francisco Vigilantes of 1856. Returning East, he found himself regarded as a military intelligence expert, and War Secretary Edwin Stanton, succeeding Simon Cameron, appointed him colonel of a Washington cavalry regiment. Ordered to southern Maryland to hunt out subversives, he brought into play all the ruthless tactics at his command.

"On my arrival at Port Tobacco," Baker wrote to his Washington superiors, "I found the inhabitants complaining bitterly of their ill treatment . . . however, I found on inquiring that the inhabitants had been the first aggressors. There are residing at this place but four or five Union men, the balance either being sympathizers with the secessionists or open and avowed aiders and abettors of treason." Baker also discovered an efficient, secret postal service existing between Confederate spies in the North and the authorities in Richmond.[8]

The colonel's first act was to arrest Thomas Jones, not for operating a signal station but for ferrying fugitives across the Potomac to Virginia. Jones confessed to taking people across the river every night, sometimes ten or twelve passengers in a boatload. He spent six months in Washington's Old Capitol Prison, which during the war Stanton and Baker kept full to overflowing with, in all, some 34,000 prisoners arrested for suspected acts or statements of disloyalty.

Though oppressed, harassed, and political prisoners in their own state, south-county Marylanders had reason to rejoice. The war had started favorably for the South. Just thirty miles west of Mudd's farm, Little Joe Johnston and General Beauregard, outnumbered and outgunned, sent Irvin McDowell's Union force of 30,000 reeling back across Bull Run Creek. The retreating forces panicked the spectators with their picnic baskets who had come down from Washington to watch what Washington papers billed as "the greatest battle ever fought in the western hemisphere."

Though a marginal victory, with heavy losses on both sides, it sent Maryland spirits soaring, serving proof of the invincibility of Southern arms and Confederate élan. By the turn of the year a certain confident arrogance infected Charles County planters; they were on the winning side.

Despite the efforts of General Dix and his successor, Daniel Schenck, to ban secessionist books, journals, poems, and pictures, a new national anthem for this corner of the demi-South was born—to be sung in the tobacco fields, in prison camps, in village taprooms; to the sound of marching feet along the banks of the Potomac, to the accompaniment of Henry Lowe Mudd's pianoforte in the parlor of Oak Hill:

> The despot's heel is on thy shore,
> Maryland! My Maryland!
> His torch is at thy temple door,
> Maryland! My Maryland!
> . . . be the battle queen of yore,
> Maryland! My Maryland!

Because of the tragic circumstances of Mudd's life, very few of his private papers, letters, diaries, even farm and medical records, would survive. Those that might have thrown light on his early days at Oak Hill were destined to be destroyed, along with the farm itself, by fire. But in mid-January, 1862, perhaps inspired by Confederate successes in the war, he expressed himself at length on the conflict between North and South.

The occasion for the outburst was a trivial one. He had canceled his subscription to *Brownson's Quarterly Review,* a liberal Northern journal, and the publishers had continued to send him bills. This irritant prompted him to write at length to Orestes A. Brownson. Once he covered the matter of unwanted bills, he vented his wrath on the editor in a revealing statement of his personal beliefs and attitudes.

> Through you our country . . . has rec'd. an irreparable injury. The present Civil War now raging, was not brought about entirely by fear on the part of the South, that their property in Slaves was endangered, but more by an unwillingness to yield up rights guaranteed by the Constitution of the United States. . . . We do not object to Republicanism or Abolitionism being a State organization or party (provided they are passive). . . . But we are bitterly opposed to its being brought into National Politics . . . to execute or legislate for our Common Country.[9]

He then went on to state his views on the Union in words that would not come to light until years later. The letter would still be hidden in Brownson's files when Mudd was accused of treason—and worse than treason:

> The North on account of its pride, shortsightedness, hypocrisy and much phylanthropy [sic] has caused the destruction of one of the most glorious nations upon the face of the earth. The South even those termed Seceders and leaders of Secession—desire Union! Yes, Union! But Alas! we know not in what manner it can be brought about.
>
> One thing seems certain to us all. The Union can never be restored by war, and the North must be very blind not to know it. . . . The Success of the Federal arms does not justify a further prosecution of the war. Thus far they have not gained a single victory; they have not gained one foot of territory, other than the enemy by his prudence and defensive attitude granted. . . . The South has already man-

ifested more energy, industry, prudence and Yankeeism
than the North. They have erected foundries, manufactories of various sorts, and in a few months will be enabled
to live well, with sealed ports.[10]

So they were saying in Richmond, Charleston, and Atlanta,
where war enthusiasm mixed with Southern pride created
a euphoria of optimism. The fact that all the cards were
stacked against them, that the North had a more than two-
to-one superiority in manpower, a five-to-one superiority in
manufactories, seventy percent of the country's railroads and
similar favorable margins in the realms of coal, food and
armaments production, did not faze the men in gray. They
had the leaders, the great West Pointers Robert Lee and
Little Joe Johnston; they had men trained from infancy to
ride and shoot and live in the open, which made for good
campaigners. Sam Mudd had seen it in Charles County, where
outdoor living and willingness to fight for principles gave
support to the popular Southern slogan that "One Confederate can lick a half a dozen Yanks."

So ignore reality and focus on the glorious, improbable
possibilities, as he did, writing of the South:

> She is possessed of every ingredient to make her self-
> sustaining and powerful. All she wants is a little more time,
> and if the war should be protracted, all the better for her
> future, because her resources will be brought out. Her iron,
> lead and other mines which she is rich in, will be worked
> and cause her not to look abroad for supplies.

Turning from this rosy picture of the South, he vented
his wrath on its opponents:

> The people of the North are puritanical, long faced or
> Methodistic and hypocritical—they deal in Sympathetic lan-
> guage to hide their deception—their actions are Pharisaical,
> covert, stealthy, and cowardly. They are law abiding so long
> as it bears them out in their selfish interest, and praisers
> and scatterers and followers of the Bible so long as it does
> not conflict with their passions. They make good cow
> drivers, pickpockets and gamblers. . . . Your people have
> so degenerated, that were it not for the foreign element

—which you possess—there would be only war on parchment. . . . They [the Union soldiers] fight very hard when there is no danger of being hurt and for the want of some visible exemplification of the destruction of shell and shot, they turn their pieces upon each other, resulting in the death of many, which fortunately is more gain than loss to the Federal Government.

He concluded his diatribe against the North—before going on to a personal castigation of its religious leaders—with statements that, if revealed, might have weighed heavily on his future:

I regret sincerely to see such a lack of Patriotism in the Present Administration and in the representatives of the North. . . . I confidently assert that if there was any other man [than Abraham Lincoln] at the head of the Government . . . the Revolution would immediately cease so far as the South is concerned.[11]

It is hard to see in Mudd's words the timid, retiring, ever-loyal citizen his contemporaries pictured. At least two neighbors with no reason to be biased, John L. Turner and Joseph Waters, saw the doctor as "a good, peaceable, and quiet citizen," harboring no sympathy for the rebellion, loyal to the Union. One can only assume that Samuel Mudd had two sides to his character—one that he showed to the world, as a good Union man; the other, kept to himself, which nurtured a festering hatred for the North and all it stood for. In that respect he may have differed from few others in Charles County, where it was expedient to stand gymnastically on both sides of the fence.

Though he was obviously bitter at being placed in this split position, he had not yet suffered materially from the outbreak of the war. Maryland's economy was still sound. Though the Union had ordered a naval patrol of the Potomac, to block off commerce with the South, the tobacco market remained healthy; prices had risen to $16 a hogshead for the better grades, though prices on consumer goods had risen in proportion. Over the farm, however, hung the threat of slave rebellion or desertion. If he lost his slaves, he might lose everything.

He tightened discipline on the farm, becoming excessively irritated by marks of slackness, overreacting to infractions of the rules. Among his seven field hands was Elzee Eglent, who was showing signs of truculence and indolence. He tried capricious threats, warning Elzee that blacks who defied their masters could be sold to Richmond to be placed at hard labor on the city's fortifications. Intimidation proved useless; and when Eglent once refused to go out to the fields, the doctor got his fowling piece from the house, gave Elzee one last chance to change his mind, then shot him through the thigh.

It was only a flesh wound, and the doctor himself removed the pellets and gave the slave a few days to recuperate. But this act of violence and sudden loss of temper turned several of the slaves against him—Elzee's brothers, Sylvester and Frank Eglent, and the injured man's sister, Mary Simms. Mary began thinking of the Confederate fugitives, Jeremiah Dyer and the Gwynns, whom Mudd had secreted in the piney woods outside his house. A slave could not with impunity speak out against his master, so Mary and the other Eglents bided their time.

At the end of that winter Thomas Jones was released from Old Capitol Prison, having served his six months' detainment and interrogation, and returned to his plantation, Huckleberry Farm, near Pope's Creek on the banks of the Potomac. In prison he had become acquainted with Benjamin Grimes of King County, Virginia, whose home was directly opposite Jones' house on the south bank of the river. As soon as he too was released, Grimes suggested to Jones that they work together in ferrying passengers and mail across the river.

After one arrest, which automatically placed him under suspicion, it was a risky proposal. "At first I refused," Jones said. "But Grimes then represented to me that Major Norris of the Confederate Signal Service had said that it was of the utmost importance to the Confederacy that it should have communications with points north of the Potomac, and that nowhere on the river was there a better location for a signal station than the bluffs near Pope's Creek, or a more suitable place for putting the mail across the river than off my shore."[12]

Jones finally accepted, on condition that he be given "entire control of the Ferry and all the other Maryland agents"; and under his aegis the basis was laid for an underground communications system stretching from Richmond, Virginia, through Zachia Swamp to Washington, New York and Canada. It was an operation without parallel in the Civil War and one that continued until 1865, when its trail led circuitously to the home of Samuel Mudd.

MARYLAND UNDERGROUND

ZACHIA Swamp, breeding ground of mystery ever since the Sacaro Indians, who had named it, disappeared within its sloughs without a trace; few but the swamp trappers knew the secrets of its trails and sumps and treacherous marshes. It was a twilight zone, a no-man's-land of decaying fens and quicksands, destined to become the setting for one of the great, largely unrecorded dramas of the Civil War. Pure circumstance, which played so large a part in Samuel Mudd's life, had placed his home in almost dead center of the stage.

Major James Rowan O'Beirne of the U.S. Marshal's office of the District of Columbia had reason to know Zachia Swamp as well as anybody could and left his own description of the area:

> The swamps tributary to the various branches of the Wicomico River, of which the chief feeder is Allen's Creek, bear various names, such as Jordan's Swamp, Atchall's Swamp, and Scrub Swamp. These are dense growths of dogwood, gum, and beech, planted in sluices of water and bog. Frequent deep ponds dot this wilderness place, with here and there a stretch of dry soil, but no human being inhabits the malarial expanse; even a hunted murderer would shrink from hiding there. Serpents and slimy lizards are the only living denizens.[1]

O'Beirne would find himself in error. For all its forbidding wastes there were more than serpents and lizards laying claim to sections of Zachia Swamp. Oak Hill and Samuel and Sylvester Mudd's plantations served as northern gateways to the area everglades. Five miles south of Dr. Mudd's was the cabin of Oscar Swann, who had served as guide to trappers and hunters before the war. Parson Lemuel Wilmer lived near and attended to the tiny chapel of Piney Church near the Wicomico River. Farther toward Port Tobacco lay the plantation of Colonel Samuel Cox, which, settled in a poor declivity, he named "Rich Hill."

Allen's Creek, the watery spine of Zachia Swamp, debouched at Allen's Fresh, above which lay Port Tobacco and below which at the mouth of Pope's Creek, on the Potomac, stood the well-positioned home of Thomas Jones. It was at Jones' Huckleberry Farm that the Maryland underground, the most effective wartime operation of its kind, began. But Port Tobacco, with its wharves, dives and sinuous dark alleys, served as its official southern terminus.

If Port Tobacco had become a cesspool, as Charles County planters thought of it, it was a convenient cesspool whose bubbling-cauldron existence covered a multitude of surreptitious operations. Colonel Lafayette Baker, arriving there on his witch-hunt for subversives, found it worthy of his best invective:

> If any place in the world is utterly given over to depravity, it is Port Tobacco. From this town, by a sinuous Creek, there is flat-boat navigation to the Potomac, and across that river to Mattox Creek. Before the war, Port Tobacco was the seat of a tobacco aristocracy and a haunt of negro traders. It passed very naturally into a rebel post for blockade runners and a rebel post office general. Gambling, corner fighting, and shooting matches were its lyceum education. Violence and ignorance had every sufferage [sic] in the town. Its people were smugglers, to all intents, and there was neither Bible nor geography to the whole region adjacent.
>
> The hotel here is called the Brawner House; it has a bar in the nethermost cellar, and its patrons, carousing in that imperfect light, look like the denizens of some burglar's crib, talking robbery between their cups; its dining room is dark and tumble-down, and the cuisine bears traces

of Kaffir origin. . . . The courthouse . . . stands in the center
of the town, and the dwellings lie about it closely, as if
to throttle justice. Five hundred people exist in Port Tobacco; life there reminds me, in connection with the slimy
river and adjacent swamps, of the great reptile period of
the world.[2]

Neither Baker's agents nor the Union gunboats patroling
the Potomac had any effect toward stifling Port Tobacco's
two-way traffic with Virginia. Though the colonel found the
adjacent countryside "wild and unsettled, a complete set of
signals had been established among the inhabitants, and
notice of our arrival had been given to the entire county,
making it necessary to move only at nighttime." The signals
came, of course, from Jones' farm, where the cliffs gave an
unobstructed view of the Potomac and the movements of
the Union gunboats, enabling Jones to alert Ben Grimes when
it was safe to send couriers and mail boats scuttling across
the river.

By this means, from the beginning to the end of the war,
the Richmond government knew as much about what was
going on in Washington and in the North as did the Northern-
ers themselves. Jones himself never met the mail boats crossing from Matthias Point on the Virginia side. The mail was
brought ashore and secreted, among other places, in a hollow
stump on the fringes of his farm. Here it was picked up
by couriers and taken to the United States Post Offices at
Bryantown, Waldorf, and Surrattsville, where the letters were
franked and the Union Postal Service took over the delivery
of Confederate mail to any point in the United States and
Canada.

One of the more trusted couriers was Dr. Stowten W. Dent
of Port Tobacco, who, like Sam Mudd, made his professional
rounds on horseback and was able to move freely through
the countryside. An old friend of Thomas Jones from Capitol
Prison days, the doctor managed to find extensive sickness
in Charles County throughout the war. He was recorded
as wearing in winter "a heavy overcoat that stretched below
his knees and provided with numerous pockets. In summer
he wore a long linen duster, also provided with a goodly
supply of pockets. He came and went unsuspected, and the

number of letters he could carry, concealed, was astonishing. The letters were delivered to other agents by him, either at Port Tobacco or Bryantown. . . ."

Dent's methods suggest how easy it would have been for Dr. Mudd to serve the underground. His farm was strategically located; he traveled often through Zachia Swamp as far as Colonel Cox's; he knew the secret trails and shortcuts leading from the end of his road to Allen's Fresh and Port Tobacco. Even though he never made illicit use of these advantages, the simple fact that they were there would invite suspicion and place him in jeopardy in years to come.

Another active courier was young John Harrison Surratt, an intelligent, sensitive, slightly built lad with a wispy blond mustache. He had inherited his father's position of postmaster at Surrattsville, thirteen miles south of Washington. John received contraband mail and packages in Richmond and crossed the Potomac from Matthias Point with the aid of the part-time ferryman, George Atzerodt, with whom he became well acquainted. Reaching Surrattsville, he affixed the necessary U.S. stamps and sent the contraband on its way; or, in reverse, steamed open official U.S. government communications, noted their contents, and relayed pertinent information to the Confederate authorities.[3]

Almost equidistant from Washington and Bryantown, Surrattsville was a principal way station in this tidewater section of the underground. Lafayette Baker, Secret Service Chief, considered it "throughout the war a seat of conspiracy. It was like a suburb of Richmond. . . ." It had been only a backwater crossroads fifteen or twenty years before. Then John Surratt, Sr., an erstwhile farmer and railroad man, had won the hand of Mary Eugenia Jenkins, a well-bred belle of Prince Georges County. John settled his wife on a farmstead inherited from his uncle; and when a disgruntled slave burned down the house, he moved to another farm on the turnpike from Washington to Bryantown and Port Tobacco.

Failing as a farmer, John turned the house into a store and then a tavern called Surratt's Villa, having obtained the concession of postmaster for the crossroads hamlet to which his name was given. He and Mary had three children: the eldest son, Isaac, joined the Confederate army as soon as war broke out; the daughter, Anna, went to public school in Bryantown; and John Surratt, Jr., attended St. Charles College near Baltimore. When his father died, in 1862, John left college (at age eighteen) to help his widowed mother. Fired from the postal service on suspicion of tampering with the mails, he became a secret contraband runner for the government in Richmond.

Young John found his role as courier exciting and rewarding. "We had a regularly established line from Washington to the Potomac," he recorded later:

> And I, being the only unmarried man on the route, had most of the hard riding to do—I devised various ways to carry the dispatches—sometimes between the planks of the buggy. I confess that never in my life did I come across a more stupid set of detectives than those generally employed in the United States Government. They seemed to have no idea whatever how to search me.[4]

John's disdain of federal incompetence was shared by Thomas Jones, who was pleasantly surprised at the ease with which Confederate communications spanned the Potomac. "This failure to discover our methods," he recalled, "gave rise to some far-fetched conjectures as to how we managed, despite the vigilance of the Federal Government, to escape detection. One idea was that by some ingenious contrivance the mail was drawn from one side of the river to the other, under water."

Jones was overconfident. Later information indicated that the federal government was not only aware of the underground operation but made use of it in devious ways. Lafayette Baker's counterspies penetrated the Confederacy by the same route, using the same facilities. They befriended Confederate couriers, helped deliver Confederate packages and mail—first opening and reading all communications, then resealing and delivering them and reporting the contents to the federal Secret Service.

In fact, a letter in the files of Secretary of State Seward in Washington, written by the U.S. Consul in Toronto, defined the operation in considerable detail:

> The Rebels in this city have a quick and successful com-
> munication with Jeff Davis and the authorities in Richmond
> in the following manner—Having plenty of money at their
> command, they employ British Subjects, who are provided
> with British passports . . . which are plainly written; name
> and date of issue on fine silk and as ingeniously secreted
> in the lining of the coat. They carry dispatches which are
> made and carried in the same manner.
>
> These messengers wear metal buttons, which, upon the
> inside, dispatches are most minutely photographed, not per-
> ceptible to the naked eye, but are easily read by the aid
> of a powerful lens.
>
> Letters are written, but are closely interlined with imper-
> ceptible ink (as they term it) which, when a certain chemical
> is employed, is easily deciphered.
>
> The messenger arriving at Baltimore receives additional
> instructions, and proceeds to Washington. Here he
> undergoes a thorough examination, is searched and per-
> mitted to pass—he takes a south-easterly course to "Port
> Tobacco" where he is sheltered . . . and at dead of night
> crosses in an india rubber boat to the south side of the
> Potomac, thence he goes to "Bowling Green" where a Rebel
> passport is issued to "Guerrilla B———" who hastens him
> on to Richmond—he returns by the same route. The last
> trip was made in fourteen days (December 14 to 28). . . .[5]

It seems evident that Jones, Dent, John Surratt and their
colleagues provided almost as much aid and information to
the Union government as to the Confederacy. The reference
in the consul's letter to "Guerrilla B———" suggests that both
sides knew of John Boyle, a notorious free-lance renegade
staked out in southern Maryland. Serving whatever cause
provided more profit, Boyle rashly pulled his gun on a Union
officer in Baltimore. The murder reduced him to the status
of an outlaw, and people like Sam and Frances Mudd were
more disturbed by men like Boyle being in their
neighborhood than by the presence of obnoxious federals.

The mention of Bowling Green in the letter to Secretary
Seward suggests that the southernmost way station on the
way to Richmond might have been the home of Richard
Henry Garrett, a farmstead destined to become a tragic footnote in the nation's history. The opposite, northernmost end

of the underground was Montreal or Toronto where a sort of Confederate government-in-exile operated to enlist aid for the South. This "Confederate Cabinet" collected Canadian money to help the Southern cause, directed espionage activities in the northwestern states, and organized guerrilla-type forays against Union installations below the border—raids that were led by such soldiers-of-fortune as George St. Leger Grenfell, a name that would someday be closely linked with that of Samuel Mudd.

When he wished, Sam Mudd could be a secretive and close-mouthed man. How much he knew about the Maryland underground is impossible to say. He could not have failed to be aware of its existence. In fact, the citizens of any occupied land are apt to be, one way or another, involved in underground activity—if only by passivity. Violate that passivity, inform on a partisan neighbor, and one becomes a more horrendous villain than the enemy himself.

If there were shadows drifting along the edges of Zachia Swamp by night, the doctor looked the other way. If broken twigs snapped on the fringes of the woods, it might be the wind—if not, he did not want to know. Footprints or hoof-prints disappeared with the morning mist, and left no traces of whatever passed. Some Union bummers on forage had found a hanged man dangling from an oak; they had cut down the body, rifled the pockets, but found no identification. A Union spy? A Confederate spy? There were many such faceless corpses in civilian clothes found in the bayous of Louisiana or the woods around Atlanta. Why not here? Mudd paid no heed and went about his business.

Certainly Sam Mudd knew or knew of many key figures in the underground. According to Cox's son, the colonel was "a personal friend" of the doctor's. Through Cox he must have known of Thomas Jones' activities. Familiar with Port Tobacco, then the county seat, he doubtless knew at least by sight George Atzerodt. The John Surratts were not family friends of the Mudds, but Surratt's Villa was a coach stop, where passengers disembarked to rest and refresh themselves on the way to Washington. And even riding alone to the capital, Sam Mudd would have stopped to water his horse and pick up the latest local news from John Surratt, Sr., in the taproom. He knew young John Surratt and Anna as public school pupils in Bryantown, but certainly not well.

Historian Osborn H. Oldroyd, in his privately published (1901) book, *The Assassination of Abraham Lincoln: Flight, Pursuit, Capture, and the Punishment of the Conspirators*, accuses Samuel Mudd of more than personal participation in the underground. He baldly links him with the plan to kidnap Abraham Lincoln and hustle the President down to Richmond via Bryantown and Port Tobacco. Following discussion of the project, Oldroyd makes this extraordinary statement: "While all these preparations were going on, Dr. Samuel Mudd and a number of gentlemen living in the vicinity of Bryantown . . . were waiting execution of the plot, ready to faithfully perform their part in securing the safe transport of the President to the Virginia side of the Potomac River."[6]

All that can be said in Oldroyd's defense is that he was writing at a time when much of the material on the Maryland underground and the several plans to kidnap Lincoln was still unavailable—forcing a writer to rely on hearsay and conjecture. The only act of participation in the underground of which Samuel Mudd could possibly be accused was sheltering Jeremiah Dyer and the brothers Gwynn when they had been threatened with arrest. Gwynn returned several times to stay at Mudd's farm on his way to Washington, but he claimed to have taken the oath of allegiance to the Union and had cleared himself of charges of disloyalty.

Some of Sam's relatives had shown themselves more considerate of Confederates and Southern partisans than had the doctor. His cousin, Dr. George Mudd, impartially played host to both sides. As Charles County became a highway for both Union and Confederate soldiers moving north or south, George kept open house for the troops regardless of what uniform they wore. Samuel Mudd's grandson writes of this impartial hospitality:

> . . . during the Civil War Dr. George Mudd's home was located in such a place as to enable him to serve both Northern and Southern soldiers; to tend horses of both armies; and to actually feed soldiers of both armies at the same time. Dr. Mudd provided means for poker and other games, and never once was his hospitality violated. Before visiting soldiers entered Dr. Mudd's home, they laid aside their

arms for the undeclared armistice that was ever present
at his home.[7]

Hospitality and even charity toward an enemy, in periods
of relative cease-fire, were not uncommon practices, perhaps
more ingrained in the Southern character than in the
Northern. While George Mudd was entertaining Yankees
at his home, a Confederate soldier named Lewis Powell was
guarding some Union prisoners of war near Warrentown,
Virginia. When an angry Southern mob threatened to lynch
the captives, Powell trained his rifle on his countrymen, ready
to protect his charges with his life. Mrs. Lucy Ann Grant
of Warrentown witnessed the incident and made a note of
it.[8]

To Powell, this honorable stance was just a reflex; he put
little stock in human life, no matter whose, and was simply
responding to a challenge. Union and Confederate uniforms
looked drearily alike to his indifferent eyes. The only high
spot of the war for him—at least the only incident that seemed
to penetrate his diffidence—was a night on leave in Baltimore
when he met the tragedian John Wilkes Booth. He would
never forget that moment when he basked in the actor's
reflected glory; and John Wilkes Booth would not permit
him to forget it.[9]

High tide for the Confederacy came in the summer of
1862, sweeping over the Potomac into Maryland and
threatening the North with deep invasion. Lee's Army of
Northern Virginia splashed across the fords and up to Sam
Mudd's former college town of Frederick, the army's
regimental bands playing a stirring call to arms:

> Come, for thy shield is bright and strong,
> Maryland! My Maryland!
> Come, for thy dalliance does thee wrong!
> Maryland! My Maryland!

It was perhaps fitting that the South should come so close
to victory, so close to independence on the soil of Maryland
where independence had such hardy roots. "Marse Robert,"
the white-haired, aristocratic Southern general, told the citizens of Maryland, "The people of the Confederate States

have long watched with the deepest sympathy the wrongs
and outrages that have been inflicted upon you. . . . We know
of no enemies among you, and will protect all, of every
opinion."[10]

Elsewhere in Maryland, in the southern counties, for
example, Lee's call to the citizens to rally round the Stars
and Bars might have been successful. But as the hungry,
ill-clad Confederates stormed the Frederick stores for socks
and shoes, leaving the city a carpet of discarded footwear,
the western Marylanders saw little in this shabby army to
encourage their support. There was nothing to attract the
flood of volunteers that Lee expected and that might have
furthered the invasion.

On evacuating Maryland for points north and west, a Confederate soldier cast aside a packet of Maryland cigars. In
the package, picked up by returning Union troops to whom
tobacco was a prize, was found—extraordinarily—Lee's
"Secret Orders No. 191" directing his generals to proceed
to Hagerstown and Maryland.

The secret of Lee's planned campaign reached General
McClellan, who moved his 70,000-man Army of the Potomac
westward in pursuit. At Sharpsburg Creek on September
17 the bloodiest battle of the war exploded; and the South,
which had never been so close to victory, was suddenly never
so close to ruinous defeat. The dead lay in windrows at
Antietam Creek and the Maryland corn was leveled by rifle
fire. Lee withdrew into Virginia, and the cautious McClellan
failed to deliver what might have been a knockout blow.

Lee would try again in ten months to invade the North,
and he would be checked again at Gettysburg; in the mean-
time the Port Tobacco *Times* saluted Antietam as a smashing
Southern victory.

Confederate successes in the East, however, did not make
things easier for Samuel Mudd. Southern Maryland was
crumbling beneath the Tyrant's Heel. The federal blockade
was tightening, though one Charles County friend of the
Mudds, Raphael Semmes, was shooting holes in the chain
as captain of the Confederate raider *Alabama*. Tobacco prices
remained high because of constricting factors: lack of transportation and lack of labor to cultivate the fields and work
in the tobacco barns. With three children now, Andrew, Lil-

lian and Thomas, Frances had only two slaves left to help her, and the doctor worked in the fields with only Charlie Bloyce and Frank and Baptist Washington.

In wartime, populations may shift geographically on major provocation. The Mudd farm population varied with each working week. Slaves came and went, were borrowed and returned. Elzee Eglent, the black whom Mudd had shot, eventually took off and disappeared with his two brothers and his sister, Mary Simms. To try to get them back was futile. A runaway slave was as good as home in this rudderless period, though home might be at best Old Capitol Prison, or at worst a sleazy colony of huts on the Potomac, south of Washington, known as "Murder Row."

Lincoln's Emancipation Proclamation, issued on the first of January, 1863, sounded a death knell for the southern Maryland plantation system. Mudd retained some of his former slaves, but Frank Washington, who had cost no more than the food he ate, now received $130 a year, which the doctor could ill afford. Frank's brother, Baptist, who doubled as carpenter, earned the same. Another ex-slave, Charlie Bloyce, worked only half-time, generally over weekends and never during the hunting and trapping seasons, when he could make good money from the products of Zachia Swamp: animal hides, furs, fish and edible game.

With fewer hands, Mudd was obliged to cut the number of acres planted to tobacco, never more than a fraction of his total land. His revenue dropped accordingly. The income from his medical practice, too, was dwindling. With prices inflated and food at black-market levels, people had no money for a doctor's care; they returned to the old folklore herbs and family-compounded remedies. Mudd confided to his horse-breeding neighbor, Llewellyn Gardiner, that he was considering selling the farm, moving to the little riverside village of Benedict, and starting a "commercial" business. He never divulged what nature of business he contemplated, possibly that of tobacco factor, but he did let it be known in Bryantown that he had good farm acreage for sale.

If prospects looked grim for Samuel Mudd, they seemed equally unpromising to Mary Surratt at the tavern some miles north. There was still plenty of traffic on the turnpike between Washington and Port Tobacco, plenty of customers in the taproom, but they seemed more concerned with transacting their clandestine businesses than with convivial drinking. Such well-known Confederate spies and couriers as Augustus Howell could be seen at the bar, along with a scatter-brained itinerant named David Herold, who hunted and fished the area. But the inn was losing money and Mary's son, young John Surratt, was rarely around to help her.

In October she leased the tavern to a hard-drinking ne'er-do-well named John Lloyd, and moved her family to Washington. She took over a three-story residence at 541 H Street, not far from Ford's New Theater, where she let out rooms to boarders. Because Mrs. Surratt was tidy and conscientious and set a good table, she was able quickly to fill the house. Her daughter Anna and her son John both had upstairs rooms, and John brought a friend from college days, named Louis Wiechmann, to the place as a paying guest. John, himself, however, to Mary's increasing distress, spent most of his time away from home and much of it in Canada.

Unlike Samuel Mudd, who religiously followed the news in the *National Intelligencer* (and in smuggled copies of the Richmond *Enquirer* when he could get them), Mary Surratt appeared to take little interest in the war or politics. She was surely aware of the Maryland underground's use of her tavern as a trysting place but not aware, as Mudd and most of Charles County were, of the stepped-up activity at the Canadian end.

The "Northwestern Conspiracy," allegedly directed by Richmond's Secretary of War, James Seddon, and led in Toronto and Montreal by such Southerners as George N. Sanders, Beverly Tucker, Jacob Thompson, William Cleary and Clement C. Clay, purposed to weld the northwestern states into a copperhead confederacy, working to end the war in favor of the South.[11] Its most daring raid was an attempt to free Confederate prisoners at Camp Douglas in Chicago. The plot was uncovered and one of the leaders, George St. Leger Grenfell, was captured, tried by Judge Advocate General Joseph Holt, and sentenced to life in Fort Jefferson Prison on the Dry Tortugas. There was no reason why the names of Holt and Grenfell should at this point mean much to Dr. Samuel Mudd; he would have time to know them better.

As the military outlook for the South grew desperate toward the end of 1864, the Canadian conspirators considered extreme measures. One was allegedly a plan to kidnap or assassinate the President of the United States. But, like the underground in Maryland, the Canadian underground was riddled with Union counterspies. A federal agent using the name of Richard Montgomery reported their goal as being "to put out of the way" President Lincoln and his cabinet. Montgomery cited as those involved in the conspiracy—and present from time to time in Canada—John Wilkes Booth, George Atzerodt (referred to as "Port Tobacco"), a Confederate deserter known as Lewis Powell or Lewis Paine, David Herold, and one John Harrison whose full name was believed to be John Harrison Surratt.

These and similar reports came from other Union agents, Sanford Conover, for one. Details and dates were different; the pattern of names was inconsistent; to get at the truth one had to select those particulars that provided the truth one wanted. Conover heard the actor Booth remark that it was time for Lincoln "to go up the spout," a statement open to interpretation; but times and dates and names were as hazy as drifting clouds to Conover.

What was wrong about all this information was that, true to the character of spies everywhere, the correspondents were inveterate liars. In addition, the War Department learned that there were two men posing as James Watson Wallace, *alias* Sanford Conover, and was at a loss as to which spy to believe. This would not prevent the department and War Secretary Stanton from bringing charges, when and as it chose, against Booth, Paine, Herold and George Atzerodt —for if their presence in Canada were purely hearsay or invention, that was beside the point. They were guilty by implied association.

Beside the point, too, as the great web of the Confederate conspiracy spread from Canada to southern Maryland, was the nature of the evidence that certain of his enemies were amassing against Samuel Mudd. How they would use that evidence was not clear at this point. But if the doctor, in discussing the war with his neighbor Benjamin Gardiner, should remark that Stonewall Jackson was "a sharp one," it would be duly noted and remembered by one of Gardiner's former slaves. If he should express agreement with Reverdy Johnson, Maryland's foremost statesman and lawyer, that an oath of allegiance forced upon one by compulsion was not binding, that too would be duly noted. In such unguarded moments one could hang oneself with words—and many did.

A STRANGER CALLS

Abe Lincoln was running for a second term as President; and Samuel Mudd, for the first time in his life, would vote Republican. It was not that he loved Lincoln, but the damage had been done. The South was on its knees. Sherman had burned Atlanta and was marching to the sea; Joe Johnston had lost command of the gallant Army of Tennessee to the intemperate Hood, and Hood was falling to pieces in the West; Robert E. Lee was fighting a losing battle in Virginia. Were he reelected to the White House, the sad-eyed, distant cousin of the Mudds of Maryland had promised conciliatory treatment for a conquered South, and that was all that one could hope for.

Rock Hill Farm, like the fields of Sylvester Mudd, Oak Hill, and Squire Gardiner's plantation, was in partial ruin, much of the acreage resigned to jimsonweed and scrub pine. Labor was harder than ever to get. Thomas Davis, from Prince Georges County, a friend of the Dyers and the Mudds, came down to the farm for extended stays. His health was poor, and Davis sought to build himself up and at the same time pay for his room and board by helping in the fields. Frances was expecting a fourth child sometime in January, and John Best, the English handyman, was confined to working at the house.

There was no doubt about the presidential ballot in November. Lincoln, with Andrew Johnson as Vice President, won over George B. McClellan by a generous popular majority and 212 electoral votes against 21 for the "Peace Party"

candidate. The outcome aroused Southern wrath from
Alabama to Montreal. In Selma the local *Dispatch* carried
an advertisement, with a mailbox number as a signature,
reading: "If the citizens of the Southern Confederacy will
furnish me with . . . one million dollars, I will cause the lives
of Abraham Lincoln, Wm. H. Seward, and Andrew Johnson
to be taken by the first of March next."

In Montreal John Wilkes Booth appeared, not, however,
seeking a million-dollar fee as volunteer assassin. He had
ample funds for now. His annual earnings over the past
several years had averaged $20,000, and he still commanded
$100 for a single night's appearance on the stage. He was
seeking a safe place to keep his money, where he could draw
on it freely without scrutiny and where it would be within
reach if he sought to leave the country. The records of his
bank deposits are the only proof of his presence in the city
at that time, apart from the dubious words of those who
claimed to have seen him there.[1]

As a bon vivant and patron of the better-class saloons,
Booth was familiar with many of the "Confederate Cabinet"
in Montreal. But if he was directly connected with the
Northwest Conspiracy or revealed to its principals any plans
of his own, there is no official record of it. He had plans,
for sure. But it was contrary to his nature to submit to group
control or to share his goals with any but subalterns. While
he boasted of striking a last-ditch blow for his beloved South,
he remained close-mouthed about the details.

But he was courting a date with destiny. The schoolboy
fantasy of gaining glory by toppling the structures of the
mighty was becoming an obsession. Lincoln's reelection raised
the target: the Colossus of the White House. Grant's refusal
to exchange Confederate prisoners of war, so badly needed
by the South, provided purpose. Like all plans of the fanatic,
his scheme was simple beyond all realities: kidnap the President and hold him as ransom for the thirty-five to fifty
thousand Confederate captives in Union prison camps.

He would need help, but not help that would detract from
or outshine his leading role in the conspiracy. Just a few
weak-willed recruits to do his bidding. He sounded out two

of his theatrical friends, John Matthews and Samuel Chester, both stock-company performers, hinting first of plans he had in mind to make them rich and famous, then revealing what the plans, in essence, were. Both shied away in horror, thereby gaining Booth's indelible contempt.

Toward the end of the year he moved permanently into Washington, taking a room with his mistress at the National Hotel on Sixth Street. He began not only to play the part of archconspirator but to dress for it. In place of the pastel-colored breeches, satin-collared mauve and russet jackets, embroidered vests and silk cravats, he wore the appropriate showboat villain's black: black tailored riding coat with flowing cape, dark slouch hat, skin-fitting breeches and black boots with silver spurs. In his belt, as theatrical props, he carried a pistol, or sometimes a brace of pistols, and a dirk.

And he began in earnest to seek recruits for his abduction of the President, starting with two schoolday friends in Baltimore. Michael O'Laughlin, who had lived opposite the Booths on Exeter Street, was working as a feed store clerk in the city. Now twenty-seven, Mike was described as "a small, delicate-looking man, with rather pleasing features, uneasy black eyes, bushy black hair, a heavy black mustache and imperial, and a most anxious expression of countenance, shaded by a sad, remorseful look."[2]

Samuel Arnold, a year older than O'Laughlin, had been a classmate of Booth's at St. Timothy Hall in Catonsville. Like O'Laughlin he had a black mustache, pointed beard, and dark bushy hair; and his soft brown eyes reflected a sensitive intelligence. Both he and O'Laughlin had served for a while in the Confederate army and had either deserted or been discharged; Arnold was now working as a field hand on a farm outside of Baltimore.[3]

Booth arranged a meeting at Barnum's Hotel, a hotbed of conspiracy in the rebel-minded city of Baltimore. All that can be gathered of that secret meeting is that he told the two men of his plot to snatch the President and gained their unqualified support. Some financial persuasion was added to Booth's promises of fame and glory. He bought Arnold a new suit of clothes, gave O'Laughlin spending money, and told them both to stand by; he would send word when the opportunity for action came.

In planning the abduction of the President it was only natural that Booth should think of Ford's New Theater—"new" because the original had burned down in December 1862 and had since been rebuilt. There was an obvious reason for the choice of scene: Booth saw himself playing a great dramatic role and wanted a stage for the performance. The selection of the theater made a modicum of sense. If Lincoln ever left the White House in the evening, it was generally to occupy his private box at Ford's. Secondly, Booth knew the brothers Ford from long association and had plenty of friends in the theater who would innocently serve his ends. Ned Spangler, the former farmhand at the Booth estate in Bel Air, was working in the building as a stagehand. Booth had gotten him the job, and Spangler would do anything to accommodate the actor in return.

What else did Booth need? He needed to know and plan the abduction route from Washington to the Potomac. He needed fast horses, maps, a carriage in which to smuggle his hostage to Virginia, and a boat to cross the Potomac from Port Tobacco. And he would need to make contacts in southern Maryland, establish possible relay stations where arms could be stashed, where horses could be changed, and where he and his cohorts, if they became separated, could arrange to meet.

These matters of familiarizing himself with the abduction route he could handle on his own, posing as a wealthy country gentleman looking for a piece of land to settle on.

Ever since Major-General Robert C. Schenk had taken over command of Maryland from Dix and his brief successor, General Wool, St. Mary's Church in Bryantown, like all other houses of worship, had been ordered to fly the Union flag above its door. Father Courtney had protested that this implied a union of state and church, in violation of the Constitution. But the Constitution, so long as Secretary Stanton was in office, had been suspended for the duration of the war. Even the President was superfluous, in Stanton's mind, although the War Secretary regarded Lincoln's safety as his personal responsibility and was haunted by rumors of conspiracies to assassinate the President.

Not changed by the war was the custom of sociable assembly before and after Sunday services on St. Mary's westward-

sloping lawn. Since Frances Mudd was eight months pregnant, the doctor attended church alone on that third Sunday
of the month, November 20. All the clan were gathered:
the Mudds of Oak Hill and its satellite plantations, the Gardiners, the Dyers, the Edelens and Boarmans. Despite the
times, they put up a brave front: the young girls dressed
like Christmas-tree bells in flowered basques and cone-shaped
hoopskirts; mothers and matrons in black bombazine and
lace; men in gray broadcloth breeches, mustard or ginger-
colored coats, wide silk cravats. They had seen each other
in these same Sunday clothes for four years; but with Maryland still in the Union they had not come to the butternut-
dyed, homespun garments that one saw in Richmond or
Atlanta.

Dr. George Mudd, the only social deviate, attended St.
Peter's, close to his home; but Dr. William T. Bowman was
among those congregating on the lawn along with Dr. William
Queen and his son-in-law from Baltimore, John Thompson.
With Thompson and Queen was a striking-looking stranger
in dark breeches, long black riding coat with satin collar,
black silk cravat and diamond stickpin. His animated talk
and gestures made him the center of attention among those
within his hearing.

During the service the stranger shared a pew with Dr.
Queen and Thompson; and after church Thompson hailed
Dr. Mudd and presented his guest: John Wilkes Booth, a
visitor from Washington.

Booth's entrance on that peaceful scene, so exclusive to
Mudds and their kinsmen, appears more or less fortuitous.
According to Thompson he had simply shown up at Queen's
house the night before with a letter of introduction from
a man named Martin in Montreal. Since half the Americans
in Montreal, most of them loyal to the South, went under
assumed names, the writer might have been anybody—even
D. Randolph Martin, a New York banker with Montreal con-
nections. Certainly none of Queen's family had ever seen
or been apt to have heard of Booth before.

His visit to southern Maryland, the letter said and Booth
reiterated, was to get acquainted with the countryside with

a view to buying an estate there. He inquired of Thompson about the roads around Charles County and the price of land in the vicinity. Thompson told him that land varied from five to fifty dollars an acre, depending on location, and mentioned Henry Lowe Mudd as the county's principal landholder. When Booth asked about horses for sale, Thompson assured him that Maryland owners preferred to sell their stock in Washington.

Regarding the stranger's financial credit, Thompson recalled:

> Booth told me, on the evening of his arrival at Dr. Queen's, that he had made some speculations or was a shareholder in some oil lands in Pennsylvania . . . he told me he had made a good deal of money out of it, and I did not know but that he came [to southern Maryland] for the purpose of investing.[4]

As Dr. Mudd acknowledged his introduction to the stranger, he saw before him an athletic-looking, well-built man in his middle twenties with extraordinarily white skin and teeth, wavy black hair that looked professionally curled, a long pointed mustache such as that affected by Confederate cavalry officers, and deep-sunk, penetrating hazel eyes. With easy familiarity, Booth reaffirmed that he was looking for land to buy and Mudd acknowledged that he had acreage for sale. He would be glad to show the visitor around his farm.

It was agreed that after noonday dinner and some mandatory visits in the afternoon, the doctor would call for Booth at Montgomery's Hotel in Bryantown. Booth was much obliged. The group broke up, and Mudd rode back to the farm to pick up Frances and the two older children for the ritual of Sunday dinner at Oak Hill with his father, mother and sisters. Sam's younger brother, Henry, was away at college and his younger sister, Cecelia, had married Dr. Joseph Henry Blandford and was living with her husband in Brandywine, some miles south of Washington.

It was the week of Sam's and Frances' wedding anniversary, and while celebrations seemed out of place in these severe times, Frances had invited friends for supper. At five o'clock Sam told her of his promise to the man named Booth, and warned her that she might have a visitor and that they would probably be late. He told John Best to saddle two horses, mounted the gray mare he generally rode, and led the extra horse to Booth's hotel in Bryantown where he found the stranger waiting. Together they rode back to the farm at twilight.

Strangely Booth made no further reference to buying land. He appeared more interested in buying horses and suggested that Mudd might know of someone with a good stable in the area. He had a buggy in Washington, and with a suitable horse he could tour Charles County, get acquainted with the neighborhood, and look for available land. Mudd mentioned George Gardiner, who lived next door and had one of the best stables in the county. If Booth cared to spend the night at the farm, they could ride over in the morning. Booth expressed himself again as much obliged.

Though they arrived late at the farm, Frances arranged extra plates of food for the visitor, who mingled easily and with hypnotic charm among the assembled guests. Frances recalled, "The conversation was on general topics. Nothing relative to the Administration or the war was spoken by anyone present." After supper Booth and the doctor remained at the table, smoking and sipping whiskey—though Booth confessed that brandy was his drink—while the ladies repaired to the adjoining parlor.

How much Mudd knew about his visitor he does not say. By now the actor's name was well known south of the Potomac; well known, too, in Washington City, where he had appeared erratically at Ford's in *Richard III* and *King Lear* (and had been criticized for his "theatrical gymnastics" and "bombastic declamation"). What they discussed in privacy that evening is not, of course, recorded, although Mudd himself wrote later of their conversation:

> . . . Booth's visit, as expressed by himself, was for the purpose of purchasing land and horses; he was inquisitive concerning the political sentiments of the people, inquiring about the contraband trade that existed between the North

and the South, and wished to be informed about the roads
bordering on the Potomac, which I declined doing. He
spoke of his being an actor and having two other brothers,
who were also actors. He spoke of Junius Brutus as being
a good Republican. He said they were largely engaged in
the oil business, and gave me a lengthy description of the
theory of oil and the process of boring, etc. He said he
had a younger brother in California. These and many minor
matters spoken of caused me to suspect him to be a government detective. . . .[5]

This strange suspicion, which does not seem warranted
by Mudd's description of their conversation, did not temper
the doctor's cordiality toward the actor. The next morning
he walked Booth over to George Gardiner's stables, where
Booth told Squire Gardiner that he "wanted a horse to run
a light buggy to travel over the lower counties of Maryland"
in search of land to purchase. Gardiner had only one buggy
horse, which he used himself and which was not for sale.
He showed Booth several saddle horses, and the actor settled
for an unprepossessing bay. The animal was old and blind
in one eye, but Booth explained that he "only needed it
for a year." Gardiner's nephew, Thomas, agreed to deliver
the horse to Montgomery's Hotel that morning.[6]

Back at the farm, Booth collected his overcoat and prepared
to return to Washington. He thanked his hostess for her
hospitality, and the doctor rode with him back to Bryantown
to pick up the newly purchased horse. A chance incident
made Frances suspicious of her late guest and sowed in her
mind a gnawing apprehension and distrust of Booth, a man
normally given to captivating women's hearts with ease. As
she recorded of Booth's departure:

> After he had gone I went to the parlor to put things
> in order. Lying on the floor by the chair that had held
> his overcoat was a letter, not enclosed in an envelope, that
> had fallen from his pocket. I picked it up and almost
> involuntarily glanced at the headlines. These lines con-
> vinced me that some poor man's home had been wrecked
> by the handsome face and wily ways of Booth. The letter
> was from New York; but I did not look at the name of
> the writer, and I do not know to this day who she was.

I laid it on the table, hoping to be able to find some means
of returning it to him. As he never returned, I subsequently
threw it in the fire.[7]

The mysterious women in Booth's life would fill a volume;
at this single period in his biography the list was long. Besides
Ella Turner, the mistress he kept at the National Hotel in
Washington, there was his socialite, secret fiancée, Miss Bessie
Hale, daughter of Senator John P. Hale. And strung along
the eastern seaboard, which the young Adonis traveled as
a performer, there was a sometimes-nameless girl in every
port, from the Montreal "Jenny" to Sally Andrews in
Manhattan, from "Red Lura" and "Miss X of Baltimore"
to one who signed herself "yours and yours only, Etta." His
conquests in boudoir and brothel formed a sordid, repetitious
catalog, and the marriage bed was not immune to
exploitation. He had been stabbed for infidelity by the actress
Henrietta Irving and been horsewhipped out of Syracuse
for seducing a local tycoon's wife. Yes, he had broken many
homes and was about to shatter another, that of Samuel
Mudd. Perhaps Frances, curiously sensing it, was justified
in her aversion for the actor. Her suspicion of Booth that
morning in November would return, with dreadful meaning.

Yet, however depraved, Booth never lost his seemingly
hypnotic charm. That Monday after Sam Mudd dropped
the actor off at Bryantown, Booth took the newly purchased
bay to the local blacksmith, Peter Trotter, to be reshod. Trotter recalled that as townsfolk and customers gathered in his
shop while he was working on the horse, the actor held them
spellbound with a histrionic monologue recounting his amor-
ous triumphs, his adventures in the theater, quoting Shakespeare, Sheridan, and no doubt his favorite lines from Colley
Cibber:

> The aspiring youth that fired the Ephesian Dome
> Outlives in fame the pious fool that raised it.

When the horse was done, Booth purchased a silver-
studded saddle from the blacksmith and took his leave. He
was headed for Washington and then to New York for a
theatrical engagement, but he stopped off briefly in

Philadelphia to leave a sealed letter "for safe keeping" with his sister, Asia, and his brother-in-law, John Sleeper Clarke. The envelope, opened by provocation more than six months later, contained a strange, long-winded, hyperbolic testament of Booth's intentions. He was apparently anxious to commit himself to a course of action about which he himself was vague. Addressed "To whom it may concern," it read in part:

> Right or wrong, God judge me, not man. For be my motive good or bad, of one thing I am sure, the lasting condemnation of the North. . . . For four years I have waited, hoped and prayed for the dark clouds to break and for a restoration of our former sunshine. To wait longer would be a crime. All hope for peace is dead. My prayers have proved as idle as my hopes. God's will be done. I go to see and share the bitter end.
>
> I have ever held the South were right. . . . But Lincoln's policy is only preparing a way for their total annihilation. . . . The South can make no choice. It is either extermination or slavery for themselves (worse than death) to draw from. I know my choice. . . .
>
> My love is for the South alone. Nor do I deem it a dishonor in attempting to make for her a prisoner of this man to whom she owes so much of misery. If success attends me, I go penniless to her side. . . .
>
> A Confederate doing duty upon his own responsibility.
>
> J. WILKES BOOTH[8]

In its entirety the letter reads like that of a tormented mind. So he intends to "make a prisoner of this man," presumably Abraham Lincoln, to whom the South "owes so much of misery." But by what means and to what purpose, other than perhaps revenge, it is hard to fathom. Hard to know why he wrote the letter to begin with and delivered it to Asia for safekeeping. A verbal release for inner turmoil? A sort of last will and testament? While bent on conspiracy, Booth never failed to leave plenty of clues and plenty of evidence that, whatever happened, he should get due credit for his actions.

He was scheduled to appear at the Winter Garden in New York on Friday, November 25. Three of the Booths—Edwin, John, and Junius—were announced as playing in Shakespeare's *Julius Caesar*, John Wilkes appearing as Mark Antony.

The house was a sellout; but the performance on the stage was outmatched in drama and excitement by the holocaust outside. One by one, New York's hotels and public buildings exploded into flame, including the structure adjacent to the theater. The Astor House, the Belmont, the mammoth St. Nicholas, the Fifth Avenue Hotel, and more than a half-dozen other famous hostelries were set ablaze, while hundreds of persons were injured in the fire that ravaged Barnum's Museum.

The following morning the press headlined the attempt to burn the city as part of a vast Confederate plot. Time proved the headlines right. The conflagration was one of the last sparks in the smoldering Northwest Conspiracy. But John Wilkes Booth, whose name was linked with that conspiracy—and whose presence in New York that night was cited as convincing proof—was probably only annoyed that New York's fire shifted the public spotlight from his own appearance at the Winter Garden. To destroy a city was beneath his aims. He set his sights on larger goals.

If Sam Mudd felt encouraged by Booth's interest in his property, which might make possible the move to Benedict, he had to draw on his supply of patience, which was getting low. He heard nothing further from the actor, but he learned from William Bowman that Booth had returned to Bryantown in the succeeding weeks, staying once with Dr. Queen, and always with the same avowed purpose: to become acquainted with southern Maryland, learning about its roads and the Potomac River crossings, and looking for good farm acreage to buy.

There was reason to be disillusioned about Booth's intentions. Five days after the actor left for Washington and then New York, the doctor ran into William Bowman in Bryantown. They discussed their common problems and Mudd's hope to move to Benedict if he could sell his property. Bowman announced that he was about to sell his own land. Whom to? Why, that actor John Wilkes Booth. Booth, it seemed, had consulted Bowman on the matter that same weekend he had stayed at Mudd's and had promised shortly to return to close the deal.

"That fellow promised to buy my land!" said Mudd indignantly. Actors were a mercurial lot, said Bowman—which was little consolation.

Mudd's prospects toward the end of 1864, like those of the other south-county planters, looked no better with the waning of the war. In the counties north of Washington conditions were improving; Maryland's economy was moving toward stability and peace. Prices were high, but business was prospering. In Charles County prices were high but largely because of the loss of free slave labor; income had dwindled with the dwindling production of tobacco.

Replacing Schenk as commander of the Maryland military district, General Lew Wallace—known later as the author of *Ben Hur*—was no better than his predecessor, which is to say, no less intolerant. He shut down southern-slanted newspapers "for their own protection," and concocted a plan to confiscate all land and property belonging to Charles County citizens suspected of disloyalty. More than that, he undertook to supervise Maryland's emancipation of her slaves, making it more difficult than ever for the planters to retain, by threat or persuasion, a modicum of Negro labor.

Perhaps Mudd shared the conviction of Charles Countians that one could not win. A foreign government, foreign in life-style and tradition, had taken over and was occupying southern Maryland. In the lower counties freedom had been stifled by intimidation, by men like Dix and Schenck and Wallace and Lafayette Baker's skulking agents searching not only for subversives but for men striving to uphold the Southern way of life. Under such conditions it was better to submit; to suppress one's emotions; to keep silent and to cooperate with the federal authorities only as much as necessary to stay out of trouble.

So when a new constitution was proposed for Maryland, officially ending slavery, and all would-be voters were obliged to take an Oath of Allegiance to the United States, Mudd took that oath. So did the other members of the clan. How much did it mean? No less a patriot and diplomat than Reverdy Johnson, one of Maryland's great statesmen-lawyers, regarded the compulsory oath as a violation of Constitutional rights. Mudd himself would be accused of using stronger words. He might have been speaking lightly when he did so. But in these times, light words were grave words, in more ways than one.

There was little on the surface to connect southern Maryland with events in Canada or to link Samuel Mudd with the Confederate conspirators collecting in Toronto at the Queen's Hotel. Yet in that city and later in Chicago a drama was unfolding, which, with its resolution and many of its cast, would be replayed in Washington with Samuel Mudd as one of the principal antagonists.

It had begun in 1859 with the hanging of John Brown and its aftermath. The plot of the drama had been publicly proclaimed by Ohio's Clement L. Vallandigham: "The day which divides the North from the South . . . decrees eternal divorce between the West and the East . . . we will not remain, after separation from the South, a province . . . of the East, to bear her burdens and pay her taxes; nor, hemmed in and isolated as we are, and without a sea-coast, could we long remain a distinct confederacy."[9]

From this premise was born the idea of a Northwest Confederacy, or Northwest Conspiracy, bound to the South by the common goal of independence from the Union. Its champions were called the Knights of the Golden Circle, recruited from the midwest states of Ohio, Illinois, and Indiana, whose populations came in large degree—up to forty percent—from the South. These were the copperheads who would challenge men like Lafayette Baker and War Secretary Stanton with a strong fifth column in the Great Lakes corner of the Union.

By November of 1864 the organization's name had changed from the Knights of the Golden Circle to the Order of American Knights to the Sons of Liberty. But the goals remained the same. The Sons of Liberty were led principally by the twenty-three-year-old Thomas Hines, late Confederate captain with John Hunt Morgan's rifles, taking orders from Jacob Thompson in Toronto with the sanction of President Davis in Virginia.

They were militant, and thought that they were strong, and by now they had a target, provided by Ulysses S. Grant. That spring, with Sherman poised at Chattanooga ready to move toward Atlanta and the Army of the Potomac prepared to strike at Richmond, Grant ordered a halt to the exchange of prisoners. On humanitarian grounds it was a cruel decision. On military grounds it could be justified: The North had ample reserves, the South did not. To release men to rejoin the Confederate army would, in Grant's mind, prolong the war.

Though the North complained bitterly of conditions in the Southern prison camps—overcrowding, lack of sanitation, near-starvation diet, and dreadful medical care—stories of equal horror reached the South from Northern prison camps. In the Dry Tortugas, Fort Jefferson had been turned into a Devil's Island for the more recalcitrant, a point of no return. One shuddered to think what the dreadful heat of the central Gulf, held in the pocket of that decaying fort, could do to men's bodies and minds. The prison camps of both sides were death traps, not so much by deliberate intent as by the harsh realities of war. Andersonville below Atlanta. Fort Jefferson in the Dry Tortugas. They would stand, or hopefully decay, as monuments to man's inhumanity to man.

Two miles outside Chicago stood Camp Douglas, holding some eight to twelve thousand Confederate prisoners of war, and nearby was the Rock Island Penitentiary with four or five thousand more. The Sons of Liberty would storm these prisons, arm the inmates, destroy Chicago and such other Northern bastions as were in their way, and attack the Union on its northwest flank. The date for this great offensive shifted, through discouraging postponements, from mid-July to early November of 1864. Captain Hines was the administrative general, and the military action, when the time came, would be led by the British soldier-of-fortune George St. Leger Grenfell.[10]

Fifty-six years old but still in his prime, Grenfell was rapidly becoming a legend in his time. The crusty, bearded, granite-faced giant with the build and posture of a Viking had served with Confederate troops as a volunteer without rank or pay since the spring of 1862. He had ridden with Morgan the Raider, with Fighting Joe Wheeler of the Army of Tennessee, with Jeb Stuart of Lee's Army of Northern Virginia. He had sought danger as if starving for it, had been wherever the bullets whistled thickest, had charged alone and berserk into

Union lines to slash at the enemy with his bloodied saber.

But when hit-and-run cavalry tactics became outmoded in the course of a war that was taking to the trenches, Grenfell had gone north to join Tom Hines, where the action was more promising. Posing as an English sportsman looking for legitimate game with his shotgun and hunting dog, he holed up in Toronto while Hines recruited his men for the offensive on Camp Douglas which the Britisher agreed to lead. Then came postponements, disappointments, and desertions. The thousands supposed to rally to the great cause dwindled to a paltry hundred, then to a mere twenty-five. Desperate, Hines refused to abandon the plan and set November 8 as the date for the attack.

It was already far too late. For months, if not years, the War Department in Washington had known of the conspiracy, through spies and informers—Grenfell himself had unwittingly roomed with one of the informers. On the night of the sixth St. Leger, with his hunting dog sleeping beside him, was arrested in his room in Chicago's Richmond House. The English crusader was pitched into a Camp Douglas cell to await trial and execution, the two regarded as synonymous. The dog fared better. He was coddled and exhibited around the city of Chicago, at twenty-five cents admission to the public, under the billing of "St. Leger Grenfell's savage bloodhound."

The widely publicized affair made colorful reading. But there were grimmer reports of Grenfell's subsequent trial in Cincinnati. Of the eight conspirators captured, reduced to six by one escape and a suicide, only Grenfell held nonmilitary status. He was a British subject, never officially enrolled in the Confederate army. Yet he would be tried with the others by a military tribunal with the writ of *habeas corpus* denied.

Grenfell's lawyers protested this violation of their client's rights: Civilians should be tried in a civil court. The War Department ruled that Grenfell's alleged crimes against the government were plotted "within the military lines and theater of military operations of the army of the United States, at a period of war and armed rebellion." Assistant Judge Advocate Henry L. Burnett, who would make his reputation on this case, went further. He declared that all six would be tried in a legal lump; the testimony brought against any one of them, the guilt that convicted any one of them, would apply to all.[11]

It was a custom-shattering decision, and one that would have a tragic aftermath. For sixty days St. Leger Grenfell languished in a tomblike cell awaiting trial, bound in shackles with a sixty-pound ball and chain around his ankle. Suffering from an attack of dysentery to which he was prone, he asked for a bowl of mush, declaring that the putrid prison fare would kill him. The officer in charge had an eloquent answer: "Then let him die, God damn him, he deserves nothing else."[12]

A pattern for unprecedented terror in America was being set, and Samuel Mudd would not escape it.

6

SPINNING OF THE WEB

There was not much to look forward to, that Christmas of 1864, as the holidays approached. Not in southern Maryland, at any rate. The war news for the South was gloomy. Hood's Army of Tennessee had fallen apart at Nashville; Grant's forces were massing before Petersburg; Sherman was at the gates of Savannah, having driven a wide wedge through the heart of the Confederate States from Chattanooga to the sea.

There was talk of secret peace negotiations between North and South, and the end began to seem a little closer. But even a negotiated peace was not one that Charles County planters could look forward to. Poverty, bordering on despair, was pressing hard on southern Maryland. The cost of everything had soared outrageously. Black labor wages were prohibitive—which made the rising demand and higher prices for tobacco more of a mockery than a promise. At Port Tobacco Christmas turkeys were selling for from fifty to a hundred dollars each. The farm was providing Mudd's family with poultry, eggs, and enough dried vegetables for comfortable subsistence. But unless the actor John Wilkes Booth came along with cash instead of promises to buy their land, it would be a lean holiday and winter for the Samuel Mudds.

Still one had to make an effort at providing Yuletide cheer. Sam arranged to ride to Washington City with Jeremiah Dyer to do some Christmas shopping: toys for the children, small gifts for John Best and the Washingtons, and above all a new cook stove for Frances to replace the potbellied monstrosity in the kitchen annex.

He and Dyer left for the city after noon on Friday, December 23. It was mild and pleasant for that time of year, and the pair rode at a leisurely pace up the old stage road to Surrattsville, stopping at Surratt's Villa for a glass of punch. Mrs. Surratt was no longer in charge, of course, having moved her family to Washington and opened the boarding house on H Street. The tavern had been leased to John C. Lloyd, and a new barkeep named Joseph Nott presided in the taproom.

John Lloyd, it turned out, was a former member of the metropolitan police who had moved to Prince Georges County purportedly to take up farming. After leasing the tavern, he found social drinking was more suited to his temperament. He consumed almost as much in spirits as he sold. The inn was jammed with holiday travelers and topers, none of whom Sam Mudd or Jeremiah Dyer knew. Lloyd was too far gone in liquor to provide good company, but he warned the two of Washington crowds this time of year. Keep a sharp eye out; trust nobody. Pennsylvania Avenue was fraught with murderers and crooks. . . .

Close to dusk, Sam and Jeremiah crossed the Navy Yard Bridge. They decided to take the Ninth Street horsecars into the city. The stables would be crowded and the rates high for the holidays; they could leave their horses cheaply near the Navy Yard. In the city they checked in at the unpretentious Pennsylvania House on C Street, a seedy, inexpensive hotel that sometimes crowded guests six to a room, although Dyer and Sam were able to get a modest suite for two. After registering and leaving their saddlebags, they went out to have supper at Dubant's Restaurant, which featured Rappahannock oysters for the first time since the war had begun—a reminder that the Rappahannock was now in Union hands.

Having finished supper, the pair stopped off at Brown's Hotel on Sixth Street, a favorite rendezvous of Maryland farmers and planters. Finding nobody there they knew, they moved on to the National, the mammoth caravansary across the street, where sooner or later everybody who was anybody made a point of showing up. The red-carpeted, red-draped lobby, with maroon upholstered chairs and glistening spittoons, was jammed with Congressmen and out-of-town visitors, and in no time at all Sam and Jeremiah became separated—Dyer later explaining that he had been buttonholed by a passing acquaintance whose company he could not shake.

Alone, Mudd went down to Pennsylvania Avenue for an evening's stroll. The wide, muddy thoroughfare, paved only on the north side, was crowded with Christmas shoppers and officers and men in uniform. The pall of gloom that had shrouded the capital all that fall had suddenly been lifted by the good news from the battlefronts. Newshawks shouted the headlines, "Savannah Evacuated!" "Richmond in a Fever!" The carillons of fifty churches pealed their messages of joy and Peace on Earth. Store windows decked with greenery were filled with gold and silver pen and pencil cases, prayer books, chess and backgammon boards, Morocco leathers, mink and sable scarfs, candies and children's toys. Posters on walls and lampposts advertised balls and parties sponsored by Washington organizations and societies.

There occurred at this point an incident that would not be brought to light until the trial of Dr. Mudd the following summer, and that would later be pieced together from the accounts of two of the participants, the doctor being one of them. Approaching Seventh Street, Mudd heard his name called. He stopped and turned. Even in the unaccustomed gaslight there was no mistaking that arresting figure in the velvet-collared greatcoat with its flowing cape, the sharply contrasted features of abnormally white skin and teeth, dark wavy hair and scimitar mustache. John Wilkes Booth, his guest at Bryantown six weeks before.

After exchanging pleasantries, Booth chatted about his purpose in the city. He was gathering information about the counties south of Washington "in order to be able to select a good locality for a country residence." To this end he was anxious to meet one John Surratt at—and here he consulted a pocket memorandum—541 H Street, a few blocks from where they stood. Perhaps Mudd would be good enough to go with him to Surratt's house and introduce him to the man. It would only take five minutes at the most.

Mudd was not certain that John Sur.att was even in the city, though he had heard that John had taken a job with the Adams Express Company operating between Baltimore and Washington. Besides, he had heard Booth's claim of "looking for a country residence" before and was beginning to wonder how sincere the actor was. Booth was no close friend of his; he owed him nothing. On the other hand, he still might be a prospective purchaser of Mudd's land. Taking out his pocket watch, Mudd observed that he was due to meet his brother-in-law at eight, and his time was limited; but he agreed to show Booth the way to the Surratt house.

They had started north on Seventh Street and had reached the Odd Fellows' Hall when another coincidental meeting took place. Approaching them on the same side of the street was John Surratt, accompanied by a slightly younger-looking stranger with a neat, triangular mustache. Small world. Smaller than the law of averages indicated. He hailed Surratt, and the two parties came abreast. Mudd introduced Booth and Surratt presented his companion, Louis Wiechmann.

With his natural sense of command, Booth took over the meeting and invited the foursome back to his room at the National for refreshments. Mudd scratched his eight o'clock appointment to meet Jeremiah, which he had mentioned only as an alibi. But as they reached Booth's floor in the hotel, he drew Surratt aside. He felt compelled to explain that this meeting with Booth was not his idea and apologized for introducing Surratt "to a man about whom I know so little." Acting on his previous impression, he also warned John that he suspected Booth of being a government agent or federal detective.

Inside Booth's room the actor pulled the call bell and ordered the bellboy to bring milk punches and cigars for four. The group settled in chairs around a central table for convivial conversation.

Of this strangely fortuitous meeting, Mudd and Wiechmann later gave different versions, though agreeing on some major details. According to Mudd's account Booth started doodling on the back of an envelope or letter, explaining that he had become lost on his latest visit to southern Maryland and wanted to get the roads straight in his mind, especially the route from Washington to the Potomac. He made some sketches and asked Surratt to verify them; Mudd was simply an interested observer of these lessons in geography.[1]

Wiechmann sat slightly apart, hearing and seeing nothing except that Booth was "drawing lines on paper." Wiechmann later recalled that Booth and Mudd excused themselves at one time and repaired to "a dark passage," remained there for some moments and then called to John Surratt to join them as the three engaged in further secret colloquy.[2]

After three-quarters of an hour Mudd prepared to leave, but out of politeness asked the others to return with him to his hotel. They all walked back to the Pennsylvania House and settled around the open fire in a downstairs sitting room. Here the group divided, Booth engaging John Surratt in private conversation. Mudd found himself paired with Louis Wiechmann—at this point a nonentity to Samuel Mudd but one who would play a greater part in the doctor's destiny than any other man alive, save John Wilkes Booth.

The Baltimore-born Wiechmann, crowding twenty-three, was a somewhat effeminate, overingratiating lad with characteristics of Uriah Heep. Slightly pudgy with auburn hair and the neat triangular mustache, he seemed sly, shy, ineffectual, and quick to shift allegiance according to how the wind blew. Early in life he had studied for the priesthood at St. Charles Academy with John Surratt. In fact, he had introduced Surratt to one of his cronies at the school, Henri Beaumont St. Marie. It was a casual three-way meeting and one that Wiechmann might soon forget. But John Surratt, reminded of that encounter five years later, would never forget the face of Henri Beaumont St. Marie.[3]

After leaving St. Charles Academy, Wiechmann had taken a teaching job in Washington and later, in January, 1864, had become an eighty-dollar-a-month clerk in the War Department's Commissary General of Prisoners, where he was now employed. During this period he had resumed his friendship with John Surratt and had visited the Surrattsville tavern several times. When John's mother moved to Washington and opened her door to lodgers, John invited Wiechmann to share his third-floor bedroom and Louis became a thirty-five-dollars-a-month boarder in the H Street house.

He and John had been close at first; and though Wiechmann had been puzzled by his roommate's frequent absences and strange preoccupations, he apparently never suspected John of underground activities. They had started out this evening on a Christmas shoppers' tour of Pennsylvania Avenue before encountering Mudd and Booth.

Now, seated together in the hotel sitting room, Wiechmann and Mudd chatted politely, sharing views and impressions on the progress of the war. Mudd spoke of Hood's defeat in Tennessee at the hands of General Thomas as a disaster from which the South would never recover. Wiechmann, quoting War Department figures, assured the doctor that Hood's losses were not as severe as reported and his defeat at Nashville not by any means disastrous. From this exchange each formed a deceptive opinion of the other's sentiments —Wiechmann sizing up Mudd as a "good Union man," the doctor finding Wiechmann "a good Southerner." Later they would both profess surprise at these extraordinarily erroneous judgments.

The party broke up at ten o'clock. Mudd left his guests in the hotel lobby and returned to his room, where he found Jeremiah fast asleep. The next morning the two pursued the purpose of their visit, Christmas shopping. Mudd purchased the stove for Frances from a dealer named MacGregor, then considered the problem of getting so heavy an object back to Bryantown.

He and Jeremiah toured the market stalls along the south side of the avenue where Maryland farmers displayed their produce, until they located Francis Lucas, farmhand and teamster for James Montgomery, proprietor of the Bryantown hotel. Lucas agreed to transport the stove to Bryantown if he could get rid of his employer's poultry that he was there to sell. In one of his occasional displays of prankishness, Mudd offered to help dispose of the feathered livestock, donned a street vendor's apron, and hawked his wares to passersby in the manner of a tobacco auctioneer. He failed to get rid of all the birds but in return for his efforts gained Lucas' promise to see that the stove was carried back to Bryantown.

After a little more shopping together on the avenue, Sam and Dyer went back to the Navy Yard for their horses and left the city around three o'clock.[4]

That winter, sickness descended on the Mudd farm like a dark miasma from the swamp. Except for a family party at George Henry Gardiner's the last Thursday of the month, to which the couple made the wintry trip on foot, Sam and Frances rarely left their home. Tom Davis, their frequent visitor from Prince Georges County, had joined the household the first week in January, moving into the guest room on the second floor. It was thought he could take up some of the work load of the servants who were leaving for the higher salaries Mudd could not afford.

Baptist Washington had abandoned the room he had built off the kitchen and returned to the city that bore his name. Charles Bloyce and Julian Ann were there only on weekends, so Mudd had little help from Charlie. The aging John Best was occupied in caring for the horses and in work around the stables. Betty Washington, though she sometimes helped at cutting brush and even at seeding the tobacco beds, was more generally needed for housework. To say that the farm was shorthanded was an understatement.

Davis was the first to come down with the strange malaise affecting the community, an illness that Mudd apparently could not diagnose. Davis took to his bed in mid-February, to remain on his back for six weeks. The doctor visited the sickroom twice a day, Frances brought the patient his meals, and brother John brought him a supply of perch from Prince Georges County to see him through a meatless Lent.

Mornings and afternoons, Mudd and Frank Washington worked alone preparing the seedbeds for spring planting. But on March 2 came the first of many interruptions. Mudd was routed out of bed at dawn, with news that his sister Mary had been taken ill. He hurried over to Oak Hill, concluded that Mary had only a slight spring cold, and advised that she stay in bed and rest.

The following day, a Friday, it rained heavily. Mudd worked alone in the tobacco barns, stripping the leaves that had been curing since the late fall harvest. Word came that Mary had suffered a turn for the worse, and without taking time to wash the tobacco gum from his hands, he hurried back to Henry Lowe's. The patient's face had broken out in pustular sores. Smallpox, almost certainly. Having come over emptyhanded, Mudd returned to the farm for his medicine kit and was back at his father's attending Mary by midafternoon.

As soon as he had Mary under regular, daily treatment, according to the best of his knowledge of this scourge, one of his father's blacks came down with typhoid pneumonia. The doctor added her to his list of patients. Though the seedbeds suffered, and the cured tobacco would be slow in reaching market, he was working harder at his true profession, medicine, than he had worked in many months. Undoubtedly this was a source of satisfaction to him; and before three months had passed, he would have further reason to be grateful for this chance preoccupation.

He was probably not in Washington—where John Wilkes Booth was spinning an imperfect web.

After the introduction Samuel Mudd had somewhat unwillingly arranged, Booth had little trouble enlisting John Surratt in his conspiracy, and Surratt brought in two more recruits. He recommended that George Atzerodt, the Port Tobacco carriage maker, be added to the band. Surratt himself, in sneaking back and forth across the Potomac on errands for the Richmond government, had used Atzerodt's services as part-time boatman. Booth agreed and gave or sold to Atzerodt the one-eyed bay he had bought when visiting with Samuel Mudd. The bay was kept at Naylor's stables near Ford's Theater, for future use.

Surratt also introduced Booth to twenty-year-old David Herold, a pharmacist's clerk who lived with his mother and seven sisters near the Navy Yard. Little more than a juvenile delinquent with a twelve-year-old mind, Herold was nonetheless affable, pliable, and totally captivated by the famous actor's charm. He knew Charles County like the palm of his hand, from riding and hunting in the area, and had met Surratt from time to time at his mother's tavern. Though not one to undertake a serious assignment, Davey would be useful as a guide and escort.[5]

At this point Booth had not considered the stagehand, Edward Spangler, as a possible accomplice. Ned owed him, of course, for the job at Ford's. Spangler had refurbished a rickety stable behind the theater where Booth kept his horses from time to time. And here Ned lived with his scant possessions—a bottle, which Booth replaced as needed, and a length of rope with which to fish for crabs on his time off. He was devoted to the actor, and Booth might find him useful one way or another when the time came.

The first big chance to kidnap Lincoln, the chance Booth had been praying and waiting for, had promised to come some time in January. Edwin Forrest, an actor known to be a favorite of the President's, was appearing at Ford's in a production of *Jack Cade*. Lincoln rarely missed Forrest when he came to Washington. A trap was quickly prepared, with Forrest as the bait.

Booth sent an urgent summons to O'Laughlin and Arnold in Baltimore. John Surratt, resigning his job with the Adams Company, hurried to Port Tobacco to arrange with George Atzerodt for a barge that could carry their party across the river to Virginia. David Herold procured the kidnap vehicle, and Lloyd's tavern was stocked with gear they could pick up on their flight—guns, ammunition, handcuffs, and a length of rope. When the announcement came that the President would attend the theater on January 18, Booth briefed his henchmen on their roles—all except Arnold and O'Laughlin, who had not responded to his summons.

The kidnap plan was so naïvely simple as to be ridiculous, At a given point in the performance, Surratt would extinguish the theater lights by means of a basement switch, then hurry to aid Wilkes as he invaded Box 8 to seize the President. They would truss their quarry with rope, lower him by more rope to the stage, then hustle the President out the back entrance into Herold's waiting carriage. In a trice they would be at the Navy Yard Bridge, then across the Potomac and

soon at Lloyd's. There they would pick up the strand of
rope to stretch across the highway as a means of tripping
up pursuing cavalry.

No other possibility was contemplated, no obstacles
foreseen. How the tough and sinewy President would be
so easily subdued, what the audience and actors would be
doing all this time, how they would evade the President's
guards, the Washington police, and the inevitable band of
volunteer pursuers, were details not, apparently, considered.
Perhaps the abductors relied on the element of surprise to
throw potential adversaries off balance.

One would never know. At the last moment the President
canceled his engagement to attend the theater.

Booth could only rant at unkind fate and those of his
followers who had ignored his call. The plan's miscarriage
only whetted his resolve to try again. He persuaded
O'Laughlin and Arnold to come to Washington and take
rooms in a boarding house on D Street; coaxed Atzerodt
up from Port Tobacco and installed him, at the actor's
expense, in the Pennsylvania House; made John Surratt's
bedroom, in his mother's boarding house on H Street, a
headquarters for clandestine meetings and exchange of information and a cache for weapons, maps, theatrical disguises,
extra boots and spurs and other equipment fitting to the
cloak-and-dagger operation.

Chance brought another conspirator into the fold. In Baltimore on theater business the first week in March, Booth
ran into a familiar figure from the past. In front of Barnum's
Hotel he recognized the ex-Confederate soldier Lewis Powell,
whom he had met when Lewis was on leave in Baltimore
some three years earlier. They greeted one another like long
separated brothers, the ex-soldier flattered by the famous
star's attention.

Being a Southerner in Union territory and anxious to hide
his identity, Powell was going by the name of Paine. But
there was no mistaking the backwoods gladiator: a giant of
twenty-one, with coarse dark hair encroaching on his
forehead, pouting lips and jutting underjaw, with nerves and
muscles of honed steel. A man with the single-track mind

of an automaton, unable to think for himself and a slave to anyone who did his thinking for him. The perfect tool for Booth's conspiracy.[6]

Born Lewis Thornton Powell, the son of a backwoods Alabama preacher, Lewis had enlisted at the age of sixteen in the Southern army, had fought on the Peninsula, at Antietam and at Chancellorsville, and had been taken prisoner at Gettysburg. Escaping, he had free-lanced as a Confederate guerrilla, then tired of the arduous life and drifted through enemy lines to Baltimore. After almost beating to death a black servant for what he considered impudence, he was ordered by the provost marshal to leave the city, at which point Booth appeared like a star of hope on the horizon.

As before, Paine was captivated by Booth's flattering attention. He was destitute, footloose, threatened with arrest. Booth fed him, clothed him, brought him to Washington, and got him to take a room at Mary Surratt's house, where he posed as "the Reverend Mr. Wood," a Baptist preacher. The band of conspirators, though not yet integrated, was complete: John Surratt, David Herold, George Atzerodt, Sam Arnold, Mike O'Laughlin, and the lone wolf, Lewis Paine. This oddly assorted cast of characters had yet to be shaped into a well-performing troupe.

Time was running out. The President's inauguration on March 4 made the need for sudden action seem imperative. Booth attended the ceremony with a ticket given him by his fiancée, Bessie Hale. As Lincoln moved through the Capitol rotunda to the platform, a dark-coated figure in a black slouch hat broke through the crowd and lunged toward the President. Guards overpowered the intruder and rushed him to a guardroom in the basement. The man was later identified by an arresting officer as John Wilkes Booth. But that Booth should so obviously show his hand, to so little purpose, was patently absurd. Evidence indicates that he never left his seat.[7]

Booth later confided to fellow thespian Sam Chester, however, that he had been close enough to the President to shoot him. Already the idea of assassination was festering in his mind. But he stuck to the plan of abducting the President as a hostage for Confederate prisoners of war and still believed it could best be accomplished at Grover's or Ford's theaters. On March 15 he held an after-theater dinner for his motley band at Gautier's Restaurant on Pennsylvania Avenue. Here for the first time Arnold and O'Laughlin met John Surratt, Atzerodt, and Herold, and all were introduced to Lewis Paine. And here for the first time Booth ran into mutiny.

Sam Arnold remarked that to try to kidnap the President in a crowded theater was ridiculous; he wanted no part of such an ill-considered prank. Outraged, Booth threatened to shoot him as a renegade. Arnold observed, "Two can play that game," and they glowered at one another till Booth simmered down.

An alternative procedure was proposed. It was known that the President frequently drove around the capital, either for pleasure or on business, often traversing lonely roads on the outskirts of the city. It would be a relatively easy matter to intercept his carriage, get rid of the driver and guards, and hustle the coach by back streets out of Washington.

Booth acquiesced and discovered from actors at Ford's that Lincoln planned to attend a benefit performance at the Soldier's Home on Seventh Street, outside the city, on March 20. Once again the kidnap machinery was set in motion. Horses were engaged, carbines, rope and other gear were readied at Lloyd's tavern, a barge was warped to the wharf at Port Tobacco. And on Monday noon, March 20, the highwaymen rode north up Seventh Street in pairs—Booth and Surratt, Arnold and O'Laughlin, Atzerodt and Paine—armed with pistols, primed with brandy, with faces half-concealed by floppy slouch hats—to wait beneath trees at a curve in the road for the President's carriage to appear.

Right on cue a smart-looking coach drawn by a spirited team of horses clattered round the bend. With pistols drawn, Booth and Surratt descended on the target like a pair of Western outlaws; they would seize and subdue the driver, while the other four took over the carriage and its occupant. The coachman turned on his seat in dumb amazement; wheels screeched and horses reared; the window curtains were pulled aside and a pale and startled face peered out at the surrounding highwaymen.

It was not the President. Surratt believed it to be Salmon

Chase who was, in fact, on his way to the performance at
the Soldier's Home. No one would ever know for sure. All
that was certain, as Booth discovered later, was that Lincoln's
schedule had been rearranged to allow him to attend a military ceremony at Booth's own hotel, the National, in down-
town Washington.[8]

For the first time real fear, bordering on panic, shook
the little group. Had they been recognized? Would the
attempted holdup be reported to the War Department? Had
they so far shown their hand that they and the whole
conspiracy were now suspected and endangered?

O'Laughlin and Arnold fled back to Baltimore, Arnold
later taking a job as sutler's clerk at Fortress Monroe in
Hampton Roads. Atzerodt took off for Port Tobacco, Paine
headed for New York, Herold went home to hide behind
the skirts of seven sisters. Surratt renounced the abortive
scheme; he wormed his way back to Virginia to resume his
role as courier between the Richmond government and Montreal. Booth might still use the boarding house on H Street
as a place of rendezvous, but John had washed his hands
of the affair for good.

At Oak Hill, Sam Mudd's sister Mary had recovered; so
had the pneumonia patient; Tom Davis was back on his feet;
and the threat of smallpox faded with the milder weather.
By the last week in March Mudd felt entitled to a break
from farm routine and on Thursday, the twenty-third, he
and Lewellyn Gardiner rode up to Washington, starting
shortly after breakfast. Their purpose was to attend a sale
of government-condemned horses scheduled for Friday
morning.[9]

Reaching Robert Martin's lodging house just south of the
Navy Yard Bridge at noon, they learned from Martin that
the sale had been postponed to Tuesday. They assuaged
this disappointment with a dinner of fresh Potomac perch
and a bottle of claret, Martin joining them at the table. Mudd
had not been in the capital since Christmas Eve, when he
had stumbled into John Wilkes Booth. He proposed that
they at least cross the bridge and do a little window-shop-
ping.

He and Lewellyn left their horses at the Inn and took

the cars to Pennsylvania Avenue. They visited Young's Carriage Factory, where the doctor looked over the display of wagons, then toured a number of livery stables to price the same type of vehicles available at secondhand. Though Mudd had never owned a carriage of any sort, if he were moving to Benedict—a still uncertain project—he would need some sort of transportation to get his possessions over there, carry provisions, and take his family to Bryantown from time to time.

A cautious and prudent man, Mudd spent no money on a carriage. His curiosity satisfied, he and Lewellyn began rounding up some cronies for an evening game of whist. They started with Frances' cousin, Henry Alexander Clark, a retail merchant in the city, and went on to the office home of Dr. Charles Allen, a longtime acquaintance of the Mudds. Allen recruited eight other men for the evening's entertainment. Never so happy as when playing cards, Mudd along with the others lost all track of time and it was after one in the morning when they were jolted out of their pleasant occupation.

None would ever forget that night. It began with a low keening sound, such as returning soldiers spoke of when describing the whine of an approaching rocket. Then the noise rose in a crescendo, and the house shook, rattling the apothecary's glass vessels in the doctor's office. Not far away, in the ghetto along the Potomac, whole shanties were lifted from their marshy roots and overturned; a black was thrown to his death; and even in Washington city proper the roofs of houses were sent spinning through the air. In these uncertain days perhaps one might expect the unexpected. A freak tornado coming from the west had struck the capital.

It seemed unwise to try to return to Martin's over the Navy Yard Bridge, and Mudd and Gardiner spent the night at Clark's. The next morning after breakfast they visited the Capitol to view some paintings on exhibit, afterward taking a streetcar to the Navy Yard and returning to Martin's in time for noonday dinner. That afternoon they rode home, Mudd arriving to discover that the night's tornado had descended on Charles County, and his tobacco barn had been leveled.

* * *

In Washington more than a freak tornado threatened the horizon. The authorities had only to heed the warnings and take precautionary measures to stave off catastrophe. Perhaps the wolf cry had been raised too often—so often that it was hard to take any single warning seriously. Lincoln himself, as reported to close associates, had dreamed of his own impending death. New York newspapers had reported his "assassination" as a *fait accompli*, while the supposed victim was alive and well. Crank letters by the score poured into the War Department, stating the time, the place, and the method by which the President would meet his death. In Lincoln's desk was a current file labeled ASSASSINATION, containing more than fifty such sinister documents.

Once these threats came close to consummation, if hearsay evidence can be believed. Crossing the ice-coated White House lawn one night with Major Thomas Eckert of the War Department, and passing close to a bush where his would-be assassin waited with a rifle, Lincoln jestingly called to his companion, "Spread out! Spread out, or we shall fall through the ice." At the cry "Spread out!" the murderer thought himself detected and took flight. His name: Lewis Paine, appointed by John Wilkes Booth (according to Paine's story) to ambush and shoot the President on the latter's customary nighttime walk from the War Department to the White House.

War Secretary Stanton was himself a man obsessed with death. As a child he had cherished a skeleton given him by his father to abet an interest in anatomy, and he had taken macabre satisfaction in placing lighted candles in the sockets of the eyes. As a youth, when his landlady's daughter died, he waited till the mourners had left the graveside, then dug up the corpse to make certain she was truly dead. When his own daughter passed away, he had her body placed in a special leaden casket, which he kept beside his bed for months. And when his wife died, the family feared that in the violence of his distraction he would either kill himself or go insane.[10]

Now the death or murder of the President was an obsession with him. He urged Lincoln to avoid public appearances, especially at the theater of which he was so fond. Should the President try to organize a theater party, ignoring Stanton's warning, the Secretary would secretly urge the guests to decline as a precautionary measure. Of no comfort was Lincoln's often quoted statement, "I cannot possibly guard myself against all dangers unless I shut myself up in an iron box."

Yet when an early warning came, it was largely ignored. The March attempt to kidnap the President near the Soldier's Home brought no response from the authorities. But the preparations of the conspirators and their subsequent panic was noted by Mary Surratt's star boarder, Louis Wiechmann. Wiechmann's motives are obscure. Was he jealous of John Surratt's friendship for the actor Booth? Was he irked at being disbarred from the tight conspiratorial society? Or was he a patriot doing his duty as he saw it?

Ever since meeting Samuel Mudd at the National the previous December, Wiechmann had wondered at the composition and behavior of Booth's little group. Why were Surratt and Booth so interested in south county farmland and topography? What went on at the secret meetings at the boarding house on H Street, from which Wiechmann was excluded? What was the meaning of the guns, knives, extra spurs and boots, and even a false mustache, which he found hidden in the room he shared with John?

Shortly after the holdup fiasco on Seventh Street, Wiechmann spoke of his suspicions to a fellow clerk at the Commissary General of Prisoners, Captain D. H. L. Gleason.

"By God, that is strange!" Gleason exclaimed. "There's something going on there."

The captain reportedly passed the word on to the War Department, while Wiechmann himself told his story to an army recruiting officer who supposedly informed his superiors. John Surratt, later explaining his defection from the group, stated that he believed the government had been informed of their activities. Yet no steps were taken by government officials, at the time at any rate, to investigate or act on Wiechmann's charges.

John Wilkes Booth, however, took steps to reassemble and

reactivate his shrinking band. John Surratt was lost to him; but he kept in touch with Mary Surratt, finding the widow an obliging, unsuspecting intermediary in his devious transactions. He sent a telegram to O'Laughlin in Baltimore, urging him to hasten to Washington with "Sam." Mike ignored the summons, and Samuel Arnold wrote an indignant letter addressed to "Dear John," denouncing and rejecting the whole scheme.[11]

But three of his henchmen remained faithful. He installed George Atzerodt in the Kirkwood House, where Vice President Andrew Johnson lived, and lured Paine back from New York to the Herndon House hotel near Ford's. Herold, of course, was still living with his family near the Navy Yard, but followed his master around the city like a fawning and devoted slave.

Booth bided his time; followed Lincoln's movements like a hawk; and started drinking more heavily than usual at Peter Taltavel's Saloon.

Two weeks after his late March visit to the capital, Sam Mudd rode north again with his brother, Henry, who was back from college and hoping to become a farmer. He was still anxious to take advantage of the government's wholesale disposal of its surplus horses. Leaving Bryantown on the morning of April 10, they spent the night in Brandywine, a few miles south of Washington, with the Blandfords—Joseph Blandford and Sam Mudd's younger sister, Cecilia, Blandford's wife. But this time Mudd shunned the capital itself. Instead, he and Henry attended an auction at Giesboro, midway between Blandford's and the city. Blandford left them there, having business in Washington, and Sam and Henry inspected the horses that were up for sale, found them "very inferior," and rode up to Martin's inn for dinner, where Blandford was to meet them. After the meal all three set out for home. Henry and Sam dropped Blandford off at Brandywine and rode together back to Bryantown.

If the two trips to the vicinity of Washington had led to nothing, the days between were far from uneventful for Charles County and the nation. Richmond fell to the Union besiegers on April 2, and one week later, on Palm Sunday, Robert E. Lee surrendered the Army of Northern Virginia to Ulysses S. Grant. In that simple ceremony at Appomatox died the dreams of a nation that itself had been a dream. In southern Maryland the Mudds, the Gardiners, the Dyers, and the Boarmans accepted the inevitable. Wasting little time on grievance for the past, they looked with a certain dread toward the future. If Lincoln had meant what he said of binding up the nation's wounds, "with malice toward none; with charity for all; with firmness in the right, as God gives us to see the right," then perhaps there was hope for justice for the South. If Lincoln lived. . . .

Coming on top of the fall of Richmond, Lee's surrender turned Washington into a carnival of jubilee. Crowds surrounded the White House shouting for the President. Impromptu parades were formed on Pennsylvania Avenue with marching bands that impishly played "Dixie." From a casement window of the White House, Lincoln briefly addressed the throng. There was no hint of venom toward a vanquished enemy, only a plea that all should work together for a reconstructed Union in which, he suggested, ex-slaves—all blacks, in fact—should have the right to vote.

In the crowd before the White House, burning with fierce hatred at those words, stood John Wilkes Booth. Lewis Paine was at his side, and would later testify that Booth, in a paroxysm of rage, urged him to shoot the President on the spot. Paine refused; the hazards of capture were too great; he had no yen to be a martyr. As the two moved off, with Booth still seething from the President's words, the actor said between his teeth, "That is the last speech *he* will ever make!"

It was.

NO DEED SO FOUL

GOOD Friday, April 14, was not a holy day of obligation, but at St. Mary's Church from dawn to dusk Father Courtney was conducting services. Mudd would have liked to attend the special service in midafternoon. But this was a critical period in his planting schedule. The tobacco seedlings were high in the protected beds on the south slope of the farm. Before the May rains, the fields below had to be tilled and hilled and fertilized and generally made ready to receive the tender shoots.

Throughout the morning he and Frank Washington, with some help from Thomas Davis, worked beneath a hazy and uncertain sky. As usual they were shorthanded. Throughout all of southern Maryland, with news of Lee's surrender at Appomatox, blacks had been taking off for Washington like pilgrims hastening to Mecca. Extra labor, had Mudd been able to afford it, was impossible to get.

In the capital city John Wilkes Booth, shaved and groomed at Charlie Wood's barbershop near the National, started walking to Ford's Theater to collect his mail. Ordinarily a man of manic confidence and self-conceit, his faith in God and in himself, often synonymous, was badly shaken. He felt, he later told fellow thespian John Matthews, like a man without a country. His beloved South was lost and he had failed in his designs to save her. All he could strive for now was justice, which began with vengeance.[1]

His original plot to kidnap the President was, of course, of no use now. But to kill the despot who had killed the

South appeared almost ordained by God, the only act that measured up to proper retribution. Rightfully, Lincoln's cabinet should die as well, bringing chaos if not total ruin to the North.

In this nightmare dream he mentally chose his victims. Secretary of State Seward should be marked for death, and that would be a job for Lewis Paine. Vice President Johnson, Lincoln's natural successor, should be disposed of, and that would be George Atzerodt's assignment. Stanton might be difficult to get at in the well-guarded War Department, but possibly other military figures, such as Ulysses Grant, now being publicly feted in the capital, could be destroyed.

The actor still favored Ford's or Grover's as the trap for Lincoln, counting on the President's fondness for the theater. Seward, invalided by an accident, was bedridden in his home. Andrew Johnson lived unguarded at the Kirkwood House where Atzerodt was now installed. Stanton and Grant? Possibly some public ceremony or reception would leave them vulnerable. But Booth's band was down to only three beside himself—Paine, Atzerodt, and Herold—which meant a careful disposition of his forces.

At Ford's that morning, acting manager James R. Ford was fretting with anxiety. His older brother, John, who owned the place, was in Richmond on family affairs, and James faced the prospect of a dreary evening at the ticket office. Just three blocks west the competitive Grover's Theater was celebrating General Grant's victorious arrival in the capital with a gala evening of patriotic songs and sketches tuned to the occasion. All Ford's had to offer was Tom Taylor's tired comedy, *Our American Cousin,* starring Laura Keene in a role that had played itself out by repetition. James would be lucky if he sold a third of the 1700 seats.

It was ten thirty when the news came. A White House messenger brought word that Mrs. Lincoln would like to engage the Presidential box that night for herself, the President and General Grant!

Ford's spirits soared. The President's presence alone would boost attendance. But Grant—the hero of the war! The house that night would be a sellout!

Like a general directing his lieutenants on the field, Ford snapped out orders. He directed James Gifford, the theater's carpenter, to have the partition removed between the two upper, stage-left boxes, numbers 7 and 8. He sent handyman Joe Simms to fetch from the Ford's apartment the high-backed cushioned rocking chair the President was used to. He arranged with William Withers, orchestra conductor, to compose a song saluting General Grant and his victorious army, and ordered special costume accessories for the singers. An announcement of the President's and Grant's appearance was prepared to reach the evening papers.

Meanwhile, since the small flags kept below stage hardly suited the occasion, Ford decided to go to the Treasury building and borrow two larger sizes of the Stars and Stripes along with an all-blue flag of the Treasury Regimental Guards.

About to leave the lobby, he encountered John Wilkes Booth and obligingly went back to get the actor's mail. Handing it to him, Ford could not repress the glorious news. The President and General Grant would be attending the performance.

"Is that so?" said Booth with studied indifference, and sat on the steps outside to read his mail. He was seen, however, to pause in his reading and break out in sudden, exultant laughter.

Inside, the play was in rehearsal and Booth, with the freedom permitted any actor well-known to the theater, watched from a back row of the orchestra. He caught the second scene of Act Three, in which the conniving Mrs. Mountchessington and her daughter Augusta learn that the visiting Yankee, Asa Trenchard, may not be the millionaire he posed as. They reject both his marriage proposal to Augusta and the earthy language of the suitor.

MRS. M.:   Mr. Trenchard, you will please recollect you
            are addressing my daughter, and in my
            presence.
ASA: Yes, I'm offering her my heart and hand just
            as she wants them, with nothing in 'em.
MRS. M.:   Augusta, dear, to your room.

AUGUSTA: Yes, Ma, the nasty beast.
MRS. M.: I am aware, Mr. Trenchard, you are not used
to the manners of good society, and that, alone,
will excuse the impertinence of which you have
been guilty.[2]

Booth watched the familiar scene with heightened interest.
Harry Hawkin, playing the part of Asa, was alone on the
simple uncluttered set. The wings and passageway that
flanked the theater were clear of all but one or two actors
waiting for the next scene. Coming up was Hawk's line that
had always drawn explosive laughter and applause:

ASA: Don't know the manners of good society, eh?
Well, I guess I know enough to turn you inside out, old gal—you old sockdologizing
man-trap. . . .

The perfect cue. Almost certain laughter to drown out any
irregular sound. A nearly emptied stage. The house lights
dim.

Booth pocketed his mail, left the lobby, walked up G Street
and east to Seventh. The strands of the web were falling
into place. At James Dumphrey's livery stable behind the
National Hotel he asked for and hired a speedy saddle horse,
a small bay with a black mane and a white star on her forehead.
From this moment on, keyed up and inspired, he was on
the move. Next stop: Mary Surratt's boarding house on H
Street. He found Mrs. Surratt and Louis Wiechmann about
to leave by buggy for John Lloyd's tavern in Surrattsville.
Mrs. Surratt was hoping to collect some money that was owed
her in the village. Booth asked her to deliver to Lloyd a
small package, which he handed to her. It contained, he
said, "glasses."

Thereafter Booth's erratic movements in the city become
hard to follow. Certainly he tried to contact the scattered
members of his band to tell them that the moment had
arrived. He stopped at the Kirkwood House to find that
Atzerodt was out. And Vice President Johnson? Also out.
Booth took out his personal card, wrote on the back, "Don't

wish to disturb you; are you at home?" and asked the clerk
to see that Mr. Johnson got it. The clerk slipped it into
Johnson's box.

It seems likely that the cryptic message coupled with the
name of John Wilkes Booth was designed to implicate the
Vice President in whatever subsequently happened. True,
according to Booth's crystallizing plan, Johnson was slated
for murder at the hands of Atzerodt. But if the unpredictable
Atzerodt failed in his assignment, here was evidence that
the Vice President was linked to the conspiracy. It might
be another way of ending Johnson's government career.

Booth would never know it, but the ploy of the calling
card fizzled when Johnson's secretary, Colonel William Browning, picked up his employer's mail. Browning had met Booth
once, knew the actor was in Washington, and was flattered
to think that the note was meant for him. He put the card
in his pocket and forgot about it.[3]

Wilkes next appeared at Deery's Billiard Saloon adjoining
Grover's, where he downed a bottle of brandy in swift, hard-
hitting draughts, then went to the theater office to borrow
a pen and stationery. The letter he wrote, addressed to the
"Editor, National Intelligencer," would only be brought to
light much later, from memory. It outlined his plans for
the night's assassination of the President, and closed with
the signatures: "John Wilkes Booth—Payne, Atzerodt and
Herold."

The fact that Booth was willing to share billing in the outstanding act of his career, suggests that he wanted his supporting cast to share the penalty if things should go awry. But
like the card he had left at the Kirkwood House for Johnson,
the letter was never to reach its intended destination.

Riding back toward Ford's, past Willard's hotel on Pennsylvania Avenue, the actor passed John Matthews, one of the
players in *Our Country Cousin*. He drew up beside him and
handed Mathews the letter addressed to the *National Intelligencer*. Would he deliver it to the paper sometime in the morning? Mathews, though doubtless puzzled at the request,
agreed to do so.[4]

At that moment an open carriage passed on its way from
Willard's evidently headed for the railroad station. In it sat
General Grant and Mrs. Grant. Was one of his projected

prey escaping? Booth entered Willard's and questioned the desk clerk. He learned that the Grants had checked out and were on their way to visit their children in New Jersey.

One prize catch had escaped the net. Booth would make doubly certain of the other, and would count on Paine to make sure of Secretary Seward, too.

It was approaching sundown; there was work to do. Booth rode into Baptist Alley behind Ford's and summoned Spangler from the theater. He showed Ned the lively bay he had hired for the evening and asked him to see that she was fed and watered and kept in the stable till he called for her. Meanwhile—was anyone else in the theater at this hour? If so, he would like to treat them to a drink. Spangler brought out two of his stagehand cronies, and Booth led them into Taltavul's, provided them with a bottle that would keep them busy for a while, and returned to the empty theater.

Though the hall was dark, he knew his way like a cat in the night and moved swiftly and surely on his self-appointed rounds. In the passageway from door to stage he picked up a wooden bar, part of a music stand, then climbed the stairs from the lobby to the mezzanine. The door to the President's box was closed but opened easily. The lock, as Booth was well aware, had been broken weeks before and never repaired.

Passing into the narrow hall behind the box he used the bar to measure the distance from the outer door to the opposite wall, then drew his penknife and cut a mortise in the plaster wall. One end of the bar would fit in the notch, the other would be propped against the door to prevent it from being opened from the outside.

At the end of the hall was the second door to the box, also with a broken lock. Booth noted the position of the President's rocker, drew an augur from his pocket and bored a hole through the panel at eye level with the chair top. He used his penknife to widen the hole, then swept up the shavings with his handkerchief, along with the plaster from the mortised wall, pocketed the debris, laid the wood bar in a corner, satisfied himself that all was well, and left the theater.

Only one vital task remained: to brief his three lieutenants,

Herold, Paine, and Atzerodt, on their orders for the evening. Though most of Booth's movements that afternoon were subsequently traced and documented, the place and time of that final meeting remained undisclosed. Herold later suggested that they met in Paine's room at the Herndon House, but nothing Herold said could be believed; Herndon House was too close to the theater for a secret rendezvous. In any event, Booth brought them together and instructed each on his assignment.

Appropriate to his stature, Booth himself would play the starring role. At ten thirty, timed by his knowledge of the play, he would enter the theater, shoot the President, and ride the wind to the Navy Yard Bridge. At the same time Paine, escorted by Herold, would wangle his way into Seward's house, shoot the Secretary, and follow the same escape route. Atzerodt, meanwhile, would force his way into Johnson's chambers at the Kirkwood House, kill the Vice President, and follow the escape route of the others.

Only Atzerodt, who had spent the day in the Kirkwood bar, first fortifying and then stupefying his delinquent courage, balked. He had no taste for blood. Kidnapping had been one thing, murder was another. Booth silenced him with a warning. Atzerodt was implicated by the letter to the *Intelligencer,* whether he actually killed or not, and would suffer the consequences with them all. No use to back out. Atzerodt sniveled in acquiescence. He was the weak link in the chain, Booth knew, but perhaps the note that Booth had left for Johnson at the Kirkwood House would have the effect at least of character assassination.

Meeting adjourned.

Some thirty minutes after the curtain had risen on the first act of *Our American Cousin,* the President's carriage rolled up Tenth Street to the main door of Ford's Theater. With the Lincolns, replacing the New Jersey-bound Grants, were a popular young couple, Major Henry Rathbone and his fiancée, Miss Clara Harris, daughter of Senator Ira Harris of New York. Upon their entrance, conductor William Withers cued the orchestra to strike up *Hail to the Chief.*

The President's party climbed the stairs to the dress circle, moved down to the unlocked doors of Box 8. Lincoln slouched into the appointed rocker with Mary on his right; Miss Harris had a cane-bottomed chair in the corner nearest the stage; Major Rathbone sat on a sofa just behind her. Guarding the entrance to the box was Constable John F. Parker, whose record on the city police force was disgraceful. Parker was not the President's choice for the assignment but was, for curious reasons, a personal favorite of Mary Lincoln. Lincoln himself had requested an armed guard for the theater party, but War Secretary Stanton had refused. Though Stanton had thought it risky for the Lincolns to attend the theater, with Washington overrun by strangers, rebel sympathizers and suspected spies, he needed all extra uniformed guards for police work on the city streets.

As the presidential party took their seats and the action of the play resumed, Parker left his post at the box door and moved up the side aisle to watch the play. Once the performance was underway, he could sneak out for a drink. Nursing a hangover, he was naggingly in need of one.

Nine o'clock was the customary bedtime for the farmers of Charles County. Each hour of the lengthening days was precious at this time of year, and the morning's work began at seven. Samuel Mudd climbed into bed beside his wife, complaining of sore muscles, weariness, and a debilitating headache, a composite malaise that may have been a consequence of overexertion, a treacherous sun above a hazy sky, or something he had eaten. He hoped for a night of undisturbed sleep, if he could rid his mind of nagging money worries and concern over what would happen to him, to them all, now that the war was over and the South had been defeated.

A nearly full moon rose over Zachia Swamp, and one by one the lights were going out all over southern Maryland—as they were going out in Washington, except for the illuminated Capitol, the all-night candles in the White House, and the cluster of streetlamps outside Grover's and Ford's theaters. In the office of General Christopher C. Augur on Fourteenth Street near Secretary Seward's home, the lights burned late. As head of the military forces in the capital, Augur had the weighty responsibility of maintaining order and security in a community growing more and more unruly with the lifting of wartime restrictions.

Half after nine o'clock John Wilkes Booth, after having dined at the National Hotel, walked the short distance to Ford's, still smartly attired in black tailored riding coat, black trousers tapering to highly polished boots, even silver spurs. Inside his coat he carried a dagger, and in his belt was a stubby, single-shot derringer, both well concealed. The only discordant note was the plaid shawl under his arm, which carried among other things a brace of pistols and some articles of stage disguise.

In Baptist Alley, passing the shanties where blacks lounged in open windows, he fetched the bay mare from his stable and led her to the stage door. Opening the door, he called for Spangler. When the stagehand appeared, Booth asked him to hold the horse. Ned told him his duties demanded that he be on stage throughout the play; he summoned a stand-in, little John Burroughs, known as "Peanuts John," to hold the horse and went back to his job.

Wilkes strapped the shawl on the pommel of the saddle and looked at his pocket watch. He was early. Circling around to Taltavul's Saloon, he ordered a bottle and fortified himself with brandy. Between the rapid-fire drinks he may have pondered the curtain line for what he believed would be the greatest starring role of his career. The motto of the state of Virginia had always appealed to him—*Sic Semper Tyrannis,* "Thus Always to Tyrants." It had a certain ring.

He spun a silver dollar on the bar and left.

There were no guards outside the theater. No one, anyway, would have questioned the well-known actor's entrance through the main door. Mounting the stairs to the gallery, he walked down the aisle toward the stage-left boxes. John Parker's seat beside the entrance to the hall was empty. At least one witness thought he saw the actor hand a card or note to the President's messenger seated on the aisle. If so, Booth did not wait for an answer but pushed through the unlocked door into the inner hallway leading to the presidential box.

Closing the door, he picked up the wooden bar and propped it between the middle panel and the mortise in the opposite wall. He tested it; firm as a bolt of steel. Any pressure from people trying to force their way into the hall would only serve to make it more secure.

So far so good. He stepped over to the inner door leading directly to box 8, and peered through the hole he had cut that afternoon. Lincoln was seated, as expected, in the high-back rocker in a corner of the box. Above the collar of his frock coat, the President's head was bent slightly forward, as if he were watching the audience more closely than the play.

Booth opened the door quietly, slipped in, and stood like a shadow behind his victim. He followed the play for a moment. On stage, Harry Hawk was projecting the lines that would cue the crime of the century: "Don't know the manners of good society, eh? Well, I guess I know enough to turn you inside out, old gal—"

Booth reached for the derringer and leveled it at the President's head.

"—you old sockdologizing man-trap!"

An explosion of laughter all but smothered the flat snap of the derringer as the ball ploughed through the President's skull behind the ear. Some heard it and were only puzzled by the sound. But to Major Rathbone the dull report and the arabesque of smoke that curled around the President's head had deadly meaning. He rose and grappled with the assassin. Booth hurled aside the single-shot derringer, and slashed at Rathbone with the knife, missing his heart but wounding him in breast and shoulder. As Rathbone staggered back, Booth leaped to the railing of the box, shouted "Vengeance for the South"—and swung himself to the stage below.

For an agile, athletic man like Booth, known on the stage (and criticized) for his theatrical gymnastics, it was no great leap. But his right spur caught on the Treasury Regimental Flag and he landed on his left leg, sprawling on all fours. There was a second of silence as Harry Hawk gaped at the intruder, and the audience wondered if this peculiar bit of business was part of the comedy. Then Booth rose to his feet, dagger in hand, and delivered the line "Sic Semper Tyrannis." Though the audience was stunned into a deathlike silence, the words were barely heard.

Limping slightly, with a piece of blue fabric clinging to one boot, the assassin loped across the set and down the passageway at stage right. Orchestra leader William Withers was in his path, and he slashed at Withers with the knife, only tearing his clothing. One other man threatened his clear flight toward the back door. Joseph B. Stewart, a Washington lawyer in the audience, had instantly sensed something criminally wrong. He leaped over the footlights in pursuit, shouting repeatedly, "Stop that man!"

Booth reached the stage door ahead of Stewart, slipped through, and slammed the door in Stewart's face. Others would later claim that Spangler had been previously posted at the entrance, had opened the door for Booth and closed it upon Stewart. In the split-second action and confusion, no one would be absolutely certain who did what.

Peanuts John was sprawled on a bench outside the stage door with the horse's bridle in his hand. He rose as Booth snatched the reins. The actor leaped to the saddle and struck Peanuts down with the handle of the knife.

Stewart was in the doorway now, still shouting, "Stop that man!" Booth spurred the filly viciously, too viciously. The skittish mare started whirling in eccentric arcs, hooves rattling like pistol shots on the stones. Stewart almost reached her flank before Booth brought the animal under control, lowered his head, and raced down the alley toward F Street. From there he presumably followed Ninth to Pennsylvania Avenue, turned south at Capitol Hill down New Jersey and Virginia Avenues, seeking the shortest route to the Navy Yard Bridge.

The streets were unlighted and deserted now. Booth could afford to slow the horse to a canter; the critical seconds of his flight had passed. Approaching the bridge he became aware, for the first time, of a sharp pain in his left leg. He must have hurt it in leaping from the box.

Sergeant Silas T. Cobb was on guard duty at the bridge gates and reported later that "at about half past ten or eleven o'clock a man approached rapidly on horseback. The sentry challenged him, and I advanced to see if he was a proper person to pass. I asked him:

" 'Who are you, sir?'

" 'My name is Booth,' he said.

" 'Where are you going?' I asked him. And he told me, 'I am going home.' "

Asked where his home was, Booth placed it vaguely in the neighborhood of Beantown in Charles County. As to the rule forbidding anyone to cross the river after nine, the traveler said he had not known about it; he had been detained in Washington on business, and since it was a dark night he had waited for the moon to guide him home.

"I thought he was a proper person to pass, and I passed him," Sergeant Cobb said.[5]

Roughly synchronized with the movements of John Wilkes Booth, Atzerodt and Herold rented horses from John Fletcher, foreman of Allison Naylor's livery stable on E Street, where Paine picked up the one-eyed bay that Booth had bought in Bryantown. All three then took to their appointed rounds, assuring Fletcher they would have the horses back by eight o'clock.

Atzerodt returned to the Kirkwood House. On his mind was anything but the murder of Vice President Andrew Johnson; what he wanted was a drink. Paine and Herold rode up to Lafayette Square and came to the converted clubhouse where William Seward was recovering from the injuries sustained some days before. The patrician, sixty-four-year-old Secretary of State had been thrown from his carriage and suffered a broken arm and fractured jaw. Now he lay sleeping in a third-floor bedroom off the stairs, his neck protected by a metal collar designed to keep his jaw in place.

Outside the house, Herold briefed his colleague on the mission. The small prop package Paine was carrying was medicine from Seward's physician, Dr. T. S. Verdi. Paine repeated the name, dismounted, tied his horse loosely to a sapling, and rapped at the entrance to the clubhouse.

Young William Bell, one of Seward's black servants, came to the door. Paine showed him the package, mentioned the name of Dr. Verdi, and pushed his way inside. Though Bell remonstrated with the intruder, Paine clumped noisily up the stairs, wondering behind which door his victim lay. Seward's younger son, Frederick, obliged him by coming out of a bedroom at the stairhead. Frederick offered to take the medicine to his father but refused to let the unknown visitor into the patient's bedroom.

"All right," said Paine, turning on the top step, "if I can't go in, then—"

Whirling, he yanked out his pistol and fired. The hammer clicked harmlessly. Paine grabbed the barrel and smashed the butt of the gun on Frederick's skull, hammering at his head and neck as he crumpled to the floor. The terrified William Bell raced out of the house and into the street, spreading abroad the cry of "Murder! Murder!"

Paine hurled aside the pistol, which had broken in the furious attack, drew his knife, and turned toward the half-dark sickroom. George Robinson, Seward's male nurse, blocked the doorway, alerted by the noise. The assassin slashed at him with the knife, and as Robinson fell he pushed through the door and hurled himself at the prostrate figure on the bed. A woman, Seward's daughter, screamed; Paine took no notice of her. He slashed at Seward's bandaged cheek, then with the instincts of a jaguar went for the throat, stabbing repeatedly at Seward's neck.

There was no time to wonder why the knife blade met such stiff resistance, as if striking metal. Major Augustus Seward, the Secretary's younger son, had come to the rescue of his father, grappling with the intruder. Paine used the knife again. "I'm mad! I'm mad!" he shouted as he struck the major down. Then Paine vaulted down the stairs, injuring another servant as he passed, and left the house.

The one-eyed roan was still at the curb, but Davey Herold, alarmed by Bell's cries of "Murder!" had taken off; and already soldiers from General Augur's headquarters on Four-teenth Street were responding to the outcry. Paine climbed into the saddle and, seemingly unperturbed, trotted down Pennsylvania Avenue, the frantic Bell following at a distance, shouting "Murder! Murder!" Near the Capitol, for reasons of his own, the assassin dropped his knife, abandoned the one-eyed horse, strode down a wooded side street and disappeared among the trees.

George Atzerodt, too, the appointed assassin of Andrew Johnson, had disappeared—but without completing his assignment or attempting to complete it. His brain conveniently numbed by alcohol consumed all evening at the Kirkwood bar, he decided he wanted no part of this nefarious adventure. He fuzzily left the hotel, discarded the knife, dropped the bay horse at Naylor's stable, and took a streetcar to the Navy Yard. He had a friend there who he hoped might put him up until the brouhaha blew over.

At this point the assassins' tally was ticked off by hastily summoned doctors. The President dying and in coma. Seward severely wounded, but expected to recover. Frederick Seward insensible from a fractured skull. Three others among Seward's household badly injured. Only one intended victim, Andrew Johnson, remained undisturbed and unaware of the attacks. He was sleeping in his bedroom at the Kirkwood House when a messenger from Stanton pounded at his door with news that Lincoln had been murdered; the Vice President should be prepared to take the oath of office.[6]

Two others, innocent of these heinous acts with which their names would be associated, were variously occupied that night. Michael O'Laughlin had come to Washington from Baltimore, lured by the bright lights and the carnival amusements of the jubilant capital. O'Laughlin had arrived the day before, spent the first night with friends in bars and brothels, and passed most of Good Friday in Lichau's bar, trying to ward off the effects of too much liquor with a few more drinks.

Several of his companions would assert that Mike had visited the National Hotel, inquiring for "a man named Booth." But none was certain if he had ever actually found his friend. There were also reports that O'Laughlin had been seen at William Seward's home on K Street, where the Grants were staying; that he had asked to see the Secretary and the General and had been turned away.

But as for Good Friday night, O'Laughlin had a solid alibi. John Giles, bartender at the Lichau House, had kept track of Mike's presence at the saloon from early evening until midnight.

Samuel Arnold had no trouble proving where he was that night—120 miles away in southern Virginia. John Wharton, his employer in the sutler's store at Fort Monroe, saw him go up to his room above the shop at about the time that Lincoln's body was being carried from the assassinaton box. Unpreoccupied with Booth's mad schemes for murder in the capital, he would sleep soundly with, for some strange reason, a revolver and extra ammunition in the carpetbag beside his bed.

At Ford's the scene was one of fury, bedlam, grief, and terror. Armed guards ringed the auditorium, imprisoning the audience and actors and the theater personnel for questioning. Outside a milling crowd demanded instant vengeance. "Hang the murdering rebels!" "Burn the theater!" Doctors called to the scene helped carry the bloodied President from the box to the lobby and across the street to the house of tailor William Petersen. There, in a second-floor chamber, Lincoln was stretched diagonally across the bed, his height making it impossible for him to be placed full length, while surgeons labored hopelessly to save his life. The bullet had passed through the President's brain and settled behind the left eye. He never regained consciousness. His death, nine hours later, was saluted by Secretary Stanton's requiem, "Now he belongs to the ages."

Stanton had been early on the scene at Petersen's. An archopponent of many of Lincoln's wartime policies, he was instantly his archavenger. Settling himself and his aides in an adjoining room, he began dispatching orders like a general in the field—placing the city under martial law, organizing all available facilities for the apprehension of the criminals. At his disposal were the army regiments stationed in the city under General Augur, including cavalry patrols; naval units on the Potomac and at the Navy Yard; along with the federal Secret Service under Lafayette C. Baker. Also concerned in the crime, of course, were the metropolitan police, perhaps the most efficient and least easily distracted of the lot.

In that frenzied hour and in the frenzied days to come it would be a miracle if all these forces could work in harmony to bring the criminals to bay. And miracles were not likely to occur. Instead, a reign of senseless terror had begun.

David Herold, having deserted his colleague in front of Seward's residence, spurred his horse in flight down Pennsylvania Avenue. He might have gone unrecognized, but stableman Fletcher had started worrying about the horse he had

rented Herold, as well as the one-eyed horse of Atzerodt's
that should have been returned. He started looking around
the neighborhood and was approaching Willard's Hotel when
Herold galloped past.

"You get off that horse, you have had it long enough,"
he shouted.

Herold only spurred the roan to top speed toward the
Capitol. The indignant Fletcher ran back to Naylor's, grabbed
a horse, and started in pursuit.

Crossing the Navy Yard Bridge on the planned escape
route, Herold, as Booth had been before him, was challenged
by Sergeant Cobb. And like Booth, he smooth-talked his way
around the guard, claiming he had lost track of time in a
prostitute's arms and, like any respectable citizen, was anxious
to return home to his family. Cobb let him by.

John Fletcher, arriving minutes later with a valid reason
to cross the river in pursuit of stolen property, was less successful. He could go over the Bridge, Cobb said, but not
come back. Fletcher gave up and returned to the stable, vow-
ing that Herold would pay for this obliquity.

Down the Bryantown road from Washington cantered John
Wilkes Booth, with Herold in his wake. Both, in sequence,
passed a stranger on his way to Washington. Polk Gardner
noted the urgency with which the two successive riders
pressed their mounts, but thought nothing much of it at the
time. At some point close to midnight David overtook his
master. He told Booth of Seward's probable assassination
and of Paine's uncertain fate, but he had no news to report
of Atzerodt. Booth dropped the missing henchmen from
his mind; they were expendable now, and his own flight
was made easier without them.

The actor's leg had begun to pain him badly. At Surrattsville
they stopped at John Lloyd's tavern for the field glasses and
the carbines that were cached there. Booth, too crippled to
dismount, told Herold to ask for whiskey, and the chronically
inebriated Lloyd brought out a bottle. Booth drank copiously
to ease the pain. The two then headed south toward the
little town of Tee Bee.

Their direct escape route, down the post road from the
capital to the Potomac, with possible crossings at Allen's Fresh

and Port Tobacco, was a six-hour ride from Washington. If they adhered to that route, they would be in Virginia before any news of the assassination reached the lower counties or caught up with the two of them. It was after three now, with only two more hours to go. But the pain in Booth's leg had become excruciating. They switched horses, Booth taking the more docile roan, but nothing seemed to help.

Plainly the leg needed medical attention. The ankle, swelling, felt like scorched flesh in the taut boot; Wilkes told Herold that he thought the leg was broken. The only doctor either of them knew in the vicinity was Samuel Mudd, and Herold prescribed a seven-mile detour that would take them to the doctor's farm. They would have the leg set quickly and be on their way. Mudd would not yet know of the assassination, nor was this projected visit part of their calculated flight. It meant delay, and delay was dangerous, but there was no alternative.

How Booth anticipated his reception at the doctor's house at that hour of the morning is impossible to say. To what extent he trusted Mudd, or was willing to confide in him, is also hard to judge. An observant man, he must have been aware of Frances' chemical dislike of him, and he knew from his previous visit that the Mudds had several servants. Since this encounter was unplanned and risky, some precautions were in order. The fewer who knew the direction of their flight, the better.

To keep Herold's identity a secret would be easy. For Booth it would require ingenuity. They agreed on an explanation for the call, and on other simple strategies. Booth lifted the shawl from the pommel of his saddle, and from long practice with disguises, made himself up as a passable Shylock. Then he wrapped the shawl around his lower face and shoulders, shoved the brace of pistols lower in his belt, and nodded his head forward.

The moon was still high but its brightness was beginning to meet challenge from the east. The bone-weary fugitives on near-spent horses bore left at Gallant Green Road toward a rendezvous that for Dr. Mudd would be a point of no return.

8

AN ASSASSIN RETURNS

THE moon was still high over Zachia Swamp, slanting through the window of the downstairs farmhouse bedroom, where Samuel Mudd had spent the better part of a sleepless night. Since his return from the trip to Giesboro on April 11, three days before, he had worked extra hours in the field, tugging at obstinate weeds between the rows of hills. His muscles ached; his stomach felt queazy; he wondered if he, like Mary some weeks before, were coming down with something.

He heard the ormolu clock on the mantel strike the hour of one, then two, while Frances slept in enviable oblivion beside him. He was still awake at three o'clock, that darkest hour of the soul. But he must have dozed off, for a full hour or more had somehow passed when he next was conscious of a pounding on the front door in the hall. He waited, hoping he might have been mistaken. Then, again, the imperious pounding. He checked the clock; the hands seemed to point to a little after four. It could be a passing stranger who had lost his way, or an anxious neighbor worried about a sudden sickness in the family.

Frances, too, had been wakened by the sound. He asked her if she would mind seeing who it was. He wasn't feeling up to it himself.

Ordinarily, perhaps, she would have gone. But there had been rumors of John Boyle and his renegade guerrillas being in the neighborhood, and she felt a sudden twinge of apprehension. No, she told her husband, he had better go himself.

Wearily the doctor pulled himself out of bed, stumbled through the dining room and parlor to the hall. Once again the pounding sounded, a little louder and more insistent. "Who is it?" he called through the door.

A youthful, chirpy voice replied that they were two strangers on their way to Washington, and his friend had been injured in an accident.

Mudd stepped into the parlor and peered through the curtains of the window. In the moonlight that flooded the yard he saw a young man holding a horse on which slumped another stranger, gaunt, dirty, and disheveled. He looked for all the world like a figure of Death, needing only a scythe to supplement the white skull shrouded in some dark material and a black cloak covering his skeletonlike frame. Off to one side, another horse was tethered to a tree. The flanks of the horses pulsed with their breathing and their hooves and legs were streaked with mud.

Reluctantly the doctor opened the door and, still in his nightclothes, stepped outside. What sort of an accident, he inquired, and what was the nature of the injury?

The limp figure on the horse was silent, but the other explained that his friend had fallen from his horse. They thought his leg was broken.

Mudd told Frank Washington, aroused by the disturbance in the yard, to take care of the horses. Then he and the younger man lowered the injured stranger from the saddle and helped him into the house, easing him down on the sofa in the parlor.

Mudd lit one of the coal-oil lamps and inspected his visitors. Both were hollow-eyed, mud-spattered, and unshaven. It seemed strange that in that condition they were on their way to Washington at such an hour of the morning. He asked the younger man, who seemed the more ready to talk, how they had found his farm and how they knew he was a doctor?

Well, said the youth, they had passed a couple in the village, a gentleman and lady, who had given them the doctor's name. Later a passing black had directed them to the house.

If the doctor was tempted to ask how these convenient passersby had happened to be abroad at such an hour, he kept his silence. More to the point was an injured man who needed medical attention, and he was ethically obliged to treat him.

He called to Frances in the bedroom, explaining that he had a patient with a broken leg, and asked her to tear some strips of cotton cloth for bandages. Then he turned to the man on the sofa. The bearded face was half concealed by a plaid shawl wrapped about his shoulders, but his mouth was twisted with agony. From the stifled, barely articulated words, the doctor gathered that he had hurt his back as well.

Who was the injured man? he asked the skittery youngster who hovered around like an attentive slave. His name was "Tyson," the youth said, presenting himself as "Henston."

The undersized sofa was no place for a medical examination. Mudd told the young man they would have to get the patient upstairs to a proper bed. The stairway was steep and narrow, but they managed to trundle the injured man up to the guest room above the parlor and place him on the nearer of the two beds.

Tentatively, Mudd tried to remove the muddy boot, but a stifled cry warned him that the ankle was badly swollen. He took a pair of surgical scissors and slit the leather down the side from rim to instep, gingerly peeled off the boot, and dropped it in a corner. A few painful probes of the injured and discolored leg told him that there was a straight break about two inches above the instep. The adjoining tissue and bone, however, were undamaged. A painful but not a dangerous wound, nothing resembling a compound fracture.

Having no proper board for splints, Mudd found an old bandbox, took it apart, and pasted together sections of the proper size. As he worked at applying and tying the splints, the young man urged him to hurry. They were anxious to be on their way, and could have the leg examined later by the patient's regular physician.

Mudd shook his head. He told the young man that he and his companion would be going nowhere that night. The patient, his breath short from exhaustion, needed rest, and since he complained of an aching back, there might be complications. The doctor would know better in the morning.

Throughout his examination and the binding of the fracture, the doctor noticed that the bearded man spoke little, except for stifled grunts of pain, and left the talking to his garrulous companion. The stranger also kept his head averted and clung to the shawl around his head when Mudd attempted to remove it. The doctor decided to let him be.

Even the average country physician was, by training, an observant man. How much did Mudd observe about his patient in this instance? Exactly one week later he recorded his impressions of the stranger:

> He was a man I should suppose about five feet ten inches high and appeared to be pretty well made; but he had a heavy shawl on all the time. I suppose he would weigh 150 or 160 pounds. His hair was black and seemed to be somewhat inclined to curl. It was worn long. He had a pretty full forehead & his skin was fair. He was very pale when I saw him and appeared as if accustomed to indoor rather than outdoor life. I do not know how to describe his skin exactly, but I should think he might be described as dark, & his paleness might be attributed to receiving this injury.[1]

As to the bearded man's companion, Mudd found him "a very fast young man and very talkative. He was about five feet two or three inches high . . . had a smooth face and appeared as if he had never been shaved; his hair was black, & I would consider his complexion dark. I did not notice his eyes very particularly. He wore a dark-colored business coat."

Having done what he could, Mudd left the two men in the bedroom. The sun was up by now, and he went out to the yard to get Frank Washington and Davis started on the day's work in the field. At seven Frances sounded the horn for breakfast. Davis and Washington went to the kitchen, and Mudd sat down in the dining room with Frances. They could hear footsteps in the room above, and Mudd called to the young man Henston to come down and join them. Then Frances surprised him by saying that he had the visitor's name wrong. The younger one was "Tyson" and the older

one was "Tyler"; at least that was what the younger man
had told her earlier that morning. Mudd let it pass.

As Frances sent a breakfast tray up to the sick man, telling
Betty Washington to put it on the table by the bed, Tyson
joined them in the dining room. The talkative youth appeared
to be an encyclopedia of information about southern Maryland, rattling off the names of people that he knew in the
vicinity—among others, the merchants William Moore and
E. L. Bean in Bryantown, Colonel Cox and Thomas Jones
at Port Tobacco, and Parson Lemuel Wilmer at Piney Church
a few miles south of the doctor's farm. He professed to have
heard of Samuel Mudd and had seen the doctor in the village,
although Mudd had no recollection of the youth.

Frances was prompted to ask, "Do you live here in the
county?"

"No, ma'am," said Tyson, "but I've been playing around
in this neighborhood for the past six months."

Even in one so obviously immature, Frances did not
approve of irresponsibility.

"All play and no work makes Jack a bad boy," she remarked.
"Your father ought to make you go to work."

"My father's dead," the youngster said cheerfully, "and
I'm way ahead of the old lady."[2]

Guided by the young man's questioning, the conversation
turned to roads in the southern part of the county. There
were some the visitor was not familiar with. How far was it to
the river? What was the shortest route that they could take to
Parson Wilmer's, whom they planned to visit?

Mudd answered patiently, but with growing suspicion and
bewilderment. Upon their arrival the two had announced
that they were on their way to Washington; now they were
interested in roads that led in the opposite direction.

Nevertheless, he obligingly took the young man out to
the yard and pointed to the narrow road, little more than
a riding trail, that led from the end of his driveway directly
through Zachia Swamp. He had used it many times, he said,
as a shortcut to Allen's Fresh, to Port Tobacco, or to Parson
Wilmer's for that matter.

After breakfast the young man made a curious request.

He asked the doctor if he had a razor he could lend them; his companion had remarked that he might feel better after shaving. Mudd provided razor, soap, and a basin of water. Then Tyson asked if there were a crutch available to help the patient move around when he was able.

The doctor consulted John Best on the matter, and the Englishman set to work to fashion a crutch from planks kept in the barn. Mudd himself spent the balance of the morning in the fields by Sylvester's property and returned for noonday dinner. Tyson came down to join them, having spent the intervening hours at the bedside of his friend. Frances prepared another tray for the patient and asked Betty Washington to take it up to him.

During dinner, Tyson asked the doctor about the chances of getting a carriage for the injured man, so that they could be on their way. This time the doctor offered no objection to his patient being moved. He agreed that the invalid would have a hard time riding with a broken leg, and perhaps a carriage would be better. He himself was going to Bryantown, he said; he had some errands to do and calls to make. The young man was welcome to come along and see what he could hire in the village.

Before leaving the house for Bryantown, the doctor went upstairs to check on his patient. The curtains had been drawn, presumably to let the man sleep, and the light was dim. But he observed that the black mustache was gone, giving the stranger a nakedly pale appearance, the lower face still covered by the shawl. As he came downstairs, Frances asked if she might visit the sickroom in the doctor's absence, to see if there was anything that she could do. Yes, of course, the doctor said.

In the yard Mudd asked Frank Washington to bring the horses—his own, the gray, and the visitor's mare with the white star on her forehead. The two mounted, waved to Frances, and turned at the gate for the road to Bryantown.

Betty Washington had come downstairs with both the dinner tray and breakfast dishes she had taken to the patient in the guest room. Nothing had been touched. Yet an injured man must eat to recover his strength. Frances prepared another tray that might prove tempting; a cake, two oranges, and a decanter of red wine. She carried it upstairs, knocked on the guest room door, and entered.

The room was in twilight, the patient lying turned toward the wall. She approached the bed, somewhat fearful of the black head on the pillow, with the face, as much of it as the shawl revealed, a ghastly pallor. She set the tray gently on the bedside table, and asked the stranger how he was feeling.

"My back hurts me dreadfully," the man said in a husky, labored voice. "I must have hurt it in falling from the horse."

Frances suggested that he try the cake and wine she had brought; it might help him feel a little better. He shook his head, but asked if the doctor had any brandy. There was no brandy in the house, she told him, but they had some whiskey; she would be glad to get him some. Again he shook his head: No.

A man not wasteful with words, but doubtless he was still in pain.

'I'm afraid you must think me pretty inhospitable," she said, "to have left you so long alone like this. Is there anything that I can do?"

No answer.

Discouraged, she went downstairs to the kitchen where the servants were preparing for tomorrow's Easter Sunday dinner. There was a playful rapping on the kitchen window. She turned to see Tyson peering at her like a grinning gargoyle. She motioned him to the front of the house and went around to let him in.

Had he succeeded in getting a carriage? she asked.

"No, ma'am," he said. "We stopped over at the doctor's father's and asked for his carriage, but tomorrow being Easter Sunday, his family had to go to church, and he could not spare it. I then rode some distance down the road with the doctor, and then decided to return and try the horses."[3]

He went upstairs, and Frances heard the two men moving awkwardly about the room above the parlor. Then there were tentative, scraping footsteps on the staircase. She stood in the hall at the foot of the stairs and watched the two descend, the injured man holding the crutch with one arm and clinging to his escort with the other. Step by painful step they pressed down between the wall and banister, the older man's face contorted with agony. Then there was suddenly something strange about that face; not only was the mustache gone, but the side whiskers of his beard were hanging at a curious angle, as if detached.

The impression passed with instant pity for the suffering patient. In spite of herself she said to Tyson:

"If you must go, leave your friend here with us. He's not fit to travel. We would take good care of him."

Tyson shook his head. "If he suffers much, we won't go far. I have a lady friend not far from here."[4]

Helpless, she opened the front door, and watched the pair hobble toward the waiting horses. Watched while Tyson lifted the older man onto the saddle of the bay, then mounted his own horse, placing the crutch at an angle on the pommel. Together they plodded slowly down the roadway toward the swamp.

Watching them as they disappeared, Frances thought again of that fleeting glimpse of whiskers gone awry. It was something she must remember to tell Sam about.

Sam Mudd, as well as Frances, was puzzled by the manner and conduct of his visitors. It had been an impulsive, unsuccessful visit to his father's farm, where Tyson had hoped to borrow a carriage. Henry Lowe Mudd had been curt about the matter. He had only one carriage in good repair, and he needed that to take his family to church on Easter Sunday. Perhaps the young man could hire some sort of conveyance in the village.

They had ridden off with that intention. But halfway to Bryantown Tyson had had a sudden change of mind. He and his friend would forget about a carriage and make use of the horses after all. Without waiting for the doctor's comments, he swung the little mare around and galloped back toward the farm.

Mudd was glad to be rid of the scatterbrained youngster and his curious companion. He had not been paid for his medical services, but no matter. Ethics had required that he admit the injured stranger to his home and treat the broken leg as best he could. The incident was ended; he was happy to forget it.

The day had turned gray and drizzly as he entered Bryantown, and he was surprised to see a troop of blue-coated Union cavalry lounging along the hitching rail in front of Montgomery's Hotel. The street seemed more crowded than usual, even for a Saturday, with people talking excitedly in animated groups. At the news stall on the corner, men were grabbing at lately arrived copies of the Washington papers. He stopped to stare, first in amazement, then with incredulity, at the black-bordered page of the *Intelligencer*. In type of diminishing boldness the short, staccato headlines read:

LINCOLN ASSASSINATED

●

ACTOR BOOTH HUNTED

●

Accomplice Stabs Seward

●

North Stunned by Tragedy

For once he did not buy a paper. Possibly he needed time to absorb the single, tragic fact itself, without recourse to details. Nearby was the general store of E. L. Bean, where Frances had asked him to pick up some cotton cloth. He entered the store, nodded to Frank Bloyce, a former slave who was at the counter, and asked Bean if he could see some bolts of calico.

Bean told him there had been some news. "Very bad news."

"Yes," the doctor said gravely. "I am very sorry to hear about it."[5]

There was much more he could have learned, had he tarried long in town. Lieutenant David D. Dana, younger brother of Assistant War Secretary Charles A. Dana, was commanding the cavalry headquartered at the inn. Among the first to be dispatched from Washington in pursuit of the President's assassins, he had led his troop south by way of Piscataway and Surrattsville, to search the area of Prince Georges and Charles counties. They had arrived at Bryantown around one P.M. with news of the assassination.

Dana would later say that in answer to excited questioning from citizens of the village, he had identified the murderer as John Wilkes Booth. Yet on leaving Washington he had been advised that at least one of the assassins was a man called Boyle, guerrilla Boyle. No single name registered with his questioners. Those who heard "Booth," thought the name was "Boone" or "Boose," and for a while the name of Boyle, already direly familiar in the neighborhood, was widely circulated.[6]

In Washington Secretary Stanton had launched the greatest manhunt in the nation's history. He had also taken over the country by assuming, unchallenged, more absolute authority than any man had ever exercised before him. While Andrew Johnson had been duly sworn in as President, it would take a while for the former Vice President to shape up to the office. Stanton was in control for now—a frenzied, hyperkinetic man who saw spies and assassins behind every tree and was determined none would escape his vigilance.

Dispatching Lieutenant Dana's cavalry to southern Maryland was only one move in this mass pursuit. Police detectives under Major A. C. Richards, army detectives from General Christopher Augur's office, and the secret-service agents of Lafayette C. Baker, all under Stanton's ultimate control, scoured the city and surrounding countryside for clues. More than a dozen witnesses appeared at Stanton's kangaroo court in the basement of the War Department to identify John Wilkes Booth as the man who had fled from the scene of the murder. At four in the morning, Stanton issued a bulletin officially naming Booth as the assassin.

Other witnesses came forward. Stableman John Fletcher was brought to General Augur's quarters, complaining of a stolen horse. The guilty man's name, he reported, was Herold—David Herold. The guard at the Navy Yard Bridge, Sergeant Cobb, was able to substantiate the story. The thief's description did not match that of John Wilkes Booth, so Herold's name went down as an accomplice.

Fletcher was grilled about other possible accomplices. He mentioned Booth and John Surratt as clients of the stable. Detectives were rushed to Mary Surratt's boarding house on H Street, but found that John had disappeared, quite

probably to Canada. By the saddle taken from a horse abandoned near the Capitol, Fletcher also pointed the finger at
a man named Atzerodt—but Atzerodt's role in the conspiracy
was hard to figure out. It was believed that John Surratt
had been the knife-wielding assailant in Secretary Seward's
home.

Thus, by the time Lieutenant Dana had arrived in Bryantown, three men were known to be key figures in the crime:
Booth, Herold, and Surratt. And they were now further
implicated by the testimony of John Lloyd, who had been
questioned by Dana's men as they passed through Surrattsville. Lloyd confessed that Booth and Herold had
stopped at his tavern for guns and whiskey, and that John
Surratt had earlier used his attic as a cache for weapons
and supplies.

Plainly then, Booth's planned escape route was through
southern Maryland. Six hours of hard riding would have
taken him to Port Tobacco and across the river to Virginia;
but intensive questioning of residents in Port Tobacco, admit-
tedly an unreliable lot, seemed to indicate that no one that
night had crossed the river. Dana resolved to concentrate
his search in the vicinity of Bryantown, or at any rate in
the undeveloped, semiwild area between Piscataway and
Allen's Fresh.

After leaving Bryantown, Mudd followed the main road
to his home, avoiding the cross-country trail that would have
saved him half a mile. He meant to stop at John F. Hardy's
farm to see about some fence rails he had asked the man
to split and hold for him that winter. But as he was passing
the roadside home of Francis R. Farrell, Hardy came out
of Farrell's house and stopped him. With some chagrin, the
farmer explained that the rails had been purchased by Mudd's
cousin, Sylvester. He had assumed that the doctor had forgotten their deal and no longer wanted them.

Mudd interrupted to say that he had "terrible news; that
the President and Mr. Seward and his son had been assassinated the evening before."

Excitedly Hardy called to Farrell, who came out and joined
them. Both men were eager for details of the assassination,

but Mudd was not prepared to be specific. The doctor believed that Seward's killer had been John Boyle, the notorious guerrilla, and that Lincoln had been murdered by a man named Booth.

Was that the same Booth they all had seen at St. Mary's Church in mid-November? Hardy asked.

Mudd said he thought so, but he wasn't sure. There were several brothers named Booth, he understood, and it might have been any one of them.

The doctor said nothing about the two men who had visited his home that morning. But as Hardy later reported, "He seemed to be in earnest when he said it was one of the most terrible calamities that could have befallen the country at this time."

Farrell, too, declared, "Dr. Mudd said that he thought at this time that the killing of the President was the worst thing that could have happened . . . things would be a great deal worse now than while the war was going." Farrell had noticed that the doctor seemed sincerely grieved and troubled by the crime.[7]

The conversation lasted some fifteen minutes, after which Mudd rode on toward his home. Fifty yards from the gate he saw two figures by the roadside: the crippled and splinted stranger seated on the roan, the other on foot and holding the horses. They seemed to be waiting for him. The younger man mounted the mare and rode back to the gate to inquire again of Mudd the way to Parson Wilmer's.

It was five miles by the main road they were on, Mudd told him; four miles by the trail that cut through the swamp just opposite the farm. He pointed to the beginning of the narrow trail, warning Tyson that it might be difficult to follow—night came early in the swamp—and there might be fences to take down or circumvent.

Tyson thanked him; then, pressing a wad of bills into the doctor's hand, he rode back to join his friend. Mudd watched them disappear into the tunnel of trees that marked the beginning of the trail, then glanced at the bills in his hand. Twenty-five dollars.

Back in the house he told Frances the news. The President had been assassinated; Bryantown swarmed with soldiers looking for the culprits. Though obviously as shocked and exercised as he, she was more immediately concerned about the strangers who had just left. She told her husband about the beard she now suspected of being false. The doctor agreed that the two men had seemed suspicious, but neither he nor Frances mentioned the name of John Wilkes Booth. Perhaps that nightmare possibility—that the assassin and the stranger they had sheltered were the same—was too horrendous even to consider, a specter that would disappear if not acknowledged.

Or—how much did the doctor know? Or suspect beyond a reasonable doubt?

That a physician, trained to be observant, could examine a man he had seen and talked with only weeks before and still be fooled by a false beard and a shawl was a matter to be weighed and pondered—and it would be. True, the light was dim; the stranger spoke rarely and then only in a husky whisper; he kept his face averted; he was an actor skilled in the art of dissimulation. Still . . . there was a question mark over Mudd's head like a barbed, inverted hook.

Mudd was, however, instantly concerned. He told Frances he thought he should return at once to Bryantown and report the incident to Lieutenant Dana and his officers.

Now it was Frances' turn to draw back from the threat of an unpleasant truth. She begged him not to. Not tonight, at any rate. She was frightened by the thought of being left alone, she said. There were too many strangers wandering abroad, too many rumors of John Boyle being loose with his guerrillas in the neighborhood. Tomorrow was Sunday; Sam could send word to the officers when he went to church.

A clumsy substitute for prompt, decisive action. But Mudd had been up since four; the day had been a tangle of distressing developments; perhaps he wanted to let his mind clear and to think things through.

All right, he told Frances, he would let it go until tomorrow.[8]

It was the first of many moments of delay, many incidents of postponed obligations, that would only accelerate the malignant forces closing in on him.

9

DRAGNET

THE bells of St. Mary's rang sweet and clear on the still air of that Easter Sunday, 1865. But they spoke not only of the glory of the resurrection; they tolled as well for the passing of a murdered President. An Easter draped in black; as dark an hour as America had ever known.

In pulpits throughout the nation, priests and pastors prayed for the soul of the departed leader in words of grief, compassion and humility. Not a few, however, warned their congregations that the crime was just a symptom of a greater evil—a vast conspiracy to destroy the North and all its sacred institutions.

Ordinarily Sam and Frances would have attended morning service at St. Mary's. It was the high spot of their week, and Easter Sunday made it an occasion. But the doctor skipped the traditional Easter ritual at his customary church, an act that is hard to understand considering that he was a man of deep-rooted habits. Was it because he shunned exposure? Did he fear to meet too many people he knew—inquisitive friends and relatives questioning one another, pressing for answers, anxiously seeking clues to Good Friday's tragedy? Whatever the reason, his evasion on the surface seemed to be motivated by a sense of guilt.

Frances did not leave the house that day, and the doctor broke routine by riding to St. Peter's Church in the piney woods about two miles from the farm. His only connection with St. Peter's was that his father had donated the land on which the neat white chapel had been built. He knew few of the congregation beyond his cousin George, a man he trusted and respected despite their differences in politics.

The first man he saw outside the church was Benjamin Gardiner, who asked him if he had heard the news of the President's murder, and did he believe it was true? Yes, Mudd said unhappily, he believed it was true. They discussed the possibility of organizing a home guard, or impromptu militia, to "hunt up all suspicious persons in the county and arrest them." According to Gardiner, the doctor told him that he had had two suspicious visitors at his house the night before, but did not elaborate on the incident.

Riding home after church, Sam Mudd caught up with his cousin George, whose home was in the same direction. Trotting side by side at an easy pace, he found that George seemed to know more than anyone about the President's assassination. George had been in Bryantown all day Saturday; had talked at length with Lieutenant Dana who respected his opinions as a loyal Union man; had heard that it was Booth who had shot the President and that Seward's assailant was probably the outlaw Boyle.

With this as an opening, Sam told his cousin of the man with the broken leg whom he had treated, and described his young companion. He included every detail he remembered: how he had set the leg, provided the razor with which the patient shaved off his mustache, supplied him with a crutch, helped the younger man look for a carriage by which to continue their journey, and finally directed them to Parson Wilmer's.

He had not known what to make of them, he said. There was a lot that seemed queer and even suspicious. He felt that the authorities should be informed.

George agreed. The authorities should definitely be informed. He offered to relay the information to Lieutenant Dana, since he knew the man.

"I would be glad if you would," said Sam, explaining that he would willingly go to town himself to talk with Dana, but was fearful of his life and of the safety of his family, with men like Boyle reported in the neighborhood. George understood his reluctance. He himself had received threats from the guerrillas but was not intimidated. Since, however, it was Easter Sunday and George had guests to entertain, he would wait till the following morning to talk with Dana.[1]

Thus relieved of immediate responsibility, Sam Mudd returned home to a ceremonial Easter Sunday dinner which the family shared with Thomas Davis and his brother John, who were spending the rest of the weekend with them. All day Monday passed without incident, and the doctor wondered if his report of the visiting strangers had seemed too unimportant to be followed up; certainly George, a highly dependable man, would have relayed the message to Lieutenant Dana. Tuesday morning, April 18, he was in the fields early with Frank Washington, when John Davis came down from the house to tell him that he had visitors: his cousin George and "four men from Washington." He strode briskly home, and George met him a short distance from the house.

"These men want to ask you some questions, Sam," he said, "about the two visitors you had on Saturday." George, as promised, had already reported the matter to Lieutenant Dana, but Dana had wanted to hear more details from Sam Mudd himself.[2]

In front of the house the doctor was introduced to the men who he gathered were detectives in civilian clothes: Lieutenant Alexander Lovett, William Williams, Joshua Lloyd, and Simon Gavacan. He repeated to them what he had said to George on Sunday. He described the two visitors, the man with the broken leg and his companion, as total strangers to him, though he gave what details he could of their appearance. One of the officers asked him more about the razor. Had he not thought it strange that the man should want to shave off his mustache? Yes, said Mudd, he had thought it suspicious at the time.

The name of John Wilkes Booth did not come up. Lovett, of course, knew who his prey was, and he thought that by now everybody in the region did, "even the darkeys." He believed from what George had told him that the man with the broken leg was Booth. If he expected to hear this opinion from Dr. Sam, he was disappointed—and perhaps for that reason reported later that Mudd "did not at first seem inclined to give us satisfaction." In short, he thought the doctor was holding something back.[3]

The four officers returned to Bryantown with George, and Mudd returned to his tobacco fields. With the ordeal over, he had reason to be thankful. The men had seemed reasonable; he had done his duty in reporting what he knew; most likely that would be the end of it.

Every weekday, ordinarily, Sam Mudd or a member of the family or a servant rode to Bryantown to pick up the mail and the Washington *Intelligencer*, which arrived from the capital shortly after noon. This week, however, the doctor never left the farm. Doubtless the mail and the daily paper were, as always, brought to the house, and from the latter he was kept informed of rapid developments in the pursuit of the assassins.

It was a three-pronged operation virulently directed by the Secretary of War but pursued with varying degrees of intensity, efficiency, and zeal. Pursued also with little coordination between the separate authorities, each of which was eager for glory and jealous of the rival faction. General Augur had 8,000 troops at his disposal with which he threw an iron cordon around Washington, blocking the bridges and exits and placing the city virtually under martial law. For his part, Lafayette Baker of the Secret Service alerted his network of agents as far north as Canada. But it was Major A. C. Richards, superintendent of the metropolitan police, with only 155 men at his command, who was earliest on target.

Among the first to be apprehended were two of the least important of Booth's henchmen. Even before Lincoln, after a nine-hour fight for life, succumbed to the assassin's bullet at 7:22 on Saturday morning, Richards' detectives had raided Booth's room at the National. They had discovered in the actor's trunk along with handcuffs and disguises, the "Dear John" letter from "Sam" in Baltimore, which referred to "Mike." They also uncovered a copy of the telegram sent on the same day to O'Laughlin urging him to hasten to Washington with "Sam."[4]

With these linked clues, along with prevalent information on who Booth's recent companions were, agents had little trouble in tracking down Michael O'Laughlin in Baltimore and Samuel Arnold in Fort Monroe. By Monday noon both were in custody in the Old Capitol Prison at First Street and Constitution Avenue.

On information provided by stableman Fletcher, George Atzerodt's room at the Kirkwood House was also searched, with no tangible results. For the moment Atzerodt was an unknown quantity. He must be connected some way or other, but there were no clues as to what his role had been or where he had gone. Atzerodt had simply disappeared.

From witnesses among the actors and the audience at Ford's, the stagehand Ned Spangler was identified as a crony of Booth's who had helped him escape from the theater after the assassination. Spangler was reported as once having said, "Lincoln deserved to be shot," and police detectives searching the stable where he slept discovered in his carpetbag an eighty-foot length of rope. It was the kind of rope crab fishermen used on the Potomac, from which lines could be suspended to hold the bait. But detectives ignored this likely use, and held it as incriminating evidence.

By late Monday afternoon, then, three small fry had been caught by the dragnet, Arnold, O'Laughlin, and Spangler, with the hunt still on for four more principal suspects, Booth, Atzerodt, Herold and Surratt. But the evening was still young for Major Richards. The detectives who raided Mary Surratt's boarding house immediately after the assassination, only to find that John Surratt had fled to Canada, hit pay dirt in a voluble informer, Louis Wiechmann. Wiechmann reminded the men that as early as March he had reported strange doings at the boarding house—clandestine meetings, weapons, disguises, handcuffs and other suspicious paraphernalia cached in the room he shared with John.

Weichmann was almost too happy to tell it all again; he linked not only John Surratt and Herold to the plot, along with a onetime boarder, Lewis Paine, but also incriminated Mrs. Surratt. As a friend of Booth, according to Wiechmann, the widow had allowed her home to be used as headquarters for the gang and at times had served as courier between the group in Washington and John Lloyd's tavern at Surrattsville, a sort of out-of-town base for their operation.

Weichmann was promptly sent with a party of detectives on a wild-goose chase to Montreal in pursuit of John Surratt (who had gone safely underground in Canada). But prompted by his testimony, detectives attached to General Augur's office raided the boardinghouse again, late Monday evening, this time to arrest the widow Surratt and her daughter, Anna.

While there, they got an extraordinary break. A knock on the door admitted a slouching giant in workman's clothes with a clownish homemade turban on his head and a pickaxe on his shoulder. He gaped vacantly at the officers who fired questions at him.

What did he want? What was he doing here?

Mrs. Surratt had asked him to come, to dig a gutter for her.

At this hour of the night—eleven thirty?

Well, he wanted to see what hour she might want him in the morning.

Mary Surratt was asked if she knew the stranger.

"Before God," she said, "I have never seen the man before."

Called upon to produce identity papers, the husky workman handed the detectives a certificate of the Oath of Allegiance, on which appeared the name of "Lewis Paine." Mary and Anna Surratt were taken to the Carroll Annex of the Old Capitol Prison, and Paine was rushed to General Augur's office for further grilling. He remained obstinate, unperturbed, and inarticulate. Finally William Bell, the page at Secretary Seward's home, was called in; he identified Paine as the knife-wielding madman who had broken into Seward's bedroom Friday night.

Augur's men took no chances with the muscular young giant. With hands and feet shackled by irons, Paine was placed in the brig of the Union monitor *Saugus,* anchored in the Potomac off the Navy Yard.

Just as Paine was delivered to the authorities by a piece of luck, so luck played a role in the capture of George Atzerodt. There were probably not half a dozen people in America with that unlikely foreign name. One of them, however, George's brother, was a Baltimore policeman. John Atzerodt had no love for the wayward George, who had once been his partner in the carriage shop at Port Tobacco. He suspected him of underground activities, and when questioned now regarding their relationship, he gladly told all he knew—including the fact that George had another relative, named Richter, in nearby Rockville, Maryland.

On Thursday, the day after Lincoln's funeral in Washington—as the President's body started its long journey by train to Illinois—detectives closed in on the Rockville home of Hartman Richter, to find Richter's cousin, George Andrew Atzerodt, hiding in a bedroom. For five days the addlebrained Atzerodt had wandered around Washington, seeking any sort of refuge, until he remembered Hartman Richter, a cousin he barely knew and who showed no enthusiasm for his visit. At his arrest he put up no resistance, even seemed stupidly relieved when the officers took him away to be shackled and placed with Paine in the bowels of the *Saugus*.

The roster of prisoners at that point came to six in all, after Anna Surratt's release for lack of incriminating evidence: Samuel Arnold, Michael O'Laughlin, Edward Spangler, Lewis Paine, George Atzerodt and Mary Surratt. For safekeeping, Arnold, O'Laughlin, and Spangler were removed from the Old Capitol Prison to the hold of the monitor *Saugus*, to be placed in irons along with Paine and Atzerodt, their heads covered with canvas bags extending to the collar bone, with slits that permitted them only to breathe and eat but not communicate with one another.

Still wanted, of course, were Booth, Herold, and John Surratt; and that Thursday a shot of adrenalin was given to the manhunt by a proclamation from Secretary Stanton:

War Department, Washington, April 20, 1865
$100,000 REWARD
THE MURDERER
of our late beloved President, Abraham Lincoln
IS STILL AT LARGE.

Displayed on billboards throughout the nation and reprinted in the *Intelligencer* and other papers, the broadside showed a reasonable likeness of Booth in satin-collared greatcoat, with wavy black hair and trim mustache. Flanking the actor was a photo labeled "John Surratt"—which, never identified, proved to be the wrong man—and a daguerreotype captioned "Harold" showing Herold as an adolescent school-boy by a classroom desk. The erroneous photo of Surratt was later corrected, and a more recent picture of Herold, still captioned "Harold," replaced the classroom photo.

If Samuel Mudd saw the proclamation, and he must have if he read the papers, he might well have been chilled by the awesome notice appended to it. Signed by Stanton, it stated that all persons "harboring or secreting Booth and Herold, or aiding in their concealment or escape, will be treated as accomplices in the murder of the President . . . and shall be subject to trial before a military commission, and the punishment of DEATH."

Unofficially the War Secretary suggested that the $100,000 reward might be doubled to $200,000 through funds contributed by zealous patriotic groups and individuals throughout the nation. Even apportioned to $50,000 for Booth and $25,000 each for Herold and Surratt, the sums made a tidy fortune for informants of whatever class. The monetary incentive, although it intensified individual initiative, helped to obscure and further confuse the chase. Cooperation between the military, the secret service, and the police, inadequate at best, turned into outright rivalry. Information was often withheld; false clues were planted to throw off the competition; it was every man for himself with a keen eye trained on possible reward.

Even worse was the effect on civilians. Neighbor informed on neighbor, ex-slaves on former masters, hired hands on their employers. Truth as a responsibility or principle went out the window; a slight suspicion or a calculated guess was reported to authorities as known fact. The penalties for perjury were slight compared with the tempting opportunities for gain. The nation went on a massive witch hunt, and the hunt eventually centered on Charles County.

Crank letters poured like snow into the War Department. Some were signed "John Wilkes Booth" and taunted the authorities to come and get him at the postmaster's address. Some were anonymous; some from well-intentioned citizens. Booth was seen simultaneously in a dozen or more places. He reportedly had escaped from Washington in female disguise, had been identified in New York, St. Louis, Montreal,

New Orleans, even on a transatlantic steamer bound for Europe. Despite these inventions both General Augur and Major Richards continued to believe that he and Herold were holed up somewhere in southern Maryland and had not succeeded in crossing the Potomac to Virginia.

The interview with Doctor Mudd on Tuesday, April 18, helped confirm that opinion and suggested that their capture was assured. Booth had broken his leg and was maneuvering on crutches. That would not only slow down the pair but would make them doubly conspicuous. Mudd had predicted that if the actor traveled far without attention to the injured leg, the wound would fester and render him incapacitated. The pair were quite apt to lose their way, even following Mudd's directions through Zachia Swamp, and the injured Booth would be further debilitated by hunger, exposure and dampness.

The doctor's prognosis had been accurate. After plunging into the thickety path that led across Zachia Swamp, the pair were forced to lead their horses on foot through the undergrowth, Booth hobbling on the crutch and leaving a trail of punctuation marks behind him. They had evidently had no intention of calling on Parson Wilmer or of sticking to the route Mudd had recommended. Instead, about a mile inside the swamp, they veered sharply to the east, and by nightfall were totally lost near a tiny chapel in the woods.

Booth sat on the steps of the chapel, nursing the injured and aching leg, and writing in his pocket diary while Herold scoured the surrounding country to try to determine their whereabouts and discover a trail they could follow. He returned to his companion with a frightened black in tow, a swamp guide he had met by accident. Oscar Swann was the man's name, and he professed to know the region well; his sister, in fact, was a servant for Colonel Samuel Cox who lived at a place called Rich Hill just a few miles farther south.

Perhaps Booth, and almost certainly Herold, had heard of Colonel Cox, a man of known Southern sympathies and a part of the Maryland underground. The fugitives persuaded Oscar to take them there.

There are several versions of their reception at the colonel's house, based on conflicting reports and speculations. One is that Cox welcomed them with open arms; another, that he regarded them as suspicious, undesirable characters and shut them out. Certain facts are evident, however. The fugitives did not remain long at the house and spent that night hiding in the woods. The next morning Cox found them, apparently took pity on their plight, and led them to a more secure refuge in a nearby thicket.

Cox, in fact, became the fugitives' most helpful ally, although he admitted knowing of the President's assassination. He sent word to his stepbrother, Thomas Jones, asking him for help in smuggling the pair into Virginia. Jones was at first reluctant. The Maryland underground had virtually ceased its operations after Lee's surrender at Appomatox; why risk his neck again at this late date? He agreed, however, to meet with them and discuss the matter.

He found Booth huddled in the pine grove, head in hands, like the statue of a wounded gladiator. Once again the actor's charm proved inescapable. "Murderer though I knew him to be," said Jones, "my sympathies were so enlisted on his behalf that I determined to do all I could to get him into Virginia, and so assured him, but told him he would have to remain quiet for the present; I would bring their food every day, and at the earliest moment would get them across the river."[5]

For five days Booth and Herold huddled in the thicket, with food from Jones and blankets provided by the colonel, while Jones hunted around Port Tobacco for a boat and a boatman to ferry them across the Potomac.

There is some indication that an attempt was made, during that period, to cross the river but was thwarted by the federal patrol boats. Continuing the diary he had started before the assassination, Booth wrote at the end of that tormented week:

Friday, 21—After being hunted like a dog through swamps and woods, and last night being chased by gunboats till I was forced to return, wet, cold, and starving, with every man's hand against me, I am here in despair. And why? For doing what Brutus was honored for—what made William Tell a hero; and yet I, for striking down an even greater tyrant than they ever knew, am looked upon as a common cutthroat. My act was purer than either of theirs.

I do not repent the blow I struck. I may before my God, but not to man. I think I have done well, though I am abandoned, with the curse of Cain upon me, when, if the world knew my heart, that one blow would have made me great, though I did not desire greatness. Tonight I try once more to escape these blood hounds. Who, who, can read his fate! God's will be done. . . .[6]

His fate at that moment was hanging in the balance. Thomas Jones had found a boat with which to cross the river and his ex-slave, Henry Woodland, had helped secret it on the banks near Allen's Fresh. But afterward Jones had stopped in the taproom of Brawner's Hotel and there had run into Captain William Williams, one of the detectives who had questioned Samuel Mudd on Tuesday of that week. Williams told Jones of the reward now being offered—$100,000, maybe $200,000, for the apprehension of Booth and his accomplices.

"That's a lot of money," Jones said thoughtfully. A word to Williams about Booth's whereabouts would solidify his finances for life.[7]

That same Friday Samuel Mudd again had callers. He was dining at Oak Hill with his father's family and their neighbor John F. Hardy. A messenger brought word that some men were asking for him at the farm. The doctor and Hardy excused themselves and rode back to the doctor's house.

The four detectives he had talked with earlier that week—Lovett, Williams, Lloyd, and Gavacan—were back and chatting with Frances in the parlor. A troop of two dozen Union cavalry were lounging in the yard. They had arrived at the doctor's house, according to Lovett, "for the purpose of arresting him," but nothing to that effect was said to Mudd himself. Instead, Lovett asked to see the razor the bearded man had shaved with. Frances started upstairs obligingly to get it; then, according to Mudd, the doctor asked his wife to bring as well the riding boot he had cut from the injured man's leg while tending to the broken ankle.[8]

Frances returned with the articles requested. The four detectives examined the boot, and noticed the half-obliterated name inside the rim: "J. Wilkes————," along with the trademark, "Henry Lutz, Maker, 445 Broadway, New York." Lovett pointed out that the last name of the owner had been scratched out; Frances believed there had been no last name; the doctor said he had not noticed the inscription up to now.

Again Mudd was asked if he had recognized the strangers. No, he had never seen the men before. Specifically he was asked if he knew the actor, John Wilkes Booth, and he mentioned Booth's visit to Bryantown in mid-November. Lovett produced the photo of Booth appearing in the "wanted" poster and showed it to the doctor. Did this look like the man in whiskers with the broken leg? Mudd said he did not recognize the figure in the photograph, "but there was something about the forehead or the eyes that resembled one of the parties."

Without further searching the house, as they had planned, the detectives decided, because of the discarded boot, that the man with the broken leg was Booth. They set out for Bryantown with Mudd in tow. During their ride to the village, the doctor acknowledged that his visitor on the night of the assassination was most probably John Wilkes Booth. He made no explanation of why he had not confessed this earlier, nor did his custodians ask him. They had still not charged Mudd with any overt crime. They were simply taking him to Bryantown for further questioning by Lieutenant Dana and Dana's superior, Colonel H. Wells, of General Augur's office.

In his interview with Wells, Mudd apparently regarded the colonel as unsympathetic. Wells' notes on the several interviews, however, show at least a conscious desire to cover all grounds and assess the truth. Possibly the doctor's understandable nervousness at all this questioning made an unfavorable impression on his interrogators, though Wells kept a reasonably open mind.

"Dr. Mudd's manner was so extraordinary," Wells recalled, "that I scarcely know how to describe it. He did not seem unwilling to answer a direct question; he seemed embarrassed, and at the third interview alarmed, and I found that, unless I asked direct questions, important facts were omitted. . . . It was at the last interview that I told him he seemed to be concealing the facts of the case, which would be considered the strongest evidence of his guilt, and might endanger his safety."[9]

Possibly to give Mudd every chance to state his case with sober reflection, Wells asked him to make a written deposition that could be filed with the authorities in Washington. To this the doctor readily agreed. He was seated at a desk, provided with a pen and ink and a stack of foolscap, the top sheet of which bore the legend: *April 21st, 1865. Dr. S. A. Mudd, residing four miles north of Bryantown, Md. being duly sworn deposes and says.*

He adjusted his reading glasses, dipped the pen in the inkwell, and began to write. *Last Saturday morning, April 15th, about four o'clock, two men called at my house and knocked . . .* [10]

With no break for paragraphs, with no apparent pause to rest his fingers, he wrote two thousand words, recording in detail every step and sequence of that fateful Saturday morning and its aftermath. The arrival of the strangers, his treatment of the injured man and a description of the patient; five feet ten inches high, well made, long dark hair inclined to be curly, full forehead, fair skin . . .

> *I have been shown the photograph of J. Wilkes Booth and I should not think this was the man from any resemblance to the photograph; but from other causes I have every reason to believe he is the man whose leg I dressed . . .*

Going back to his meeting with Booth in mid-November, he noted that the horse Booth had purchased from George Gardiner was not the bay the stranger rode last Saturday, then added: *I have never seen Booth since that time to my knowledge until last Saturday morning.*

He should have pondered well that sentence; for history would question and debate it for a century or more. But without apparent pause he went on writing.

There were six pages more in his small, precise, and delicately slanted penmanship, until he reached that point when the two men left his house between four and five o'clock that afternoon. *I do not know where they went. . . . I have not seen either of them since.* He concluded the deposition with a medical diagnosis of the fugitive's injury, the complications that might develop, the possible need for future treatment, showing a doctor's concern for an intransigent patient. And concluded with a typically modest statement: *I do not know much about wounds of that sort; a military surgeon would know more about those things.*

Why, as a general practitioner of seven years' experience, he should not know much about a fractured leg, or why an army physician should know more, was a puzzle only he could answer.

It was after six when Mudd finished his written statement and was allowed to ride back alone to the farm to dine with his family and spend the night at home. The next day, Saturday, April 22, the *Intelligencer* carried a barbed edict that must have originated from the War Department or from General Augur's office:

> The counties of Prince Georges, Charles and St. Mary's have during the whole war been noted for hostility to the Government and their protection to Rebel blockade runners, Rebel spies and every species of public enemies; the murderers of the President harbored there before the murder, and Booth fled in that direction. If he escapes, it will be owing to Rebel accomplices in that region. The military commander of the Department will surely take measures to bring those Rebel sympathizers and accomplices to murder to sense their criminal conduct.[11]

The finger of blame was pointed squarely at that region of southern Maryland that Mudd called home, and its inhabitants stood accused of harboring the assassins not only after but before the crime. The tentacles of the greatest manhunt in the nation's history stretched out from Bryantown to every corner of the region, snaring the unwary who would talk too much or fail to talk enough.

Innkeeper John Lloyd, formerly questioned, was now arrested. With a pistol at his head he was forced to tell all he knew—which proved more damaging to Mary Surratt than anyone else, since the widow had made frequent trips to Surrattsville to collect the rent and other monies due her, and, as a courtesy, had performed odd errands for John Wilkes Booth. John Surratt was already so thoroughly

incriminated, as were Booth, Herold and Atzerodt, that
Lloyd's information about their frequent meetings at the
tavern added little new.

Some 1,400 soldiers stationed at Chapel Point in southern
Maryland, under the command of Major John M. Waite,
combed Charles County in three detachments, concentrating
on Zachia Swamp. The dragnet also included a naval patrol
of the Potomac, though the river's many coves and inlets
made it difficult to cover. By Friday of that first week one
of Waite's detachments was scouring the woods within a
stone's throw of the thicket hiding Booth and Herold. Fearful
that the horses' neighing would betray them, Herold took
the animals to an area known for quicksand, clubbed them
to death (to shoot them mercifully would be noisy), and let
the carcasses sink in the morass.

The fugitives' position was, however, plainly perilous. Tom
Jones—having eschewed the temptation of the prices on their
heads—decided that the time had come to act. On Friday
a false rumor called the soldiers to St. Mary's County; the
field was briefly clear; the night was overcast and cloudy.
Jones led Booth and Herold to the boat he had hidden at
Dent's Meadow near the river. There he gave them a compass
and shoved them off. A spring tide carried the craft upriver
and back to the Maryland shore, where the conspirators hid
out over Saturday and that night succeeded in crossing the
Potomac to Virginia.

Samuel Mudd returned to Bryantown that Saturday for
further questioning but again was allowed to return home
for the night and to attend church with the family on Sunday.
Sunday afternoon he took Colonel Wells and two of the detectives on an expedition to try to retrace the track of the fugitives
after they had left his farm. They walked some distance into
the swamp, the indentations of Booth's crutch leaving an
easily marked trail, until they came to a slight hill where
the ground was firmer. Here there were indications that the
pair had suddenly left the wagon road that led to Parson
Wilmer's and had veered off to the east—but the traces were
too indistinct to follow. Wells called the search off. The coming week he would order a systematic crosshatch combing of

the area on the conviction that the two were hiding some-where in Zachia Swamp.

If Mudd had reason to hope that his role in the matter had been satisfactorily explained, and that he was relatively in the clear, that hope was dashed on Monday morning when six mounted men appeared in the yard. Four were in uniform, an officer and three soldiers he had not seen before; the other two, in working clothes, were black retainers from his father's farm. The doctor was told to pack what he thought was necessary; they were taking him to Washington.

Frank Washington was told to saddle horses for himself and the doctor, while Mudd went into the house to pack. Though Frances had, in the presence of all these inquisitive strangers, been calm and stoic up to now, she broke down visibly at the sight of Sam mounting the gray with his packed portmanteau. The officer, whose name she later wished she could remember, came over to her.

"Don't worry, ma'am," he said gently, "don't grieve too much. I'll see that your husband soon returns to you."[12]

The party then trotted down the driveway and swung left on the road to Washington. If Samuel Mudd had turned for one last farewell look at Frances, he would have seen her standing by the gate, as he would see her in imagination, standing by the gate for years to come.

10

THE SHAPE OF DESPAIR

GRAY, moldering, echoing with the footsteps of a thousand condemned ghosts, the Old Capitol Prison in Washington was often compared with the Bastille of the Bourbons. In terms of human misery there was basis for the parallel. Yet the square brick building on First Street, with its slotted windows, decaying plaster and creaking stairways, was not the impregnable, dungeonlike keep of the Terror. Though carrying the stench of death within decaying walls, it was essentially a makeshift repository for political dissenters, spies, wartime grafters, and contraband blacks the government did not know what to do with.

Built in 1815 to house Congress after the British had destroyed the Capitol in the War of 1812, it still wore some of the badges of its ancient glory: the arched entrance surmounted by a triple window, and the wide high-ceilinged halls that had resounded to the oratory of John Calhoun and Samuel Houston. When Congress moved back to the reconstructed Capitol, the building became a roach-infested boardinghouse until in 1861 it was needed to hold Confederate prisoners of war. The broken windowpanes were flimsily replaced with wooden slats, the two upper floors partitioned into tiny cells. As more space was needed, civilian housing behind the building was added to the complex, a part of which was known as the Carroll Prison or the Carroll Annex.[1]

In the South, where it was expedient to ignore such horrors as Andersonville and Richmond's Libby Prison, the Old Capitol was cited as a vicious example of the Northerner's inhumanity to man. Among the inmates, many would agree.

According to one familiar with the jail, the small, barred cells, with three-tiered bunks along the walls, were filled with "filth of every imaginable kind, and entirely destitute of any furniture or other accommodations indispensable to the humblest cabin." With ten prisoners jammed into a room, the ventilation was described as stifling, "mould, must, and heat were oppressive," and the bunks were so infested with vermin that the inmates preferred sleeping on the floor.[2]

Behind this mausoleum was a high-walled yard for exercise, mostly unpaved, which became a dust bowl in dry weather, a quagmire when it rained. Adjoining were the latrines or so-called "sinks," which in the words of one prisoner "consisted of wide trenches partially covered over, but open in front, with long, wooden rails on which the eighteen or twenty persons using them were obliged to stand. The months' accumulation of excrement of several hundred men—many of whom were suffering from diseases of the intestines produced by these sinks—sent forth an offensive effluvium that poisoned the atmosphere of the whole prison, and disgusted and sickened the senses of its inmates."

Another prisoner protested more temperately: "The presence of these sinks . . . did not contribute to the beauty of the scenery or add sweetness to the tainted air."[3]

The food served to the prisoners fitted the surroundings. Rancid pork or beef, "a disgusting mass of putrid meat," half-cooked beans or rice, were piled on the slat-board tables like so much refuse. "The odor which assailed the nostrils," wrote one prisoner, "seemed as if coming from an ancient garbage heap."[4]

The general slovenliness had some advantages. While trigger-happy guards patroled the streets outside the jail to thwart escapes the wooden slats could never have prevented, the prisoners within were free to make the best of dragging time. Systematic, cooperative efforts to exterminate the bedbugs were the only organized activities. The largest room, once used for seating Congress, offered a place of general assembly, where men killed time by playing cards, writing letters, smoking, singing, or drinking smuggled liquor purchased from the guards. Boredom and despair were the archenemies. As one prisoner recorded, "The worst misery in the Old Capitol was the helplessness and uncertainty which made the men . . . dull their minds with endless games of bluff poker, and toss wakefully at night on their shakedowns. . . ."[5]

Although the jail was operated by the War Department and hence under the aegis of Secretary Stanton, it was in effect run by forty-five-year-old Superintendent William P. Wood. In that respect the prisoners were lucky. Though a close friend and favorite of Stanton, the Virginia-born Wood had a mind of his own that was characterized primarily by inconsistency. A former private in the Union army, he detested discipline and was partial to Confederate prisoners. He stole from his charges, cheated them wherever possible, sympathized with them, and indulged them. An avowed atheist, he encouraged a similar lack of faith in others. Sunday-morning services conducted by both Union and Confederate chaplains were announced by Wood's bullhorn voice echoing down the halls: "All ye who want to hear the Lord God preached according to Jeff Davis, go down to the yard; and all ye who want to hear the Lord God preached according to Abe Lincoln, go down to number sixteen!"[6]

Warden Wood and the Old Capitol had played host to a number of distinguished guests throughout the war, many of them gentlemen planters from lower Maryland, statesmen, bankers, lawyers, doctors, editors, merchants, guilty of uttering ill-advised criticism of the government and subject to detention without trial. "The great majority, however, were dirty, lousy half-clad soldiers," wrote civilian prisoner George H. C. Rowe of Fredericksburg, Virginia. "The condition of many of the captive soldiers can be conceived when I state that many of them were actually scraping lice from their persons with knives and sticks."[7]

Not a few women had occupied the cells. Maryland's Rose O'Neal Greenhow, the aristocratic Confederate spy the admiring Warden compared with Marie Antoinette, was granted special dispensations. "The Wild Rose" was allowed to keep a pistol on her person, which she could point at federal guards outside her cell, but was not permitted to have bullets. The intrepid Belle Boyd, who had aided Stonewall Jackson's operations in the Shenandoah Valley, entertained the prisoners with ringing choruses of "Maryland, My Maryland!" coming down strong on the line, "Huzza! she spurns the Northern scum!" While the inmates shouted and applauded, exasperated Union guards shouted, "Shut up, you damned bitch, or I'll shoot you!"[8]

By the time that Samuel Mudd arrived at the Old Capitol's Carroll Annex, Rose and Belle, having served their terms, were long gone. Mrs. Greenhow had drowned in a shipwreck off North Carolina, weighted down by the English sovereigns she was smuggling into the Confederacy; Belle Boyd was on her way to fame as an actress on the London stage.[9]

But Mudd found plenty of company among others accused of involvement in John Wilkes Booth's conspiracy. Mary Surratt shared a cell with her daughter Anna, until Anna was released for lack of incriminating evidence. Also among the inmates were innkeeper John Lloyd from Surrattsville; entrepreneur John Ford, whose only crime had been to own a theater at an unfortunate time in history; various members of Ford's staff; Louis Wiechmann, in custody as a potential witness; Edward Spangler; and a score of Charles County witnesses and suspects.

As they had been rounded up and escorted to the jail, angry mobs had followed the cavalcade, as mobs had followed the tumbrels carrying prisoners to the guillotine in Paris' Reign of Terror. The popular rumor was that those in custody were John Wilkes Booth and his accomplices, and cries of "Kill them! Lynch them!" summoned eager additions to the crowd. Stones and bottles rained on the heads of the entourage until soldiers were obliged to turn and face the mob with bayonets fixed while the captives were hustled through a side door of the jail.

The arresting officers had learned their lesson by the time that Mudd was escorted over the Navy Yard Bridge to Washington in the early afternoon of Monday, April 24. They followed back streets up to the Old Capitol, arriving without incident. And because the doctor was regarded by his captors as "a professional man and a gentleman," he was taken not to the main building but to the Carroll Annex, where the clientele, either by design or accident, was of a somewhat higher caliber than in the Old Capitol itself.

Except for greater privacy, however, and some sense of detachment from the prison atmosphere, conditions were not a great deal better than in the Old Capitol Prison. Accustomed to the spartan furnishings of his bedroom at the farm, Mudd could not have been too uncomfortable with the straw-covered bunk, pine table and bench. But his fastidious nature must have recoiled at the grimy walls, the vermin-infested bedding, the oppressive, airless heat infested with the odors of the cookhouse and latrines, the coarse language of the guards and inmates coming to him from the street and yard.

Though kept from communicating with the other prisoners —"condemned to living death," said the *National Intelligencer*—and not permitted to leave the cell for air or exercise, he was allowed to see the newspapers that made the rounds of the prisoners, many of them days old by the time they reached him. Warden Wood showed him enough consideration to make him feel, perhaps, that he was more of a guest than a prisoner; that his stay would not be long; that he was there to give testimony regarding his fellow inmates; that it was matter of protective custody. At the end of the week, on Saturday, April 29, he asked for paper and pen and composed a letter to his wife:

Carroll Prison
April 29, 1865

My dearest Frank:

I am very well. Hope you and the children are enjoying a like blessing. Try and get some one to plant our crop. It is very uncertain what time I shall be released from here. Hire hands at the prices they demand. Urge them on all you can and make them work.

I am truly in hopes my stay here will be short, when I can return again to your fond embrace and our little children.[10]

How Frances answered that letter, along with many to follow in the years to come, we have no way of knowing. All Mudd's personal papers, from childhood to 1869 were, with a few exceptions, confiscated by the federal authorities. Presumably they were destroyed, though to what purpose, for what reason, it is hard to say. If there were any incriminating revelations in his letters, records, diaries, notes, that would have helped to convict him, surely the government would have made the most of them. If, on the other hand, his personal documents, of whatever kind, proved him a generally blameless, well-motivated citizen, they might weaken the case against him, might invite suppression by those anxious to convict him.

To a biographer seeking to form an accurate picture of the man and his life it is, to say the least, a handicap. One must work through indirection, through the eyes and ears of others, and rely on hearsay or try to draw conclusions from the often insufficient, fragmentary facts.

In replying to her husband's letter, Frances would certainly not mention the true state of affairs at home. As his letter indicated, the doctor was a worrier. And he had enough to worry about; the farm particularly—a support for Frances and a hearthstone for his children. Once the doctor had been taken into custody and was seen riding through Bryantown flanked by federal officers, the pressure was not eased from Frances' shoulders. Quite the contrary. She became the unprotected target. Charles County friends and neighbors, by tacit agreement, stayed away. When a fellow citizen was charged with offenses against the Union, he or she might gain sympathy and even secret commendation. But few were willing to stick their necks in the same noose.

Frances was not left alone, however, although she might have wished she were. Upon her husband's removal to the Carroll Annex, a company of soldiers had been stationed at the farm, much as a strong guard had been placed at Mary Surratt's boarding house in Washington. It was doubtless more to check on any unsuspecting visitors than to protect the inmates, for lower Maryland was primed with Southern sympathizers. Nevertheless, the presence of the military proved small comfort. As Frances later recorded of those stationed on the farm:

> They burned the fences, destroyed the wheat and tobacco crops; pulled the boards off the corn-house, so that the corn fell out on the ground, and all the corn that the horses

could not eat was trampled under their hoofs in such a way as to render it unfit for use. The meat-house was broken open and the meat taken out. All that they could not eat was left scattered on the hillside where they had pitched their camps.

A day or so after their arrival my husband's sister came over to see me. She wanted some garden seeds, and asked me to go down with her to the old gardener, Mr. John Best, to get them for her. When we went out no soldiers were in sight. We carried a basket, and the old man tied up some seeds in packages, put them in the basket, and then asked us to go see his garden.

A few moments after we entered the garden we were surrounded by soldiers. One officer came over and demanded to know what we had in the basket. The little packages of seeds were unwrapped, their contents examined. With a crest-fallen look he remarked, "I thought you were carrying food to Booth."[11]

Frances' ordeal was one made familiar by reports of Sherman's occupation of Atlanta and subsequent march through southern Georgia to the sea. Almost word for word the stories were dismally the same: soldiers camping on farms and plantations, rifling the barns for food and fodder, and wantonly destroying what they could not use despite the orders given to their officers. After Mudd's removal, Warden Wood of the Old Capitol stationed two detectives on the property, and Wood himself shortly came down to Bryantown and made the house his headquarters for investigating Booth's escape and possible refuge in Zachia Swamp. While he was there he gave orders for his men to shoot anyone trying to enter the house or yard.

But Wood and his men were often absent during the day, and Charles County crawled with soldiers and detectives sweeping the area from Bryantown to Allen's Fresh and Port Tobacco. Besides the troops from Chapel Hill, additional cavalry units arrived from Washington until as many as 10,000 men, according to one estimate, were combing the small area, knocking on house doors, grilling the occupants, threatening, cajoling, sometimes dragging off bewildered citizens for detention and questioning in improvised jails in villages throughout the county.

Came the day when Warden Wood was recalled to Washington, and Frances found herself a virtual prisoner with her four small children and Betty Washington, forbidden to communicate with relatives or neighbors or to leave the farmhouse. There followed a night of terror, which, for all she knew, was only the first of more to come:

> Some of the soldiers came around the house and began talking impudently to the colored woman. I called her in, locked the door, and drew down the curtains, not knowing whether I would be dead or alive the next morning. I lighted the lamp in the dining-room, put the children to bed, and with the colored woman sat there till two o'clock in the morning. At this time I heard a rap on the door, and a familiar voice called me. It was a cousin of mine, Sylvester Mudd, who had risked his life by coming within the lines, knowing I was alone. I could not have been more glad to see an angel from heaven than I was to see him.[12]

If Sylvester's presence was a temporary comfort, a real relief did not come till the day following, Wednesday, April 26, when a bugle sounded, the troops fell into formation and the roll was called—after which the tents were folded, and the column marched down the dusty roadway to the turnpike from Bryantown to Washington.

The word had come. John Wilkes Booth and David Herold had been captured in Virginia.

As throughout the Maryland manhunt, a mixture of fortune and misfortune plagued Booth's flight into Virginia.

When Thomas Jones and Henry Woodland shoved the flatboat out into the Potomac, an incoming tide carried the craft six miles upstream, shelving it in Nanjemoy Creek, still on the Maryland side of the river. Booth and Herold hid in the overhanging bluffs throughout that Saturday and successfully crossed the river after nightfall.

If Booth had expected to be greeted in Virginia as a hero, he was quickly disillusioned. David Herold was out of his depth in this part of the country, and the couple were forced to stop at whatever farms they came to for directions, food, and water—leaving behind them a devastating trail of clues.

Though they wisely tried to conceal their identities, posing as Confederate veterans returning to their homes or regiments, they were regarded with open suspicion and distrust; if food and help were given, it was offered grudgingly.

They were able to pick up a horse for the injured Booth at a squatter's cabin but not far beyond the Potomac were turned away from the home of Dr. Richard H. Stewart, where Booth had sought treatment for his festering leg. After spending the night in a black's cabin, they were directed to Port Conway on the Rappahannock. They crossed the river by a ferry carrying three of Colonel John Singleton Mosby's raiders, disbanded after Lee's surrender. The loquacious Herold revealed their identity as the assassins of the President, and the soldiers' reaction was to shove them off on someone else.

One of the veterans, Willie Jett, conducted the fugitives to the farm of Richard H. Garrett on the road to Bowling Green, presenting the actor to Garrett as a "Mr. Boyd." What happened between Garrett and the two conspirators is pure conjecture, except for the fact that Booth and Herold either chose, or were obliged, to spend the night not in the farmhouse but in Garrett's barn.

Hot on their heels, had they known it, were Major James R. O'Beirne's cavalry from General Augur's office, who had picked up the trail by accident at Port Tobacco and had followed the pair across the Potomac to Virginia. O'Beirne had telegraphed Washington of his progress and, surprisingly, was recalled to the capital. There he was ordered to turn over the pursuit to Lafayette Baker's Secret Service, seemingly because Baker preferred that his agents get the credit (and reward) for the assassins' capture.

Baker dispatched by steamer to southern Maryland a company of twenty-five cavalry, commanded by Colonel Riverton Conger, Lieutenant Edward P. Doherty, and Lieutenant Luther C. Baker, the chief's cousin. At Port Tobacco they crossed the Potomac to Virginia. There they picked up the trail by unnamed clues—the black cabin owner? the ferryman on the Rappahannock? Dr. Stewart?—and tracked the fugitives to Garrett's farm. Under pain of torture and death, Garrett's son directed the pursuers to the barn. Conger's orders were to take Booth alive. He commanded Corporal John Corbett to form a cordon around the building while others set fire to the wooden framework. He would smoke Booth and his accomplice out.

As flames licked up the walls and turned to plumes of smoke above the barn, Herold emerged to surrender, simpering with fright, pleading for his life on grounds that he had liked the murdered President and had even "laughed at Mr. Lincoln's jokes." Booth, however, only hurled wild challenges through the bolted door, taunting his besiegers to come and get him; he would never be taken alive. It was a scene from Götterdämmerung, with the black-cloaked posturing hero of the tragedy declaiming behind a screen of flames, needing only a chorus of fire maidens to orchestrate the grand finale.

In the cordon surrounding the barn, Corporal Corbett, a self-emasculated religious fanatic, watched the tragedian's last performance in the smoldering proscenium. He heard other voices than Booth's. Creeping closer, up to the very wall, he raised his pistol to a crack, and shot the actor through the head. Asked later why he had disobeyed orders to take Booth alive, Corbett had an unassailable reply. "God spoke and directed me to shoot him," Corbett said.

Hauled out of the burning barn, Booth took a long time dying on the Garrett's porch, pleading with his captors, "Kill me! Kill me!" At daybreak he whispered a final message, "Tell Mother I die for my country," followed by the two words, "useless . . . useless . . ."

Conger rifled the dead man's clothing, found and pocketed Booth's diary, the contents of which would never be fully known—critical pages were at some time and place removed. A wobbly buckboard hauled Booth's body and the captive Herold back to the Potomac; a steamer carried them upriver to the waters off the Navy Yard. Here both were placed aboard the *Montauk*, Herold in chains in the brig, Booth's body lying and putrefying on the iron deck.

As thousands of ghoulish sightseers came down the river to view the "death ship," one sneaked aboard to cut a keepsake lock from Booth's hair. From this incident, Stanton decided that the body might become a problem. There should be no marked grave to become a shrine for Booth's idolators, no enduring tomb, no record of burial. After a hasty autopsy and identification of the corpse, Lafayette Baker and his cousin Luther, aided by sailors, brought a flat-bottomed skiff alongside the *Montauk*. Before the gawking crowd, Booth's body was lowered to the boat, followed ostentatiously by a ball and chain. The skiff was then rowed two miles downriver to Geeseborough Point, beyond which, and out of sight, stretched a malevolent slough where the Army was used to dumping the carcasses of dead mules. Here the sailors waited until midnight, to be certain that none followed.

Plainly, it seemed, Booth's body was to be buried in this cesspool of the sea. Early next morning scores of fishermen hovered like vultures above the site, dredging and grappling for the body or any portion, or bits of clothing that might be marketed as souvenirs. But a reporter on the *Evening Star* warned them of scant success:

> Out of the darkness Booth's body will never return. In the darkness like his great crime, may it remain forever; impassable, invisible, nondescript, condemned to that worse than damnation—annihilation. The river-bottom may ooze about it, laden with great shot and drowning manacles. The fishes may swim around it or the daisies grow white above it; but we shall never know.[13]

Booth's death and burial did not put an end to the wild rumors that swept the capital and country; and the press was glad to give them circulation. Even his demise was questioned. Had the actor really been cornered and shot? Or was the report of his capture and burial at sea merely a ruse to conceal the fact that the government had been outwitted, that their quarry had escaped?

Booth was seen alive in countless cities, in New York State, Mexico, and Canada. He was found to be living in luxury in Europe. Or, acknowledged dead, his remains had been given a gruesome immortality. His mummy was displayed at county fairs and sideshows. His skull was in the possession of a farmer out in Idaho. A body known to be that of Booth's was buried in Oklahoma, death caused by suicide from an overdose of strychnine.

For a few, Booth would never die, but would walk the

earth like an inescapable, vindictive phantom. Samuel Mudd was one of those few.

Not until years later would Dr. Mudd know that when he was moved to the Arsenal Penitentiary, he was only a stone's throw from where his nemesis lay beneath six feet of earth. Booth's sea burial had been a hoax. Long after midnight, when the crowds had gone, Baker's party had rowed back to Greenleafs Point and had carried the body ashore to the grounds of the ancient arsenal. There, in the yard of the penitentiary, Booth's body was hastily dumped into an unmarked grave, with the burial party bound by solemn oath to secrecy.

Mudd's removal from the Carroll Annex to the penitentiary was a first step in the War Department's plan to bring the criminals to justice. Like the Old Capitol Prison, the penitentiary, on the peninsula between the Eastern Branch and the Potomac, was something of an afterthought. Built in 1803 as part of the Washington Arsenal, it had been converted to prison use during the Civil War to accommodate the overflow from the capital's jails. While one would hardly have called the Old Capitol a dungeon, the penitentiary might qualify. Mudd's cell on the second floor was barely ten by fourteen feet in size. There was a cot, a bucket, a plank bench, nothing more. A narrow barred window looked out on the yard in which the baked air mixed with the miasma of the river marshes.

In contrast to the corrupt but indulgent administration of Warden Wood at the Old Capitol, security at the penitentiary was of the overkill variety. Setting up the machinery of justice, Stanton had appointed Brevet Major General John F. Hartranft supervisor of the prisoners. Though a thick wall twenty-five feet high surrounded the prison, and another wall embraced the arsenal grounds, Hartranft took no chances. He ordered an infantry brigade, a battery of field guns, and a cavalry battalion to proceed to Greenleafs Point and set up camp outside the grounds. From this formidable force, a regiment of infantry was selected each day to guard the prison. As a precaution, no regiment stood guard more than once, and no soldier held the same position twice.

The eight accused conspirators were scattered throughout the second-floor tier, each in a solitary cell, with empty cells between them to forestall their signaling to one another by tapping on the walls. Two soldiers stood guard before each cell, twenty-four hours a day, with a company of infantry guarding the entrance to the tier of cages. According to officer R. A. Watts of Hartranft's staff, "The company of soldiers was relieved each morning, others always taking their place, and as in the case of the outside guard, the same men never returned a second time and no soldier ever stood guard at the same post twice nor more than two hours."[14]

The excessive security of the jail itself, however, was nothing compared with the physical restrictions on the prisoners. Up to this point Mudd had been treated with some consideration. Neither he nor Mary Surratt had been thrown into the floating tombs on the Potomac, the *Saugus* and the *Montauk*, where the other six had been buried alive below decks. The widow and he arrived at the penitentiary by carriage one midnight in early May. At the same time the captives from the monitors, hooded and shackled, with seventy-five-pound weights attached to their ankles, were prodded across the arsenal grounds into their cells.

Once in his cell, however, the doctor became a victim of one of Stanton's ingenious forms of torture. A canvas hood, extending to the middle chest, was lowered over his head and tied with cords around his neck. He may have heard of the Navy's custom of "bagging" prisoners to render them helpless and keep them incommunicado. But in this case some refinements had been added. While slits for nose and mouth made it possible to breathe and eat, cotton padding was pressed against the eyes and ears to make the wearer deaf and blind.

If the doctor did not protest—what good would it have done?—Samuel Arnold, whose resentment of the injustice being dealt him had begun to fester and would grow like cancer in the years to come, recorded this form of torture for posterity:

> The covering was made of canvas, which covered the entire head and face, dropping down in front to the lower portion of the chest. It had cords attached, which were

tied around the neck and body in such a manner, that
to remove it was a physical impossibility ... it being with
the greatest difficulty, and frequently impossible, to place
food in my mouth, a sentinel kindly volunteering his services
to perform that for me. ... Daylight never lit upon the
eye, they not even permitting the cap to be withdrawn for
the purpose of washing the swollen, bloated, and soiled
visage.[15]

As a doctor, Mudd might have asked himself how long
before the face became infected from the pressure and the
skin decayed for want of oxygen? How long before this torture drove a man insane? Pertinent questions. First submitted
to this treatment in the bowels of the *Montauk*, George
Atzerodt had been driven to temporary madness and had
tried to beat his brains out on the vessel's iron wall. Though
Mudd did not complain, Dr. George Loring Porter, the prison
surgeon, protested to Stanton that if this continued, he was
apt to lose his charges before they could be brought to trial.

As a consequence, a lighter, less constrictive hood was substituted for the heavy canvas cowling, minus the cotton padding over eyes and ears. In addition Mudd was granted relative
exemption. The other male prisoners were "stiff-shackled"
and "leg-ironed." Rigid metal bars were chained to their wrists
to limit movement of arms and hands, and the seventy-
five-pound cone of lead attached to their ankle chains had
to be lifted and carried if they changed position. Mudd wore
only conventional shackles on his wrists.

During this period of suspension, no visitors were permitted; and much as the doctor must have worried about Frances
and the children, the fate of the farm, and perhaps his own
fate, he had no way of getting information. Guards did not
talk to prisoners, or answer questions directed at them. The
captives could not read or write, and communications of any
sort were not delivered or received. Mudd and his fellow
inmates lived in dark and silent limbo, blind and dumb and
half-deaf in a brick tomb where only the clanking of chains,
of iron keys turning in iron locks, and the tramp of feet
on echoing stone, told of a world beyond their trapped existence.

* * *

In his proclamation of April 20, announcing the copious rewards for Booth and his accomplices, Secretary Stanton had declared that the culprits, when found, would be tried before a military commission. Since such a trial was without precedent in times of peace, certainly without precedent in the prosecution of nonmilitary suspects, he and his staff anticipated possible objections. The prosecution would claim that the conspiracy was hatched in time of war, and the conspirators were part of the Confederate army of soldiers, spies, and saboteurs that sought to overthrow the Union.

If this argument were not sufficient, Stanton added a codicil. The court would not be trying these prisoners alone. It would also be trying, in absentia, Jefferson Davis and "others unknown" who had conspired "to kill and murder within the Military Department of Washington." The national climate being what it was, with the public demanding summary vengeance, it was easy to gain credence for the proposition that Booth and his associates were merely tools of a great Confederate conspiracy. Stanton believed he was on firm ground in proceeding with a military trial.

It remained for President Johnson to appoint the members of the commission. It would take time for Johnson to challenge Stanton's assumption of authority, but he hesitated on this move. Two of his cabinet, Gideon Welles of the Navy and Treasury Secretary Hugh McCulloch, favored a civil trial. Johnson asked Attorney General James Speed for his opinion. Speed double-talked around the issue—"on the one hand," "on the other hand"—but concluded that the defendants were probably "public enemies," and if so "they not only can, but ought to be, tried before a military tribunal."[16]

Stanton had his own vigorous reasons for favoring a military trial. There would be none of the delays, postponements, and appeals available in civil courts. Moreover, as one of the defendants noted, this, in Stanton's mind, was to be "a court of conviction," not a court of justice. The secretary had all but said as much himself, in declaring of the defendants, "The proof is clear and positive as to their guilt."

On May 1 came the presidential order directing that a nine-man commission, composed of "competent military officers," be selected by the Assistant Adjutant General, and that "the Judge Advocate General proceed to prefer charges against said parties for their alleged offenses, and bring them to trial before said Military Commission."

With a swiftness that suggested the nine members had already been selected, the commission was enrolled. Its roster:

Major General David Hunter
Major General Lew Wallace
Brevet Major General August V. Kautz
Brigadier General Albion P. Howe
Brigadier General Robert S. Foster
Brevet Brigadier General James A. Ekin
Brigadier General T. M. Harris
Brevet Colonel C. H. Tomkins
Lieutenant Colonel David R. Clendenin

All but Clendenin, a professional soldier, had served in the Union Army, and might be suspected of being prejudiced against those accused of murdering their Commander in Chief.

But would any other military court have not been prejudiced? The method of trial had decided the issue. The beribboned and decorated officers would give the verdict dignity and a semblance of authority.

Senior member of the court and therefore president of the commission, was the handsome, headstrong David Hunter, a former West Pointer now in his early sixties. It was Hunter who, as Union commander of conquered coastal regions in the South, had arbitrarily freed all the slaves in his department prior to Lincoln's Emancipation Proclamation. The President had annulled the order; but for his action Hunter had been branded a war criminal in the South, slated for execution when the war was over. The war was over, and the situation, at least as regarding Hunter and the eight defendants, was reversed.

Hunter had been a close friend of the martyred president, as had been General Albion Howe. Both had accompanied Lincoln's body to its final resting place in Illinois, and had only recently returned. Lew Wallace, former Indiana lawyer and potential novelist, aspired secretly to be an artist; at the start of the war he had formed a volunteer regiment of fellow Indianans to join the Union Army, in which had served another commissioner on the panel, Robert Foster.

German-born General Kautz, still in his thirties, had had a brilliant war career; among other accomplishments he had headed a cavalry brigade that had captured Confederate raider John Hunt Morgan in Kentucky. Serving with Morgan at the time was that flamboyant English soldier-of-fortune, George St. Leger Grenfell, now a Union prisoner of war, who would have a curious connection with the trial and with the ultimate verdict passed on Samuel Mudd.

The others lacked any particular distinction, apart from certain idiosyncracies that hardly commended them as jurists. General Harris was an amateur phrenologist and pursued the pseudoscience with the fervor of a dedicated quack. He believed that a man's character and behavior could be determined and analyzed by the configurations of his cranium. One needed no other evidence in a court of law. Throughout the trial he would study the bumps on the heads of the eight defendants, take notes on same, and arrive at his infallible conclusions.

The authority of the members of the court was hazily defined, a condition that admitted of convenient flexibility in their procedure. The nine commissioners were judges, jurors, and prosecutors, as occasion warranted. Basically, however, they were there to decide and convict on the evidence. The word "convict" is not misused. Judge Advocate Holt had injudiciously remarked "we are here to *convict* [*italics added*] according to the laws of war." One can assume that all nine commissioners had reached their verdicts.

Counselors "for the government" and hence for the prosecution were Judge Advocate General Joseph Holt, appointed by Vice President Johnson, and Holt's chosen assistants, Judge Advocate Henry L. Burnett and Special Judge Advocate John A. Bingham.

They were a formidable trio. As Judge Advocate of the Army since 1862 and a close friend of Secretary Stanton, Holt smoldered with hatred for anything that could be branded "rebel." None with such a tinge of Southern sympathy as Dr. Mudd could be accused of should be spared the righteous vengeance of the Union. "There have not been enough Southern women hanged in this war," he allegedly had said—and before him came a likely candidate in the form of Mary Surratt.[17]

Navy Secretary Gideon Welles, who had deplored the trial by military court, declared that Holt was intent on "hanging the conspirators before Lincoln was buried." And Thomas Ewing warned his clients Mudd and Arnold, "You have a damned hard court to try you, and as for Judge Holt, he is a god-damned murderer."[18]

Henry Burnett had been a key figure in the investigation of Samuel Mudd and other suspects since the assassination. He collected and collated evidence and, like a hound on the fox's trail, he had brought his quarry to bay and meant to make the most of it. The verbose Bingham, inclined to become lost in his own oratory, was by tactic an obstructionist; he prepared to sow objections like so many weeds on the courtroom floor to delay the growth of reasonable argument.

The trial was set to open on Tuesday, May 9. Samuel Mudd, kept in suspense and ignorance throughout the first hot week in May, got a glimpse of the coming ordeal the day before. General Hartranft, lantern in hand, called at his cell at midnight, ordered the prisoner's hood to be removed, and presented the doctor with a paper containing the formal charges lodged against him. They were farreaching, comprehensive, unequivocating. The same charges had been leveled at his co-defendants. Thus, they were not appearing in court as individuals, entitled to individual consideration, but as cancerous cells of one malignant growth, collectively doomed and indivisible.

For the first time Mudd read that he was accused of "maliciously, unlawfully, and traitorously . . . conspiring together with one John H. Surratt, John Wilkes Booth, Jefferson Davis, George N. Sanders, Beverly Tucker, Jacob Thompson, William C. Cleary, Clement C. Clay, George Harper, George Young, and others unknown, to kill and murder . . . Abraham Lincoln . . . Andrew Johnson . . . William H. Seward . . . and Ulysses S. Grant".[19]

With eyes unaccustomed to the light, even dim light, he

must have stared at the page with numbing incredulity. Sanders? Tucker? Thompson? Cleary? Clay? Harper? Young? Who were these people and the "others unknown?" How did Jefferson Davis come into the picture; or, for that matter, General Grant?

Mudd returned the paper without comment. None of the words and names could be made to fit reality, but what was there to say? The hood was replaced on his head, the gate clanged shut, the key turned in the lock. Through the cowling he could hear the footsteps retreating down the brick-lined passageway.

11

COURT OF CONVICTION

The stone hulk of the penitentiary, discolored by the damp, miasmic air of the Potomac, seemed to belong to the Middle Ages, when a country's greatness was determined by the thickness of its walls and justice was measured by the depth of its dungeons. Yet the scene outside, as described by the New York *World* reporter George Alfred Townsend, belied that grim impression. Wrote Townsend on a typical May morning:

> A perfect park of carriages stands by the door, and from these dismount major-generals' wives in rustling silks, daughters of congressmen attired like the lilies of the milliner, little girls who hope to be young ladies and have come up with "Pa" to look at the assassins; even brides are here in the fresh blush of their nuptials . . . they chatter and smile and go up the three flights of stairs to the courtroom. . . .[1]

The view from within hardly seemed suggestive of the greatest test of justice in the nation's history. During the week before the trial painters and carpenters had improvised a makeshift courtroom on the third floor of the graying penitentiary. It was little more than a converted cell, less than forty-five feet long and thirty wide; but the walls had been freshly plastered and whitewashed and the floor planks covered with coconut matting. Four grated windows, offering little ventilation, bathed the high-ceilinged room in chiaroscuro, and gaslights were installed in case the sessions lasted through the evening.

169

Furniture was new but spartan, the only concession to comfort being scores of much-patronized spitoons. Three wooden posts divided the chamber lengthwise—tables, chairs, a half-dozen benches east to west. At one side was placed a long green-beige covered table for the nine men of the military commission, with seats for the three judge advocates. To the right of this, across the west end of the room, ran the prisoners' dock, a raised platform fenced by a four-foot-high railing with a door at one end leading to the tiers of cells. Between the central pillars was a witness stand, with tables for the defending lawyers placed below the dock. The defense counselors could barely see, and not communicate with, the prisoners behind them.

Across the room from the commission was a table for the court reporters and newspaper correspondents. Among the court reporters, once the trial got underway, was the British-born Benn Pitman, whose brother Isaac had invented the first shorthand system for the English-speaking world. Pitman's record of the court proceedings, which he transcribed word for word with the aid of six assistants, became, and still remains, perhaps the most authoritative record of the trial. Reporters for the *National Intelligencer* also compiled a word-for-word transcript of the inquiry, published daily in the paper, colored, however, by the correspondents' personal impressions.[2]

Behind the reporters' table were chairs for a limited number of spectators, never adequate for the morbidly curious crowds, mostly congressmen and wives and daughters who used their influence to gain admission and whose chattering, whispering presence was a constant irritant to the reporters, lawyers, and commissioners. Most had come not to see the processes of justice but to catch a glimpse of the "fiendish assassins" in the dock.

The court convened on May 9, minus reporters and lawyers for the accused. At ten that morning, Samuel Mudd and the other male defendants, still shackled but with hoods removed, filed into the dock—Arnold, Mudd, Spangler, O'Laughlin, Atzerodt, Paine and Herold, with a soldier between each. They were followed by Mary Surratt, unchained but heavily veiled, who had a seat at the far end of the enclosure closest to the prisoners' entrance. The nine military men of the commission, decorated and bemedaled and in full-dress uniform, took their seats along with the three judge advocates.

The first session was one of brief formality. The accused were asked if they wished to be represented by counsel—a belated question, considering they had already been in jail for several weeks. All replied that they did, and court was adjourned to give them time, precious little time, to do so.

Working through the conscientious offices of General Hartranft, Mudd requested the services of Maryland Congressman Robert J. Brent, an acquaintance if not a close friend of the family, a man whose loyalty and Union sympathies would favor him in court. Brent was in Washington, and Hartranft promised to inform him of the doctor's choice.

Brent turned the request down with the explanation that he had another case pending. It is doubtful he was tempted. If he thought Mudd guilty, even a guilty man deserved representation in court; but to defend a man accused of such a crime would not enhance Brent's reputation. The doctor tried two more Maryland lawyers then in Washington, James E. Morgan and Henry A. Clark. Like Brent they declined, unwilling to run the risk of soiling their reputations in his behalf.

As a last extremity he got word to Frederick Stone, the Port Tobacco lawyer who had handled minor legal matters for him in the past. That he accepted the case would prove a boon for Samuel Mudd. But Stone was still a relative unknown in Washington; and perhaps for that reason, or because of pressure from her family and friends, Frances felt her husband would also need a man like Thomas Ewing, Jr., who had just resigned his commission of brigadier general in the Union Army.

How Frances achieved this coup, she did not divulge, saying only, "I engaged General Ewing to defend my husband." But the doctor could not have had a more able, sympathetic counsel—nor one better equipped to display courage, wisdom and conviction before a hostile court. His credentials were impressive. Son of a nationally distinguished father, brother-in-law of war hero William Tecumseh Sherman, Ewing had risen swiftly in the ranks of Union generals, winning military laurels for, among other courageous services, the defense of St. Louis in 1864. The Radicals on the commission might not like him, would in fact do their best to squelch him, but he would not be intimidated.

Mary Surratt was also fortunate. To her defense came Reverdy Johnson, one of the most brilliant attorneys in Baltimore and Washington, with a mind aloof from prejudice and passion. The commission would not relish Johnson either. Like Thomas Ewing, he saw things with a piercing clarity—and in a court already harboring its verdict, piercing clarity was something to discourage. The commission early set its sights for Reverdy; rather than try to refute his arguments, they would try to refute his right to appear at all.

The other attorneys for the defense, though not so well known, were surprisingly able. Frederick Stone, working with Mr. Ewing, extended his services to David Herold. O'Laughlin was represented by Washington lawyer Walter S. Cox; and Paine and Atzerodt by William E. Doster, a former city Provost Marshal, who had in the past crossed swords with Lafayette Baker in defense of the Secret Service leader's persecuted victims. General Ewing agreed to handle, along with Mudd's case, those of Samuel Arnold and Edward Spangler, two whose connection with the assassination conspiracy was as tenuous as Dr. Mudd's.

The lawyers had little time to round up witnesses and prepare their briefs. Defense strategy had to be played by ear as the trial progressed. The attorneys did not even know what the specific charges against their clients were until they were read at the second session of the court on May 10. Samuel Mudd, having earlier been presented with general charges by General Hartranft, now learned, that he did, prior to April 20,

> . . . advise, encourage, receive, entertain, harbor and conceal, aid and assist the said John Wilkes Booth, David E. Herold, Lewis Paine, John H. Surratt, Michael O'Laughlin, George A. Atzerodt, Mary E. Surratt, and Samuel Arnold, and their confederates, with knowledge of the murderous and traitorous conspiracy aforesaid and with the intent to aid, abet, and assist them in the execution thereof, and

in escaping from justice after the murder of the said
Abraham Lincoln, in pursuance of said conspiracy in
manner aforesaid.[3]

He had never, before mid-April, heard the names of
Herold, O'Laughlin, Paine, and Arnold; had known John
and Mary Surratt simply as Charles County residents; and
was aware of Atzerodt only as a Port Tobacco drifter. Now,
as essentially the same charges were read against each of
them, they were bound together inseparably in the court's
eyes. Asked how they pled, all responded, one by one, with
the same reply: "Not guilty."

Rules of procedure were established for the court:
"Convene at 10 A.M., to sit until 1 P.M. and then take a recess
for one hour. Resume business at 2 P.M." Dropped from
these procedural rulings were instructions to bathe the prisoners before their court appearances. After an initial dunking
in nearly ice-cold water, the defendants were allowed to go
unwashed, the hoods making it impossible even to cleanse
their faces in the days and weeks to come.

At ten o'clock the following morning, the door in the western corner of the third-floor room swung open, and the
dismal procession of prisoners filed in by order: Arnold,
Mudd, Spangler, O'Laughlin, Atzerodt, Paine, and Herold.
Each was attended by an armed guard and, on being seated,
was flanked on either side by guards. Once again, Mary Surratt entered last and occupied a seat at the far end of the
row, slightly apart from her fellow prisoners. Heavily veiled
in mourning black, unlike the others she still wore no shackles
though some lurid-minded press reporters believed they
heard the clanking of chains beneath her voluminous skirts
each time she moved.

It was the first time any of the alleged conspirators had
been seen in public since their arrest, the first time many
had been seen at all by the three hundred people, spectators
and members of the court, that filled the chamber to capacity.
George Townsend, at the reporters' table, focused his attention on the composed and quiet form of Dr. Mudd and noted
that he "has a New England and not a Maryland face." He
observed that the doctor was "neatly dressed in a grass-green
duster and white bosom collar" and "keeps his feet upon

the rail before him in true republican style and rolls a morsel of tobacco under his tongue." Elaborating further, Townsend wrote:

> He has a sort of homebred intelligence in his face, and socially is as far above his fellows as Goliath of Gath above the rest of the Philistines. . . . His high oval head is bald very far up, but not benevolently so, and it is covered with light, red hair, so thin as to contrast indifferently with the denseness of his beard and goatee. His nose would be insignificant but for its sharpness, and at the nostrils it is swelling and high spirited. His eyes impinge upon his brows, and they are shining and rather dark, while the brows themselves are so scantily clothed with hair that they seem quite naked.[4]

Noah Brooks of the Sacramento *Union*, who referred to the accused doctor as "the companion and associate of Booth," described Mudd as a man who was "about thirty-five years of age [he was thirty-one], and had mild blue eyes, a good, broad forehead, ruddy face, hair scanty and thin, a high head, and a sanguine temperament. He sat in his shirt sleeves, with a white handkerchief knotted loosely about his neck, and attentively regarded the proceedings with the air of a man who felt sure of himself."[5]

Colonel Henry Kyd Douglas, ex-Confederate colonel, waiting to appear as witness for the defense of Mrs. Surratt, was reminded by the courtroom scene of the drumhead trials that fed the guillotine in France's Reign of Terror. It was, he wrote, "the most severely solemn tribunal" he had ever witnessed, a court "organized to convict" and "a Court of Death," in which justice sat "with unbandaged, bloodshot eyes." Totally absent was any "judicial decorum, fairness, calmness . . . passion decided everything." Of the spectators, "ladies of position, culture and influence," their "scowls and scorn, white teeth and scorching eyes, augmented the general horror." Though as a Confederate veteran, Douglas' views were doubtless colored by personal bias, many mustered-out veterans of Grant's and Sherman's armies, in Washington for the Grand Review that May, shared the widespread abhorrence at trying civilians in a military court.

Before the first full session of the trial got underway on May 12, General Harris of the commission challenged Reverdy Johnson's right to appear in the court for Mrs. Surratt. Six months before, Johnson had questioned the law requiring the people of Maryland to take an oath of allegiance to the United States before voting on the state's new constitution. That, claimed Harris, put Johnson's loyalty in question.

Reverdy rose to his own defense by pointing out that he had taken the oath in the Senate, in the Supreme Court, and in all the courts of the United States in which he had appeared. What more could the commissioners demand of him as proof of loyalty? The objection was withdrawn; but Johnson, perhaps sensing that his usefulness to his client had been diminished, remained thereafter in the background, leaving Mrs. Surratt's defense primarily to junior counselors Frederick Aiken and John W. Clampitt.[6]

Whereupon the court got down to business, the first matter being an attempt to link the eight defendants, as before charged, to a master Confederate conspiracy headed by Jefferson Davis and his representatives in Canada. Witnesses testified to the appearance of Booth, Surratt, and even Lewis Paine in Montreal, where Booth had consulted with Jacob Thompson, Clement Clay, and others on a plan "to put the President, Mr. Stanton, and General Grant out of the way."[7]

Jefferson Davis was linked to the plot for reportedly having said, on hearing of the murder of Lincoln and the stabbing of Seward, "If it were to be done, it were better it were well done." It was hearsay evidence, but to the prosecution hearsay evidence was acceptable.

The testimonies, which ranged far afield—to the St. Alban's Raid, the burning of New York, even the treatment of Union prisoners in Confederate camps—seemed aimed partly at inflaming the minds of the commissioners and public, partly at reiterating the justice of trying the defendants in a military rather than a civil court. For that purpose, perhaps, the matter was not disposed of in one session, but was scattered throughout a full month of the proceedings, without particular relevance or order.

For that matter, there was no order whatever to the trial.

More than 480 witnesses were called in bewildering sequence, without it always being clear in whose behalf they were appearing. The defendants themselves were not allowed to take the stand or answer questions in their own behalf; they were there, to all appearances, simply to hear themselves torn apart by perjured or purchased testimony.

Dr. Mudd was quickly brought into the proceedings by the most devastating witness of them all, Louis Wiechmann. On the third day of the trial Wiechmann appeared for the prosecution—a crafty witness, avoiding direct accusations, striving to give the appearance of one who wished nobody harm but was obliged to tell the truth.

The truth, as Wiechmann saw it, was not a matter of fact but of hazy impressions presented in suggestive innuendos. "I saw Mr. Booth at Mrs. Surratt's. They were alone; they talked in whispers." He noted that John Surratt had considerable sums of money in his possession "when he came back from Canada or just before leaving for Richmond." He saw strangers at the house who "might have been blockade runners," but of course he didn't know for sure. He was just an innocent boarder with a penchant for keeping tabs on people, checking the postmarks on the letters they received, going through bureau drawers, and looking behind pictures.

Dr. Mudd was seeing most of his fellow defendants and accusers for the first time. But he had, of course, met Wiechmann at the National Hotel at Christmastime, and from that encounter had no reason to distrust or fear him. Now, however, there was something eerily chilling in the government clerk's testimony. With a shrug, a shift of emphasis, a choice of words, Wiechmann seemed able to say one thing and suggest another.

Asked by the judge advocate if he were acquainted with the defendant, Wiechmann replied that they had met "about the fifteenth of January last." He was wrong, of course, about the date; but he described with fair accuracy his and John Surratt's encounter with Dr. Mudd on December 23:

WITNESS: He and John Wilkes Booth were walking together. Surratt introduced Dr. Mudd to me,

and Dr. Mudd introduced Booth to both of us. . . . Booth invited us to his room at the National Hotel. When we arrived there, he told us to be seated, and ordered cigars and wine for four. Dr. Mudd then went out into a passage and called Booth out, and had a private conversation with him. When they returned, Booth called Surratt, and all three went out together and had a private conversation, leaving me alone.

JUDGE
ADVOCATE: Can you state the nature of their conversation?

WITNESS: I did not hear the conversation; I was seated on a lounge near the window. On returning to the room the last time Dr. Mudd apologized to me for his private conversation, and stated that Booth and he had some private business; that Booth wished to purchase his farm, but that he did not care about selling it, as Booth was not willing to give him enough. Booth also apologized, and stated to me that he wished to purchase Dr. Mudd's farm. Afterward they were seated round the center table, when Booth took out an envelope, and on the back of it made marks with a pencil.

JUDGE
ADVOCATE: What sort of marks? You mean, writing?

WITNESS: I should not consider it writing, but from the motion of the pencil it was more like roads or lines.[8]

Cross-examined by Ewing about the date of January 15, Wiechmann testified, "I could fix the exact date, if reference could be had to the register of the Pennsylvania House, where Dr. Mudd had a room at the time. I am sure it was after the first of January and before the first of February."

Wiechmann's confusion about the date was the only loophole in his damning testimony. And damning it was. For Mudd had up to now maintained that he had met with Booth only once, at Bryantown in mid-November, and *had had no contact with the actor since that time*. Cross-questioned further by Ewing about his conversation with Dr. Mudd in

Booth's hotel room, Wiechmann said only, "He expressed the opinion that the war would soon come to an end, and spoke like a Union man," and added:

> I had never seen Dr. Mudd before that day. I had heard the name of Mudd mentioned in Mrs. Surratt's house, but whether it was this Dr. Samuel Mudd I can not say.

Not until the defense had had its turn in court some four weeks later would Ewing and Stone have a chance to challenge Wiechmann's testimony, principally on the grounds of his confusion of dates. Meanwhile, the prosecution bent all efforts to prove that Mudd had not only failed to divulge this meeting with Wiechmann, Booth and John Surratt in Washington, but had indeed been in touch with Booth right up to the time of the assassination, and for many times before.

Two people who had been in Washington for the inauguration were called to the witness stand. A New York pastor, William A. Evans, appeared for the prosecution and was asked to identify himself. "I am a minister now, and have been for fifteen years. I hold a secret commission under the Government to arrest deserters and disloyalists wherever I find them." Evans professed to have seen Dr. Mudd numerous times in Washington in "some kind of dark brown overcoat, and a dark slouch hat" driving "a two-seated carriage, what is termed a rockaway" drawn by "a fiery horse." He fixed the date as sometime during the winter and remembered the incident and circumstances because their vehicles had almost collided in the street.

Evans testified to having seen Mudd enter Mrs. Surratt's house at the time Judson C. Jarboe, a "rebel," was coming out. He identified the house by asking a policeman whose it was. He remembered the hour, eleven A.M. but could fix the date only as during the winter, possibly in February. He also believed he had passed Mudd on the road to Washington with David Herold. "It might have been a year ago." Cross-examined by Ewing, who hammered at his vagueness on facts and dates, the witness confessed, "I am so confused at present that I can not recollect. I have been so confused since the death of President Lincoln that I really at times am bordering on insanity almost."[9]

A visitor to Washington from Troy, New York, Marcus P. Norton, testified that on the morning of March 3, "I think," a stranger had accidentally entered his room in the National Hotel. He identified the intruder as Dr. Samuel Mudd "either he or a man exactly like him," pointing to the prisoner, and testified that:

> He appeared somewhat excited, made an apology, and said that he had made a mistake; that he wanted to see Mr. Booth. I told him that Booth's room was probably on the floor above. As he went down the flight of stairs to the floor below, he turned and gave a look at me.[10]

Why a person looking for Booth's room and directed to the floor above should proceed *down* the stairs to the floor below, did not strike the court as inconsistent. But Ewing and Stone were taking notes pending their appearance for the defense.

General Harris of the military commission was also taking notes, observing the shapes of the prisoners' heads and forming his conclusions. His phrenological analysis of Dr. Mudd was quite positive:

> He might just as well have admitted his complicity in the conspiracy. Mudd's expression of countenance was that of a hypocrite. He had the bump of secretiveness largely developed, and it would have taken months of acquaintance-ship to have removed the unfavorable impression made by first scanning of the man. He had the appearance of a natural born liar and deceiver.[11]

General Lew Wallace engaged himself in drawing thumb-nail portraits of the prisoners, doing a reasonable likeness of Dr. Mudd. General Holt sat like a Western Buddha, eyes closed as if in sleep or meditation. The other commissioners sat in stony impassivity. A witness to the sessions described the legislative atmosphere as "grim . . . none of the Commissioners ever smiled."

Mudd's character and loyalty were early brought into the prosecution's testimony, when he was accused of having harbored dissenters and draft evaders on his property since 1861, the first year of the war. In that segment of the testimony the doctor's reprehensible loss of temper in June of 1863, when he had shot Elzee Eglent in the thigh and threatened him with extradition to a work gang building batteries in Richmond, came back to haunt him. Eglent himself testified to both the incident and the threat, but it was Elzee's sister, Mary Simms, also a onetime slave of Dr. Mudd's, who was the most voluble witness among the doctor's former servants.

Mary had reportedly heard Dr. Mudd say, in effect, that he would shoot Mr. Lincoln if he had the opportunity. She also stated that "a man named John Surratt came very often" to the Mudd Farm during the preceding summer. "He was there almost every Saturday night to Monday night; and when he would go to Virginia and come back he would stop there." Surratt did not sleep in the house, said Mary, but in the woods, with "a Captain White from Tennessee; a Captain Perry, Lieutenant Perry, Andrew Gwynn, Bennett Gwynn and George Gwynn. . . .

> When they came into the house to eat, Dr. Mudd would put us out to watch if anybody came; and when we told them somebody was coming, they would run to the woods again, and he would make me take the victuals. . . .
>
> Some men that were lieutenants and officers came from Virginia and brought letters to Dr. Sam Mudd; and he gave them letters and clothes and socks to take back.[12]

Other relatives of Eglent, also former slaves of Dr. Mudd's, confirmed and embroidered Mary's testimony. The fourteen-year-old Milo Simms averred that he had overheard the doctor agreeing with Benjamin Gardiner's statement "that Abe Lincoln was a God damned old son of a bitch, and ought to have been dead long ago." Milo, too, had seen rebels hiding in the woods on the doctor's property, as had Milo's brother, Sylvester Eglent, and Melvina Washington, another of Dr. Mudd's ex-slaves.

There were some glaring holes in this testimony, which Ewing carefully observed. Mary Simms said that the "rebels" had used the farm as a hideout during the previous summer, 1864. The others said the incident took place in 1863. Nothing approximating such a band of fugitives could be proved to have been on Mudd's property after 1861. Aside from tossing out names that could have been overheard, few of the witnesses could accurately describe the truants. Mary Simms saw them "dressed in gray coats, trimmed up with yellow; gray breeches, with yellow stripes down the leg." Elzee Eglent saw them "some in black clothes and some in gray; gray jackets, coat-like, and gray breeches." Milo Simms observed that they had "plaid gray clothes, and one had stripes and brass buttons." To Rachel Spender "they were dressed in black and blue."

The tenth day of sessions, May 18, brought to Dr. Mudd's case the most devastating testimony to date, if it could be believed—particularly damaging when linked with Wiechmann's earlier testimony indicating that Mudd had met Booth in Washington that winter. Daniel J. Thomas, whom Mudd had known in his Bryantown schooldays as a sneak and a liar and who now was posing as a self-appointed Union agent hunting down Maryland subversives, appeared and testified for the prosecution:

> About two months ago, some time in the latter part of March, I had a converstion with Dr. Mudd at John S. Downing's, who lives close by me and about a mile and a quarter from Dr. Mudd's. We were engaged in conversation about the politics of the day. I made a remark to Dr. Mudd that the war would soon be over; that South Carolina was taken and I thought Richmond would soon be, and that we would soon have peace. He then said that Abraham Lincoln was an abolitionist, and that the whole cabinet were such; that he thought the South would never be subjugated by abolition doctrine, and he went on to state that the President, Cabinet, and other Union men in the State of Maryland would be killed in six or seven weeks.

Frederick Stone was quick to cross-examine:

MR. STONE: Did you think that he was speaking in earnest?
WITNESS: I cannot judge whether a man is earnest or not from the language he uses; but I should think a man was in earnest to talk of the President being assassinated.[13]

Thomas recalled that he was shocked by the statement,

saying to Mudd that a man who had taken the oath of
allegiance "ought not to say such things about the President.
He [Mudd] said he did not consider the oath worth a chew
of tobacco." Asked if Mr. Downing had been present at this
particular turn of conversation, Thomas confessed that he
was not, but that two or three weeks later he had repeated
it to Mr. Downing and Downing had said simply, "I am glad
I was not there."

As the prosecution moved forward, jumping from defendant to defendant and back again, with witnesses called in
helter-skelter fashion, the examination came to the morning
after the assassination—the twelve hours when Mudd confessed to having given innocent sanctuary to the injured Booth
and David Herold. Testimony came principally from the four
detectives who had visited Mudd's house the following
Tuesday, April 18, and again on Friday, April 21: Lovett,
Gavacan, Lloyd, and Williams—along with their superiors,
Lieutenant Dana and Colonel Wells.

The key questions examined were: Did Dr. Mudd recognize
Booth when he arrived at the farm with a broken leg, and
was he aware that Booth, six hours earlier, had assassinated
the President? Collateral with these was the more general
query, How soon did Mudd become aware that he had treated
and aided an assassin, and did he do all possible to further
the capture of the culprit?

On the matter of recognition, Colonel Wells testified that
at first, "Dr. Mudd said he did not recognize the wounded
man. I exhibited to him a photograph of Booth, but he said
he could not recognize him from the photograph." Later,
after discussing Mudd's introduction to Booth in November,
Wells testified:

> In answer to a question, he admitted that he could now
> recognize the person he treated as the same person he
> was introduced to—Booth. *He had never seen Booth from the
> time he was introduced to him in Church until that Saturday
> morning* [italics added].[14] Herold he had not seen before.

Both the Judge Advocate and General Ewing pounced on
the discrepancy that Mudd had said first he did not recognize
the actor, later that he did. What was the explanation for

this change of mind? According to Wells, who admitted he could not remember the exact words of the interview, Mudd had said that "he did not know Booth or remember him when he first saw him; but that on reflection he remembered that he was the man who was introduced to him November last; but he did not say whether this reflection, from which he recognized the wounded man as the one to whom he had been introduced, occurred before or after the man left; but the impression made on my mind was that it was before the man left." In short, the doctor "did not . . . say that reflection or memory came to him at any particular moment."

Lieutenant Lovett told essentially the same story, that during the two visits to the farm the doctor had first said that he did not recognize the man with the broken leg, but subsequently said that it was Booth. Of their initial visit, Lovett recalled:

> When we asked Dr. Mudd whether two strangers had been there, he seemed very much excited, and got as pale as a sheet of paper, and blue about the lips, like a man that was frightened at something he had done.[15]

As to the question of whether or not Mudd knew of the assassination and Booth's part therein prior to Booth's departure from the farm, Lieutenant Lovett insisted that he had proclaimed Booth as the murderer as soon as he arrived in Bryantown, and that "even the darkeys knew about it." Two persons, Frank Bloyce and John H. Ward, testified that they had seen Dr. Mudd in Bryantown at about that time. Ergo: Dr. Mudd must have heard the news and the name of John Wilkes Booth that afternoon. Only detective William Williams offered contradictory testimony: "I think he [Dr. Mudd] stated that he first heard of the assassination of the President at church, on Sunday morning."

Mudd himself, in his statement to Colonel Wells, made no mention of when he first heard of the President's assassination. But, as noted earlier, both the storekeeper Bean in Bryantown and John Hardy, whom Mudd encountered outside the village on that Saturday afternoon, testified to the doctor's speaking of the murder and expressing horror at the deed.

This matter of timing was important. Did Dr. Mudd know or suspect, before Booth and Herold left his farm, that he might be harboring assassins? If so, he could be found guilty as charged of protecting and aiding the fugitives.

The prosecution completed its case against the eight conspirators around May 30, though chronology was hard to follow in this trial. The general impression left upon the public and the commissioners was that Dr. Mudd was guilty, with only the degree of guilt indefinite. If one accepted the given testimony, certain facts stood out in bold relief.

Mudd had met Booth not once, as originally stated, but at least twice before the assassination.

The doctor had belatedly recognized the injured man as Booth during the time that he was tending to the actor's leg.

The chances were good that Mudd had heard of Booth's participation in the crime while Booth was still at the farm or in the neighborhood of Bryantown. Although he had, through the services of Dr. George Mudd, reported the presence of "two strangers" at his house on the morning of April 15, he had not reported Booth's identity—which he now said he had been aware of. The detectives suggested that he had changed his testimony only when the discovery of the boot with Booth's name on it made further evasion futile.

In short, the doctor had lied at least once regarding the number of times he had seen the actor prior to April 15; and had seemed to evade the truth when he stated first that he had not recognized the actor when Booth called at the house with a broken leg, then reversed himself by saying that he had. At that point in the trial the press and its correspondents, such as Howe and Townsend, expressed the belief that things looked dark for Samuel Mudd.

Except for the letter received from her husband from Carroll Prison on April 29, Frances had been out of touch with Sam since his departure from Bryantown the preceding Monday. She was not allowed to visit him at the penitentiary or at any time during the trial, but was kept informed and comforted, to a degree, by General Ewing. The attorney proved to be "a true friend during my husband's trial and imprisonment. Whenever he saw the least shadow of hope, he would write me nice friendly and cheering letters, which I sometimes think must have kept me from despair."

Her brother, Jeremiah Dyer, and Henry Lowe Mudd's family rallied to her side during this period of loneliness and deprivation. Dyer helped with the management of the farm, and Mary, the doctor's sister, helped with the housework and the children. John Davis became a surrogate foreman of the tobacco fields, Betty Washington still helped in the kitchen, and the English retainer, John Best, maintained a chin-up attention to his duties.

As the daily copies of the *National Intelligencer* reached the farm, all were "shocked and surprised at the base and false testimony" given against the doctor by Daniel Thomas on May 18. Frances concluded:

> His reason for giving the false evidence was to secure a part of the large reward offered by the Government for the capture and conviction of Booth and those thought to be his accomplices. Norton, Evans, a number of the negroes, and several others, also swore notoriously false.[16]

Several times during the month of May she was called to Washington to consult with General Ewing, and on one such occasion at the lawyer's office was introduced to the wife of Orville Hickman Browning, former Senator from Illinois and a close friend of the late President. The two established an instant rapport, and Mrs. Browning went out of her way to comfort the distraught and worried wife. She related to Frances a meeting with Commissioner Lew Wallace at a restaurant where she was breakfasting with Orville. Discussing the trial in progress, and the case against Samuel Mudd, General Wallace remarked, "If Booth had not broken his leg, we would never have heard the name of Dr. Mudd."

"If that's so," Mrs. Browning said, "why don't you send the doctor home to his family and children?"

"The deed is done," pontificated Wallace. "Somebody must suffer for it, and he may as well suffer as anybody else."[17]

Though the statement was later denied by Wallace through

his secretary-daughter, one thing seemed clear in that atmosphere of "frenzied madness" (General Ewing's words) that permeated Washington during May and June. Cheated by Corporal Corbett's bullet of their leading victim, John Wilkes Booth, the commissioners were resolved that no suspect should escape their vengeance if there were any chance of gaining a conviction. Many did escape the net—people like John Lloyd, Samuel Cox, Thomas Jones, and others who had actively helped the assassins to escape—but only by testifying against those in custody.

The last week in May a curious incident occurred, never satisfactorily explained. An army ambulance drove up to the farmhouse. Out of it stepped Lieutenant Luther Baker and, with infinite gall, none other than Daniel Thomas, who had just completed his testimony against Samuel Mudd.

"We've come to take you to Washington," Lieutenant Baker told Frances. "I presume you know Mr. Thomas."

Astonished and puzzled, Frances settled for a withering reply.

"Knowing Mr. Thomas as I do, and not knowing you, I must look upon you as a gentleman. If I must go to Washington, it will be under your protection and not that of Daniel Thomas."

As it turned out, she had to make the trip with neither. Her brother, Jeremiah Dyer, was expected at the farm that evening, and Frances asked permission to wait for his arrival and then go to Washington with Dyer in the morning. Baker nodded his consent. "I will trust you," he said; and he and Thomas departed in the ambulance.[18]

The following morning Frances and Jeremiah took the early stage to Washington. On its arrival at Capitol Hill, a group of cavalry officers with clanking swords surrounded the coach and escorted Frances and Jeremiah by carriage to Lafayette Baker's office. This, apparently, was to be an interview of prime importance—with the head of the federal Secret Service! But Baker had barely commenced talking when he was called away on urgent business. Before leaving, he told Frances to go to a hotel and send the bill to him. She asked if, instead, she could stay with her cousin, Alexander Clark.

"Yes," Baker said, "but return here tomorrow morning at ten o'clock."

What happened at ten o'clock and after was recalled by Frances some years later, as recounted to her daughter Nettie:

> The next morning, at the hour mentioned, I went to General Baker's office, and was not kept waiting many minutes before he came in. I told him if there was any information I could give him, please to let me get through as soon as possible, as I had left four little children at home, and no responsible person to take care of them. Without asking me a question he remarked, "Mrs. Mudd, stay over till two o'clock, and if I do not send for you, you can go home." No messenger came, and my brother hired a carriage and brought me home.[19]

To try to attach any purpose to this brief, abortive confrontation would lead only to pure conjecture. But operating as a team, Stanton and Baker had a system of selecting potential witnesses and grilling them in secret sessions, with the aim of making a deal whereby they would testify for the government in return for certain concessions: principally immunity for themselves, their families or their associates. It had worked, among others, with Louis Wiechmann, with John Lloyd, with Atzerodt's policeman brother, all of whom were vulnerable by reason of their acquaintance with the principal conspirators. That it would never work with Frances may have been apparent to the inquisitors the moment they laid eyes on her.

It may well have been, too, that Stanton and Baker, like the commissioners, felt they had enough against Mudd, from the testimony so far given, to convict him. He might not hang—that would be up to the court—but there were some fates worse than death.

If, as the prosecution's case developed, things looked bad for Dr. Mudd, they looked worse for most of the other defendants in the dock. George Atzerodt, while he had balked at committing the crime for which he was on trial, was easily indicted for criminal intent. He had been seen at the Kirkwood house on the night of April 14, had occupied a room just above that of Andrew Johnson's, had inquired about the Vice President's habits and schedule, and had boasted some time earlier at a drinking party that he would soon become famous and have "enough gold to last a lifetime." A search of his room had revealed incriminating documents linking him to John Wilkes Booth. The knife with which he had allegedly intended to kill Johnson had been found; and stableman John Fletcher testified to his flight on horseback just after the turmoil in Ford's Theater.

David Herold had been easily disposed of, since he had been captured in Booth's company and Fletcher had seen him fleeing Washington after the assassination. Lewis Paine, of course, had been identified by Seward's doorman, as well as by the Secretary's nurse and Major August Seward, as the knife-wielding intruder on the night of havoc. Fifteen witnesses testified against Paine for the prosecution; only four were called to testify against Herold and no more were needed.

The bewildered stagehand, Edward Spangler, who had done little to aid the cause of the conspirators, found himself all but hung by the rope found concealed, along with a dirty collar, in his carpetbag. Was it used for crab fishing? Or was it intended for tying up a kidnaped President? There were other charges against Spangler. He had been a flunky of Booth's and had worked on the family farm in Bel Air. He had reportedly slapped a stagehand after Booth's escape from Ford's and warned the man, "Don't tell which way he went!" Some witnesses, as noted, thought Spangler had opened the door for Booth as the actor fled the theater. On top of these vague and hearsay charges, he looked the part of a ne'er-do-well, a rheumy-eyed, unshaven, skid-row bum, with a sullen, truculent manner.

A principal witness against Arnold and O'Laughlin was Mrs. Mary Van Tine who ran the D Street rooming house where both had lodged the previous winter. She reported that John Wilkes Booth had been a frequent visitor and talked "in low tones" with her roomers. The pair had also been seen with Booth at Barnum's Hotel in Baltimore; and there were the telegrams and letters found in Booth's room implicating both of them. Besides that, three witnesses testified to having seen O'Laughlin outside Seward's home the night of Paine's attack, and Arnold reportedly kept a loaded revolver and extra ammunition in his room at Fort Monroe. It was not highly incriminating evidence, but it would do for a conviction-minded court.

Mary Surratt suffered badly at the hands of two men she had generally trusted and befriended, John Lloyd and Louis Wiechmann. Wiechmann, while professing the greatest admiration for the widow and her Christian qualities, gave a deadly account of her association with the actor Booth. Mrs. Surratt had used the obliging Louis to summon Booth to the boardinghouse when she wished to see him, "on private business." Or Booth would call on his own initiative. "Mrs. Surratt would sometimes leave the parlor on being asked by Booth to spare him a word. She would then go into the passage and talk with him."

Wiechmann told of Lewis Paine's arrival at the boardinghouse under the name of "the Reverend Wood"; of Atzerodt's appearance there and David Herold's frequent visits; of the several apparent blockade runners who had stopped at the place from time to time; of the spurs, knives, and revolvers he had found in John Surratt's room, along with such articles of disguise as spectacles and a false mustache. He told of having driven Mrs. Surratt to John Lloyd's tavern the week of the assassination, Tuesday, and again on Friday, once in a buggy supplied by John Wilkes Booth.

John Lloyd's testimony on the same day added barbs to Wiechmann's pointed revelations. He told detective George Cottingham of the carbines, rope, and ammunition that John Surratt, Atzerodt and Herold had left at the tavern some weeks prior to the assassination; and how Mrs. Surratt on her Tuesday visit had asked about the articles that Lloyd had hidden and specifically about the "shooting-irons." On her Friday visit, hours before the assassination, Mrs. Surratt had told him, "Mr. Lloyd, I want you to have those shooting-irons ready; there will be parties here tonight who will call for them."[20]

For all practical purposes the prosecution wound up its case against the prisoners during the final week in May, having questioned 131 witnesses in nine days at court. The testimony of approximately half those witnesses had been directed at linking Jefferson Davis and his "Canadian Cabinet" to the conspiracy. Of the other half, the testimony of nineteen witnesses had been directed specifically against Dr. Samuel Mudd—more than were brought to testify against any other defendant, (seventeen against Paine, eleven against O'Laughlin, eight against Arnold, seven against Mary Surratt, and four against Spangler).

Herold, Paine, and Atzerodt seemed plainly condemned by the evidence presented. Testimony against Arnold, Spangler, and O'Laughlin appeared flimsy. Mary Surratt was perilously caught between the damning evidence of Lloyd and Weichmann and the human sympathy of court and public for the fact that she was a woman. Though many thought she might be guilty, none felt she should be made to pay the extreme penalty for her guilt.

As for Samuel Mudd, a reporter for the New York *Times* concluded, "Dr. Mudd is doubtless guilty, but with what degree of punishment he will be adjudged remains with the commission to determine." Similarly, correspondent George Alfred Townsend observed, "Dr. Mudd, if he be innocent, is in only less danger than if he were guilty." Mudd by now must have been sufficiently disillusioned to agree with both of them. But Mudd's attorneys had yet to have their day in court, and an army of witnesses had been assembled to defend him.[21]

At the farm on the hill overlooking Zachia Swamp, the nights were heavy with mist and redolent with the scents of spring; night creatures croaked in the marshes; and in the upstairs bedroom three small children, Andrew, Lillian, and Thomas, whispered to one another about strange presences and absences they did not understand. Only Sam, Jr., was too young to sense that anything was wrong. But in the back room downstairs, Frances knew that almost everything was wrong—dreadfully, unfairly wrong.

12

THE WEIGHTED SCALES

THE legions of victory, a million strong, had come and gone. Grant's Army of the Potomac, Cump Sherman's "dashing Yankee boys," had marched down Pennsylvania Avenue in the Grand Review, then dispersed in drunken riot through the city, finally drifting back to homes up North. Washington sank into exhausted apathy, all passion spent. The jubilee that had followed Richmond's fall and Lee's surrender; the tragic shock of Lincoln's murder and its aftermath of terror; and finally the artificial stimulus of the returning troops had left the city worn and limp, drained of all emotion.

The same malaise pervaded the dim, forbidding courtroom where the heat remained oppressive. Moist fingers stuck to tabletops and papers. Commissioners ran their fingers around binding collars. Prisoners sweated in the prison clothes they had worn since early May. Spectators listlessly fanned themselves with their hands.

And the trial droned on. Even the newspaper editors found their interest, and the interest of their readers, dwindling, bannering their columns with such alliterative headlines as:

PROTRACTION PROTRACTED AND
PATIENCE TIRED OUT

THE OLD, OLD STORY OVER
AND OVER AGAIN

The prosecution had wound up its case, and the prisoners, to the public satisfaction, stood condemned. What was the need of prolonging the trial? Get it over with. Build the gallows and hang the wretches! It was not a receptive climate in which Thomas Ewing and Frederick Stone, along with Reverdy Johnson and his associates, began to present their defense of Samuel Mudd, Mary Surratt, and the other six defendants.

Taking up first the charge that Mudd had harbored Confederate partisans on his property, Ewing called as witnesses Jeremiah Dyer and Benjamin Gwynn, two of the fugitives named by the prosecution. Dyer testified that he had indeed been "in the neighborhood of Dr. Mudd's house for about a week" in early September, 1861—not in the summer of 1863 or 1864 as testified by the prosecution witnesses:

> It was about the time Colonel Dwight's regiment was passing through, and there was a perfect panic in the neighborhood; the report was that everybody was to be arrested. Mr. [Benjamin] Gwynn and his brother [Andrew] came down in a fright stating that officers had been in the house to arrest them. . . . I also received notice that I was to be arrested. So for several nights we slept in the pines between Dr. Mudd's house and mine. . . .The party consisted of Benjamin Gwynn, Andrew Gwynn, and myself. . . . We were all dressed in civilian clothes.[1]

Bennett Gwynn testified for his brothers, Benjamin and Andrew, and himself, to the effect that they three with Jeremiah Dyer were the only ones hiding in the woods that autumn; there had been no "Captain White" or "Captain Perry" or any of the others charged with being there. It was about the time "General Sickles came over into Maryland, arresting almost everybody."

MR. EWING: You felt, therefore, that it was likely you would be arrested?

WITNESS: Yes, I understood there was an order for my arrest.

MR. EWING: You slept there in the pines for the sole purpose of escaping that arrest?

uel Alexander Mudd in his early
rs as a Maryland tobacco planter
country physician.

Sarah Frances ("Frank") Dyer, wife
of Dr. Samuel Mudd, as she appeared shortly after marriage.

ah Ann Reeves, Sam's mother,
e of Henry Lowe Mudd.

Henry Lowe Mudd, father of Dr.
Samuel Mudd.

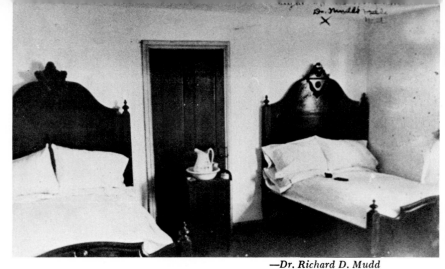

—Dr. Richard D. Mudd

Second-floor guest room of Dr. Mudd's house; Booth was treated in bed on right.

Farmhouse of Dr. Mudd in Charles County, Maryland, near Bryantown. Front porch was added in later years.

—Dr. Richard D. Mudd

hn Wilkes Booth at about age twenty-
ven, shortly before the assassination of
esident Lincoln in April, 1865.

fayette C. Baker, head of the United
ates Secret Service. Baker's force was
rgely responsible for the arrest of Dr.
udd.

Vice President Andrew Johnson was slated
for assassination but was unharmed.

Edwin M. Stanton, Lincoln's Secretary of
War, initiated and supervised the relent-
less hunt for the President's assassins.

SURRAT. BOOTH. HAROLD.

War Department, Washington, April 20, 1865,

 # $100,000 REWARD!

THE MURDERER

Of our late beloved President, Abraham Lincoln,

IS STILL AT LARGE.

$50,000 REWARD

Will be paid by this Department for his apprehension, in addition to any reward offered by Municipal Authorities or State Executives.

$25,000 REWARD

Will be paid for the apprehension of JOHN H. SURRATT, one of Booth's Accomplices.

$25,000 REWARD

Will be paid for the apprehension of David C. Harold, another of Booth's accomplices.

LIBERAL REWARDS will be paid for any information that shall conduce to the arrest of either of the above-named criminals, or their accomplices.

All persons harboring or secreting the said persons, or either of them, or aiding or assisting their concealment or escape, will be treated as accomplices in the murder of the President and the attempted assassination of the Secretary of State, and shall be subject to trial before a Military Commission and the punishment of DEATH.

Let the stain of innocent blood be removed from the land by the arrest and punishment of the murderers.

All good citizens are exhorted to aid public justice on this occasion. Every man should consider his own conscience charged with this solemn duty, and rest neither night nor day until it be accomplished.

EDWIN M. STANTON, Secretary of War.

DESCRIPTIONS.—BOOTH is Five Feet 7 or 8 inches high, slender build, high forehead, black hair, black eyes, and wears a heavy black moustache.

JOHN H. SURRAT is about 5 feet, 9 inches. Hair rather thin and dark; eyes rather light; no beard. Would weigh 145 or 150 pounds. Complexion rather pale and clear, with color in his cheeks. Wore light clothes of fine quality. Shoulders square; cheek bones rather prominent; chin narrow; ears projecting at the top; forehead rather low and square, but broad. Parts his hair on the right side; neck rather long. His lips are firmly set. A slim man.

DAVID C. HAROLD is five feet six inches high, hair dark, eyes dark, eyebrows rather heavy, full face, nose short, hand short and fleshy, feet small, in-step high, round bodied, naturally quick and active, slightly closes his eyes when looking at a person.

NOTICE.—In addition to the above, State and other authorities have offered rewards amounting to almost one hundred thousand dollars, making an aggregate of about TWO HUNDRED THOUSAND DOLLARS.

—Library of Congress

Original reward poster circulated by Secretary Stanton showed a wrong man in place of John Surratt and a schoolroom photo of David Herold with name misspelled.

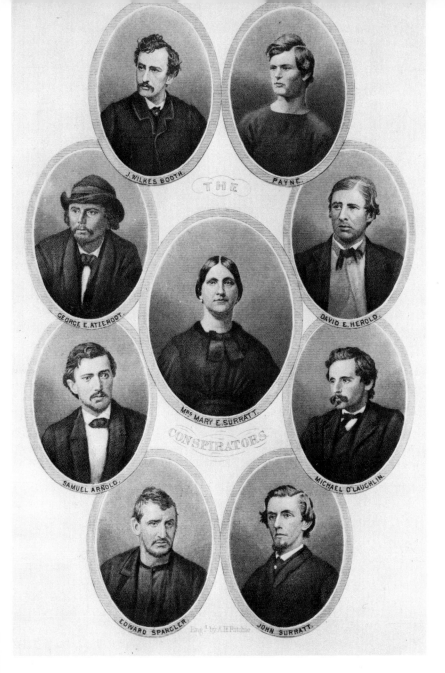

This gallery of Booth's alleged accomplices was published by court stenographer Benn Pitman, who omitted Samuel Mudd for lack of proof that the doctor was involved.

—*National Archives*

Sketch of Dr. Mudd made by an unknown spectator during the trial.

Louis Wiechmann, whose testimony helped to convict Dr. Mudd.

The military commission and judge advocates who conducted the trial of the Lincoln conspirators (left to right): Col. David R. Clendenin; Col. Charles S. Tompkins; Gen. Thomas M. Harris; Gen. Albion P. Howe; Gen. James A. Ekin; Gen. Lew Wallace; Gen. David Hunter; Gen. August V. Kautz; Gen. Robert S. Foster; Hon. John A. Bingham; Col. Henry L. Burnett; Hon. Joseph Holt.

—*Library of Congress*

Aerial view of Fort Jefferson showing single bridge over moat leading to portcullis; officers' barracks are in upper center of yard.

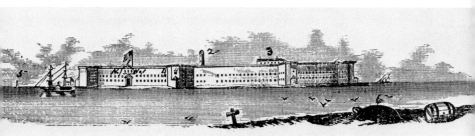

Of this marked drawing of Fort Jefferson the doctor wrote: "No. 1, marked in ink, shows you the location of our quarters. . . . The door below is the sally port, and is the only entrance to the Fort. No. 2 is the lighthouse; 3, officers' quarters; 5, Logger Head Lighthouse, about three miles distant; No. 6 represents Hog Island . . . and a barrel used to carry water to hogs.

George St. Leger Grenfell, British soldier
of fortune, was imprisoned with Mudd for
his part in the ill-fated Northwest Conspiracy.

John Surratt in the uniform of a papal
Zouave, photographed while hiding out
in Rome.

Thomas E. Ewing, former general in t
Union Army, acted as attorney for I
Mudd during and after his trial.

Dr. Mudd in the carpenter shop at Fo
Jefferson prison.

WITNESS: Yes, sir. Dr. Mudd knew why we were hiding
                  in the pines, and why he was feeding us
                  there.[2]

While General Ewing admitted that this testimony was not "a complete answer to the allegation," it indicated that the incident "took place in 1861, at the beginning of the war, at a time of general terror in the community, and that some of the persons alleged to have been concealed there, were not there."

To support the contention that the incident had been misrepresented, Ewing called six more witnesses to testify that either there had been no fugitives in Mudd's woods or that their number had been limited to Dyer and the Gwynns. All swore, too, that John Surratt had never been seen on Mudd's property or in his house.

It was not an entirely satisfactory defense, and Ewing switched his tactics to an emphasis on the doctor's favorable reputation. Jeremiah Dyer, who had lived from childhood next door to Samuel Mudd, was questioned about the doctor's character:

> I have known Dr. Mudd since he was a boy. I have never heard the slightest thing against him. He has always been regarded as a good citizen; he has a good reputation for peace, order, and good citizenship. I never knew of any thing to the contrary, except his shooting his servant, which he told me of the day it happened.[3]

Eglent had suffered "only a flesh wound," Dyer testified. Still, the incident did not inspire sympathy for Dr. Mudd. Ewing tried to counteract it by calling other ex-slaves of the doctor to the stand. Frank Washington testified of Mudd that, "He treated me first rate. I had no fault to find with him." Baptist Washington declared, "He always treated his servants very well." Charles Bloyce stated,

> I call Dr. Samuel Mudd a first-rate man to his servants. I never saw him whip any of them, nor heard of his whipping them. They did pretty much as they pleased, as far as I saw. I never heard a word of his sending or

threatening to send any of his servants to Richmond.
ASSISTANT JUDGE
ADVOCATE BINGHAM: Did you ever hear anything about his shooting any of his servants?
WITNESS: I did hear that.
ASSISTANT JUDGE
ADVOCATE BINGHAM: Do you think that is first-rate business?
WITNESS: I do not know about that.[4]

Bloyce's response, which concluded his testimony, prompted one of the rare outbursts of laughter in the court.

While he had Jeremiah Dyer present, Ewing switched again to the more serious accusation made by Daniel Thomas: that Mudd had forecast the murder of Lincoln and his cabinet during the conversation at Mr. Downing's house and therefore knew of the plot to assassinate the President. Since the court had only Thomas' word for the doctor's prescience, Ewing directed his attack against the witness's credibility. Jeremiah testified:

> I have not seen a great deal of Mr. Thomas for the past two or three years. . . . I know he has not borne a good reputation for truth in that neighborhood since he was a boy. I have heard him spoken of as one who would tattle a great deal, and tell stories, and say a great many things that were not true.

Dyer, however, was a friendly witness, and Ewing sought more powerful ammunition to discredit Thomas. He presented as a witness John H. Downing, the man in whose home and in whose presence Mudd allegedly had made his damning statement. Testified Downing:

> No such words were spoken in the house to my knowledge, and I stayed there all the time. . . . Dr. Mudd and Thomas could have had no conversation at that time but what I heard. . . . The President's name was not mentioned during Dr. Mudd's stay. . . . Nor was any reference made to any member of the Cabinet, nor to killing anybody; I am sure I should have remembered it if a word of the kind had been mentioned.[5]

The defense went further in bringing Dr. John C. Thomas, brother of Daniel Thomas, to the stand. Under questioning by Frederick Stone, Thomas testified that his brother had repeated Mudd's statement to him, but only after the news arrived of Lincoln's assassination. Not at the time that Mudd had allegedly made the statement. Stone sought to underscore this point.

MR. STONE: State whether he ever mentioned that conversation to you before that time.

WITNESS: No, never before that time.

Had Daniel Thomas concocted Mudd's statement after the fact, as a mischievous means of embarrassing the doctor? Or as a means of qualifying for some ultimate reward? Was Thomas himself confused, unstable, even possibly insane? Stone pursued this line relentlessly.

MR. STONE: State whether you have or have not attended your brother professionally.

WITNESS: I have, in some serious attacks. He had a very serious paralysis attack with paralysis of the body. He was for some time laboring under considerable nervous depression and was mentally affected by it so that his mind was not exactly right for a long time.

MR. STONE: State whether your brother's mind is now sound at all times.

WITNESS: I am under the impression that it is not at all times.[6]

With that, the credibility of Daniel Thomas crumbled, even in the eyes of the commission. In all, some dozen witnesses testified that Daniel could not be believed, even when under oath, but their corroboration was superfluous. Even the press, which tended to favor the prosecution, labeled Thomas "entirely unreliable."

On the momentum of this triumph, Stone and Ewing went after the credibility of other witnesses who had placed the doctor in Washington, with Booth and/or John Surratt, in

* * *

the weeks immediately before the assassination. One prime target was the Troy attorney, Marcus Norton, who had testified that Mudd had mistakenly entered his room at the National Hotel in quest of John Wilkes Booth. A fellow lawyer from the upstate city declared, "It is the general opinion of the people of Troy that Mr. Norton is not to be believed." He based this statement on the fact that some eighty attorneys in that city had petitioned for Norton's impeachment after his questionable handling of a case.

As for the Reverend William Evans, who had seen Mudd entering Mary Surratt's house "sometime during the winter," he proved a shadowy, unhinged witness under General Ewing's hammering:

MR. EWING:	When do you say you think you last saw Dr. Mudd in Washington?
WITNESS:	Several days before the inauguration.
MR. EWING:	Three or four days before?
WITNESS:	About the latter part of February. I I always like to discharge my duty, I have a certain amount of work to do, and . . .
MR. EWING:	We do not want your personal history.
WITNESS:	You seem to be so precise, I want to give you everything connected with it.
MR. EWING:	We are not so precise as to your personal history.
WITNESS:	A little of it will not do you any harm.
MR. EWING:	I do not think it will do any good in this case.
WITNESS:	We are all free and equal men and can talk as we please.
MR. EWING:	If the court wishes this examination continued perpetually, this witness may be indulged in his lucubrations as to his history and answers to everything except the questions that I propose. I ask the Court to restrain him to enable me to get through the examination.
THE PRESIDENT:	The witness has been told once that he must reply to the questions.
WITNESS:	Very well, I will answer them.

THE PRESIDENT:	If you do not do as you are directed, we will try—
WITNESS:	And make me do it?
THE PRESIDENT:	Yes, sir.[7]

The fact that the court shared Ewing's impatience with the witness, and for once supported his objection, was enough to assure that Evans as a witness had been disqualified. What he told the court thereafter was regarded as mere drivel. Even the imperturbable Benn Pitman, keeping his word-by-word record of the proceedings, saw fit to inject an uncustomary, parenthetical footnote in his transcript:

> (*This witness was exceedingly discursive, and his examination was consequently very lengthy. . . .*)

> Across the Potomac, the guns had fallen silent. The guards were gone from the Washington bridges. Virginians were no longer enemies, but farmers who trundled their crops to the city markets. Rich with the wastage of armies, the perennial fields were green. On the Capitol dome, Armed Freedom rested on her sheathed sword.[8]

As Margaret Leech noted, the war was over for the capital. But the residues of bitterness and moral laxity remained. The city was a "pest hole" to General Sherman, who left it on the first of June, declaring, "Washington is corrupt as Hell, made so by the looseness and extravagance of war."

Looseness and extravagance, corruption and distortion, were hallmarks of the continuing trial of the conspirators. For them and for their prosecutors the war was far from over. By presidential proclamation Andrew Johnson, beginning to assume the moral cloak of Lincoln, had decreed that with a few exceptions amnesty and pardon should be granted to all persons who directly or indirectly had participated in the late rebellion. But amnesty was far from the thoughts of the commission sitting in the hot June air in the third-floor courtroom of the penitentiary. Nerves were growing edgy, tempers short. Time and again the prosecutors objected to the valid arguments of the defense; time and again Judge Advocate Holt rose from his seeming stupor to pronounce, "Objection sustained!"

The remaining principal witness for Ewing's and Stone's defense of Samuel Mudd was Dr. George Mudd, called to the stand on May 29. At issue now was the doctor's guilt or innocence in receiving Booth into his home on April 15, mending the actor's broken leg, and thereafter reporting (or failing satisfactorily to report) the incident to the authorities. Ewing and Stone had laid the groundwork well for his appearance; a half-dozen witnesses had testified that George was a "good Union man" whose loyalty had been beyond reproach throughout the war.

After testifying to the character of Samuel Mudd, "I know of none whose reputation is better," George told of Dr. Sam's riding home with him from church on Sunday morning, April 16.

> MR. EWING: State whether he said anything to you about any persons having been at his house.
>
> THE JUDGE
> ADVOCATE: You need not answer that question. The Government has not introduced the declarations of the prisoner, Dr. Mudd, at that time.
>
> MR. EWING: I propose to offer that statement for the purpose of showing that Dr. George Mudd . . . was informed by the prisoner at the bar that there were two suspicious persons at his house on Saturday morning; he told him of the circumstances of their coming there; expressed to him a desire that he should inform the military authorities of their having been there. . . . I can imagine no declaration of a prisoner more clearly admissible than this.
>
> THE JUDGE
> ADVOCATE: If the court please, the principle here is almost too well settled to discuss. . . . The transaction in which the prisoner was involved, and is the subject of his arraignment, had closed the day before. That consisted of his having received and entertained these men, and sent them on their way rejoicing, having fed them, having set the leg of the

one whose leg was broken, having comforted and strengthened and encouraged them, as far as his hospitality and professional skill could do, to proceed on their journey.

That transaction was complete at four o'clock on Saturday evening. To introduce a declaration by the prisoner made twenty-four hours afterward, by which he seeks to relieve himself of the imputation which the law attaches to his previous conduct . . . is not competent. . . . The great principle which says that a criminal shall not manufacture testimony for his own exculpation, intervenes and forbids that this Court shall hear that testimony.

MR. EWING: The Judge Advocate says that the transaction was completed. Not so. The charge here is of concealment, as the prosecution has sought to prove; a concealment not only of the suspects' presence *while* they were in the house, but a concealment *extending until Tuesday or Friday*. . . . Two of the witnesses for the prosecution who were at the house on Tuesday have testified that Dr. Mudd denied the presence of the suspects in his house. That was not irrelevant testimony. But now your propose to exclude us from proving that he informed the Government the previous *Sunday* that they had been there . . . which is explicitly and clearly to the point.

THE JUDGE
ADVOCATE: If the gentleman will frame his question so as to bring out simply the conduct of the prisoner in the act he did, I shall not object; but I must object to the prisoner's declarations.

MR. EWING: I cannot prove how he informed the government without proving the words he used.

ASSISTANT
JUDGE
ADVOCATE
BURNETT: The question could certainly be asked of the witness, "Did Dr. Samuel A. Mudd direct you to go to the authorities, and inform them that these parties had been there?"

MR. EWING: I claim more than that; I claim the whole statement.[9]

The commission sustained the judge advocate's objection. No words or statements made by Dr. Mudd in his defense after the act of harboring Booth and Herold in his house—in other words, after four o'clock on Saturday—would be allowed. George Mudd, however, was a skillful and crafty witness, stating in his own words what the doctor had told him about Booth's and Herold's visit, his innocent treatment of the stranger's broken leg, his desire that George should report the incident to the authorities.

Then came the matter of when Dr. Mudd had known of the President's assassination and would have had reason to suspect the strangers who had visited his house that morning. What information could George provide?

MR. EWING:	Did you have any conversation with Dr. Samuel Mudd at the church as to what he knew of the assassination?
WITNESS:	No, sir. I heard—
ASSISTANT JUDGE ADVOCATE BINGHAM:	You need not state anything you heard the doctor say at church.
MR. EWING:	I think it admissible, as explaining the conduct of the accused at the time of the offenses charged—concealment beyond that Sunday—as showing his frame of mind, his information, his conduct.
ASSISTANT JUDGE ADVOCATE BINGHAM:	If the Court please, that is not the point here. The declaration of a defendant, made *after* the crime he is charged with, is not admissible . . . criminals shall not make evidence, at their pleasure, and in their own behalf, and adduce it in court to exculpate themselves from crime.
MR. EWING:	I wish to call the attention of the Court to the fact that the declaration as to which I am now inquiring

> was made *during* the time of the
> alleged offense of concealment. . . .
> I ask the decision of the Court on
> Judge Advocate's objection.[10]

The commission sustained the objection—which, to all significant purposes, wound up George Mudd's testimony on the case. Witnesses were called to testify that while Samuel Mudd had been seen in Bryantown on the afternoon of Saturday, April 15, it was not generally known in the village—contrary to Lieutenant Dana's statement—that the President's assassin had been John Wilkes Booth.

Unresolved was what was said during Mudd's meeting with Booth in Washington on December 23. Regarding this, there was only Wiechmann's deadly testimony that he had been present. Considering the potential significance of that meeting, especially in view of the fact that Mudd had denied seeing Booth at any time after the actor's visit to Bryantown the previous November, it is strange that the prosecutors did not hammer harder on this point. That they did not took some of the burden off the defense. In his summation for the defense, General Ewing pointed out:

> It will be observed that the only men spoken of by this witness as having seen the accused on this occasion are Booth who is dead, and Surratt, who is a fugitive from the country. So there is no one who can be called to confirm or refute his statements, as to the fact of these men being together, or as to the character of the interview.[11]

The defense attorney attempted to undermine Wiechmann's testimony by pointing to the witness' confusion about dates. Wiechmann had testified that Mudd had met Booth in Washington during the third week in January, at a time when evidence demonstrated that Mudd had never left his home in Maryland. Craftily linking Wiechmann's testimony with that of other discredited witnesses—Daniel Thomas, Lucas Norton, William Evans—Ewing pointed out that if Wiechmann had erred about the date, then his entire testimony was in doubt. "The mildest thing that can be said of him, as of Norton, is that he was mistaken. . . ."

Ewing further tore apart the testimony of the four de-

tectives who had called at Mudd's house on Tuesday and
Friday, April 18 and 21. Two had claimed that Mudd denied
having strangers at his house the previous Saturday. Yet at
the same time they confessed to having visited the farm because of Samuel Mudd's report to the authorities, via Cousin
George, that he *had* had strangers at his house. Would he
send such a report to Dana's officers and then contradict
the report when they arrived? Surely the detectives were
confused or had made false statements to the court.

"I venture to say that rarely in the annals of criminal trials
has the life of an accused been assailed by such an array of
false testimony," Ewing summarized.

Not content with attacking individual witnesses, Ewing
challenged the intentions of the court itself, quoting the
judge advocate as saying that he expected to convict under
"the common law of war." This was a term, the counsel
said, "unknown to our language—wholly undefined and incapable of definition. It is, in short, just what the judge
advocate chooses to make of it. It may create a fictitious
crime, and attach to it arbitrary and extreme punishment."

Throwing doubt upon the court's intentions could not
have endeared the lawyer to the commission, but doubtless
Ewing knew the scales were weighted against him and was
looking beyond to a time when he might obtain a writ of
habeas corpus and could appeal his case in the civilian courts.
In any event, he based the rest of his summation on Mudd's
innocence on the basis of common law: Dr. Mudd had not
been proved guilty, beyond reasonable doubt, of any of the
charges pressed against him. Not guilty of taking any part
in the assassination of the President, since "at the time of the
tragedy Dr. Mudd was at his residence in the country, thirty
miles from the place of the crime." Not guilty of *conspiring*
to assassinate the President, since a score of witnesses (and
here Ewing reviewed their testimony) had indicated, or
striven to prove, that Mudd had not been in touch with
Booth and John Surratt, the principal conspirators, prior to
the assassination.

Then Ewing reached the close of his summation:

> Can, then, Dr. Mudd be convicted as a conspirator, or an
> accessory before or after the fact, in the assassination? If

this tribunal is to be governed in its findings by the just and time-honored rules of law, he cannot; if by some edict higher than constitutions and laws, I know not what to anticipate or how to defend him. With confidence in the integrity of purpose of the Court and its legal advisers, I now leave the case to them.[12]

For David Herold and Lewis Paine, little defense was possible. Both had been caught, in effect, red-handed. The best that Frederick Stone could elicit from nine witnesses appearing in behalf of Herold was that the prisoner was of "a light and trifling" nature, "more of a boy than a man." A onetime employer found him "unreliable" and apt to "play a joke on anybody." A former quartermaster in the War Department who had known Herold since boyhood declared him "immature" and "easily persuaded." His sister testified that they had quarreled over a pitcher of water she was carrying and "we both got wet from the water being spilled."

In short, Stone seemed to be trying to prove that David Herold was too trifling to be taken seriously, too stupid to have known what he was doing, had been a victim of Booth, and was too much of a child to be condemned to die. The defense was the briefest of the trial.

For Paine's defense, William E. Doster announced that he was entering a plea of insanity for his client. When Assistant Judge Advocate Bingham objected, Doster enumerated Paine's bizarre acts before, during, and after the attack on Seward up to his return to Mary Surratt's, of all places, in a "crazy disguise; because who in the world ever heard of a man disguising himself in a piece of his drawers as a hat." Paine had not only shown a lunatic indifference to his fate throughout the trial, but at one point had "laughed at a moment when his life was trembling in the balance."

For corroboration Doster called to the stand two doctors specializing in mental disorders. With the first, Charles B. Nichols, superintendent of the Government Hospital for the Insane, Doster established a definition of insanity. Then:

MR. DOSTER: If one should try to murder a sick man in his bed, without ever having seen him be-

	fore, would it not be presumptive proof of insanity?
WITNESS:	It would give rise, in my mind, to the suspicion that the man was insane. . . .
MR. DOSTER:	If the same person should besides try to murder four other persons in the house without having seen them before, would it not strengthen that suspicion of insanity?
WITNESS:	I think it would.
MR. DOSTER:	If the same person should make no attempt to disguise himself, but should converse for five minutes with a negro servant, walk away leisurely, leave his hat and pistol behind, throw away his knife before the door, and ride away so slowly that he could be followed for a square by a man on foot, would not such conduct further corroborate the suspicion of insanity?
WITNESS:	I think it would. . . .[13]

Another physician sustained Dr. Nichols' conclusions, while two guards who attended Paine since his arrival at the penitentiary testified to the prisoner's peculiar manner and condition. Paine had expressed the wish that "they would make haste and hang him; he was tired of life," and had complained of being constipated for thirty-four successive days, or ever since the assassination—a seemingly bizarre defense. In rebuttal the government produced three Army surgeons who concurred that the prisoner was sound and sane.

In defense of George Atzerodt, Doster attempted to present a statement, in the prisoner's own writing, declaring "his guilt in this transaction, if there is any guilt, and of his innocence if there is any evidence of it." The judge advocate "deplored" the tactic of submitting a confession, and refused to accept the statement. With that, the crux of Doster's defense, whatever the confession may have said, went out the window.

The lawyer tried another strategy, attempting to prove that Atzerodt, by his very nature, was incapable of committing the crime that he was charged with. He brought to the stand Samuel McAllister, clerk at the Pennsylvania

House, who had testified earlier that Dr. Mudd had not stopped there at any time after Christmas. McAllister had known Atzerodt as another patron of the hotel.

MR. DOSTER:	Do you know any thing about his reputation for courage?
ASSISTANT JUDGE ADVOCATE BINGHAM:	I object to that. I do not think we are going to try his character for courage.
MR. DOSTER:	May it please the Court, I intend to show that this man is a constitutional coward; that if he had been assigned the duty of assassinating the Vice President, he never could have done it; and that, from his known cowardice, Booth probably did not assign him to any such duty. Certainly it is just as relevant as anything can be.
ASSISTANT JUDGE ADVOCATE BINGHAM:	If the counsel wishes to prove that the prisoner, Atzerodt, is a coward, I will withdraw my objection.[14]

Thus conciliated by a rare concession from the prosecution, Doster presented three other witnesses to substantiate Atzerodt's "remarkable lack of courage." It was the best that he could do with what he had to work with.

Throughout these last days of the trial Dr. Mudd, hands resting on the rail before him, jaws working on the wad of tobacco in his mouth, appeared to the reporters as serene and confident. Certainly the sort of evidence aimed at hanging Herold, Paine and Atzerodt could not be brought to bear on him. His case fell into the category of the remaining four defendants, who to one degree or another had been victims of circumstance or dupes of that homicidal maniac John Wilkes Booth.

Considering his obviously minor role, if any, in the conspiracy, Ned Spangler was given an exceptionally stout defense. A score of witnesses, including the brothers Ford, testified that his duties in the theater would not have given the stagehand any opportunity to aid in the assassination or in Booth's escape. He had been on the opposite side of the stage throughout the evening and had not even had time to tend Booth's horse. John Ford also commented on the rope found in Spangler's possession, to which the prosecution had attached a sinister significance. "That rope might be used as a crabline," said Ford. "I understood he was a great crab fisher."

As to Jacob Ritterspaugh's statement that Spangler had slapped him after Booth's flight, and said, "Don't say which way he went," Ewing produced scene-painter James Lamb, who testified that Ritterspaugh had given him a different version of the incident. According to Lamb, Ritterspaugh admitted having said, "I know him; I will swear that man was Booth," and Spangler had said, "Hush up, what do you know about it?"

Things were going too well for Spangler in Assistant Judge Advocate Bingham's estimation. Resorting to tactics he had used throughout the trial, he did his best to confuse the witness, James Lamb:

BINGHAM: That is what Jake said?

WITNESS: That is what Spangler said to Jake.

BINGHAM: Are you now reporting what Jake said, or reporting what Spangler said?

WITNESS: I am reporting what Spangler said and what Jake said.

BINGHAM: We are not asking you for what Spangler said, we are asking you what Jake said.

WITNESS: Jake said: "I followed the party, I was close at his heels, or near to him, and I said 'That is Booth. I know him, I know him.' "

BINGHAM: Jake said he followed the party close to his heels.

WITNESS: Near to him.

BINGHAM: Did you or did you not swear that he said he followed the party close to his heels?

WITNESS: You know whether I swore it or not.

BINGHAM: I ask you whether you did swear to it or not?

WITNESS: I say he said he followed the party close to his heels.

BINGHAM: Very well, stick to it. . . . What more did Jake say? Did he say he came back after following the man close to his heels?

WITNESS: No sir.

BINGHAM: Why not?
WITNESS: Spangler was standing in the way.
BINGHAM: While Jake was following the man close to his heels?
WITNESS: No, not at all.
BINGHAM: How was that?
WITNESS: Spangler, I suppose—
BINGHAM: You need not state what you suppose. State what Jake said.[15]

In defense of Michael O'Laughlin, Walter Cox called to the stand O'Laughlin's fellow participants in the thirty-hour binge that had lasted from Thursday night to the Saturday morning when the President had died. Their account was a Baedeker of Washington gin mills, from Lichau's bar in Rullman's Hotel to Welch's Saloon to the Canterbury Music Hall to the Metropolitan, back to Lichau's and around again.

Never, all three testified, had O'Laughlin been out of their company, and never had they been close to Secretary Seward's house. The proprietor of Rullman's had seen O'Laughlin drinking at the bar when news of the President's murder had arrived, and O'Laughlin had been overheard to say that the assassination was "a dreadful thing." The rest of the witnesses stressed the fact that O'Laughlin had willingly and voluntarily surrendered to the authorities, which proved, said Cox, "his entire innocence in this affair."

To defend Mary Surratt, Crampitt and Aiken had the agile mind of Reverdy Johnson to direct them, although Johnson himself remained in the background to avoid antagonizing the commission with his questioned presence. What they did not have, as it tragically developed, were carefully investigated, well-selected, well-coached witnesses. Wiechmann's testimony regarding Mary Surratt's acquaintance with Booth and the presence of Booth's conspirators at the boardinghouse was circumstantial evidence. Aiken and Crampitt could handle that. But John Lloyd's statement that Mary had brought the conspirators' firearms to his tavern, as confessed to detective George Cottingham, was dangerous unless discredited. And Aiken believed he had it licked.

Accordingly, detective Cottingham was called on May 25,

as the first big gun for the defense. Cottingham dropped a
bombshell in Aiken's lap. The attorney asked him what the
tavern keeper had confessed to him at the time of Lloyd's
arrest.

> WITNESS: Lloyd stated to me that Mrs. Surratt had come
> down to his place on Friday between four and
> five o'clock; that she told him to have the fire-
> arms ready; that two men would call for them
> at midnight. . . . He commenced crying and
> hallooing out, "O, Mrs. Surratt, that vile
> woman, she had ruined me."

This was not what Aiken had anticipated; not the story
Cottingham had agreed to tell the court: namely, that Lloyd
had made no such declaration. Aiken asked the witness to
repeat in "precise language" what Cottingham had told him
earlier. Was it not very different from what he was now re-
lating to the court? Cottingham replied that as a detective he
was entitled "to gain an objective by the use of strategy."

> MR. AIKEN: Then you are ready now to swear that you told
> me a lie?
> WITNESS: Undoubtedly I told you a lie, because I
> thought you had no business questioning me.
> MR. AIKEN: No business! As my witness, had I not a right
> to have the truth from you?
> WITNESS: I told you you might call me into court, and I
> state here that I did lie to you. But when put
> on my oath I will tell the truth.[16]

Aiken and Crampitt did their best to salvage their case
after this initial sabotage. Five Washington priests were
called to the stand and swore to Mary's character as a devout
and loyal Christian but, on cross-examination, were unable
to testify as to her loyalty to the United States. Mary's
daughter, Anna, as well as several boarders in the H Street
house, described Mary's hospitality to the conspirators as
no more than inherent graciousness. As to Mrs. Surratt's
insistence that she had not recognized Lewis Paine when he
had sought refuge after the assassination, a number of witnesses testified to the widow's failing eyesight. She could not

work when the light was dim; she could not thread a needle; she often passed friends on the street and failed to recognize them.

Mary's brother, John Zaddoc Jenkins, was expected to be a powerful witness for the defense, able to swear from life-long knowledge to Mary's good character and conduct. But before the trial he had run amok, trying to intimidate prospective witnesses for the prosecution, threatening to "see in Hell" anyone who testified against his sister. He tried to recant by asserting in court, "I was angry and excited, and I didn't mean it anyhow." Too late, the damage had been done.[17]

Counting as much against Mary as anything was the fact that John Surratt was heavily implicated in the plot with John Wilkes Booth and was now rightfully believed to be a fugitive in Canada. John might be a loner, beyond his mother's influence, but he was still her son. Having been cheated for now of bringing John to justice, the court would take the widow as the only available substitute. To a degree she was tried and would be sentenced as much for her son's transgressions as for any wrongdoing the commission could attribute to her.

And to the same degree Samuel Mudd was being tried and would be sentenced for the "disloyal" attitude and sentiments expressed throughout the war by southern Maryland. Vengeance needed a victim among south-county planters, and at last it had one.

Benn Pitman, who for thirty days had been transcribing the proceedings and had written more than a thousand pages, recorded in his meticulous hand: "Each of the counsel for the accused here announced, on behalf of his client, that the defense was closed." On sharp command the eight defendants rose wearily from their chairs and shuffled in single file, with a clanking of chains, through the rear door and down the dreary passage to their cells—to await the verdict of the court.

13

JOURNEY INTO DARKNESS

IT was all over but the shouting—the shouting for vengeance from the streets, the quieter demands of General Ewing making a last appeal for his client, Dr. Samuel Mudd.

At the beginning of the trial, Thomas Ewing, as well as Reverdy Johnson, had protested the authority of the improvised commission. The protests had been overruled, with Assistant Judge Advocate Bingham later presenting an elaborate defense of the procedure. Now Ewing argued that the charges against his client had not been defined. They did not specify the crime. Rather, they specified four different crimes: conspiracy against the government, assassination of Abraham Lincoln, the assault upon Secretary Seward, the intent to murder Andrew Johnson.

Of which of these several crimes was Samuel Mudd accused?

All four, the judge advocates replied, in effect saying that Ewing was trying to confuse the issue and resorting to technicalities to obstruct justice. Bingham offered to reiterate to Ewing "what he already knows, that the act of any one of the parties to a conspiracy . . . is the act of every party to that conspiracy; and therefore the charge that the President was murdered by the hand of Booth, is a direct and unequivocal charge that he was murdered by every one of the parties to this conspiracy."

MR. EWING: It is then, I understand, *one* crime with which they are charged.

JUDGE
ADVOCATE
BINGHAM: One crime all round, with various parts per-
formed.

MR. EWING: The crime of conspiracy.

JUDGE
ADVOCATE
BINGHAM: It is the crime of murder as well. It is not
simply conspiring, but executing the conspiracy. . . .

MR. EWING: I should like an answer to my question, if it is
to be given. How many crimes is my client
charged with and being tried for? I cannot
tell.

JUDGE
ADVOCATE
BINGHAM: We have told you, it is all one transaction.

MR. EWING: I am as much in the dark as ever. . . .[1]

The court would not enlighten him, and Samuel Mudd
was in the dark as well. What the court's verdict might be,
what fate lay in store for him, he had no way of knowing.
The testimony he had heard in the past five weeks had generally been damning though confused by contradictions. The
commission had overruled almost every objection raised to
clarify obscurity. Its members would reach their decision by
what they wanted to believe. They would feel justified in
that they had no other choice; one could not untangle truth
from fiction.

The matter of trying civilians in a military court was still
a moot issue. The conspiracy to abduct or assassinate the
President—and Jefferson Davis' name was still linked to that
charge—had been hatched in time of war. Peace had since
intervened. Some notable jurists in America, in addition to
Reverdy Johnson and Thomas Ewing and others engaged
in the case of Samuel Mudd *et al*, were beginning to express
doubt about the Constitutional ethics of this military trial
and its conclusions. Perhaps in anticipation of further protest,
Special Judge Advocate Bingham delivered to the court an
immensely long-winded defense of the military's jurisdiction,
which Benn Pitman took down word for word and which
Edwin Stanton filed in his office for future use.

At the close of business on Monday, June 14, the court adjourned for two weeks. Samuel Mudd and the other male defendants remained for the most part in their cells, shackled and hooded, dwelling in a half-world of uncertain dread. They were permitted two hours of exercise in the yard, hoods and chains removed, but under close guard; they were not allowed to speak. Round and round the enclosure they were marched in single file. Their counselors had had their say; nothing further could be done to help them; the quality of any mercy to be shown by the commission would, for a certainty, be strained.

The court reassembled on Thursday, June 29, to deliberate on the evidence and reach a verdict. The prisoners' dock was empty. The defense attorneys were, of course, excluded, and the doors were locked and guarded. However, not only were the nine commissioners present, but the three Judge Advocates as well—a little like having the district attorney and his assistants sit with the jury while it deliberated on a civil case. Special Judge Advocate Bingham made a sweeping condemnation of the opposing counselors' defense, blasting recklessly at the "alibis" offered in behalf of Samuel Mudd; after which the twelve-man council of judges, jurors, and prosecutors began to draft their verdict. By the end of the day the prisoners were unanimously found guilty of conspiracy and murder, with the sole exception of Edward Spangler, who was pronounced guilty of conspiracy alone.

Herold, Atzerodt, and Paine were sentenced to "hang by the neck until dead." O'Laughlin and Arnold were given life at hard labor. Spangler received a lenient term of six years in prison. But when it came to Samuel Mudd and Mary Surratt, the commission, despite Bingham's impassioned plea that all should receive the maximum penalty, hesitated. Both were declared guilty, but the degree of guilt and the penalty were matters for further debate.

In Mary Surratt's case the vote was four for death to five for life imprisonment, short of the two-thirds majority needed to send her to the gallows. How the death sentence was arrived at is impossible to say; the meeting was secret; there was no Benn Pitman taking notes. Yet somehow Mary was condemned to die. There were many theories advanced as to why the verdict was slanted against the widow while Dr. Mudd was spared the gallows. But none of the theorists was present at the secret session. No one would ever know for sure.[2]

However, the four dissenting commissioners drafted, in Mary's behalf, a plea for clemency to be reviewed by President Andrew Johnson. Colonel Burnett agreed to deliver it to the chief executive. So far Johnson had expressed no sympathy for Mrs. Surratt, remarking only, "Hers was the nest in which the plot was hatched."

Samuel Mudd was spared from hanging by a single vote— five to four, again short of a two-thirds majority. Decision on the doctor's sentence was postponed until the next day, June 30, at which time the following notation was entered in the court's private records:

Court-Room, Washington D.C.
June 30, 1865, 10 o'clock A.M.

The Commission met, with closed doors, pursuant to adjournment.
All the members present; also the Judge Advocate and the Assistant Judge Advocates.
The Commission do hereby sentence the said Samuel A. Mudd to be imprisoned at hard labor for life, at such place as the President shall direct.
The Commission thereupon adjourned *sine die.*
J. Holt   D. Hunter[3]

Colonel Burnett was true to his word—up to a point. The following day, according to his own account, he attached the petition or recommendation of mercy (for Mary Surratt) to the findings and sentences applying to the other prisoners and delivered them not to Johnson, but to Judge Advocate Holt. Holt promised to submit them to the President for his approval.

What happened next is part of the mystery surrounding the entire case. Johnson was ill and able to see no one until July 5. On that day, according to Holt, the Advocate General placed the written conclusions of the trial before him, and the President signed them "with a shaking hand." Some would say that Holt withheld the petition of mercy for Mary Surratt, or that Johnson felt the prisoner's sex was not an adequate reason to commute the sentence. The final document with which Holt left the White House read in part:

> Executive Mansion
> July 5, 1865
>
> . . . It is ordered that the sentence of David E. Herold, G.A. Atzerodt, Lewis Payne [sic], Mary E. Surratt be carried into execution by the proper Military Authority, under the direction of the Secretary of War, on the 7th day of July, 1865, between the hours of 10 o'clock A.M. and 2 o'clock P.M. of that day.
>
> It is further ordered, that the prisoners Samuel Arnold, Samuel A. Mudd, Edward Spangler and Michael O'Laughlin be confined at hard labor at the Penitentiary of Albany, New York, during the period designated in their respective sentences.
>
> Andrew Johnson,
> President[4]

If the nation, both North and South, was shocked to learn that a woman would be executed by the government, regardless of her crime, lower Maryland was outraged by the sentence passed on Samuel Mudd. Southerners by tradition and heritage, the natives all but apotheosized him as a martyr to Northern prejudice. From the depths of his own resentment the doctor felt himself betrayed; speaking later of the commissioners who had sentenced him, he said:

> Not a man of them sat on my trial with an unbiased and unprejudiced mind. Before a word of evidence was heard, my case was prejudiced and I was already condemned on the strength of wild rumor and misrepresentation. The witnesses perjured themselves and while I was sitting there in that dock and listening to their monstrous falsehoods I felt ashamed of my species and lost faith forever in mankind. That men would stand up in the court and take an oath before heaven to tell the truth and the next moment set themselves to work to swear away by unright perjury the life of a fellow man was something that I, in my innocence of the world, never thought possible.[5]

* * *

Conceivably his greatest crime had been an innocence of the world: his failure to recognize the patent, fanatic villainy of John Wilkes Booth; his belief that one could be a Southerner by sentiment in the Northern prison camp of Maryland; his clinging to the childish code of silence or excessive caution when confronted by authority. Peculiarly, of all the commissioners, David Hunter seemed to understand the nature of the man and his position. A friend of Hunter's quoted the general as saying:

> The Court never believed that Dr. Mudd knew anything of Booth's designs. Booth made him a tool, as he had done with the others. Dr. Mudd was the victim of his own timidity. Had he acknowledged to the soldiers whom he saw in search of Booth the day after the assassination that Booth had got his leg set at his house and went off, and had he like a man come out and said he knew Booth instead of flatly denying it to the courts, he would have had little trouble.[6]

There were to be many such statements, revelations and confessions reported in the aftermath of the trial. Most of them were hearsay and served only to confound the existing doubt about the degree of guilt or innocence of Samuel Mudd and Mary Surratt. No longer under oath, witnesses changed or elaborated on their testimony; beyond further punishment, prisoners eased their minds with alleged confessions, which their father-confessors may have reported accurately, may have altered to improve the story, may have invented out of whole cloth as a sop to public interest.

As soon as Frances heard of her husband's sentence on the morning of June 6, she took the first coach to Washington and applied at the War Department for a pass to visit the doctor at the penitentiary. She did not see Stanton himself, but a member of Stanton's staff provided a carriage to take her to the arsenal gate. As she entered the grounds, the sounds of hammering and sawing reached her ears. Rising from one end of the yard was the framework of a gallows. Work on the superstructure was being supervised by the executioner, Christian Rath, a name that suggested a character from a sixteenth-century morality play.

The government was losing little time. Four prisoners, one a woman, would be hanged at two o'clock the next day.

General Dana, acting for Secretary Stanton to expedite the execution, greeted Frances at the prison and sent her under escort to the anteroom on the third floor, where she waited with two soldiers for her husband to be brought in from his cell. What the couple talked about in that brief time together under guard can only be surmised. The doctor told her he had heard of his sentence from a guard, though none of the prisoners had been officially informed. "He was in his shirt sleeves," Frances recollected, "and wore a pair of carpet slippers without socks. . . . I noticed that his ankle was sore, and I asked if it was caused by the chains he had to wear. He paused a few moments, then answered, hesitatingly, as though afraid to say otherwise in the presence of the guards, 'No.' "[7]

What must have been a seeringly painful interview, a final farewell if the doctor's sentence were accepted literally, ended on order of the corporal of the guard. On her way down the narrow, circular stairway, Frances met "a poor girl who was weeping bitterly," and was told it was Anna Surratt, Mary's daughter. Anna had been at the White House, banging at the gates until admitted to the grounds, then pounding on the White House door until admitted to the hallway leading, on the left, to the executive wing.

Here her passage had been blocked by two stout guardians of the President, Senators Preston King of New York and James H. Lane of Kansas. Shoulder to shoulder they told her, No, she could not pass; no one was allowed to see the President that day.

Perhaps for Anna it was just as well. For Johnson, of course, had taken no action on the commission's petition for mercy for her mother. Reverdy Johnson had applied for a writ of *habeas corpus* and that had been denied as well. There was no hope for Mary Surratt, and little hope for Frances Mudd as she returned to southern Maryland and four small children and a lifetime without a husband.

* * *

Friday, July 7, was a steamy, cruel, midsummer day in Washington; the temperature had reached ninety-eight degrees by early morning. Haze did not temper a scorching sun. The leaves of the poplars along Pennsylvania Avenue drooped listlessly; the stump of the Washington Monument seemed to float in waves of heat. On the soggy flats of the Potomac, between Capitol Hill and the penitentiary, war-surplus cattle grazed beneath a veil of insects. On the eastern horizon storm clouds gathered; the world seemed to listen for the sound of thunder.

Outside the penitentiary grounds the crowds had been gathering since dawn. They came by special train from Baltimore, by streetcar and carriage from Washington, by the sooty excursion steamers churning up and down the dank Potomac from the piers between Georgetown and the Long Bridge. Like so many crows, they waited beneath black umbrellas, hopeful for the relief of rain, and told one another reassuringly that this would be the greatest hanging in the nation's history.

Actually, only a hundred civilians, along with reporters and military personnel, were admitted to the yard. The rest were obliged to get their thrill vicariously, seeing only the musket-carrying soldiers, a thousand strong, ranged along the top of the wall, catching a glimpse of the single beam above the scaffold with its lethal fringe of rope.

In the yard Captain Christian Rath was making last-minute preparations. Bribed with a promise of whiskey, a squad of soldiers had hacked four graves from the hard-baked soil at one side of the scaffold. Alongside the piles of excavated earth plain pine coffins stood open. With a sack of lead shot, Rath tested one of the new ropes he had purchased for the hanging. As the trap was sprung, the knot slipped its fastening and the sack plummeted earthward, nearly killing the executioner. The soldiers whooped with glee and derision. But Rath was satisfied; the rope itself was sound.

Samuel Mudd and his fellow prisoners had no view of these proceedings. They had been told only that their exercise period was suspended for that day. But since dawn they had been aware of strange disturbing sounds; the multiple footsteps in the yard, the hammering and carpentry, the muffled orders. To these were added, as the day wore on, the wailing of David Herold's sisters from the tier below, the uncontrollable sobbing of Anna Surratt in Mary's cell, the prayers and incantations of the Catholic priests trying to bring consolation to the condemned.[8]

Shortly after two o'clock, the death march commenced. The iron door of the penitentiary clanked open and, preceded and followed by soldiers, the four prisoners filed slowly and silently toward the scaffold: Mary Surratt in black bombazine and heavy veil, supported by two black-robed priests; George Atzerodt, gibbering like a monkey in a comical pointed nightcap; David Herold, childishly tearful and bewildered; Lewis Paine, unfearing and disdainful. Clowning for the audience, Paine snatched a straw hat from a spectator's head and placed it rakishly on his own. The witnesses tittered.

The storm clouds drifting from the west obscured the sun, and at long last a soft rain came. The black umbrellas added a touch of mourning to the scene at the procession mounted the thirteen steps to the platform and the prisoners took their seats beneath the ropes. In a ceremony agonizing for the four condemned, General Hartranft laboriously read the findings of the commission, to reassure the dying of their guilt and the justice of their execution.

A gust of wind whisked the straw hat from Lewis Paine's head, but he had no further use for it. White hoods were placed over the prisoner's faces, through which Mary Surratt pleaded to her guard, "Don't let me fall!" George Atzerodt shouted bravely, "Good-bye, shentlemens!" And Christian Rath whispered to Paine as he tested the noose, "I want you to die quickly," and Paine answered, "Thank you, Captain."[9]

Since early morning General Hartranft had waited for word from the White House staying Mary Surratt's execution. Rumors that it would arrive momentarily had sustained his hope time after time. He waited a few seconds more; decided it was no use; raised his hand. The traps banged down. Four bodies dropped and swayed and shuddered for a while. Lewis Paine, whose stout neck had remained unbroken, writhed convulsively for several moments, then grew still.

Samuel Mudd learned of the executions from Thomas

Ewing, who called at his cell that afternoon. Schooled by his boyhood idol and mentor, William Tecumseh Sherman, Ewing was a fighter of bulldog tenacity. He had far from given up on his client. His plan, as he outlined it to the doctor, was to wait till the latter had reached the Albany Penitentiary. Then Ewing would go to New York State, file a plea of *habeas corpus* and seek a new trial in the civil courts. The chances were that the prosecution would not dare again to produce such thoroughly discredited witnesses as Daniel Thomas, Evans, Norton, and Mary Simms. Before a civil judge Mudd's attorneys would not face the arbitrary restrictions imposed by the military commission. In fact the legality of the military trial might be effectively reopened as a point in question.

If that failed, they could carry the case to the Supreme Court, where the constitutionality of the military trial might well be challenged. It would take time, but that would allow the present climate of "frenzy" and "madness" (Ewing's words) to give way to a calmer atmosphere. The sentence of life imprisonment might be reduced if not rescinded. Lawyers' fees would mount, of course, and that might mean selling off some of the doctor's land in Maryland and drawing eventually on his father's savings. So be it. That, and faith in the Lord, was all he had left.

During the next two weeks, which dragged interminably through the heat of mid-July, Mudd and the three remaining prisoners, Spangler, Arnold, and O'Laughlin, were again allowed their two-hour period of exercise and fresh air in the yard. But meeting their gaze as they stepped out the door was the still-standing scaffold, ropes dangling, and, beside it the four mounds of new-piled earth that marked the graves of their less fortunate companions.

Had the hideous structure been left there deliberately as a sort of intimidation? If so, it achieved its purpose. The prisoners could not keep their eyes from the hanging traps and the severed ropes; but Mudd tried to turn his thoughts to the prospect of their transfer to New York. The Albany Penitentiary might be no better for human comfort—it had an infamous reputation as a jail for army deserters—but at least it would not bear the stench of death.

Ewing would never have the chance to carry out his project

for a new trial. At some point during the period Secretary Stanton altered the specific sentences President Johnson had initialed, changing the details of the prisoners' incarceration. On the afternoon of Monday, July 17, the prisoners were summoned before General Hartranft who read the respective sentences imposed by the military commission—hard labor at the Albany Penitentiary. It was a curious ceremony, since by now each must have learned, one way or another, of his fate; but in the light of subsequent events it had its purpose.

That midnight the prisoners were marched from their cells between a double row of guards, still chained and hooded, down to the arsenal wharf, where a vessel waited with a head of steam. Once they were aboard and led below with shackles clanking, the ship got underway, moving swiftly down the Potomac with the tide. At noon the next day the steamer anchored off Fortress Monroe, Arnold's old stamping ground, where General George B. McClellan had launched his ill-starred peninsula campaign three years before.

There their ankle chains were temporarily removed. They clambered aboard a tugboat that chugged out to where the gray hull of the *U. S. S. Florida,* a Union gunboat, lay at anchor and then climbed up the side of the vessel to the main deck, where the shackles were restored.

Dr. Mudd kept no log of the journey he began that day. But Samuel Arnold, festering with bitterness, recalled their descent into the hold:

> . . . it requiring in our shackled condition the greatest care, owing to the limited space 8 inches of chain allowed between our ankles. After leaving the second deck, we were forced to descend upon a ladder whose rungs were distant so far apart that the chains bruised and lacerated the flesh, and even the bone of the ankle.
>
> We remained in this sweltering hole during the night, in an atmosphere pregnant with disagreeable odors arising from various articles of subsistence stored within, and about eight o'clock the next morning we passed through the same ordeal in our ascent to the upper deck, which was attended with more pain than the descent owing to the raw condition of my wounds.[10]

They remained on deck throughout the day, surrounded

by guards under the command of Captain George W. Dutton. The ship was curving in a slow arc toward the south, and even its crew and officers seemed puzzled by their course. At noon Captain Budd of the *Florida* informed the prisoners he was sailing under sealed orders and would announce their destination on the following day. He directed them to bring their bedding up on deck; plainly it would be warm where they were going.

Arriving off Hilton Head, South Carolina, that evening, the captain brought some "guests" aboard, which cued an evening of carousal. While the prisoners were herded to a roped-off section in the bow, to eat their first full meal of hardtack and salt pork, sounds of music and dancing and drunken laughter came from the afterdeck until the early hours of the morning. One could surmise that Budd had opened his sealed orders, and the crew were either rejoicing or seeking consolation.

At noon on the twentieth, still steaming southward, Captain Budd announced their destination: the Dry Tortugas in the Gulf of Mexico—which meant Fort Jefferson, the "Devil's Island" of America. It was a name that brought the same shuddering sense of horror as did Libby Jail or Andersonville, which were as much extermination camps as prisons.

Dr. Mudd knew of Fort Jefferson only through the columns of the press. Few people survived long there, and those who did survived only in a form of living death. Perhaps Captain Dutton of the guards was only curious or perhaps he was needling his prisoner for a reaction when he asked the doctor if he knew where the island was. And what it was.

"It is the end of all hope for me," Mudd told him. "I cannot live in such a place."

When Thomas Ewing heard the news of the prisoners' removal to Fort Jefferson, he knew he had been cheated. It seemed probable that Stanton had anticipated his designs for a new trial in the civil courts, and had persuaded Johnson to place the prisoners not in a civil penitentiary but in a military jail, where they would still be under military law. No appeal would be possible; the outcasts would be as good as buried in a tomb.

Still Ewing did not abandon hope. "If their destination is as supposed," he wrote to an associate, "they are beyond the reach of law. We will have to await the course of events to bring their relief."

What possible course of events he could have had in mind is hard to figure out.

Frances did not hear of her husband's fate until the end of July. He had written to her when the *Florida* stopped at Charleston, but the letter could hardly have arrived before she learned from the papers that the prisoners were destined for Fort Jefferson. On the same day she received a letter from Mary Rose, the sister of Dr. George Mudd, who was now a mother superior in the Frederick Monastery. Sister Mary quoted her brother George as saying, "The Government in all its endeavors has been unable to prove anything against our own dear friend and relative, Sam."

Sister Mary had been too sick at heart to write earlier, she wrote to Frances, but now she echoed the attitude of that pious family by adding:

> Our poor dear Sam! What a siege of suffering he has gone through for an act of charity. How wonderful and hidden are the ways of God! And it is not for us to question these mysterious ways of His providence. It is our part only to join hands in humble submission, deeming ourselves happy even to be thought worthy to suffer for His Holy Name's Sake.[11]

But Frances was not ready to submit and suffer. She secured affidavits of her husband's innocence from Dr. Blandford, Sylvester and Jeremiah Mudd, and forwarded them to General Ewing with an affidavit of her own, which reviewed in detail her knowledge of Sam's brief relationship with John Wilkes Booth. It had all been presented and discussed before, interminably, but Ewing nonetheless submitted the papers to President Johnson. Johnson reviewed them and stated curtly that Mudd's sentence was subject to no change.

Ewing wrote to Frances on the last day of July to express regrets that his planned efforts for Sam's release had been frustrated "by the removal of your husband beyond the jurisdiction of an established State Court, and [by the fact that] the President will not give to your evidence the weight it deserves." He offered what little consolation and hope he could:

> You should seek comfort, however, in the reflection that the vindictive and energetic effort to take his life failed, and that he will be returned to you before many months in spite of all that can be done by the Administration to keep him imprisoned.
>
> If he is sent to the Tortugas, the place is better for his health than almost any other. The island is dry, and the climate good. Rely on it, wherever he has gone his sanguine temperament will buoy him up, and preserve his health and strength.[12]

Even allowing for Ewing's good intentions, his optimism was of the hollowest variety. There was not the slightest hope that Mudd would be returned to Frances "before many months"; and the Dry Tortugas, far from enjoying a "good" climate, were insect-ridden islands of excessive, enervating heat. Though Ewing had heard reports that his client was in "excellent spirits," Captain Dutton, throughout the voyage, had found him morose, resentful, and despairing. In fact, Dutton, making a point of interviewing the convicts in his charge, began taking notes he thought might interest his superiors when he returned to Washington.

All day Sunday the steamer bucked the Gulf Stream as it passed the string of Florida Keys, whose twisted, tortured-looking pines had given them the name, in Ponce de Leon's time, of *Las Islas de Martires*, the Islands of the Martyrs. At sundown they rounded Key West where the weathered houses loomed bone white beneath the slanting clouds. Sixty-eight miles to the west lay the clustered islands of the Dry Tortugas, which Ponce de Leon had named for the edible turtles his crew had discovered there, adding the "dry" to warn future mariners that no fresh water would be found.

All night and through the morning of July 24 the *Florida* crawled through the tricky channels of a shallow, glassy sea, through the brown sargassum weed and floating driftwood, seeing occasional sharks' fins slicing through the water. In midafternoon they left to starboard the little Marquesas, lost islands in a mangrove wilderness, and an hour later sighted the top of the Loggerhead Lighthouse on the westernmost reef of the Dry Tortugas.

Then, thrusting up from the sea like some diluvial monster, rose Fort Jefferson, its ocher bricks turned blood red in the setting sun. It seemed to float by sorcery on the surface of the water, hexagonal walls soaring more than fifty feet, with no visible land or vegetation to give perspective to its monolithic height.

As the ship drew closer, the other small islands of the archipelago took shape. Loggerhead to the west; then Sand Key, Middle and East keys in the distance. East of the approaching harbor, Bush Key and Long Key, black with the rookeries of sooty terns, pressed close on the twenty-five-acre Garden Key, the central island, on which the prison stood. All were scattered over ten square miles of shoals and reefs and channels that varied in hue according to depth and temperature, from blinding white, to blue, to green, to rust and ocher and vermilion.

The *Florida* fired a salute as she approached the harbor, and a gun from the fort replied. It was a ritual surviving from the war. Fort Jefferson had never been called to fire on the enemy; in fact Confederate marines could have simply walked ashore and taken possession of the ill-manned, ill-gunned stronghold. But on at least one occasion her trigger-happy artillerists had sunk a friendly Union vessel that had failed to salute on passing.

Within minutes, the officer of the day rowed out in a dory to discuss the cargo with Captains Budd and Dutton. The four prisoners were then taken ashore, led over the draw-bridge across the moat, and into the dark labyrinth of casemates, bastions, and interminable high-arched corridors. Passing the first door inside the gate, they were confronted by a crudely painted sign, *All Hope Abandon, Ye Who Enter Here*. History books would later say, mistakenly, that this legend marked the cell of Samuel Mudd; that he had, in fact, inscribed it in his own hand. No matter, it would have applied as well to any cell or any prisoner condemned to living death within the fort.

14

DEVIL'S ISLAND

IN the early nineteenth century the Dry Tortugas, of which Fort Jefferson on Garden Key was the imposing center, had been the lair of the Caribbean pirates who preyed on Dutch, French, and Spanish traffic with the Isthmus and the Mississippi Delta—until David Porter, commanding the U. S. West India squadron, drove them out of the area in 1822. Even then the strategic importance of the islands had been recognized, underscored by the British invasion of Louisiana in the War of 1812. Enemy possession of the islands would menace the growing commerce to and from the Mississippi Valley and would mean their control of all navigation in the Gulf.

With trouble in Cuba, revolt in Latin America, wavering loyalty in Texas, and a threatened war with Mexico, the Army Corps of Engineers began in 1846 the construction of Fort Jefferson as a principal link in the nation's chain of coast defenses. It was a massive undertaking, so ill-considered and ambitious that it would never be completed. Plans for the hexagonal monster that would occupy two-thirds of Garden Key's twenty-five acres called for walls eight feet thick and fifty feet high, a half-mile in perimeter. Three arched tiers would mount 450 guns and provide for a garrison of 1,500 men.

Laborers and artisans were imported from the North, but much of the heavy work was done by slaves from Key West, who were better able to survive the heat and hardship. Almost all material had to be brought by ship from the mainland: lumber from Georgia and Louisiana, granite from New Hampshire, cement from Boston, millions of bricks from

Maine, and, when the supply ran out, from Florida and Alabama. Of the scores of vessels carrying supplies to the construction site, it was amazing that only four were lost in the treacherous waters of the Gulf.

Progress was slow. In that tropical climate it took two men to do the work of one. And oval-shaped Garden Key rose at its highest point only three feet above the sea. With the foundations extending fifty feet below the water line, and little known about submarine construction, tons of mortar were poured into the frames, year after year. Having failed to hit bedrock, the engineers eventually realized they were building on virtual quicksand. Six years after the War with Mexico only the rims of walls on this "Gibraltar of the Gulf" began to show above the island's surface.

On the eve of the Civil War the fort was only half-finished. Though its tiers upon tiers of corridors and casemates and its six protruding bastions were things of beauty and marvels of brick and masonry, the walls were cracking. The fort was not only sinking and shifting on its treacherous foundations, its monolithic weight was pressing the whole island back into the sea.[1]

Still the work continued, accelerated by the outbreak of the war. Eventually 89 of the proposed 450 cannon were mounted at embrasures, on wooden platforms that rotted with the dampness and collapsed on firing. In January, 1861, Major Lewis Arnold with a company of artillery arrived from Boston to pronounce the fort "secure to the United States."

It was a boast that was backed by little more than nerve. When the armed Confederate privateer *Wyandotte* appeared in the harbor and sent a white flag ashore to demand the fort's surrender, the peppery Arnold bellowed at the messenger, "Tell your captain I will blow his ship out of the water if he is not gone in ten minutes!" The schooner discreetly withdrew. Arnold could only wipe the sweat from his brow and thank God that his mounted cannon—which, if fired at all, could not have reached the vessel—probably looked good from a distance.

Throughout the war, though the ordnance remained about the same, the garrison varied in number from 800 to 1,500. Barracks were built for the troops, and in the sixteen-acre yard were special quarters for the officers. Rainwater trapped by basins on the battlements was carried by ducts to a hundred storage cisterns built in the foundations. A hot-shot furnace was constructed in the yard, and a subterranean powder magazine made an excellent dungeon for offending troops and prisoners.

By late 1861 the first contingent of military prisoners arrived, to grow throughout succeeding years as President Lincoln commuted the death sentences of Army deserters to long terms on "the terrible Tortugas." It was as good a use as any for the decrepit stronghold, already virtually obsolete. Before many months had passed, the federal bombardment of Georgia's Fort Pulaski demonstrated that even massive walls of brick could not withstand the penetrating shells of rifled cannon.

The prisoners took over much of the work around the fort, including completion of the seventy-foot-wide moat between the bastion and the seawall. One of these inmates, known only as "Fat Charley," had gained distinction at First Manassas. "It was this way," a prisoner told Samuel Mudd. "When the colonel gave the order to retreat, Fat Charley never stopped till he got clear to Vermont. That was a little too far, y'understand, so they jailed him in the Dry Tortugas."[2]

It was fun-loving Charley who captured and dumped the first man-eating shark into the moat, apparently for entertainment. Troops and prisoners amused themselves by throwing cats into the ditch and watching the grisly consequences. Known as "provost marshal," the shark was permitted to remain as a psychological deterrent to potential escapees. The effect was more psychological than real. Made sluggish by the tepid water, the shark often failed to attack the cats.

By the time Dr. Samuel Mudd arrived with Spangler, Arnold, and O'Laughlin, the moldering fortress held about 600 prisoners charged with a wide range of offenses, from desertion and theft to murder and treason. For the most part they were a hard-core lot whose satisfaction lay in guts survival and in trying to outwit their guards. They moved about the yard in chains, some carrying the iron balls attached to their ankles, wearing heavy gray-flannel overalls, as much for protection against the insects as to conform to prison rules.

Yet their plight was not much worse than that of the garrisoning troops, many of whom were as apt to take flight or rebel against restriction as were the prisoners themselves. There had been at least one serious mutiny among the troops before Sam Mudd arrived. Consequently they were rotated frequently before dissatisfaction built to the exploding point. The present garrison consisted of four companies of the 110th New York Volunteers, under Colonel Charles Hamilton, Post Commander.

Samuel Arnold, the chronic complainer of the group, was surprisingly tolerant of Hamilton's administration, writing that "our treatment was as good as could be expected under the circumstances."

Mudd's quarters, which he shared with his three cellmates, while far from comfortable, were not intolerable. The second-tier casemate was domed with high brick ceilings. Each man had a wooden bench and "a soft plank" for a bed; Ned Spangler, with his skill at carpentry, fashioned the planks into bedsteads raised above the stone floor. There was no light save for three slits, which Mudd called "port holes," seven feet above the floor. These were six inches wide on the inside, spreading to two feet on the outside and, as Dr. Mudd observed, "served better the purpose of ventilation than agreeable breeze." By standing on one of the benches one could look across the moat to the harbor sheltered between twin piers, beyond which the sea stretched for three hundred miles to the invisible coastlines of West Florida and Louisiana.

The four captives were briefed on their arrival by Colonel Hamilton. They would not be required to wear chains but would be under constant supervision. They could not consort with prisoners other than each other. Any breach of discipline would lead to solitary confinement in the dungeon or the guardhouse. They would be allowed to receive mail and packages from outside but these, as well as any letters they themselves wrote, would be opened, inspected and censored. So long as they remained on good behavior they could enjoy the freedom of the island, which meant the eight sandy acres outside the walls as well as the sixteen-acre prison yard.

Even the hard labor to which they had been sentenced did not prove oppressive. Because of his medical training, Dr. Mudd was assigned to the prison hospital as combination steward, nurse, and dispenser of supplies. Samuel Arnold, the most literate of the other three, was made a clerk in the Provost Marshal's office. Ned Spangler was given carpentry assignments, while O'Laughlin switched from sweeping and sanding the bastions to cleaning the bricks that were stacked in the yard for construction yet to be completed. Neither Mudd nor Arnold, because of the nature of their assignments, was obliged to wear ball and chain while working. The clanking bothered their supervisors. O'Laughlin and Spangler had their chains removed at night.

From their initial impressions, it was not the Dry Guillotine that had been pictured in the North—an intolerable Devil's Island whose natural and man-made horrors few survived. The climate was steamy, enervating and oppressive, and one warred incessantly against the bedbugs, vermin, and mosquitoes. Yet Mudd wrote that he could be content there except for the dreadful yearning to be with his family.

Efforts, some doomed to failure, had been made to improve the surroundings of the prison yard. Spanish grass grew between bisecting paths; some butternut trees and date palms had been planted; jasmine and morning glory grew around the officers' barracks. Gulls perched and nested on the lofty crenellations. Giant frigate birds swooped over the island in graceful arcs. The crystal-clear sea was animate with waving coral and marine life. Giant turtles were captured and put in the moat among the sharks, to be butchered and eaten from time to time.

Fresh fish for the prisoners, however, was a rarity. There were few offerings besides the salt pork, salt beef, potatoes, bread, and coffee that made up the standard prison fare. Mudd eschewed the beef and pork, which he believed to be contaminated, and stayed with the potatoes, bread and coffee. Fresh vegetables and fruits could, if one had the money, sometimes be purchased from the supply ships arriving once a week from New Orleans and twice a week from Key West. Wines and liquors were not sold except to officers.

Such was the superficial picture of their prison life, surely not intolerable. But a sensitive man, such as Samuel Mudd,

sank quickly below the surface to a bottom of despair. Letters
from Frances, like his own to her, took from two to three
weeks to arrive and then were so often censored that he
never knew whether what she had meant to say to him, or
what he had meant to say to her, appeared in the versions
that each received. Packages from his brother-in-law, Thomas
Oswald Dyer in New Orleans, were robbed of their contents
if they included such luxuries as fruits or sweets or brandy.
His only company throughout the long tropical evenings were
three men, strangers up to now, with whom he had little
in common. His guards, though not intimidating, kept their
distance.

Above all, with crushing weight, was the sense of a lifetime
in this god-forsaken place, apart from his wife and children.
"My heart almost bleeds sometimes," he wrote to Frances,
"when I think of you and our dear little children, and the
many pleasant hours we used to enjoy together. . . . I can
only hope, through the mercies of God, to live through these
hardships and return to my family." In time this longing
and loneliness would color the whole picture of the island
in his mind.[3]

His cellmate, Samuel Arnold, needed no other influences
than his inner bitterness to come to his conclusions. In his
recollections of Fort Jefferson he wrote:

> Without exception it was the most horrible place the eye
> of man ever rested upon, where day after day the miserable
> existence of man was being dragged out intermixed with
> bodily suffering, want & pinching hunger, without the addi-
> tional acts of torture and inhumanity that soon I became
> a witness of. . . .
> Subsistence issued was horrible in the extreme. Many
> were suffering dreadfully from scurvy and chronic diar-
> roeha. The bread was disgusting to look upon, being a
> mixture of flour, bugs, sticks and dirt. Meat whose taint
> could be traced by its smell from one part of the fort to
> the other, in fact, rotten and to such an extent that dogs
> ran from coming in contact with it. No vegetable diet issued,
> of any description, and the coffee . . . was made into a slop
> by those who had charge of the cook house. . . .[4]

The heat, the damp, the solitude and boredom—yes, they were almost as hard on the garrisoning troops as on the prisoners. But the garrison could be rotated, and few were forced to serve a term of more than six months. Shortly after Mudd's arrival, the 110th Regiment was replaced by four companies of the 161st New York Volunteers, which, according to the prisoners, treated them somewhat better than their previous guardians, "no change however occurring in the nature and kind of food issued, it still being of the meanest and coarsest nature."

He relieved the monotony by writing innumerable letters, often several a day, to Frances, Jeremiah Dyer, Ewing and Stone, his parents at Oak Hill, and his cousin Thomas in New Orleans—one of the Mudds who had migrated west and, in Thomas' case, had become a successful merchant in the Crescent City. He kept careful track of dates, in order to check up on his correspondents and make sure that each of his letters was properly and speedily acknowledged.

Although incoming mail that he received either rotted or vanished in the prison climate and confusion, most of his letters to Frances survived the years of his confinement. One is tempted to quote from them at perhaps more length than they deserve, if only because they constitute the only surviving words, in bulk, that Mudd consigned to paper in his lifetime. Whatever he had written earlier was confiscated when the Union authorities occupied the farm, or was burned when Oak Hill was destroyed by fire.

More than the value of rarity, however, is the fact that the letters reveal the changes in his character through prison years, under the pressure of confinement. Nervous and temperamental by nature, such mercurial ups and downs could be expected. But beneath the surface vibrations ran a deeper undercurrent of emotion, almost steadily downhill, from initial hope and optimism to growing exasperation with prolonged confinement, and finally bitter despair and vilification of his family and friends for failure to effect his release.

For the first several weeks of his confinement he was subject to the worst of mental tortures—he was kept incommunicado from his family, his friends, the outside world. He was not allowed to receive mail or read papers. He fretted with anxiety over Frances' welfare, the health of the children, the condition of the farm. When she seemed to ignore his letters, he suffered spiritual agony. "Frank must be sick—the little children are sick—some may be dead, or some other misfortune has happened . . . and the dear ones at home are unwilling to break the cruel intelligence to me."

Please, please write! he begged her. "I have written to you by every mail that has left this place, and surely some have been received. . . . I have written to Jere, Ewing, Stone, Ma and Papa . . . and not one syllable have I received. I am afraid when the silence is broken, the news will be too great to bear."[5]

In the officers barracks, sixty paces from his cell, the letters from home, from family and friends, piled up. The original orders of the War Department that they be destroyed were not, apparently, fully carried out. It is obvious from his letters to Frances that some of her own got through to him. How many other incoming communications of one sort or another were suppressed, it is impossible to say. The post commanders' were not fond of keeping records.

At Rock Hill Farm, Frances struggled with the problems of survival, trying to keep the establishment intact and running, seeing to the education of the children. Virtually all their savings and much of Henry Lowe Mudd's resources had gone to pay for Sam's defense. The property had been mortgaged, and while she tried to sell land to meet the payments, the market for real estate in southern Maryland was tight. Fields that had flourished with tobacco now lay fallow. Or, worse, had deteriorated into scrubby, weed-clogged wastes for want of labor. Most of the former slaves had left, and Frances was forced to settle for itinerant help when she could get it, and could afford it.

John Best, whose steadiness was like a rock and who became affectionately known as "Uncle John," took over much of the administration of the farm. Sylvester and Henry Lowe Mudd offered sympathy and counsel and sent their servants over to the house to help. Her brother Jeremiah Dyer, though living and working in Baltimore, was of indispensable assistance. Though barely literate and easygoing, he was a man of good sense and estimable conscience. Not only did he visit Frances frequently to check on the farm operation, but he also kept in contact with Tom Ewing and Richard Merrick regarding Sam's welfare and the legal aspects of his case.

At the end of July she received the first letter from her husband, written aboard the *Florida* and posted when the vessel stopped at Charleston. "In it," she wrote, "he asked me not to give up hope; to take care of the little ones and at some future day he would be at home with us. This seemed to give me courage, and I began to work with renewed efforts to try to secure his release."[6]

Throughout the summer she worked toward that goal. In late July she collected affidavits from Sam's friends and relatives, among them Dr. Blandford, George and Sylvester Mudd, and Jeremiah Dyer, testifying to her husband's innocence and loyalty. These she sent to Thomas Ewing to present to President Johnson. Ewing did so, but reported to her that "he [Johnson] read the papers and informed that the sentence would not be changed by him as at present advised. So there is no hope for Doctor's release, except from the courts or from Congress."

She resolved to take things into her own hands and carry the torch to Washington herself. Sam's mother, Sarah Reeves, was ailing, seemingly wasting away from grief and worry for her son. Perhaps her misery would soften stony bureaucratic hearts, and any resource she could summon, she would. She applied to the Assistant Secretary of War, James Hardie, for a chance to plead her case before the highest authority in the land at that time: Secretary Stanton. With Hardie she pulled out all the stops, exaggerating Sarah's illness in a letter she wrote to him:

> Could you have seen me last night, a lone watcher by the dying bed of Doctor's Mother and have known all the agonizing thoughts that passed through this poor weary brain, I think the picture would have moved you to pity. Doctor's mother has fallen under the terrible ordeal which

she has gone through, owing to the persecution of her innocent son. In a few short hours she will be insensible to the misery of this world. But alas poor me, left to suffer on, how long, O Lord, how long!

Actually Sarah, only in her middle fifties, would survive another two years, though she never fully regained her health. But Hardie was prompted to arrange an immediate meeting between Frances and War Secretary Stanton; the interview took place on August 2. It took some courage to confront the Iron Man of the War Department, whose reputation for intransigence, spleen, and hatred for the South was legendary. Ulysses Grant had said of Stanton, "It seemed to be more pleasurable to him to disappoint than to gratify." Yet, save possibly for Andrew Johnson, he was the key link in the chain that bound her husband.

Frances did not overplay her hand by making demands that might be held unreasonable. All she wanted, she told the Secretary, was permission to write to her husband, to send him some of his personal belongings, clothes and such, and a little money with which to buy whatever small comforts could be purchased at the prison.

Over his large, punctilious nose the Secretary stared at her for several minutes. Then he said curtly: "As long as Dr. Mudd is in prison the government will furnish him with what it thinks necessary for him to have, and he can have no communication whatsoever with the outside world."

Frances rose, turned her back on him, and walked out without a word.

Not many people turned their backs on Stanton, or failed to acknowledge their dismissal when the Secretary bade them good day. The silent rebuke from Frances may have given Stanton second thoughts. Some weeks later he sent word by an assistant that the prisoner, Dr. Mudd, would be allowed to receive letters from her if they were mailed unsealed to the Adjutant General of the Army in Washington. But no more. "The government provides suitable clothing and all necessary subsistence in such cases, and neither clothing nor money will be allowed to be furnished him."

Mudd's lawyers, Ewing and Stone, had adopted a wait-

and-see stance. There was not much else they could do. Public
sentiment against the alleged conspirators was still strong;
but criticism was gathering over the execution of Mary Surratt
and the arbitrary conduct of the trial. Frances, however,
worked unflaggingly against dark odds for Sam's release.
In late August, through the offices of Thomas Ewing and
possibly Reverdy Johnson, both of whom were friendly with
the President, she journeyed to Washington to call on Andrew
Johnson.

She found the White House filled with children and
wildflowers from the hills of Maryland. Cows grazed on the
grassy lawn beneath the elms. There was the scent of baking
and hot doughnuts from the downstairs kitchen. And an
atmosphere of hominess about the place. A long way from
the Lincoln era of the years before.

If she had any qualms about the meeting, they were dis-
pelled by the straightforward, easy-mannered Tennessean. He
was no longer the ogre whom even the Maryland slaves had
hanged in effigy a year ago. In five short months as President
he had erased the stains of the drunken speech at the
inauguration, of the bungling tactlessness of early days in
office. He had in fact risen to the stature of that office and
was already putting into effect Lincoln's program for the
South—provisional governments for the states below the
Mason-Dixon line, representation in Congress, almost full
restoration of their rights. The keynote of his policy was
one of the loveliest words in the English language: amnesty.

But faced with Frances' plea for leniency and even freedom
for her husband, he was helpless. He had signed the death
warrant for Mary Surratt and was already beginning to regret
it. But this was no time to concede that errors had been
made. He explained to Frances that he was not himself a
lawyer; he had signed her husband's conviction papers only
on the advice of his War Department and Attorney General
James Speed. He could not refute their recommendations
now. But he told her that if Judge Advocate Holt agreed
to sign the papers for the prisoner's release, he, the President,
would endorse them.

With this beacon of hope she raced to Judge Holt's office
in the nearby War Department. Here she collided with a

rock. The steely judge advocate, who once had remarked, "There have not been enough Southern women hanged in this war," had no more sympathy for Samuel Mudd than he had had for Mary Surratt. His face clouded at Frances' request that her husband's conviction be reviewed.

"I am sorry, Mrs. Mudd," he said, "but I can do nothing for you."

Back home, she wrote to General Ewing of her two encounters, with the President and Joseph Holt. Ewing replied that she had evidently made a favorable impression on the latter, "who has twice spoken of you highly," but so long as the judge advocate controlled the President's decision in this matter, there was nothing more that she could do. He himself would seize every opportunity to secure her husband's release by legal means. "Do not worry too much. You and the Doctor are still young, and will yet live a long and happy life together."[8]

Telling her not to worry was like King Canute directing the tides to stop pressing at the shore. And any good impression she had made on Holt provided little comfort. She knew a dead end when she saw it. Furthermore, Judge Holt was about to receive a minor bombshell that would further dampen her hopes. At the request of the Judge Advocate General, Captain Dutton, who had escorted the prisoners to the Dry Tortugas on the *Florida*, appeared at Holt's office to report on this assignment.

In a written statement Dutton recorded the conversation he had had with Dr. Mudd on July 22, after the prisoners had heard their destination was the Dry Tortugas:

> . . . he confessed to me that he knew Booth when he came to his house with Herold, on the morning after the assassination of the President; that he had known Booth for some time, but was afraid to tell of his having been at his house on the 15th of April, fearing that his own and the lives of his family would be endangered thereby.
>
> He also confessed that he was with Booth at the National Hotel on the evening referred to by Wiechmann in his testimony; that he came to Washington on that occasion to meet Booth, by appointment . . . and they had a conversation of a private nature.

I will here add . . . that this confession was voluntary,
and made without solicitation, threat or promise, and was
made after the destination of the prisoners was com-
municated to them. . . .[9]

Of this statement, released by Stanton to the public press,
there was little Frances had to say. Little that she could say.
And Sam, who would not hear of his "confession" for some
weeks, would be equally impotent.

Frances had saved all the letters Sam had sent from prison,
almost one a day. Though seemingly written for her eyes
alone, with possibly some side thoughts for the censors and
the public, the letters uniformly protested his innocence and
the unfairness of his trial—often in strong, persuasive words.
She made a packet of selected letters and sent them to Dr.
Brandford, her brother-in-law in Brandywine. Did Joe think
they might be circulated to the newspapers, to counteract
the unfavorable publicity that came from men like Dutton
and from Stanton's office?

Blandford took the matter up with Richard Merrick,
assistant attorney for the defense. Merrick responded directly
to Frances that he had the letters, "and will take care of
them, subject to your order," but expressing the opinion
that "it would be inexpedient to publish anything at this time."
To Blandford, Merrick was a little more explicit: "Let this
cruel and unfortunate affair rest quiet for the present. It
will wake with greater vigor when the time comes to arouse
it."

She had got nowhere with the affidavits. She had failed
to move either the President or Judge Holt. Her interview
with Stanton had proved futile. Sam's letters had been
rejected. What was left? As she looked ahead to a bleak and
hopeless future, she could only see, as did the poet, "Down
the long corridor of years, the quiet closing, one by one,
of doors."

A hundred miles up the Mississippi, four hundred miles
northwest of the Tortugas, New Orleans lay prostrate from
the nearly mortal wounds of war. The cotton was gone. So
was the molasses and tobacco. The ships had left or been
destroyed. Even the piers along the levees had been burned.

Under General Benjamin ("Beast") Butler's years of Union occupation, the Crescent City had seethed with cabalistic hatred, nursed its resentment, plotted its revenge.

And who could say for sure that there still were not Southern agents hiding in the Vieux Carré, conspirators around the tables in the Absinthe House, Confederate spies and European sympathizers in the waterfront cafés? Not Lafayette Baker, who arrived at the Crescent City late that summer on his way west. He looked and listened, lurked and prowled, and took notes. Perhaps he saw in New Orleans a diminutive Port Tobacco seething with traitors and Confederate collaborators.

Arriving at Louisville, Kentucky, on August 16 he sent a dispatch to Thomas T. Eckert, Acting Assistant Secretary of War, dated nine A.M. the following morning:

> I have important papers. I think the commanding officer at the Dry Tortugas should be put on his guard against an attempt to rescue the State prisoners in his charge.
> A company is organizing in New Orleans for that purpose. I have all the facts from a reliable source.[10]

The letter started on its way, directed by Eckert in Washington to General Phil Sheridan, hero of the campaign in the Shenandoah Valley and now commanding the Department of the Gulf in New Orleans; thence to Key West, and from Key West to the Dry Tortugas. Despite its seeming urgency it would not reach Fort Jefferson for more than three weeks. But it set in motion a chain of events that directly sealed the fate of Samuel Mudd.

Whether or not the doctor had heard of Captain Dutton's deposition regarding his alleged confession on the *Florida*, he drafted, on August 28, a sworn affidavit contradicting "erroneous statements" attributed to him by the press. On several points he "positively and emphatically declared to be notoriously false" the following:

> 1st. That I confessed to having known Booth while in my house; was afraid to give information of the fact, fearing endanger to my life, or made use of any language in that connection . . .

2nd. That I was satisfied and willingly acquiesced in the wisdom and decision of the Military Commission who tried me, is again notoriously erroneous and false. On the contrary I charged it [the Commission] with irregularity, injustice, usurpation, and illegality . . .[11]

Thirdly, although he confessed to having met John Wilkes Booth in Washington on December 23, he branded that encounter purely "casual or accidental." But it cannot be so easily dismissed. He had, before his conviction, denied ever having seen Booth between their first meeting at St. Mary's Church in November 1864 and the night of April 15, 1865, when he set the actor's broken leg. Now he admitted that there had been such a meeting and disagreed on only a few points with Louis Wiechmann's testimony at the trial.

"I was a mere looker on," he said. "I had no secret conversation with Booth, nor with Booth and Surratt together, as testified by Wiechmann."

Of the many puzzling facets in the case of Dr. Mudd, this is the most baffling. Why did he not concede this meeting earlier, to the questioning detectives or at least to his defense attorneys? Considering his own bitter feelings about the trial, and his charges of truth suppressed and evidence withheld, why did he himself withhold such a crucial bit of evidence —unless it was from a sense of guilt, warranted or not?

From Ewing's summation for the defense there is every indication that the lawyer had not been informed of the encounter. He was a man of known integrity, and it seems unlikely that he would have deliberately denied a truth. Yet he rejected Wiechmann's testimony on the grounds that the witness gave a false date, "by means of which his evidence against Mudd is utterly overthrown." And Ewing tried to clinch the issue, as noted earlier, by pointing out that only two men could substantiate Wiechmann's testimony, John Surratt and John Wilkes Booth. One was dead and the other had disappeared.

Historians and students of Dr. Mudd's trial have offered no explanation for this irregularity (it is hard to find a better word). Dr. Richard Mudd, recounting his grandfather's movements in those critical months, stresses simply that this—the December 23 meeting—was the *only* time that Dr. Mudd encountered John Wilkes Booth in Washington. John Surratt, when he reappeared from exile, only further obscured the issue—first confessing that he had met Dr. Mudd with Booth in Washington, then later insisting that he had met the actor through a letter of introduction given him by someone else.

Precisely what happened to Mudd's affidavit of August 28 is unclear. Frances writes only that "he was not permitted by the authorities to have it published. He sent it to me in a letter about the 1st of October, 1865."

He continued to bombard Frances, Ewing, Stone, and Jeremiah Dyer with lengthy letters, begging for newspaper clippings or any news concerning the public and legal attitude toward his imprisonment and rebuking them for their failures to reply in kind. To Frances, he wrote:

> I am well in body. I am often cast down by depressing thoughts about you and all near and dear to me. I sometimes in my dreary walks look homeward, and feel an involuntary gloom and despondency to come over me. The thought often arises, or the question is asked within myself, "Shall I ever see home again, or those fond ones left behind?" God alone knows and can answer.[12]

He knew nothing, of course, about the anxieties aroused by the alleged conspiracy to rescue him and the other state prisoners that Baker had unearthed in New Orleans. But through his work in the dispensary and his natural concern for health, he became aware of another constant threat that hung over the fort like a suspended dagger. The Dry Tortugas were sufficiently isolated to escape the plagues that from time to time struck New Orleans and Key West. Yet ships arrived from these cities regularly. If one should bring the seeds of infection to Garden Key, the closely populated stone enclosure would become a breeding ground for epidemic.

There was an outbreak in September of what was termed "bone fever," actually yellow fever—a disease Dr. Mudd had briefly encountered at the Baltimore Infirmary in student days. At one point, three-fourths of the guards and prisoners were afflicted by it. "It lasts generally but two to three days," the doctor wrote to Frances. "During the time, the patient imagines every bone will break from the enormous pain he suffers in his limbs. None has died with it."

Yet they died from other causes, which the doctor diagnosed as malnutrition, acute dysentery and chronic diarrhea. He noted bitterly that the four deaths from these sources, throughout August and September, occurred among prisoners only—indicating "something wrong, something unfair" in the distinctions made between the prisoners and guards.

At about that time, too, a grisly episode occurred. A spectral ship hove to outside the harbor and a lone boatswain rowed toward the pier, to shout through a megaphone that all hands aboard were "sick with fever of some description." Several had died, and there was none who was well enough to nurse the sick. They needed food, water, and medical attention. A plague ship! None, not even Dr. Mudd, volunteered to row back to the ship with help. Let her be gone, the quicker the better. At night, the stricken crew were able to get enough sails aloft to bear the vessel back into the Gulf, to God alone knew what fate or destination.

In Washington, War Secretary Edwin Stanton had received Baker's warning of the rescue plot. He immediately wired Major General E. R. S. Canby in Florida:

> THIS DEPARTMENT IS INFORMED THAT AN OPERATION IS ON FOOT IN NEW ORLEANS TO GO TO THE DRY TORTUGAS AND BY SURPRISE OR STRATEGEM SEIZE THAT PLACE AND RELEASE THE PRISONERS THERE. IMMEDIATELY ON RECEIVING THIS TELEGRAM PLEASE SEND A SPECIAL MESSENGER TO NOTIFY THE COMMANDER AT KEY WEST AND TORTUGAS TO TAKE STRICT MEASURES TO GUARD AGAINST STRATAGEM OR SURPRISE AND SECURE THE SAFETY OF THEIR COMMANDS.[13]

Later, Assistant Adjutant General E. D. Townsend sent more specific orders to Colonel Hamilton at Garden Key: "The Secretary of War directs that besides taking effectual measures against any attempt to rescue prisoners, you will place the four State Prisoners—Arnold, Mudd, Spangler and O'Laughlin under such restraint and with such limits inside Fort Jefferson as shall make abortive any attempt at escape or rescue."[14]

Despite these red herrings, neither Mudd nor any of the other three state prisoners was aware of any increase in security. Nor were they subjected to any additional restraints. Possibly Hamilton felt that the fort was already adequately guarded. He ordered the gun crews strengthened and posted a few additional sentinels at the two piers outside the fort, at the portcullis, at the door to the prisoners' cell, and ordered, "Muskets will be kept loaded day and night."

Unaware of these precautions or of any conspiracy directed toward his freedom, Mudd nevertheless kept track of every ship arriving at the port. Each aroused hope of a message announcing the commutation of his sentence. Colonel Hamilton would deliver it, congratulate the doctor and thank him for his patience. He would shed his prison garb, don the civilian clothes still stored beneath his bedstead, stroll out the gates and across the drawbridge and sail away to Frances. It was a game he played and replayed every time a smokestack sprouted on the horizon; and each time, the game ended, as he knew it must, in disappointment.

The longing to be with Frances and the children, the desperate need for resurrection from his tomb, became at times almost unbearable. But he held himself in check as several score prisoners left the island, their sentences completed or commuted. He had been there only six weeks but it had seemed like an eternity when, on September 5, he wrote to Frances:

> I have had several opportunities to make my escape, but knowing, or believing, it would show guilt, I have resolved to remain peaceable and quiet, and allow the Government the full exercise of its power, justice, and clemency. Should I take French leave, it would amount to expatriation, which I don't feel disposed to do at present.[15]

In place of the customary "Your devoted husband," he signed the letter "Good-by, my dearest Frank, and all."

If the words "at present" caused Frances any apprehension, or the finality of his "Good-by" seemed a little strange, it must have seemed stranger still, as the days went by, to have no further word from Sam. The letter of September 5 was followed by six weeks of silence; and silence, in a man of volatile nature, can be ominous.

15

BREAK FOR FREEDOM

FORT Jefferson was a vault of gothic mysteries. Men disappeared and no one knew precisely how or why. Fire glowed at midnight in the hot-shot furnace, giving rise to rumors that bodies were being cremated to conceal the cause of death. The corpses of drowned men washed ashore, impossible to identify, and were buried in the potter's field on adjacent Bird Key. Once a week a garland of Cuban orchids was placed on one of the markers, no one knew by whom or how it got there.

High noon created dancing mirages across the Gulf, castles and armies of cavalry and swaying forests of tall trees. Thick morning fogs peopled the enclosure with pale wraiths that looked like ghosts. In one such heavy morning mist Mudd climbed on the bench to see if the sun had filtered through the haze and saw instead a curious charade that prompted him to summon the other prisoners. They climbed up and pressed around him, trying to peer together through the slitlike port.

Almost directly beneath their eyes, between the fort's foundations and the seawall, a prisoner was making his escape. He was doing so by walking across the bottom of the moat, thirty feet beneath the surface, but was moving with no great haste. First, one lurch forward, then a pause, and one step back, as if uncertain of direction in that underwater twilight.

Watching in startled fascination, they realized that the man's feet were entangled in the Gulf weeds growing from the bottom of the moat. He must have been trapped and suspended there throughout the night. As the sun burned away the haze, the guards discovered the body and tried to snare it with lassos. This failing, they waited for the shark to take the bait. When the snub-nosed "provost marshal" only nudged the body curiously and then turned away, the exasperated soldiers pumped a round of bullets into the corpse to draw blood. That did it. The shark, attracted by the scent of blood, swam back and chewed to pieces the offending object.[1]

Another of many attempted escapes had failed. But if one kept score, an extraordinary number had succeeded. The doctor's own tally, as given by letter to Frances, seemed to vary with his mood. He first reported that thirty had escaped in the short time he had been there, and then raised the count to forty.

Not all of the escapees were convicts. The outlying key was also an escape hatch for soldiers who rebelled against their duties at the post. One regimental burial party, carrying a corpse by boat to Bird Key, dutifully dug the grave and dutifully filled it, then took the boat and started rowing to Cape Sable. A sloop from the fort set sail in pursuit; the wind dropped and the craft became becalmed; the escapees were last seen rowing off the rim of the horizon. Thereafter musket-bearing troops accompanied the burial parties to the cemetery.

On the surface the fort appeared escape-proof, with the double gates of the portcullis locked at night, the prison surrounded by a moat, sentinels posted at strategic points, and the whole surrounded by shark-infested seas. Yet guards could be bribed, the gates could be left a fraction open or prisoners could be lowered through the gun embrasures. The moat could be crossed under cover of darkness with no great danger from the lazy shark.

While the Number Two Wharf to the right of the drawbridge was reserved for transports and supply ships, Number One Wharf, fifty feet distant, berthed the garrison trawlers *Nimble* and *Rarity* and a number of other fishing boats and dories. Though rudders and oars were locked in the guardhouse after sundown, one could steal a boat and maneuver to one of the nearer keys, where some sort of steering gear and paddles could be improvised; then row to Key West or to Havana ninety miles beyond.

There was always the chance of dying of thirst or exposure on the way, or of being capsized or swamped by sudden squalls, or driven off course by vicious winds. Still, many made it.

An alternative was to swim to one of the adjoining islands, build a makeshift raft of driftwood or whatever might be found there, then hope for winds or current that might carry the raft to the Florida Keys, Cape Sable, or the Louisiana coast. The odds were uncertain, but there was always the chance of being picked up as a shipwrecked mariner by a passing French or Spanish freighter—which might mean gratuitous passage to the Bahamas or the Leeward Islands or even Europe, where without money or papers one was on one's own.

Johnny Adare, serving six years at hard labor for robbery, was considered "a very hard case" at Fort Jefferson. Dr. Mudd would get to know him well in time; but at first Adare was only a dubious prison hero with a reputation for slipperiness. Shortly before Mudd's arrival, Adare and a black prisoner had paddled on planks across three miles of water to Loggerhead Key. There they had stolen the lighthouse boat and rowed themselves to Cuba.

In Havana, Adare's self-centered avarice caught up with him. Anxious to reach Europe, he sought to raise the price of passage by selling his black companion into slavery. The black, sensing the plot, appealed to the Spanish authorities. The Spaniards, with a rare feeling for justice, allowed him to go free, but they shipped Adare back to Fort Jefferson, where he was promptly put in irons. Despite the thirty-pound ball and chain on his ankle, Adare boasted to Dr. Mudd that he would try again. Before too long, he did.[2]

What effect these breaks for freedom had on Samuel Mudd is impossible to say. They must have dangled a tantalizing bait before his eyes. In his one September letter to Frances, in the first week of that month, he wrote plaintively of the hundred or more prisoners who had served their terms or had had their sentences commuted and were going home.

Brooding over his trial and the newspapers' comments on its outcome, which Frances had sent to him at his request, he became increasingly outraged at the injustice of his sentence:

> I have lost all confidence in the veracity and honesty of the Northern people, and if I could honorably leave the country for a foreign land, I believe our condition would be bettered. There was never before a more persistent effort to blast one's character and fortune than was resorted to in my case. What could not be effected by fair means, was done by foul. I saw no love and no patriotism. Had these virtues existed, I should have had a reward . . . instead of the treatment received.[3]

During the last week of September there occurred a number of incidents, small and large, and all unfortunate for him. He had gotten on well with the officers of the garrison; his conscientious service at the hospital was noted; if not the hail-fellow-well-met, he was nonetheless appreciated. On Monday, the eighteenth, Captain William R. Prentice of the 161st Regiment left in his cell a copy of *Les Miserables*, an appropriate title at any rate, with a note saying that the New York Volunteers would shortly be replaced at the fort and that the book was a good-bye present and a token of his friendship.

Mudd was deeply touched. He wrote Prentice a note expressing his gratitude, regretting that his "present poverty" prevented his responding with an equally suitable gift; and he enclosed, as a token of his appreciation, "a small medal usually worn by members of the Catholic Church in honor of the Blessed Virgin." More to the point, he expressed deep sorrow at the regiment's departure; he had been treated with kindness and consideration by the Volunteers and suspected that any change could only be for the worse.

Five days later that change for the worse arrived. The transport *Thomas A. Scott* pulled up at Wharf Number Two and across the moat filed troops of the 80th and 82nd U.S. Colored Infantry to replace the New York Volunteers.

Black men! Mudd, who had been a slaveholder most of

his life and accustomed to humility and servitude from blacks, would now be submitted to their patronage and domination. It was the final indignity, impossible to accept and fraught, he believed, with danger. He was warned, perhaps jocularly, by the departing New Yorkers, that the blacks would not hesitate to take revenge on a Southern white man. And Samuel Arnold wrote of Mudd that "he was fearful his life would be sacrificed under their rule."

Arnold was no doubt exaggerating, as he generally did. But he was probably right in saying that under the black troops Mudd found his imprisonment "almost insupportable." He had all the ingrained racial prejudices of his class and background, and complained to Frances:

> . . . it is bad enough to be a prisoner in the hands of white men, your equals under the Constitution, but to be lorded over by a set of ignorant, prejudiced and irresponsible beings of the unbleached humanity, was more than I could submit to. . . .[4]

When a vessel arrived with troops and provisions, both garrison and prisoners dropped their normal duties to help unload the cargo. The *Scott* stood at the wharf for three days while the ship's crew and the prison population worked together at the task. In that interval Dr. Mudd became acquainted with an eighteen-year-old crewman, Henry Kelly. Precisely what bargain they arrived at is unknown. It seems quite possible that Mudd had enough cash from funds brought with him to offer the youngster a bribe for his assistance. It was later reported that some of the departing white troops, who had themselves experienced the misery of being cooped up on the island, also helped. In fact, Mudd himself wrote, "I was as much induced by them to make the attempt to take French leave as my own inclination and judgment dictated."

Around noon of Monday, September 25, as the steamer was coaling and the 161st Volunteers were preparing to depart, he went to his cell and got out the carpetbag containing the clothes he had worn on his arrival. Shedding the gray prison garb, he put on the breeches and coat of a casual civilian traveling gentleman; walked under the portcullis, across the drawbridge bustling with troops and stevedores and up the gangplank of the *Scott*.

Kelly met him as arranged and hustled him below to an aperture formed by the ribs of the hull and the loosely spaced planks of the lower deck. There he lay, anxious and sweating in the heavy clothing, waiting to hear the clank of the engines that would mark the ship's departure, hearing instead a rush of heavy-soled boots on the deck above him.

His absence from the cell had been almost instantly discovered. A coalman on the *Scott* named James Healey had seen a stranger come aboard and go below with one of the crew. Troops with fixed bayonets swarmed over the ship like a horde of locusts. Skilled in the art of detection, they thrust their bayonets at short and frequent intervals between the planks until a cry of pain gave Mudd away.

They hauled out the doctor, bleeding from a superficial flesh wound, and led him, unprotesting, to the guardhouse. There he was grilled by Major George Wentworth, the new commander of the post. Who was the crewman who had secreted him aboard the *Scott*? "Under the penalty of being shot," Mudd reported, he was forced to identify the man as Kelly.

He and Kelly were forthwith put in irons, and thrown into a small cell in the dungeon. Wentworth issued an order to the provost marshal of the prison, H. A. Harris:

> Captain: By direction of the Major Commanding, you will see that Dr. Sam'l A. Mudd is placed at "hard labor." Let him be detailed in the Engineer Dept. to wheel sand. And hereafter, when any boat arrives, he will be put in the dungeon and kept there until it departs, and in future no favors of any kind will be shown him.[5]

Mudd's humiliation and bitterness at this defeat and at his punishment can only be imagined. He was overcome not so much by remorse as by the knowledge of failure and the demonstrated hopelessness of his position. He had hit the bottom of the pit, and no light reached him from above.

A charitable historian believed that Mudd had tried to

escape in order to put himself in the hands of a civilian court, for a new trial under fairer laws. Mudd himself cites the presence of the black troops as the cause of his attempt—"the insecurity of life, the humiliation of being guarded by an ignorant, irresponsible & prejudiced Negro Soldiery. . . . Could we have had the White Regiment, the 161st. N.Y.V. to guard the place no thought of leaving should have been harbored for a moment."[6]

To Major Wentworth he gave a different reason. In an apologetic letter of, for him, unusual humility he acknowledged that he had "acted contrary to my own judgment & honor . . . more from the impulse of the moment & with the hope of speedily seeing my disconsolate wife & four little infants." He continued:

> Before I was detected I had made up my mind to return if I could do so without being observed by the guards. I am truly ashamed of my conduct & if I am restored again to the freedom of the Fort & former position, no cause shall arise to create your displeasure, & I shall always counsel subordination to the ruling authorities.[7]

Wentworth was not moved by his appeal. The doctor was shackled when in his cell and wore chains at labor in the yard. He had, of course, forfeited his sinecure in the prison hospital and was put to work, not wheeling sand as Wentworth originally prescribed but cleaning bricks. Though a guard was assigned to keep him busy, the task seemed more humiliating than exacting. "I worked hard all day," he wrote to Jeremiah Dyer, "and came very near finishing one brick."

Although he blamed Henry Kelly, his dungeon mate, for failing him in the planned escape, Kelly charitably "excused" the doctor for incriminating him in the attempt. In fact, the young seaman seemed to regard his situation as something of a challenge. He assured Mudd that Wentworth was a fool, that there was no prison strong enough to hold him. He was already planning his own break for freedom.

The alleged conspiracy to liberate the four state prisoners —of which Lafayette Baker had been informed by "a reliable source" in New Orleans—remained a mystery. There was a brief fever of excitement when a sail was sighted on the horizon and a schooner drifted slowly toward the fort. At sundown the vessel tacked and disappeared, but that night extra sentinels were posted on the wharves and the gun crews maintained battle stations. When the schooner reappeared the following morning, tacking back and forth outside the harbor, Major Wentworth sent a pilot out by boat to identify the ship and her intentions.

The pilot returned with the news that the schooner was from Portland, Maine, had been delivering ice to Panama, and was returning under ballast. Crossing the Gulf, every man on board had been afflicted with "Panama fever" and was either sick or dead; the captain had been barely able to keep the vessel on course, let alone run up a signal of distress. Wentworth sent a rescue party to board the ship, which they found was slowly sinking with nine feet of water in the hold. They pumped out the hold, brought the dead ashore for burial, and sent the schooner on its way.

A not unusual incident in the maritime history of the keys, but every insignificant event was exaggerated by suspicion and anxiety. By now the garrison, the officers, the prisoners themselves, were jittery. There was a sense of something brewing. From army district headquarters in Tallahassee, via Key West, Wentworth received a dispatch from Brigadier General Newton in command of the department:

> Sir: Official information has been received at these Head-quarters from Washington, that a plot exists to release the prisoners at Fort Jefferson. You will take the proper precautions to prevent any uprising of the prisoners and in case you find this information to be correct, take measures to ferret out the leaders and place them in irons.[8]

The "official information" would never be revealed; but whatever it was, it shifted the scene of the conspiracy from New Orleans to Fort Jefferson itself. The message triggered a regime of persecution that even Major Wentworth found distasteful. Arnold, Spangler, and O'Laughlin were thrown into irons and temporarily removed, along with Dr. Mudd, to a single cramped cell in the dungeon. The few members of the 161st New York Volunteers who had not left with their contingent were forthwith transferred, as suspects, to Louisiana.

"What has led to this treatment, we are at a loss to account," the doctor wrote to Frances. He accepted his own severe confinement as punishment for his escape attempt. But why were the three others now submitted to the same chastisement?

Samuel Arnold thought he had the answer. He considered the whole conspiracy affair to be a fabrication by Lafayette Baker or Secretary Stanton. Some years later, in his published memoirs, Arnold charged that Baker and Stanton had concocted the rumor to provide an excuse for throwing the prisoners into chains and submitting them to further tortures. When the alleged New Orleans conspiracy failed to arouse enough alarm, they invented a plot supposedly brewing among the prisoners themselves.

As clerk in the provost marshal's office, Arnold had glimpsed a copy of Newton's dispatch from Key West, ordering Wentworth to "ferret out the leaders" of the threatened uprising. Concluded Arnold, "We were therefore made the leaders so that further persecution could be heaped upon us . . . tortures already inflicted were not enough to satisfy the pent-up hatred of those against us, their defamed, traduced victims of military injustice."

Worse was to come with a visit from the mainland by General H. L. Foster, Commander of the Department of Florida. Foster, too, was pursuing the conspiracy myth. He looked over the disposition of the four state prisoners and found the security inadequate. He ordered Wentworth to provide—or construct, if necessary—a special, maximum-security cell to which Mudd and his cellmates were removed. Kelly remained where he was and was given as a dungeon mate a notorious criminal named Smith.

The other four were kept incommunicado, not allowed to receive mail, not even permitted to leave their cell to engage in prison labor, which, however arduous, would have given them air and exercise and some relief from the monotony.

The cell door was kept bolted, and an armed sentinel paced to and fro outside to guard against anyone trying to approach their quarters.

As Arnold moralized in his memoirs, the "seeds of persecution" sown among the officers and garrison were soon to bear dreadful fruit; and as the doctor wrote to Frances, "God knows what further persecutions they may have in store."

Mudd took the excessive punishment even more personally than did Arnold. He felt that because of his former good name and position, and the controversy attending his conviction, he was being singled out for persecution. There may have been some truth in that. Of the four state prisoners in the fort, he was the most prominent. And like Jefferson Davis, now imprisoned in Fortress Monroe, he had become a symbol and a target—a symbol of the Great Confederate Conspiracy and one of the few surviving targets (now that Booth was dead and his henchmen executed) on which the authorities could vent their wrath.

With some natural self-pity, Dr. Mudd tried to cultivate a modicum of resignation and acceptance. "I have learned to disregard the mocks and jeers of this cold and uncharitable world." He would put his faith for the future, he decided, in the "Grace and Providence of the Almighty," even while suggesting to Jeremiah Dyer that more practical help might come from "the Hon. Reverdy Johnson, Montgomery Blair [of Maryland, former Postmaster General], and many others whose principles and opinions are growing daily more popular."

Actually Reverdy Johnson had never stopped working on the case. He had lost his client, Mary Surratt; now his crusade was launched against the injustice of the trial. He had many partisans for there was a growing feeling that Mary Surratt had been unjustly convicted—or at least convicted on insufficient evidence. It was also felt that the trial of a civilian by a military court had been a breech of justice and that the four alleged conspirators imprisoned in the Dry Tortugas were victims of a cruel distortion of the law.

Division within the country spread to the highest level.

Secretary Stanton was having his troubles with Andrew Johnson, who was feeling his power, as President and was threatening to implement further his predecessor's, Lincoln's, policy of amnesty and leniency toward the South by granting autonomy to the Southern States. Against Johnson were pitted the Radicals, such as Stanton himself, if he admitted it, who wanted to see the South forever subject. To them the conviction of such men as Samuel Mudd was wholly warranted; the military trial had been a right and lawful one.

Most of the Canadian conspirators indicted with Dr. Mudd and his three cellmates were still at large, but Jefferson Davis, captured at Irwinville, Georgia, on May 10, was languishing in Fortress Monroe in Virginia awaiting trial for treason. Though the country was now at peace, the institution of the military trial was maintained, to wreak full vengeance upon Davis and uphold the sentences already passed on Mudd and his prison associates.

Apparently with that goal in mind, Judge Advocate Holt, acting for Stanton, printed, at the taxpayers' expense, the entire text of the long and windy argument of Special Judge Advocate John A. Bingham delivered at the conclusion of the trial of the conspirators on June 30. With it Holt included portions of the opinion of Attorney General Speed on the legality of the trial and recommended that both documents be widely distributed among the public and especially among the legal profession. The implication was that these papers comprised a bible of justice in the United States, surpassing in authority the Constitution.

There was an instant backlash to this action. A typical example: Congressman Charles A. Eldredge of Wisconsin threw the documents back at Holt, asserting that they would not prevent history "from branding military trials of civilians as infamous violations of the Constitution and laws." He continued:

> Do not, I pray you, flatter that you and the Secretary of War can, by the circulation of these documents at your own or the people's expense, convince your countrymen that arrests without warrant, imprisonment without trial, sentences without conviction, trial without indictment

or jury, and the worse than mockery of your victims in military trials, are anything but crimes—gross outrages of people's rights and liberties, and violations of the people's Constitution.[9]

*   *   *

Strong language. But it reflected a tide of indignation, in strange contrast to the earlier cry for vengeance, at the plight of the state prisoners. Dr. Mudd, though unable to see the news, seemed to detect the sound waves. He was aware that public sentiment was changing; that men of authority and stature were speaking out in his behalf. It made him that much more impatient and indignant at this durance vile.

His ankles chafing from the chains, his spirit raging against persecution, he released his choler in letters to Frances, and surprisingly they were not censored. He had not acted dishonorably in attempting to escape. "Could the world know to what a degraded condition the prisoners of this place have been reduced recently, they, instead of censure, would give me credit for making the attempt." Enlarging on this he wrote:

> Why should I be expected to act more honorable [sic] than my persecutors, who sent me here? Have they not, from the beginning to the present, endeavored to degrade and humiliate by previously unknown and unheard of tortures and cruelties even in an uncivilized community, to lower us, the victims of injustice, beneath the dignity of brute creation?[10]

His ire was further aroused when, despite the increased precautions, more prisoners successfully escaped. In fact, life at Fort Jefferson often had a comic-opera quality about it. In the excitement attending Samuel Mudd's concealment aboard the *Scott*, while the vessel swarmed with soldiers on the scent, six other prisoners found hiding places on the ship and sailed away to freedom. Subsequently two more convicts disappeard, method and destination undetected; and in early October three others snatched a boat from under the eyes of the guard, at high noon, and were nine miles offshore by the time the theft was discovered. It had seemed useless by then, or too much effort, to pursue them.

But the most provocative escape was that of Henry Kelly, Mudd's collaborator in his own abortive break for freedom. Kelly had vowed no bars could hold him, and he made good on that boast. He and the renegade Smith, confined with him in the dungeon, contrived one night to break their chains. They pried loose the iron grates across a tiny window, squeezed through, and lowered themselves from the window by means of the loosened chains.

Outside the walls they took their time, preparing to leave the place in style. There was a sutler's store beside the fort, on a sandy area west of the wharves. They woke the sutler, robbed him of fifty dollars, bound him, and helped themselves to as much clothing as they needed along with a supply of canned fruits, vegetables, and meats. Collecting, too, some fishing equipment, a water jug, and a pair of oars, they sneaked down to Wharf Number One, climbed into a boat, and rowed stealthily away.

Nonetheless, Samuel Mudd had promised Frances he would not again attempt to circumvent authority, or arouse the anger of his captors. Yet in mid-October, only three weeks after his attempted breakaway, he cautioned his wife not to regard such efforts as dishonorable. "I am a prisoner under guard, not under a parole, and under no obligation to remain if I can successfully evade and free myself." And he closed with the sentence, either naïve or ominous: "I will return home by the way of New Orleans and through the South."[11]

Several thousand miles away another would-be escapee—originally one of the three most-wanted fugitives on the War Department's list—was on his way to freedom. John Harrison Surratt, far more closely linked than Mudd with the assassin John Wilkes Booth, was placing an ocean between himself and his pursuers. It would be another year before his saga reached the American press, but John had finished the first chapter of that story.

While Mary Surratt was undergoing the tortures of the trial in the Washington Penitentiary, John was in Montreal, a price of $25,000 on his head. Enroute to Canada, he had stopped briefly at Elmira in New York, where more than 5,000 Confederate prisoners of war were being held. Whether the prisoners were any part of John's plans is debatable, but at Elmira he heard of the assassination and raced north across the border to Montreal.

Had John returned to Washington and given himself up, he might have eased the pressure on his mother. But who could know for sure, without the benefit of hindsight? Instead, using the name of Armstrong, he made his way east from Montreal to the small French village of St. Linoire, where he found refuge with the parish priest, Father Charles Boucher.

After a week with the hospitable priest, Surratt confessed all to his host, admitting that he was wanted by United States authorities for conspiring to abduct the former President. Boucher was sympathetic. He arranged with one of his clerics, Father Benedict Lapierre, to escort the young man up the St. Lawrence to Quebec. There John, his hair dyed and with spectacles as a disguise, boarded the liner *Peruvian* for Liverpool.

Frantic with grief and guilt over the execution of his mother, John all but fell to pieces on the voyage. Finally he was forced to unburden himself to Dr. George McMillan, the ship's physician; he confessed he was a wanted man, and why. He told McMillan he would wait in Liverpool for expected money to arrive for him from Canada and then would be on his way, his ultimate destination undecided.[12]

Dr. McMillan was a man of conscience. He reported the matter to Andrew Wilding, American vice-consul at Liverpool. Wilding cabled State Secretary William Seward, now recovered from his multiple wounds, that John Surratt was receiving sanctuary at the Church of the Holy Cross in Liverpool. What should be done about the fugitive? Two weeks went by. Then in mid-October Seward's secretary cabled the vice-consul:

> . . . UPON A CONSULTATION WITH THE SECRETARY OF WAR AND JUDGE ADVOCATE GENERAL, IT IS THOUGHT ADVISABLE THAT NO ACTION BE TAKEN IN REGARD TO THE ARREST OF THE SUPPOSED JOHN SURRATT AT PRESENT.

What was behind this extraordinary message is a mystery. The word "supposed" suggests a hope that the whole thing might be an error. Were Stanton and Holt afraid that John Surratt, if returned, might tell too much that was better left untold . . . such as the falseness of the charges against Mary Surratt that claimed her a partner in crime with John Wilkes Booth . . . or of the charges that Samuel Mudd was linked with Booth's escape plans? Was the Bureau of Military Justice feeling pangs of conscience about its already convicted or executed prisoners? Plainly, so long as the public did not know of Surratt's whereabouts, they preferred that it remain that way. Better that he should disappear completely.

Unaware of his gratuitous reprieve, Surratt finally received the needed funds from Montreal and made his way, uninhibited, to London. He would lie low in London for a while, and if things got dull he could always head for Paris. The only chains that bound him were those of conscience, the strongest chains that could be forged, stronger by far than those Dr. Mudd endured.

16

THE CHAIN GANG

THE sea gulls were first to herald the news, screeching and rising from the battlements to fly to sea in greeting. Then from the sentinels came the shout:

"Fresh fish!"

The soldiers of the garrison took up the cry, and the shackled convicts in the prison yard joined in. "Fresh fish!" New prisoners arriving.

From the east steamed the *Alice Carter*, a disreputable survivor of the slave trade, still reeking of death and wearing a coat of barnacles like tiny skulls. The vessel was warped to Wharf Number Two, the lines made fast. From the bowels of the hold, filing down the gangway and across the drawbridge to the sally port, came thirteen men in shackles—nine of them "common prisoners," four others political victims, or, as they called themselves, "graduates of the military inquisition."

Among the latter, feeble in step but ramrod straight, was George St. Leger Grenfell, his white hair worn shoulder length, his handsome features graven by fatigue and suffering. With Samuel Mudd he would join the dubious ranks of Garden Key's most celebrated prisoners, one whose legendary reputation would outlast the useful lifetime of the fort itself.

Now fifty-seven years of age, Colonel Grenfell's background was as stormy as the man himself. Born of an aristocratic English family whose members had ranged from poets and novelists to admirals and generals, he came from the Cornish town of Penzance. When he began pretending to push elderly townsfolk over the cliffs at Land's End just to frighten them, he was sent to Holland for his education, then to Paris, where he shifted direction to pursue a life of military buccaneering.

He joined a French cavalry regiment in Algeria, and adopted the Muhammadan religion, principally because it permitted him to have four wives. After several years of fighting Arabs, he shifted to the other side and fought beside Abd-el-Kader in the Emir's war against the French. Thereafter, according to his biographer, Stephen Starr,

> He fought the Riff pirates off the coast of Morocco, and then served with Garibaldi in South America. Finally, tiring of this irregular and barbarous strife, and desirous of settling down to a more Christian and civilized kind of warfare, he returned home . . . and obtained a commission in the English service. He fought in India during the greater part of the Sepoy rebellion, and then in the Crimean War, attaining the rank of lieutenant-colonel.[1]

When the Civil War broke out in the United States, Grenfell was drawn as by a magnet to the lost cause of the Southern cavaliers. In June, 1862, he showed up at the camp of the Confederate raider John Hunt Morgan in Tennessee. He was just right for Morgan's cavalry, among whom deeds of reckless bravery were commonplace. The troops admired him for his courage and his courtly manners but mistrusted him for his fierce uncompromising temper. Distinguished by a scarlet forage cap, he would lead them into battle, then break from the ranks in a single-handed charge upon the Union lines, going berserk and slashing at the enemy with quirt and saber. Though horses were shot from under him, he himself miraculously was not scratched.

Breaking with Morgan on the ridiculous grounds that Morgan, on Christmas day, 1863, married a Tennessee belle and thereby disqualified himself as an independent, dedicated soldier, Grenfell joined—he never formally enlisted—Braxton Bragg's Army of Tennessee, riding with Fighting Joe Wheeler's cavalry. Falling out of favor with Wheeler for allegedly stealing horses, he shifted to Robert E. Lee's Army of Northern Virginia, serving with Jeb Stuart's cavalry. But

Stuart, he found, played the banjo badly and had an atrocious ear for music. He left the corps in January, 1864.

At about that time, his old commander, John Hunt Morgan, escaped from the Ohio Penitentiary, where he had been imprisoned by his Union captors, and Grenfell hurried to his side. But the great days of the Southern cavalry were over; the war had taken to the trenches. In Morgan's command, however, was a young lieutenant named Thomas Hines. Hines persuaded Grenfell to quit the Confederate army and join him in Canada to take part in the burgeoning Northwest Conspiracy.

It was to be Grenfell's job to lead the attack on Camp Douglas on the fringes of Chicago, where thousands of Confederate prisoners would be released and armed and thereafter would aid in the assault on other prison camps and Union strongholds. Posing as an English sportsman, with shotgun and hound as theatrical props, Grenfell registered at Chicago's Richmond House and waited for the moment of attack.

That moment never came. Informed on by Union spies and Confederate turncoats, Grenfell was captured in his hotel room without a struggle and held in jail in Cincinnati until his trial before Henry Burnett's commission. Sentenced to die by hanging, he received a commutation to life imprisonment in the Dry Tortugas; the many appeals in his behalf (he was a British citizen) were fruitless. Summed up Colonel Burnett for the prosecution,

> As to this man Grenfell, I confess I have no sympathy . . . for the foreigner who lands in our country, and who takes part in the struggle against us. . . . I have no sympathy for the man whose sword is unsheathed for hire . . . his sword has gleamed in every sun, and has been employed on the side of almost every nationality. . . . He was a fit instrument to be used in this enterprise.[2]

On September 28, 1865, he was placed aboard the transport *John Rice*, bound for Key West and there, with a handful of his coconspirators, transferred to the *Alice Carter* for the trip to Garden Key.

"I cannot say that the appearance of the Dry Tortugas is very inviting," remarked Grenfell to the guard who led him to his cell. Yet out of regard for his age and ill health—he had wasted grievously in eleven months in Northern jails—he was treated, at first, with marked consideration. The post surgeon excused him from hard labor, he was allowed a daily bath and enjoyed the best food the prison provided. But like Dr. Mudd he could not accept or adjust to prison walls. The first entry in the diary he then began to keep complained:

> Why did they not hang me at once? Far better for me had they done so than to endure all the misfortune which I have since gone through, and still have to go through. It would appear that every change I make is for the worse, and when I think I am at the bottom of the pit the ground suddenly gives way under me and precipitates me still lower.[3]

He was by character his own worst enemy. When "a one-horse lieutenant" in the garrison made a slurring comment on his reputation, he dressed the man down in scathing terms, calling him, among other things, a coward. The guard lived up to the charge by retreating from the colonel's withering stare, though Grenfell wrote, "I expected to be ironed and hung up by the thumbs—a common punishment here for the most trivial offenses."

Retribution would come, but not because of him or his defiance of authority. The third week of October he was summarily transferred to the damp and airless dungeon cell shared by Samuel Mudd and the other three political prisoners. No reason was given for the move, though Arnold assured the Englishman that he, too, was a victim of the trumped-up charge of conspiracy among the inmates.

To Dr. Mudd the arrival of Grenfell must have been a stimulating change. The doctor got on well with his other cellmates, holding a paternal feeling toward Arnold and O'Laughlin and a kindly sympathy for the inarticulate, bewildered Spangler. But in Grenfell he found a refreshing kindred spirit somewhat like his own, self-sufficient and defiant. There was a resilience and durability about the Britisher that boded well for his survival on this devil's island. To Jeremiah Dyer the doctor wrote, regarding Grenfell:

> He is quite an intelligent man, tall, straight, and about sixty-one or two years of age. He speaks fluently several languages, and often adds mirth by his witty sarcasm and jest. He has been badly wounded and is now suffering with dropsy, and is allowed no medical treatment whatever, but loaded down with chains, and fed upon the most loathsome food, which treatment in a short time must bring him to an untimely grave. You will confer an act of kindness and mercy by acquainting the English Minister at Washington, Sir F. A. Bruce, of these facts.[4]

Mudd was wrong, of course, about the colonel's age—he was only fifty-seven—but Grenfell's hair had turned snow white since he had first joined Morgan in 1862. Nor was there any record of his ever having been seriously wounded. But there was a good deal of Baron Münchhausen in the colonel's makeup; he could invent wounds as easily as he invented history. Though his colorful career required no embellishment, he embellished it nevertheless, and the stories he told to his cellmates in the dungeon rivaled the Arabian Nights for length and entertainment.

Were Arnold to complain of savage treatment from the guards, Grenfell countered with tales of Abd-el-Kader, who burned out the eyes of his prisoners with flaming sticks and shoveled hot coals down their throats. And as for the hardships of prison life, what took more out of a man than riding with Morgan the Raider, skirmishing night and day, living on acorns, sleeping beside your horse to keep warm through the long Kentucky winter?

Men would later say of Grenfell that he was "a hero of romance, not of fact." But the facts were there to lend a tinge of authenticity to the romance. Assigned by Morgan to wreck the Louisville & Nashville Railroad, he discovered that the tracks passed through a tunnel in a mountain that was veined with anthracite. He did not block or dynamite the tunnel. He filled a freight train with hay, ignited the cars, and sent it rolling through the tunnel. The flaming hay ignited the veins of coal and the whole mountain turned into a smoldering volcano. It burned for days and weeks, while the Union army waited for supplies.

Exact opposites in many ways, the Maryland doctor-planter and the English gentleman of fortune had in common more than the shared miseries of prison life. They had both been exposed to Judge Advocate Burnett's inexorable skill as prosecutor and could compare notes on the testimony given at their trials—"extorted, perverted, and when necessary, manufactured" in their opinion. And Grenfell's philosophy, *il faut durer*, helped the doctor through his moments of despair. When Mudd grieved for home the Englishman reminded him, "I forget that I have no home"; when there seemed no hope for the future, the colonel recalled the motto of Morgan's rebels, "Never worship the setting sun." One could believe that for St. Leger the sun would never set.

Yet their most severe trials lay ahead. The five state prisoners had been together for only a week when they had visitors from the provost marshal's office. A squad of soldiers entered their cell, accompanied by the prison blacksmith. Chains were soldered to the ankles of each prisoner with solid iron bars between, restricting their movements to a hobble. From now on they would do their full day's stint of labor in the yard, dragging the shackles with them. The irons would be removed only at night when they were in their cell.

Even the docile O'Laughlin, who rarely opened his mouth and seemed to live a zombielike existence of his own, protested vehemently at this treatment. He told Lieutenant William Van Reed of the guard ("a vain and pompous personage," wrote Samuel Arnold) that his sentence did not call for being kept in irons, "it was not in conformity with the findings of the Court," and he, O'Laughlin, had done nothing to deserve such punishment.

Van Reed paced up and down their cell, "displaying his signal of rank," and replied:

"Sir, your sentence has nothing to do with the matter.

We can do with you, and to you, what we please." Whereupon the lieutenant withdrew the guard and the gate clanged shut behind him.[5]

Their common hardship created a strong camaraderie within the group, and Arnold facetiously christened them "the chain gang." Arnold as much as any of them felt this bond of kinship with his partners in misfortune. While the others were given physical labor by day, first cleaning bricks, then sanding and sweeping out the bastions, he was returned to his clerkship duties in the provost marshal's office. The clanking of his chains annoyed the provost marshal. He ordered them removed, and Arnold was given the special dispensation of sleeping in the guardhouse rather than the dungeon.

This seeming stroke of fortune troubled Arnold. He missed his comrades and the damp confinement of the dungeon with its human warmth of friendship. His relief from chains seemed suddenly an emblem of dishonor. Reversing O'Laughlin's procedure, he protested this unmerited favoritism that set him apart from his friends. He demanded the same treatment as the others. And had his way. Outraged, the provost marshal ordered the chains restored and threw Arnold back into the dungeon with his cellmates.

Still in the custody of "the detested and abominable negro regiment," Mudd wrote to Jeremiah Dyer that their situation "could not be much worse."

> Notwithstanding living in irons, we are closely guarded and not suffered to leave the door for the most trivial thing without having a negro guard with musket and bayonet by our side. At night, our chains are taken off, the door locked, and a sentry placed there on guard. This treatment was not brought about by any fear of escape, or the apprehension of any violence on our part, but is no doubt done to degrade and lessen us in the estimation of our fellow-prisoners and citizens, and to keep down the apparent sympathy of strange arrivals, of which every boat brings many.[6]

The doctor evidently did not share Sam Arnold's belief that the fear of a prison conspiracy had led to their misfortune, and it is certain that the post commander, Major Went-worth, did nothing to enlighten them. Little news was leaked to the press regarding the treatment of the prisoners at Gar-den Key. Escapes and attempted escapes were not reported. And the telegraph messages that passed among the War Department, Lafayette Baker, and General Sheridan in New Orleans—which had precipitated their confinement—would come to light only in future histories.

They suffered through a month of this abuse, not knowing for certain the reason. "We were worked by ourselves," recorded Arnold, "denied all intercourse with Everyone upon the desolate island, and forced in this condition to perform the most menial and degrading work upon the Key." And the food! The incredible daily mixture of maggoty bread, stale fish and coffee! "Putrid, unfit to eat," wrote Arnold, adding:

> Coffee was brought to our quarters in a dirty, greasy bucket, always with grease swimming upon its surface, bread, rotten fish and meal all mixed together, the one spoiling the other by contact, and thus we were forced to live for months until starvation nearly stared us in the face.[7]

At Rock Hill Farm, in Baltimore and Washington, Frances and her brother, Jeremiah Dyer, pressed their efforts in behalf of Samuel Mudd. Dyer hammered at Thomas Ewing and Frederick Stone to take some action, and they, more realistically, continued to reply that at this time there was no action they could take. Frances wrote her younger brother, Thomas, in New Orleans, suggesting he try to get through the curtain of secrecy that screened the prisoners' fate and find out if there were anything her husband wanted.

While the Dyer family seemed in some ways more aggres-sive in seeking Samuel Mudd's release, the doctor's youngest sister Fanny, seventh of Henry Lowe Mudd's brood, was so indignant at her brother's treatment that her letters became something of a problem. What the letters said is unknown; but they were surely opened and their contents noted by the censors. Mudd pleaded with Frances to ask Fanny "to be more prudent in her writing. The last letter that arrived was not handed me on account of insulting language." Such language, he believed, however justified, was prejudicial to his interest.

Frances and Jeremiah Dyer found promising allies in unexpected quarters. One was ex-governor Thomas H. Ford of Ohio. Ford's interest in Dr. Mudd can only be explained by the fact that the doctor was, to some extent, a victim of Lafayette Baker's spiteful tactics; and Ford hated Baker. In 1863, during one of Baker's drives to clean up Washington, attorney Ford had gone to court to defend another of Baker's prisoners, Maude Roberts, the notorious madam of a bawdy house. He got Maude off with a modest fine; and when her paramour partner was given a stiffer sentence, Ford appealed directly to President Andrew Johnson for a pardon—and eventually got it.

A champion of the underdog and a crusader for corrective justice, Ford agreed to use his influence and his acquaintance with the President to work for Dr. Mudd's release. Being from Ohio, Ford had Copperhead leanings, but to Jeremiah Dyer, who had expediently switched in loyalty from Confederate to Union, that did not matter. "Although he is a copper-head, he is a big man, and a warm friend."

It was among big men and warm friends that Dyer sought support. "I try to . . . make them talk about his [Dr. Mudd's] case," he wrote to Frances. "You know every opinion has its weight, so you must be hopeful, not too sanguine as to any particular time. My own opinion is, from all I can gather, we may reasonably expect him home between this and the first of January."[8] Dyer and Frances fed these hopes to Dr. Mudd as well-intended tonics for his troubled spirit. But the illness that beset him was Fort Jefferson itself, a malignancy for which there was no cure.

"Every day increases my hate toward the authors of my ruin," Mudd wrote to Jeremiah Dyer on November 11, "and sometimes I can scarcely withhold my angry indignation. The near approach of expected relief I am in hopes will keep me within bounds."

The expected relief had come the day before with the arrival of four companies of the 5th U. S. Artillery to replace the black regiments. Although some of the black units stayed behind to finish out their terms of service on the island, remaining a constant goad to the Maryland-born doctor, the presence of white troops gave him hope for better treatment, since, as he had written to Dyer, no treatment could be worse. In Samuel Arnold's jaundiced view, however, "we found we had traded off the witch for the devil." The officers of the 5th Artillery, in Arnold's eyes, were such that "none worse could be found on the face of the earth." Arnold commented that "cruelty now became the order of the day."

Brigadier General Bennett H. Hill, "a man of kindly instincts," however, became the new commander of the post. As a former provost marshal in the West, Hill had followed Dr. Mudd's trial in the papers and had been even more closely connected with George St. Leger Grenfell. In fact, Hill had been one of the first to learn, through an informer, of the Chicago conspiracy to liberate Camp Douglas and had helped forestall the plot.

Perhaps the fact that Hill was in part responsible for Grenfell's fate and was also familiar with the vicious distortions of a military trial made him surprisingly tolerant and sympathetic toward Grenfell and his fellow prisoners. He was horrified to find them in chains, and applied to the War Department for permission to discard the irons and move the prisoners to better quarters. Stanton wired back a stern refusal, but Hill kept after the permission till he got it—some months later.

Meanwhile, Hill gave the prisoners an allowance of three dollars a month with which to purchase provisions and minor luxuries from the sutler's store outside the fort. It did not go far—a toothbrush alone cost seventy-five cents —but it provided Dr. Mudd with his much-loved plug tobacco. Their diet was improved, and they were allowed fresh fruits and vegetables, when available, items that had been formerly denied them. Most important, Hill lifted the ban on sending and receiving mail, and also allowed them to use the prison library, with its modest collection of newspapers, books, and periodicals.

In strange contrast to Hill's leniency toward the prisoners

was the rigorous discipline he imposed upon the garrison. And for once the five members of "the chain gang" felt a twinge of sympathy toward their guards, some of them new recruits who had been duped into volunteering for this duty on a touted "tropical paradise." As the rookies tried to adjust, stumbled and fumbled in the effort, Sam Arnold recorded the consequences with a sympathetic eye:

> There was not a day passed scarcely but that ten to fifteen would be seen, carrying from morning until night, heavy cannon balls upon their shoulders and often continuing for days as well as nights. To fail to salute an officer was a sure forerunner of punishment, when in fact at times it was impossible to distinguish them, they not being clad in their required uniform.
>
> The manual of arms was drummed into the recruits, with the butt end of the musket and the different evolutions of command were first learned in the region of the back, legs & breast, the drilling officer not being particular on what part of the body the blow was given. Our close proximity to the Guard House afforded every opportunity of becoming conversant with the many different acts of cruelty and tyranny practised. . . .[9]

Dr. Mudd's letters were getting through again to Frances, as were hers to him. He wrote of being placed in shackles and being confined to the dungeon with the other prisoners, of being compelled to sweep out the bastions daily under guard, of the execrable prison diet. He complained of a cold and attacks of rheumatism and of being generally unwell.

Before Bennett Hill assumed command, all packages arriving for the prisoners had been confiscated, but now Thomas Dyer in New Orleans applied to General Sheridan for permission to send Dr. Mudd a trunkful of clothing and canned foods and twenty-five dollars cash. Permission was granted.

When the trunk arrived, the clothing turned out to be the latest in New Orleans fashions, embroidered vests, satin cravats from Paris, English tweeds and Spanish leathers. Mudd found them "inappropriate" to his situation and wrote to Frances that "it would be the height of nonsense to wear them." Dyer had also included two bottles of whiskey concealed in the clothing, which he had hoped would go unnoticed. Mudd never received the whiskey, which apparently had slaked the thirst of members of the garrison, and the money was automatically turned over to the provost marshal to cover the doctor's allowance. Otherwise—he thanked Thomas profusely, via Frances, for the thought.

As the nights lengthened from November to December, Mudd spent his long evenings making presents, he called them "souvenirs," for his friends and relatives outside. He began to gather the myriad shells and fragments of shells that carpeted the prison yard and fashioned them into picture frames. He also created collages, which he called "moss-cards," actually made of dessicated coral polyps, clustered in tight configurations like free-form engravings.

These were to be Christmas presents, for the Christmas season, its presence keenly felt among the prisoners, was close upon them. He wondered if Frances would have the money to get through it, funds to buy presents for the children. Thinking of many former medical patients in Charles County who still owed him money, he made out bills for each of them and sent the bills to Frances to collect. It seems unlikely that she ever did. Most Charles Countians, though sympathetic, were still fearful of any involvement with the doctor. The Nanjemoy Mudds—not a close branch of the family—had stopped sending their children to school on the grounds that Dr. Sam had gone to school and college both, and look where it had got him!

He had naturally dreamed of being home for Christmas, knowing it was a fantasy. "I can imagine," he wrote to Jeremiah Dyer, "the sight of all my little children, my dearest Frank and yourself, with the usual glass of egg-nog and sweet things, seated around a happy fire with no thought to mar the pleasure and joy of the greatest Christian festival. . . . It adds only a new pain to my already languishing life."[10]

General Hill did his best to make Christmas at least tolerable for the prisoners. Their dinner was the same as that served to the garrison and included, as Mudd reported, "canned roast turkey, sausage, oysters, preserves, fresh peaches, tomatoes, etc." But he wrote to Frances on December 25 that nothing could lighten his spirits during this "the darkest hour of our lives. I sometimes ask myself the question, 'what have I done to bring so much trouble upon myself and family?' The answer is from my inmost heart—'nothing.' I am only consoled to know that the greatest saints were the most persecuted. . . ."[11]

In Washington Christmas crept softly upon the city. It was a very different Christmas from that of 1864, when hope of peace was like adrenalin and news of Union victories swept like flames along the streets; when Pennsylvania Avenue swarmed with drunken officers and men in uniform; when the ubiquitous prostitutes were forced to wear Confederate colors on their bodices to shame the rebels; when Grant's and Sherman's victories in Georgia and Virginia seemed more important than the birth of Christ; and when Samuel Mudd walked down Pennsylvania Avenue to a nearly mortal meeting with the actor John Wilkes Booth.

All was calm this season, all was bright. The Civil War was over. Most of the states had ratified the Thirteenth Amendment, ending slavery in the United States, ending forever the Maryland planter's life as Samuel Mudd had known it. (Already his land was up for lease, but blessedly he would not hear of it till after Christmas.) Not for another two months would President Andrew Johnson officially declare that "the insurrection is at an end, and peace, order, and tranquility exist throughout the whole of the United States." But already, and in fact long since, some forty thousand Maryland boys had returned to their south-county homes—some from Lee's surrendered forces in Virginia, some from Grant's Army of the Potomac, some from the West and even from beyond the Mississippi. Already they were talking of early spring planting to begin, perhaps, in February.

In the candlelit White House, the second-floor living room in the west wing dripped with greenery. Children and grandchildren, some barefooted, some in slippers, swarmed around the decorated tree, and the scent of burning hickory, mulled wine, and candied fruit evoked uncountable earlier Christmases in Tennessee. The President sat in a chair apart, a writing tablet on his knees. His hair was a tinge whiter than a year before, his cheeks a little jowlier, his brow more furrowed and his eyes more tired. He leafed through the letters lately brought to his attention. They were more entreaties, he was certain; more pleas for yuletide favors; more demands upon his good will. But now was as good a time as any. He began to read:

Bryantown, Md., December 22, 1865

His Excellency, Andrew Johnson
President of the United States

Dear Sir:
I hesitate to address you, but love is stronger than fear. . . . Mr. President, after many weeks of anxious waiting for news of my innocent, suffering husband, Dr. Samuel Mudd, last night's mail brought the sad tidings that he, along with others by orders from the War Department, were heavily ironed, and obliged to perform hard work. . . . The food furnished is of such miserable quality, he finds it impossible to eat. Health and strength are failing. . . .
I saw you in September, and . . . looked into your face, and if it is true that "the face is an index to the heart," I read in it a good, kind heart that can sympathize with the suffering of others. . . . I beg you in the name of humanity . . . to put a stop to this inhuman treatment. By a stroke of your pen you can give him liberty. Think how much depends upon you . . . .
Could you look into our household, it would give you a subject for meditation. In the Doctor's childhood home, there is his father, who is old and infirm. . . . His mother has scarcely left her sick-room, since his arrest. . . . Pass from this to my little household. I, a wife, drag out life in despondency . . . suffering a living death, am miserable and have to battle with this overwhelming trouble.

There was more, much more—about an aging, ailing mother who would die in peace if she could only see her son again; about four children ranging from one to seven years of age, "the third, a delicate boy requiring constant care"; about a wife's fear that her husband might be lost to her through death in prison. And the words had the brutal strength of one in torment:

I do not love you, neither will I ask the Almighty to bless you . . . but give back to me my husband and . . . the wealth of my gratitude will be yours. My prayers shall ascend in union with my little children. . . . God of Mercy, I pray You, touch the heart of Thy servant, make him give back my husband.

Mrs. Samuel (Sarah Frances) Mudd[12]

The President put down the letter, and thought for several moments. Then he reached for his pen and drafted a reply.

17

"I HAVE GROWN OLD IN MY YOUTH"

THE rains came. Not the gentle rain of Maryland that blended with the season, promising a good spring for the crops. But hot, angry, whipping rain that stung the flesh, penetrated walls and casemates, turned the prison yard into a quagmire. Then, as suddenly as the rain had come, a lens opened in the sky, and a hot sun turned the key into a steaming caldron, firing spurious rainbows in the west.

The appeal that Frances had written to the President, if it were to bring results at all, would not have had time to pass through proper channels. The condition of the five state prisoners was as before. They remained in the damp cell in the dungeon, the condensing water forming stalactites on the vaulted ceiling, the walls coated with a green slime, pools sometimes a foot deep forming in the creviced floor. If Mudd was reminded of anything familiar, it would have been of the dank miasmas sometimes rising from Zachia Swamp, with its stench of rotting vegetation and decay.

It was that time of the year when nerves became frayed and tempers edgy. More than the usual amount of liquor was smuggled to the garrison from the supply ships, and the prisoners became its victims. The officers, Arnold wrote, performed their duties in an alcoholic daze, meting out punishments on whim, carrying persecution to extremes. For the slightest infringement of the rules prisoners were forced to tramp about the yard in circles in the torrid heat, carrying cannon balls on their shoulders. If they rebelled, they were hung by their thumbs on a gallowslike frame in the center of the yard, baking beneath the tropic sun. If they dropped from sheer exhaustion, they were carried to the dungeon to revive, then prodded out with bayonets to resume their burdened march.

Samuel Mudd had been imprisoned for less than six months, but it seemed like a lifetime when he wrote to Frances on January 22:

> I am beginning to realize the saying of the Psalmist, "I have grown old in my youth," etc. Imagine one loaded down with heavy chains, locked up in a wet, damp room, twelve hours out of every twenty-four during working days, and on all day on Sundays and holidays. No exercise allowed except in the limited space of a small room, with irons on.
>
> The atmosphere we breathe is highly impregnated with sulphuric hydrogen gas, which you are aware is highly injurious to health as well as disagreeable. The gas is generated by the numerous sinks that empty into that portion of the sea enclosed by the breakwater, and which is immediately under a small port hole—the only admission of air and light we have from the external port.
>
> My legs and ankles are swollen and sore, pains in my shoulders and back are frequent. My hair began falling out some time ago, and to save which I shaved it all over clean, and have continued to do so once every week since.
>
> . . . My eyesight is beginning to grow very bad, so much so that I can't read or write by candlelight. During the day, owing to the overpowering light and heat, my eyes are painful and irritated, and can't view any object many seconds without having to close to shade them from the light.

The glare of the tropical sun on the white shale of the island, unrelieved by any vegetation, was maddening to prisoners and garrison alike. During construction of the fort, when the supply of reddish-colored bricks from Maine ran out, the engineers had imported yellow bricks from Alabama, which were used for surfacing the outside walls. The pale bricks seemed to double the intense light of the sun, causing what was referred to as "moon blindness," similar to the snow blindness often suffered in the Alps.

* * *

With all this [Mudd continued] imagine my gait with a
bucket and broom, and a guard, walking around from one
corner of the fort to another, sweeping and sanding down
the bastions. This has been our treatment for the last three
months, coupled with bad diet, bad water, and every incon-
venience. The greatest wonder is, that we have borne up
so well.[1]

A devout Catholic, he was grieved by the lack of any religious observances on the island, a regret not shared by any
of his cellmates, least of all St. Leger Grenfell, whose irrever-
ence and blasphemy grated on the doctor's ears. After the
first of the year, however, the prison was visited by Father
William O'Hara, newly installed at Key West. "I have not
the language at my command," wrote Mudd to Frances, "to
express the joy and delight I received on the occasion of
this visit." The priest heard his confession, blessed him, and
conducted mass for the Catholics in the prison.

The doctor needed all the solace he could get. Frances,
on the advice of Jeremiah Dyer, had leased out a portion
of the farm—most of the grazing land and the tobacco fields
—keeping only the house and the vegetable gardens for
her own use. She still had with her the faithful English
retainer, "Uncle" John Best, and two of the former servants,
Baptist Washington and Alvin Brook, had returned to work
for room and board. Southern Maryland, like much of the
South, was overrun with a newly freed and drifting black
population, and Mudd was concerned over possible danger
to Frances and the children from these roving bands.

Jeremiah Dyer, of course, could be counted on to look after
Frances' welfare, an obligation he filled with unflagging conscience and fidelity. He visited Rock Hill not less than every
two weeks; checked on the operation of the farm; and served
as an intermediary between Frances and Sam's lawyers,
Ewing, Stone and Merrick, in the capital.

The last week in January, Andrew Johnson's reaction to
Frances' letter of December 22 took effect via orders to Stanton relayed to General Sheridan in New Orleans. Not only
was Dr. Mudd relieved of his chains, but so also were Grenfell,
Spangler, Arnold and O'Laughlin; and all were moved from

the dungeon to casemates on the second tier, directly above the drawbridge and portcullis. Grenfell was given a separate cell from Dr. Mudd's, with an empty chamber intervening, possibly for reasons of security—they were the prison's two prime inmates. It was not the freedom Frances had requested for her husband, but under the circumstances it was something of a victory. Never again would the doctor be subjected to inhuman treatment in the prison.

Their new quarters, Sam wrote to Frances, were larger, airier, and lighter; generally more healthful; and their diet much improved. The doctor sent her a sketch of the eastern façade of the prison, showing the three small windows or "loop holes" just above the sally port, two feet wide on the outside, narrowing to four-inch slits on the inside, positioned seven feet above the casemate floor. Under these better conditions, he observed, "I have hopes of a prolongation of the thread of life." Yet—

> My disposition is undergoing a change. The virtue of resignation to an adverse and unjust punishment is rapidly dying out within me, and a different spirit supplanting. God knows I try to control these emotions, but it seems almost in vain.
> History often reverses itself. Pilate, fearing the displeasure of the multitude, condemned our Lord to death. Is not mine somewhat an analogous case?[2]

Characteristically, St. Leger Grenfell expressed no appreciation for this marked improvement in their circumstances. He considered it the consequences of his own protests to the British embassy in Washington, where, in fact, the ambassador regarded Grenfell as an unmitigated nuisance. "He has embarrassed Her Majesty's government in every nation under the sun." Nevertheless His Excellency appealed to the President and Secretary Stanton for whatever consideration might be due an English citizen, and in time results would be forthcoming.

Meanwhile, a case of smallpox was discovered on the island, and the afflicted prisoner was placed in the empty casemate between Dr. Mudd's and Grenfell's cells. Grenfell was outraged; the post surgeon was calculatingly exposing them to the disease; otherwise the ill man would have been remanded to an isolated corner of the fort. He obtained a sizeable board and on it inscribed in heavy charcoal: "SMALL POX HOSPITAL: KEEP OUT!" He placed the board outside the door.

The provost marshal ordered the colonel to remove the board and cautioned him "to be very careful of his actions in the future." The warning fell on deaf ears. Grenfell began to keep a written list of what he considered violations of his rights, along with a record of unjust treatment inflicted on the other prisoners. Had he been more prudent, he would have known he was all but writing his own death warrant.

Samuel Arnold was no more appreciative of their better quarters and more lenient treatment. Unlike Dr. Mudd, he found the casemate on the second tier as insalubrious as the dungeon. The thick walls exuded moisture, and the floor was damp and slimy. They dug holes and trenches to carry off the water and keep pools from forming. The place was infested with mosquitoes, bedbugs, roaches, and scorpions. Even Dr. Mudd, who generally kept his complaints for Frances, was annoyed by the sentinels' pacing outside their door and calling out the nighttime hours as he tried in vain to sleep.

He also objected to being made an object of curiosity to visitors who came from the mainland to inspect the prison "zoo." His name was notorious enough to make him a specimen of more than ordinary interest. As strange eyes peered through the bars, as at an animal in a cage, his only recourse was to stand in stony immobility, not wincing or batting an eye—pretending to be oblivious to the indignity—until the spectators sighed with satisfaction and departed.

The view from the casemate, except for the glimpses of sky through the Gulf-side ports, was of the prison yard below. And like Grenfell, Samuel Arnold was an avid observer of life in the enclosure. Unlike Grenfell, he abstained from putting what he saw on paper, storing it in his mind for future reference.

The garrison suffered as much as the prisoners from sadistic treatment. A private named Wheeler, to save money on work he could do himself, took a stitch in his army pantaloons instead of giving them to the prison tailor. For this he carried a cannon ball two hours off and two hours on, day and night, for four weeks. Another prisoner so punished happened to drop the ball; his hand was nearly severed by a blow from an officer's saber. A French Canadian recruit, for impudence to an officer, was beaten to death with the butt end of a musket. A German recruit named Christian Conrad was subject to fits, and a cure was attempted by kicking his writhing body and dousing him with water. He was finally sent on a stretcher to the mainland, a maimed and totally disabled man.

The four state prisoners, Arnold wrote, had a ringside seat at this Grand Guignol:

> There did not pass a day but men could be seen tied up by their thumbs, between the sky and the earth, until the joints of their thumbs were nearly pulled from their sockets, some bound in cords and carried to the Gulf Stream and nearly drowned, others tied up in the guard house and lashed upon their naked flesh. Many of these cruelties were inflicted because they followed the example set by some of the Officers in charge of them, and dared like them to become intoxicated.
>
> There was another mode of punishment applied in many instances. Men were what they called nailed to the cross in spread eagle fashion & others tied, with their hands behind them, to swinging limbs, the tip of their toes barely touching the earth.[3]

As a consequence of these tortures, practiced or threatened, desertions were frequent, leaves to Key West were canceled, and the soldiers were virtually captives, as restricted as the prisoners. Mudd found himself sharing food he received from Thomas Dyer with his guards and other members of the garrison, winning thereby their gratitude and friendship. More than one assured him that if he wished to attempt another escape, they would do what they could to help, if they could avoid being compromised themselves. Mudd declined their offers; he was looking now not for freedom only but for pardon and the clearing of his name.

* * *

That winter and early spring the perpetually gray skies parted and the first real rays of hope shone through. The sequence of events had begun in early 1864, before Mudd's trial and before the trial of Grenfell. An Indiana copperhead named Lambdin P. Milligan, indicted for conspiracy, was tried by a military commission under Judge Advocate Burnett. Found guilty in December 1864, he was sentenced to be executed. His attorneys applied for a writ of *habeas corpus.* The case went to the Supreme Court, and in April, 1866, Chief Justice Salmon P. Chase concurred in the court's decision that trial before a military tribunal violated Milligan's rights under the Constitution. It was noted that Milligan was a private citizen, neither the resident of a seceded state nor a prisoner of war. In fact, his status was exactly that of Samuel Mudd at the time of Mudd's arraignment.

Regardless of Milligan's guilt or innocence, wrote Justice Chase, "it is more important to the country and to every citizen that he should not be punished under an illegal sentence . . . than that he should be punished at all. The laws which protect the liberties of the whole people must not be violated or set aside in order to inflict, even upon the guilty, unauthorized though merited punishment."[4]

The landmark decision was a vindication of General Ewing's argument at the trial of Samuel Mudd and Reverdy Johnson's denunciation of the military court's authority. The cases of Milligan and Mudd were almost parallel. Both were citizens of a loyal state; both were tried before a military commission rather than a civil court; and in Mudd's case—to his legal advantage—tried not during the time of war but after hostilities had ceased.

The decision at this point, however, applied to Milligan alone. It did not automatically apply to Samuel Mudd and the other four state prisoners at Garden Key. Two courses of action were open. Their attorneys could appeal for a writ of *habeas corpus* and, obtaining it, move for a retrial in the civil courts. That would mean time and money; and so long as Stanton and Holt remained adamant regarding Mudd's sentence, the War Department could fight a long, delaying action and quite possibly come out on top.

The other course was to appeal directly to Andrew Johnson

to free the prisoners of his own accord, relying on the President's expected adherence to the Supreme Court verdict —certainly the easiest and quickest move. Jeremiah Dyer hurried to Washington to talk with ex-Governor Ford. Would Ford, with his direct line to the White House, bring Mudd's case again before the President, in the light of the new circumstances?

It was an unfortunate period in Andrew Johnson's young administration. His conciliatory attitude toward the South had aroused the wrath of the Radical Republicans. It was the North, the Radicals argued, who should rule the South, and not the discredited, defeated rebels. Johnson, whom they had first regarded as a useful tool in their program of oppression, had proved to be a traitor to the cause of Reconstruction. Johnson, it was suddenly recognized and emphasized, was a Southerner by birth himself.

Under the circumstances Ford found the President reluctant to take action in behalf of Samuel Mudd. He reported to Dyer that the President had given him "every assurance that he would release Sam at the earliest moment that he could consistently do so." The President had also remarked that Mudd "was a mere creature of accident, and ought not to have been imprisoned; but in the present state of political excitement he [the President] did not think it prudent of him to take any action, as it would be another pretext for the Radicals to build capital on." In short, the President would act not upon conscience but upon political expediency. In view of the issues at stake—the fate of a single political prisoner against the future of the South—one could hardly blame him.

Meanwhile, acting on the Milligan decision, assistant defense attorney Richard T. Merrick submitted to the Supreme Court a writ of *habeas corpus* in behalf of Dr. Mudd. Grenfell's lawyer, Robert Hervey, proceeded along the same lines. He secured a Tallahassee attorney and ex-Confederate army officer, Anderson J. Peeler, to sue for the writ in Florida.

Perhaps it was unfortunate that these similar actions appeared to link the name of Samuel Mudd with that of Grenfell. The Grenfell suit especially resulted in waves of protest reaching to the halls of Congress. One speaker in the House read a resolution making Grenfell a prototype of the other appellants jailed for conspiracy. "He is one of the worst men that lives on the face of the earth. . . . He should have been hung. Never allow him to be released. Keep him in the Tortugas till he rots. . . ."[5]

What happened to Dr. Mudd's appeal is clouded by confused reports and missing records. The writ of *habeas corpus* was denied for inexplicable reasons by Salmon Chase. The Supreme Court Justice, acting alone and not consulting other members of the court, rejected the findings *ex parte Milligan* as applied to Dr. Mudd.[6]

The War Department appeared guided by this action, though it could not wholly overlook the Milligan decision. Stanton ordered the release of all state prisoners convicted in military courts, "except those under sentence in the Dry Tortugas"—Samuel Mudd, St. Leger Grenfell, Arnold, Spangler, and O'Laughlin.

So long as Holt and Stanton were in power, there was little hope for action on their cases; and little hope from a President engaged in battle with the Radicals in Congress. There would be party conventions in the summer, then the November 1866 elections. If Johnson's administration scored a victory at the polls, that would give the President the strength he needed to take action. But in the spring of 1866, autumn appeared far, far away.

It was a dismal year, a wretched year, for the doctor and the country both. A wounded nation seemed intent on picking at its scars, keeping alive the hatreds and suspicions of the Civil War. Though Johnson declared, "the insurrection is at an end," the extremists of the North remained implacable. The myths of The Great Conspiracy that had led to Lincoln's murder were kept alive, partly for political purposes, by the increasingly powerful Radical element in the Republican party.

Mudd followed events through the Baltimore *Gazette* and *Weekly Sun*, both filed a month late in the prison library. His spirits rose and fell with every rumor and report. More and more he came to realize he was the victim of an ugly political warfare, in which he and his fellow prisoners, though drastically affected, were merely insignificant pawns. The central figure in the drama was Andrew Johnson, the President who had confirmed Mudd's sentence and was now the target of the very men who had imposed that sentence.

As Johnson continued to propose ameliorative measures for the South, the Radicals throughout the nation rose in protest. Was Johnson condoning the late rebellion? Were the ex-Confederate states to be readmitted just by accepting the Thirteenth Amendment ending slavery?

The North demanded more than this mere ounce of flesh. Johnson had become a traitor, not much better than the vanquished rebels. It was the President who fired the first salvo in the war with Congress. He vetoed a bill designed to strengthen and perpetuate the Freedman's Bureau, founded in March of 1865 to implement emancipation and promote black people's welfare. Worthy aims, perhaps; but violations would be tried in military courts, now held unconstitutional. He also vetoed the Civil Rights Bill, which accorded citizenship and equality to blacks, a measure Johnson felt was an unwarranted intrusion on the states' authority.

Both bills were ultimately passed, in one form or another, over the presidential vetoes. Congress had won the first round. But Johnson continued to fight. Opposition was a tonic to him, strengthening his resolution.

As the President's hold on the government declined, so also did Mudd's chances for a reconsideration of his case. Only someone who maintained sufficient power to defy the War Department and the Congress could annul the convictions of civilians by the military courts. The President's vetoes gave the doctor momentary hope. Then despair set in. Since human nature vents its frustrations on those nearest and dearest, Mudd took his out on Frances. Unfairly, he once again charged her with indifference, withholding the truth, and feeding him false hopes.

His letters became querulous, vindictive, and accusatory. "Spare me the kisses and the promises," he begged her. "These things . . . serve only to embitter." When she saw light in the Supreme Court's Milligan decision and in the President's conciliatory attitude, he told her bluntly: "You are wrong to tolerate any such sentiment or interpretation —it only coincides with, or confirms, the verdict of the Court, who sentenced me to this hell." In the same breath he asked for forgiveness if he appeared to be a "scold." He was "naturally nervous and excitable" and nothing contributed more to this state than "severe and long suspense."[7]

Yet Frances and her brother Jeremiah Dyer were in constant touch with Sam's attorneys and others whose influence might aid the doctor's case. All believed the President might take some action after Congress recessed and the Radicals got off his back. Dyer wrote to Frances, "I am very sanguine, after the adjournment of Congress, we will be able to accomplish Sam's release."

Frances, of course, sent these words on to her husband, to sustain his spirit. Like Sam, and to almost the same degree, she was the victim of a crumbling society, a world that was falling down around her. She was one lone woman battling against harsh odds and trying to share her husband's burdens while she struggled with her own.

Jeremiah Dyer's sanguine optimism was part balm, part irritant to Dr. Mudd. Sam admitted to Frances, "Bright beams begin again to shed their light," but added:

> I shall be content until after Congress adjourns; after that, I shall be anxious, and look for some decided action to be taken by you and my friends; otherwise I will give up all hopes of ever leaving this place alive, and live only to curse my enemies.

Then he added, vindictively:

> I perceive not the slightest change in the character of your letters; it is another put off, another child's play—to torment and vex me.[8]

He appeared to be serving notice on the world—and Frances was the center of that world—that his patience was exhausted. He was still sweeping down the bastions and was otherwise in his quarters under guard. He continued to be "weak and nervous, which I attribute to the diet, want of exercise and climate, combined with reception of unfavorable news, and consequent agitation of mind." The midsummer weather was suffocating. The prison swarmed with mosquitoes, fleas and bedbugs. Sleep at night was difficult.

Mudd's dreams of being home with his wife and children had become, he recognized, "mere castles in the air." His only remaining pleasure, he wrote to Frances, was the chance to write to her. Then, in the following letter, he "felt like throwing away pen and ink, and foregoing the pleasure of ever writing again," for "Blessed are those who expect nothing for they shall not be disappointed." And he went back to blaming her for repeated disappointments:

> I know that you would not knowingly deceive me, and am rather disposed to believe you were wilfully imposed upon by those who knew better. I am in hopes you will be more guarded in the future, and not suffer your credulity to mislead you again.[9]

And later:

> Try and do not deceive me again; if you know nothing positive, have the resolution to tell me so. . . . How different have I acted toward you. I have never failed to give you . . . a true condition of my health, treatment, etc.[10]

With the War Department's pardon of prisoners convicted by the military courts, the convict population of the fort was reduced to 170. These were hard-core criminals, rapists, murderers, arsonists, and thieves, of which all but thirty were black. Moreover, since white soldiers in the garrison succumbed more readily to heat and hardship, they were replaced by black troops, which Mudd found detrimental to "my usual serenity." His patience was spent. "Fifteen months of the most brutal and degrading imprisonment has done its work. I am broken down and good for nothing. You spoke of turning gray—I am nearly bald."[11]

In spite of the tone of woe in all his letters at this time, the five state prisoners were being treated with more leniency and latitude than before. It seems likely that Stanton and Holt, determined as ever to keep them buried on the island, were anxious that they should have no publicized reasons for complaint. To placate St. Leger Grenfell, still the *bête noire* of the garrison and its commanders, they gave the English prisoner a patch of garden to cultivate. Since no soil existed on the island, earth was brought by ship from Louisiana. A small plot was surfaced at one end of the yard, surrounded by a picket fence. Grenfell wrote to a friend in Kentucky, "Be it known that they have turned my sword into a shovel & rake and I am at the head of my profession here. What I say or do [horticulturally] is law!"[12]

Mudd could only view the phenomenon from a distance, passing to and from his prison chores, but Captain T. P. McElrath of the 5th U.S. Artillery later recalled his impressions of the gladiator at his hobby:

> He was dressed in Confederate gray and surmounted by a high straw hat squeezed to a conical point at the crown and destitute of a ribbon, giving him the general appearance of respectability peculiar to the average native Southern planter of the early reconstruction days . . . to all appearances [he] performed the duties of his position with earnestness and zeal. . . . [The garden] never proved productive but for a long time it gave its captive superintendent agreeable and healthful recreation.[13]

It also gave Grenfell a perverse amusement, which was why it never proved productive. He had no outlet for his spleen, no way openly to torment his captors. But he could slyly get even with them if they did not know it; he could figuratively throw this garden in their faces. So he secretly roasted the seeds before he planted them, to make certain they would not germinate. If a few survived and sent up seedlings, he sprinkled them with seawater. Nothing blossomed. The disappointment of the garrison, in this first garden venture on the island, gave him infinite delight.

Mudd himself was relieved of his daily chore of sweeping out the bastions and assigned to more congenial work in the carpentry shop. He was above Grenfell's tactic of cutting off his nose to spite his face and took a genuine interest in the new assignment. "I occupy my time principally in making little boxes, ornamenting them with different colors and varieties of wood." In time the boxes got larger, and he encrusted their tops and sides with shells and bits of glass and coral. In a venerable Bahamian house on Key West's Whitehead Street, one of them survives today, a marvel of design and craftsmanship.

Yet, like Grenfell, he took a perverse satisfaction from events that could only lead to his misfortune. In Tom Dyer's home town of New Orleans, port of departure for the Dry Tortugas, a meeting was held in July of 1866 to choose delegates for the National Union (Republican) Party Convention in Philadelphia to be held a month later. A mob of blacks descended on Mechanics' Hall to break up the all-white caucus. In a clash with the police, thirty-five were killed, scores wounded. All but one of the dead were black. Coming on top of a similar riot, some weeks earlier in Memphis, the massacre outraged the North, where it was hailed as further evidence of Southern lawlessness and resistance to emancipation. Yet Mudd wrote to Tom Dyer in early September:

> I have been led to believe the whole South exterminated, or reduced to abject slavery, until news of the recent riot reached us. I am grieved at the occurrence, the loss of valuable lives, but proud to know there is manhood enough left to rebuke the oppression of the interventionists.[14]

By "interventionists" he could have meant the scalawags and carpetbaggers, or the Radicals—in the eyes of the Southerner they were all the same. Yet violence directed at the Radicals, who sought to keep the South enslaved, could lead only to retaliation, and Mudd would be the victim of that whiplash. In the November, 1866, elections the Radicals gained a major victory in Congress. In dealing Johnson a crushing defeat they diminished, almost to zero, the doctor's chances of a presidential pardon. In the months to come, Johnson would be fighting for his political life. He would not have time or thought to give to Samuel Mudd's survival.

In December the doctor was busy making Christmas gifts of coral for his friends and relatives; for Frances, a delicate cross of driftwood and a wreath, though what materials he used to make the wreath is puzzling. He also fashioned picture frames for the children, with detailed directions on how to fit the pictures in the frames. Then, a born worrier, he fretted about what damage they might suffer from rough treatment in the mails.

Though still under the relatively mild command of Brigadier General Bennett Hill, the prisoners enjoyed no special holiday favors, no roast turkey, oysters, or preserves as on the previous Christmas. Prison routine was uninterrupted, and perhaps that kept his mind from dwelling too much on the ghosts of Christmases long past. Michael O'Laughlin received a carton of wines and cakes and fruits from Baltimore, which he shared with his three cellmates. Mudd considered it "quite a treat."

By the year's end, though despondent, he was not without hope. In his last December letter home he noted:

We have made application to the Secretary of War, through General Hill, giving many valid reasons for our removal to some Northern prison. I am in hopes it may prove unnecessary, and that we may be released through the medium of the recent decision of the Supreme Court. God grant it may not be much longer deferred.[15]

18

WHEN ROGUES FALL OUT

JOHN Wilkes Booth was dead, according to the records of the War Department, though many still believed his reported death and camouflaged burial had been a cover-up for Stanton's failure to apprehend the criminal.

Jefferson Davis still languished in a cell in Fortress Monroe, though his irons had been removed on Johnson's orders. Presumably Davis would be tried for treason, but on what specific charge, or when, or by what court, remained a matter of contention.

Samuel Mudd, the only other convicted figure of stature in the Great Conspiracy, was alive but thoroughly disposed of in the Dry Tortugas.

Now, in the winter of 1867, another ghost from that conspiracy rose from the dead or near-dead to evoke the past. John Harrison Surratt had been captured in Egypt, and a naval vessel was bringing the prisoner back to the United States for trial. Newspapers in the prison library at Garden Key began to carry the second chapter in the curious saga of the fugitive in exile. . . .

After spending the winter of 1866 in London, on money sent from Montreal, John sojourned briefly in Paris, then trekked across the Continent to Rome. In the Italian capital his funds began to run out. Partly for reasons of economy, partly for anonymity, he enlisted in the Vatican Zouaves, using the alias John Watson. Entranced with his new image, he had a daguerreotype made of himself in papal uniform, white leggings, piped pantaloons and tunic, tasseled fez and all. Never having been in military dress before, he appeared to love that uniform so much he allowed it to betray him.

When his company was moved to Sezze, southeast of Rome, one of life's baffling coincidences overtook the ex-Confederate courier from Maryland. Henry Beaumont St. Marie, the Maryland student from St. Charles College, whom John had met with Louis Wiechmann in 1863, had also joined the Papal Guards now stationed in the tiny town. There was no avoiding the encounter. In their inevitable reminiscing, John blurted out that "had it not been for Wiechmann, my mother would be living yet."

Then the whole story poured into St. Marie's astonished ears: the plot to abduct or assassinate the "nigger-loving Lincoln," John's degree of involvement and the roles of others in the Great Conspiracy. Though John enjoined his fellow cadet to respect the secret, it was too much for St. Marie to keep to himself. He promptly relayed the information to Rufus King, American minister in Rome.

King could have made it easy for himself by dropping the whole matter and gaining the gratitude of Stanton's War Department. But, duty-bound, he wired the news to Washington. Stanton tried to ignore the cable, as did Advocate General Holt, until, after repeated evasions, the State Department prodded them to action. Six months later, in November, 1866, General King in Rome asked the Pope's chancellor, Cardinal Antonelli, to release Zouave "Watson" for arrest and deportation to America. Cardinal Antonelli began to take the necessary steps.

There followed a bizarre exchange of messages and telegrams between the principals concerned. A general of the Zouaves sent word to the colonel commanding the battalion in which John "Watson" Surratt was serving:

November 6, 1866

COLONEL: CAUSE THE ARREST OF ZOUAVE WATSON, AND HAVE HIM CONDUCTED, UNDER SECURE ESCORT, TO THE MILITARY PRISON AT ROME.

The colonel telegraphed in reply:

November 7, 1866

GENERAL: I HAVE THE HONOR TO INFORM YOU THAT THE
ZOUAVE JOHN WATSON HAS BEEN ARRESTED, AND WILL BE
TAKEN TOMORROW MORNING, UNDER GOOD ESCORT, TO ROME.

Twenty-four hours later, the colonel wired the Italian War
Minister in the Eternal City:

November 8, 1866

EXCELLENCY: AT THE MOMENT OF LEAVING THE PRISON,
SURROUNDED BY SIX MEN AS GUARDS, WATSON PLUNGED INTO
THE RAVINE, MORE THAN A HUNDRED FEET DEEP, WHICH
SURROUNDS THE PRISON. FIFTY ZOUAVES ARE IN PURSUIT.[1]

Fifty Zouaves were hardly a match for young Surratt, who
for three years had eluded federal troops in southern Maryland. With the posse hard on his heels, he made his way
to Naples. There, posing as a Canadian national unjustly
impressed into foreign service, John obtained the help of
the English consul in securing passage to Egypt aboard the
steamer *Tripoli.*

He could not, however, part with the colorful Zouave
uniform that stood out like a beacon in the crowd. He was
still wearing it when the *Tripoli* stopped for coal at Malta.
William Winthrop, U.S. consul in that city, recognized the
fugitive and relayed the news to Alexandria, the ship's next
port of call. As John stepped ashore at Alexandria he was
put under arrest by Charles Hale, American consul general,
who promptly cabled Secretary Seward of John's capture.

This time, with news of the arrest reported in America,
Stanton could not ignore the man least wanted by the War
Department. When he and Lafayette Baker had vigorously
searched for John in July of 1864, Surratt had been hard
to trace, let alone capture. Now, like a bad penny, he kept
turning up. The United States Navy was ordered to send
the corvette *Swatara* to bring the captive home in tight security. The *Swatara* anchored off Washington's Navy Yard
in mid-January, 1867, and Surratt was hustled to Dr. Mudd's
former prison, the Old Capitol on First Street.

How would Surratt's return and likely prosecution affect Dr. Mudd's situation, beyond refocusing attention on the Black Easter tragedy of 1865? Public sentiment was hard to gauge.

Mudd took a somewhat dim view of the development. The reappearance of John Surratt, he wrote to Frances, "will be the advent of a new excitement, and the reiteration of every species of lie and slander which were given currency at our trial and subsequently, and serve as a pretext to continue my unlawful and unjust imprisonment."[2]

There was more to concern the nation than the capture of Surratt. Of all the alleged conspirators in Lincoln's murder, some were free for having turned state's evidence; some had been executed; and those surviving, such as Jefferson Davis and Samuel Mudd, were locked in prison, as finally was John Surratt. But one remained not only free but in the White House! President Andrew Johnson was now cited as the mastermind behind the whole assassination plot.

Of all the shameful charges hurled so indiscriminately in the wake of Lincoln's murder, this was by far the most preposterous. Yet two congressional scavengers, James Mitchell Ashley and George S. Boutwell—enraged by Johnson's vetoes of bills humiliating to the South—were out to gain revenge on the President who, they claimed, had swept into office on the Great Emancipator's blood.

The two predators called for the President's impeachment and presented "proof" of his complicity: as a starter, Lafayette Baker reported having seen a letter from Johnson to Jefferson Davis indicating collusion between the two throughout the war. The letter, however, had somehow disappeared.

Johnson had balked at pursuing and arresting John Surratt for fear Surratt would reveal his involvement. For the same reason he had hastened the execution of John's mother, Mary, despite the commission's plea for clemency. (Johnson had never seen the plea, presumably because Stanton and Judge Advocate Holt had withheld it.)

The card Booth had left for the Vice President at the Kirkwood House the night of the assassination finally came home to roost. It was advanced as proof of their connivance.

And there was the gun, the knife and the other incriminating paraphernalia found in George Atzerodt's room at the Kirkwood House. They had been obvious plants to divert suspicion from the culprit, Andrew Johnson.

Finally, who had the greater motive? Only Lincoln stood between the ex-tailor and the White House. Eliminate Lincoln, and Johnson would have a free hand in furthering the Lost Cause of the South.

This balderdash collapsed of its own flimsy weight. But the move toward impeachment had begun; the abyss between Johnson and the Congress had been widened; and Dr. Mudd would feel the consequences. More and more he was becoming the victim of an ugly political battle. He was caught between the clashing interests of the two main agencies with the power to release him: the President and the Congress, Stanton's Bureau of Military Justice siding with the Congress.

If the President were inclined to pardon Dr. Mudd, he would only be feeding ammunition to the Radicals. If the Radicals or Stanton or the Bureau of Military Justice were inclined, in view of the Supreme Court's Milligan decision, to show leniency toward the doctor, they would be admitting they had erred in his conviction in the first place. Here was the riddle of the Sphinx, whose colossus stretched from Washington to Garden Key, which would take the wisdom of an Oedipus to solve.

Somehow life went on at Rock Hill Farm in southern Maryland. It always does, somehow, Sarah Frances Mudd was learning. Between caring for four children, ranging in age from nine-year-old Andrew to young Sam, Jr., a little over three; running the farm; doing her own cooking, sewing, cleaning, gardening, she still had time to think ceaselessly of Sam, write to Sam, work for his release and make frequent trips to Washington, the White House and the War Department to that end.

Sam's mother and father, although as much concerned for Frances' welfare as their son's, were too old and ill to be of any physical help. Or financial assistance, for that matter. Much of Henry Lowe's fortune had gone to pay for Sam's defense. As in Virginia, the big plantations were breaking up, to be sold in parcels or left to grow to jimsonweed and pine.

The state of Maryland was paying dearly for the war. The southern counties were plagued by hordes of unemployed drifters who lived by pilfering or demanded wages the planters, including Frances, could not pay. There was some income from the farmland she had leased, and she still had Baptist Washington to work the rest.

"Tell Bap. I say to pay his whole attention to the farm," Sam wrote to her. "Should he desire any carpenter work, he will find plenty on the farm, for which, should it be in my power, I will amply compensate him. A good corn-house is very much needed, also a barn or pen-house for tobacco. At his leisure he could get out the material for them, and leave it to some competent party to estimate value, and take it out from rent or otherwise."[3]

John Best, the English handyman, was getting on in years and becoming testy and difficult to handle. On that subject, too, her husband, who never stopped worrying about the farm, offered some advice. "Exercise a little of that virtue—patience. Mr. Best is growing quite old, and with bad health it is natural he should be cross and a little childish. Try to bear with him until I get home, should it be my fortune soon."[4]

The staunch rock in her troubled life was Jeremiah Dyer, and briefly she and Sam were worried about losing at least a part of his devotion and attention. The durable attraction between Mudds and Dyers persevered. Early that spring Jeremiah married Sam's younger sister, Mary Clare, and took her back with him to Baltimore. But he still returned regularly to Bryantown to help Frances in the operation of the farm, writing lightheartedly in advance (with atrocious spelling):

> . . . tell mr Bess [Best] I hope he has a Pig fat for I will certainly call on him for it at Easter   I suppose he will be able to give me beets & beans & peas also. Can you not have a s[t]uffed ham. I am tired of Balto meet. . . .[5]

Thomas Ewing, having become a back-door adviser to the President, had all but relinquished the case. But Andrew Sterritt Ridgely, closely associated with Reverdy Johnson, was working for Mudd's release as were Frederick Stone and David Merrick—when they had the time. Dyer commuted between Baltimore and Washington and prodded them with every new development.

He pursued and developed obscure leads with the genius of a Sherlock Holmes. Judge William F. Turner of the War Department's Bureau of Military Justice had sat through Mudd's trial and apparently believed in the doctor's innocence, but he failed to protest the verdict. Later Turner had written to an army friend (according to Dyer's report to Frances) that "neither he nor the Court ever believed Sam had anything to do with the killing of Lincoln but was the victim of his own timidity. . . . It clearly proves that Sam was innocent of any conspiracy."[6]

Somehow Dyer traced and found that letter and sent copies to the Baltimore *Gazette* and Washington *Intelligencer* for publication in their columns. A small coup, perhaps, but another item in Mudd's favor. Turner had died a few weeks after the disclosure of the letter, and his passing was not mourned by Dr. Mudd, who felt the judge should have spoken out in his defense. "The cause of his [Turner's] death," Mudd wrote to Dyer, "is said to be apoplexy, but more likely poison by his own hands. The fate of a guilty conscience."[7]

Despite all the efforts being made in his behalf, Mudd felt that more could be accomplished with the ammunition of the Supreme Court ruling in *ex parte Milligan*. "Milligan was tried during the existence of active war," he complained to Frances. "His case is declared illegal. We were tried after the war, and peace declared. If the trial of Milligan was wrong, then certainly ours was more so. . . ."

He could not understand why the application in his behalf for a writ of *habeas corpus* had been denied. Perhaps it had been presented to the wrong judge. Try another judge, or better yet Secretary Stanton or the President. What he could not comprehend, from the insulating distance of the Dry Tortugas, was the extent to which these various powers were locked in paralyzing battle. Rather, he chose to believe that they were all united in a plot to keep him buried in Fort Jefferson.

A plague on all their houses—on their "foul play and rascality!" Let them cut one another's throats, for "when rogues fall out, honest men get their due." There was a hint of prophetic truth in the remark.

The doctor saw many parallels between his own condition and St. Leger Grenfell's. Nonetheless, under General Hill, whom Grenfell unfairly referred to as "that bad old man," the Englishman had received, according to Mudd's letters, humane and considerate treatment: to wit, the garden he had sabotaged from spite. Yet he wrote to his sister of cruel work in the boiling sun, impossible for a man approaching sixty; of recurrent rheumatism from the dampness of his cell; of "weak spells" from the wretched food, which caused him to collapse each night, almost insensible, on the hard straw pallet of his bunk.

Sir Frederick Bruce, the British minister in Washington, finally did bring pressure on the State Department at least to investigate the treatment the colonel was receiving. This produced the statement that Grenfell was "a favorite of the officers...[who] do all in their power to alleviate his situation"; while Hill wrote to the colonel's sister that Grenfell "was completely satisfied with his life in the Dry Tortugas, and has been assigned duties which are very light."

Grenfell was indignant on hearing from his sister of this comment. "The lying old sinner knew perfectly well that by his own order I was being treated worse than any other prisoner on the island. The very day that he dates his letter I was working with niggers unloading 450 tons of coal from a vessel under a sun hotter than your hottest July weather, and kept at work till I could hardly stand."

He was not, however, treated worse than any other prisoner, as he himself would later admit. Among those unloading cargo was a common criminal named James Dunn, who with two of the soldiers guarding him discovered a cache of whiskey in the vessel's hold. All three became so drunk that they were reported to the officer of the day, C. C. McConnell. Major McConnell ignored the intoxicated guards, but ordered that Dunn be given a cannon ball to carry for several hours round the yard. Finding the prisoner too drunk to walk, he had him strung up by the thumbs on a rail beneath the windows of Dr. Mudd's and Grenfell's casemates.

For hours Dunn swayed in the broiling sun, his thumbs swelling to the size of turnips, his face discolored by the strain. At day's end he was cut down, and again given the ball to carry, with a sentinel assigned to prod the prisoner with his bayonet. Dunn's mutilated hands made it difficult to hold the weight. He finally collapsed; the ball fell on his head and crushed his face against the coral. The guard struck him with the bayonet, trying to force him to his feet, but the prisoner's screams aroused the lighthouse keeper, who protested to McConnell that the "hideous cries" were keeping his family awake.

McConnell ordered the punishment continued outside the walls of the fort, beyond official sight or hearing. Again Dunn was strung up by the thumbs and wrists and left there through the night, begging the guard from time to time to kill him with the bayonet. He was cut down the next morning, his hands bleeding and gangrenous, his face badly mutilated, unable to speak or stand. Three months of medical care in the prison hospital prevented the amputation of his hands, though he lost the use of one arm.

Dr. Mudd, Grenfell, and Arnold took due note of the atrocity, and Grenfell reported it, no doubt with some embellishment, to his lawyer Bradley Johnson. Johnson, of his own initiative, sent the letter—which miraculously passed the censors—to the antiadministration New York *World*. Picked up by other newspapers in the North, it aroused indignant public sympathy for "the helpless victims of military despotism."

When the published letter was later brought to Hill's attention, he immediately divined the author. Grenfell's quarters were searched, and a copy of the article discovered. All kindly feeling for the aging rebel vanished. "Colonel St. Leger Grenfell is kept in close confinement under guard," Mudd wrote laconically to Thomas Dyer in New Orleans. The Englishman was back in the dungeon; his cell was boarded up to admit no light and a minimum of air; he was allowed to speak to no one or to receive or send mail.

But the incident had some effect. The War Department could not ignore the published and now widely circulated charges. A committee of investigation arrived on Garden Key, heard the testimony of the officers and guards but not the prisoners, concluded that the charges had been grossly exaggerated, and proceeded, according to Arnold, to celebrate their findings with a night of drinking. However, Hill issued an order that no further cruel or unusual punishments, such as hanging by the thumbs, would be allowed. Grenfell, nevertheless, remained a marked man.

There followed a period of relative tranquility on Garden Key, during which Dr. Mudd concerned himself with reports of John Surratt's impending trial. Rumors were rife that the four state prisoners would be called to testify in Washington. "We . . . have very little hope of this small boon being offered us," Mudd wrote, but "Should Surratt have a speedy and impartial trial, I have more hopes from its results than from everything else, for I know it is bound to lead to my entire exculpation, and it will be impossible for those in power to hold me against the will of an enlightened public."[8]

"When rogues fall out, honest men get their due," the doctor had written to Frances. In Washington the rogues were falling out, though not perhaps the ones he had in mind. In the disgraceful charge of treason brought against the President and in attempts to build a conspiracy case against Jefferson Davis (with hopes of involving Johnson), false witnesses had been discredited. Sanford Conover, one of the government's leading witnesses, was jailed for perjury; other witnesses turned out to be, respectively, a former burglar, a quack physician, an army deserter, a convicted horsethief; four or more confessed to having fabricated evidence.

In the nation's eyes, at least, the War Department and the Bureau of Military Justice no longer appeared lily-white. But Stanton and the Radicals were far from fazed. Congress passed, over Johnson's veto, the First Reconstruction Act, supplanting provisional governments throughout the South with military rule; they followed that with the Tenure of Office Act, forbidding the President to remove from office any member of his cabinet.

Over the President's vetoes the Radicals had pushed through measures annulling all of Johnson's, and before him, Lincoln's program of fair treatment for the South. Stanton, along with such men as that archtraitor (in Mudd's eyes) Henry Winter Stevens of Maryland, had led the Reconstruc-

tion move. In the early summer Johnson thought of removing
Stanton, despite the Tenure of Office Act, but resisted the
impulse. Then the President made "the appalling discovery"
that a recommendation of mercy for Mrs. Surratt, which
the military commission had appended to its summary of
the trial two years before, had been withheld from him. He
could only attribute this delinquency to Stanton. He suspended Stanton and replaced him temporarily with General
Ulysses Grant—thereby defying Congress and laying the
grounds for his subsequent impeachment.

The battle lines were clearly drawn, the troops engaged.
In Dr. Mudd's eyes it was not simply a falling out of rogues,
but an army of rogues arrayed against the President—and
he was in Andrew Johnson's corner.

On Garden Key the era of restraint toward, and better
treatment of, the prisoners ended when General Hill was
transferred to a new department post at Key West. Command
of the fort was temporarily assigned to Major Valentine H.
Stone of the 5th U.S. Artillery. Stone brought with him a
rumor that all the prisoners, their number now reduced to
forty-five, would be moved to Ship Island near the Mississippi
Delta, a sandspit made famous in December, 1814, as the
bridgehead for the British invasion of Louisiana. The rumor
proved no more valid than the earlier report that Mudd,
Arnold, Spangler and O'Laughlin would be furloughed to
testify at John Surratt's arraignment.

Stone's younger brother, Henry, had served with the Confederate raider John Hunt Morgan in St. Leger Grenfell's
time. Hearing that Grenfell was in the Dry Tortugas, Henry
wrote to the major requesting that he do all possible "to
alleviate the prison life of [his] old army friend . . . a true
soldier and a gentleman." Presumably, Stone was ready to
comply. But Grenfell was his own worst enemy. Finally
allowed outside his cell to work in the prison yard, he complained that the labor was too arduous.

What happened next was described in somewhat different
terms by Dr. Mudd, Samuel Arnold and the Englishman
himself. Grenfell was seen by Arnold "moving along like

one writhing in pain, scarcely able to place one foot before the other. . . . Every feature of his face plainly showed his condition, proving in most unmistakable terms that he was quite ill."

Grenfell did in fact complain to Dr. James Holden, the post physician, that he was too racked by rheumatism and lumbago to stoop or carry bricks. The doctor examined him, found nothing seriously wrong, and sent him back to his duties. The colonel turned "sullen and refractory" and refused to obey, at which point Lieutenant Frederick Robinson, acting provost marshal for the day, took over. He again ordered Grenfell back to work and the Englishman again refused. He would perform any duties within his power, he protested, but hauling bricks was beyond his strength.

"This was all that was needed to fire the blood of his jailor," wrote Samuel Arnold, who recorded Grenfell's subsequent ordeal in purple prose. "Bound around his body, from the feet upward to his neck in cords, he was tied to the same iron bars by which the tortured prisoner Dunn had suffered martyrdom and in this erect position, unable to move hand, foot, or body, remained like a statue during the morning . . . the piercing rays of the sun shining down in full force upon his venerable gray hairs. . . ."[9]

After seven hours on this grid, "devoured by mosquitoes," Grenfell was again asked if he would carry the bricks. "I told them I could not." Robinson then ordered the guards to bring some rope and Grenfell was pushed across the draw-bridge to the waterfront. There, he related:

> I was laid down on the wharf, my hands tied savagely behind me so as to cut all the skin round my wrists, and I was thrown off into twenty-five feet of water. Unfortunately I could swim very well thus tied, so they hauled me on shore again & tied my legs. Still by great exertion I managed to float, and I was once more hauled in. . .
>
> This time they sunk me by iron weights attached to my feet and when insensible they hauled me up again. When recovered I was asked if I would carry bricks. Upon my saying I could not, in I went. . . . This was repeated three

times until . . . I fainted off entirely and was put on some
blankets to recover as best I could. Every time I was brought
out of the water Robinson would kick me. My ribs, elbows
and hands were stripped to the skin through these kicks.[10]

Dr. Mudd's account of the unsavory incident agrees in
essentials with St. Leger Grenfell's. Arnold's version adds
some dialogue that the author purportedly overheard. After
two duckings with the iron weights, Grenfell said to Robinson
and the guards: "Gentlemen, if it is your intention to murder
me, do it in a respectable manner, and I will thank you for
the act."

"Damn you, you deserve to die," an officer replied.

Said Grenfell, "I leave God to judge between us which
is worse, gentlemen, you or I."[11]

Dr. Mudd added a concluding comment: Though Grenfell
was "an old man, about sixty . . . they could not conquer
him."

Grenfell was returned to solitary confinement in the dungeon until, in late spring, Major Stone was replaced by Major
George P. Andrews, 5th U.S. Infantry. The new commander
relaxed the restrictions on the rebel prisoner, relieved him
of heavy work, and allowed him to return to the care of
his garden. Even Grenfell was forced to admit of Andrews,
"I really have not a fault to find with him." Dr. Mudd wrote
to Frances, "From the slight acquaintance I have had, he
seems quite a good man. Nearly all the older officers have
been relieved; the present number seem much kinder and
better disposed."[12]

Things were moving fast on the outer fringes of Mudd's
life. Early in May, Jefferson Davis was released on bond from
Fortress Monroe and allowed to go to Canada. Mudd
regarded this as a strange but happy development, a weaken-
ing of the despotic government that kept him in Fort Jefferson. "Rage has become impotent," he wrote to Frances,
"the bloodthirsty wretches, feeling no longer security in
their demon pursuits, have shrunk away into ignominious
nothingness, or are crying under the weight of a guilty conscience." If the government freed the leader of the Confeder-

ate rebellion, surely his own freedom was not far behind.

A few weeks later, on June 10, the trial of John Harrison Surratt began. If Mudd anticipated that Surratt would get the same sort of drumhead trial he had suffered at the Old Penitentiary, he was proven wrong. Though the trial aroused almost as much excitement, national sentiment had undergone a change. The public was crying more for justice than for vengeance. In contrast to the forbidding guardroom of the Old Penitentiary, the Criminal Court of the District of Columbia, lodged in the west wing of the City Hall, seemed to commentator David DeWitt to be "the very sanctuary of even-handed justice." Above all, it was not to be a military trial—the Supreme Court's Milligan decision had seen to that. Surratt would appear before a jury of civilians, six from the South (including Maryland), four from the North.

There is no evidence that David DeWitt was present at that trial, but he seemed to catch its intrinsic drama in the paragraph:

> One overmastering impression there was, striking awe into the heart of the most indifferent spectator. All felt that the woman who had suffered the extreme penalty of the law two years before was again on trial with her son, and, as the defendant stood in the flesh with upraised hand to answer the indictment, the ghost of his mother seemed to hover above his head, echoing with shadowy lips the plea of not guilty, with the feeble repetition of which she had tottered to the scaffold.[13]

It was a trial of fearful import for the government. If the prosecution failed to get a conviction—or worse, were the prisoner acquitted—then the previous sentence of Mary Surratt by the military commission would seem to constitute "judicial murder." Not only was John Surratt on trial but so in a sense was the court that had convicted Dr. Mudd, Arnold, Spangler, and O'Laughlin.

Significantly, one of Surratt's defense attorneys was Richard Merrick, the lawyer who was becoming increasingly involved with attempts to secure the release of Dr. Mudd. Success with Surratt would seem to foretell at least a promise of success with Mudd. "In case of his [Surratt's] acquittal," the doctor wrote to Frances, "I cannot see upon what pretext they can hold me." He could not resist, however, adding the gloomy comment that "had Surratt been on the same trial that I was, he would certainly have been hung, though innocent—no amount of evidence in his favor could have saved him."[14]

The prosecution based its case on evidence that Surratt had been in Washington on the night of the assassination. Fourteen witnesses were bribed, cajoled, and coerced into testifying to that fact. But their appearance and testimony were so unconvincing that defense attorneys Joseph Bradley and Richard Merrick tore them to shreds. Even Louis Wiechmann, reappearing for the prosecution, seemed more intent on saving his shaky reputation than on convicting John Surratt. He did not mention the defendant's name.

There was another important result of the proceedings. The diary of John Wilkes Booth, concealed during Dr. Mudd's trial, was brought forcibly to light. Lafayette Baker had privately published his *History of the Secret Service*, in which he mentioned giving the diary to Stanton after Booth's death in Virginia. The public and the defense attorneys—and even, for appearances' sake, the prosecutors—demanded that the diary be produced. It was—with eighteen pages missing! All Booth's entries leading up to the time of Lincoln's murder had been excised. By whom? Certainly not by Booth himself, who cherished the record for posterity. The finger of guilt was pointed at Secretary Stanton and the War Department.

Among the pages left intact was Booth's entry dated April 14, 1865: "For six months we have worked to capture, but our cause being almost lost, something decisive and great must be done. . . ." Worked to *capture,* not to kill. With no adequate proof of John Surratt's presence in Washington on April 14, he was obviously not involved in any murder plot. Neither, obviously, was Dr. Mudd, who could not have known, at his distant home in Maryland, of the actor's last-minute change of plans.

"I have seen Booth's diary," the doctor wrote to Frances, referring no doubt to reprints of the document in Baltimore and New York papers. "It shows clearly that I could have had no knowledge of the deed, and [it] would have tended, had it been before the Court, to establish my innocence." Certainly had the diary been produced in evidence during the trial of the conspirators in 1865 it would have given the defense some weighty, if not decisive, ammunition.

Equally significant was the record of Booth's flight through southern Maryland. Of the night of the killing the assassin wrote: "In jumping, broke my leg. I passed all the pickets. Rode sixty miles that night, with the bone of my leg tearing the flesh at every jump." Thence to his hiding in the swamp, with no mention of his having stopped at Dr. Mudd's for treatment—apparently a fortuitous incident not worthy of citing in this, his final testament.

The omission of Samuel Mudd's name from that testament was in itself revealing. Booth had pointedly mentioned Paine, Atzerodt, and Herold in the letter he gave to Matthews for delivery to the press. He had pointedly mentioned Herold again as his aid in the flight through Maryland. Considering his obvious urge to reward his accomplices with proper billing in the act, his disinclination to credit John and Mary Surratt and Samuel Mudd with any aid whatever seemed significant.

The sixty-two-day trial ended in early August with an evenly divided jury confessing itself "unable to reach a verdict." The prisoner was remanded into custody and a retrial scheduled for early in 1868. But the case against John Surratt had run out of steam, and the likelihood of a retrial seemed remote.

Dr. Mudd had followed the trial, as reported in the Baltimore *Gazette*, with extreme impatience. He fully expected, as he wrote to Frances, that Surratt, like himself, would be convicted on the basis of prejudice and perjured testimony. In letter after letter he chafed at delays in the proceedings and alternated between optimism and despair. He would be satisfied if the trial had no other consequence than "to clear away many of the mists that surround the tragic affair and lead to my early release from this place of exile and misery. . . . To this end, my darling Frank, are all my fondest anticipations centered."

At the trial's conclusion, however, with the jury hung and

no verdict reached and the whole dreary business left in limbo, he sank back into the posture of despair. "For God's sake," he wrote to Frances, "urge action on the part of those entrusted with the care of my case. Davis has been set free, and Surratt, once regarded as his prime agent, seems now without a charge against him, and here am I, having suffered the tortures of the damned, without one word of rebuke to those who have caused all—and without pity, sympathy, or consolation from an enlightened public."[15]

As the summer wore on, the weather turned hot, cloudy, and rainy in the Dry Tortugas. The doctor sank into a lethargy of discontent. With nothing immediate to complain of, he brooded upon past injustices. "We were fed like brutes for more than fourteen months, kept in chains over three months . . . under close guard day and night. . . . Had we been ordered out and shot, it would have been much kinder than the treatment we received."

In spite of the heat, he was forced to wear heavy clothing as protection against the "millions of tiny mosquitoes" that attacked the prisoners in droves. The prison fare had worsened. "We have been entirely without vegetables of every description for a considerable time, and the rations are principally salt pork and indifferent bread." The climate at that time of year he found "very debilitating in itself."

He refused the request of an unidentified photographer to have his picture taken, but, approaching age thirty-four, sent Frances a conscientious summary of his appearance:

> . . . my hair is considerably thinner, consequently the bald head more perceptible, and no doubt larger in circumference. I have no wrinkles, and wear constantly a mustache and goatee. Owing to the peculiarity of my skin, and not much exposed to the sun, I am paler or fairer than when I left home. I may be a few pounds lighter, perhaps about a hundred and forty-four or five. My manners about the same, impulsive, etc. Generally have but little to say, but think a great deal. I am very weak, though in appearance strong. This I think is attributable to the climate and the want of free exercise.[16]

Even under their new, supposedly "humane" commander, Major Andrews, Mudd found the prison rules "more barbarous than ages bygone—refusing to work or obey an order, is punishable with instant death by shooting." That this was no exaggeration seems evident in "Special Order No. 78," posted that summer at the fort, from which this extract:

> In future every sentinel must use his bayonet and cartridge, and no sentinel who faithfully tries to do his duty shall ever see the inside of the Guard House: if a prisoner refuses to obey orders, the sentinel must shoot him and then use his bayonet, at the same time calling for the guard.

Samuel Arnold quoted Major Andrews as saying that the order was not of his doing, that the edict had come from Stanton. Be that as it may, the license to murder without fear of punishment brought quick results. Two weeks later, Mudd recorded, an ex-deserter named John Winters was shot to death by Private Perry Coffman of the 5th U.S. Artillery, who claimed to have found the prisoner in a "drunk and unruly" condition. "Instead of meeting with rebuke," wrote Dr. Mudd, "the soldier was commended for his conduct."

At this low point in his life, Mudd considered the murdered Winters lucky and wondered how long before he and his fellow prisoners would meet the same fate. Writing to Frances on the last day of July, he closed with the plaint, "I don't think Job had greater misfortunes than have been visited upon us."

Greater misfortunes, however, were impending.

19

A TIME FOR DYING

TO every thing there is a season, and . . . a time to die. The autumn of 1867 was a time for dying. They had been brought to the Dry Tortugas for that purpose, the state prisoners believed. Garden Key was not an island but a place of execution; Fort Jefferson was not a prison but a tomb.

They were not merely expendable. They were, of political necessity, doomed. So long as they remained alive, with voices to be heard, the myth of the Great Conspiracy, the rule of the Radicals in Washington, was threatened. It had been evident to Samuel Arnold and St. Leger Grenfell when the prisoner stricken with smallpox had been placed in the adjoining cell. The intention had been that the ill man should infect them with the disease.

Samuel Mudd, with a better, though incomplete, knowledge of medicine, harbored no such fantasy. In fact, he considered the island fairly immune to epidemic, owing largely to its isolation. Yet he also knew the Dry Tortugas formed the buckle in the yellow fever belt that extended in an arc from Central America and Mexico across the Gulf to Cuba and the Leeward Islands.

The Yellow Jack was a curse the white man had imported to the New World on his slavers along with the greater curse of slavery itself. In 1867 none was aware that the disease was of African origin, carried by the deadly *Aedes Aegypti* mosquito. For the most part the black man was immune to the disease by long exposure; for the whites the deadly *vomito negro*, or black vomit, could prove fatal.

Down through the centuries it had claimed untold thousands of victims, with a mortality rate—sometimes as high as ninety percent—greater than the Black Death of the fourteenth century or London's Great Plague of 1665. For the West Indies' planters it had turned the sunny Caribbean into a sea of the dead, from which flight was the only escape. It had killed off two-thirds of the British forces besieging Cartagena in the War of Jenkin's Ear, and some fifty years later, in 1853, had savagely struck the city of New Orleans.

The New Orleans epidemic, like the previous plagues, was attributed to "diffusable miasma" aggravated by "the filthy conditions of the place." The solution was to keep one's windows tightly closed. A Dr. Josiah Nott of Alabama suggested it might be caused by the mosquito and was squelched by ridicule. Not until 1881 would Dr. Carlos Finley pin yellow fever on the African mosquito whose larvae found a fertile breeding ground in the water casks carried on ships from the Dark Continent.

"Flight, fumigation, cremation of corpses—nothing proved of the slightest avail against the pestilence," wrote Simon Harcourt-Smith in a recent history of the disease. "It defied all habitual methods of attack, such as quarantine and segregation." Further:

> Its symptoms were numerous and horrible—violent pains in head and stomach, sometimes also in loins, arms and legs. Then the agony would spread to the stomach, and after a few hours would come the vomit, black and greasy. Next occurred, almost inevitably, an eruption of red and purple spots all over the body. The fever seems rarely to have taken more than four or five days to reach its climax. During the last stages the victim would decline into a coma, with a rapid pulse that increased in shallowness, till death mercifully ensued.[1]

None of the cases Dr. Mudd had seen in student days at Baltimore had proven fatal, and he was not much concerned with rumors that instances of Yellow Jack had appeared at New Orleans and Key West. He was preoccupied that summer with his carpentry, making crabwood canes and cribbage boards and teaching Michael O'Laughlin, who seemed more dependent on his friendship than the other prisoners, to fashion crabwood crosses to send as gifts to friends in Baltimore.

Needless to say, he was gratified with Johnson's removal of Secretary Stanton. But unhappily—perhaps forgivably, considering the torment he had suffered—he began to side with those who accused Johnson of complicity in the assassination plot. Why had Johnson not charged Stanton with "wilfully withholding" the diary of John Wilkes Booth, a document that might have cleared the falsely convicted prisoners? "His silence upon this point leads me to suspicion that he had a knowledge of all that was going on, and lent his approval to the cruel and barbarous wrong."

The first week of August one of the garrison officers, Captain George W. Crabbe, returned from a furlough in Havana complaining of a fever. As a precaution he was isolated in the prison hospital, where the fever rose. His lips and nostrils became scarlet with congestion; his pulse grew feeble; his skin turned lemon yellow. Vomiting started, clear at first, then black with blood, accompanied by delirium. In five days Crabbe was dead.

It was a week, Mudd remembered, when the island, enveloped in a constant rain and millions of mosquitoes, was becoming "sickly." Unaware then that the infection had been brought from Cuba the doctor wrote to Frances on August 25:

> We have had one case of yellow fever since I last wrote, which proved fatal. It originated here, and was not imported. A general renovation has ensued, which for the future will prevent its recurrence. I have no fears regarding it, which is its greatest preventive.[2]

The renovation consisted principally of boarding up the south side of the fort, where the surrounding moat had been only half-completed, as protection against the "deadly miasma" originating in the moat. Since he was working in the carpentry shop, Dr. Mudd was among those detailed to this assignment. During the operation, he observed, cogitated, began taking notes and making charts.

He believed with the post physician, Joseph Smith—who admitted later that he had never seen a case of the disease —that the fever was caused by germs borne by the prevailing wind or rising with the poisonous effluvia from the stagnant moat. Further, that it was transmitted by contact or proximity. As the infection spread and more cases developed he made charts of the locations of the casemates and the disposition of the cots in each, drawing arrows to indicate the course of the disease from room to room and bed to bed. He was devising his own mistaken methods of combatting the disease, based on what he had learned at the College of Medicine in Baltimore.

The day after he had written his previous letter to Frances, which he had not yet sealed and mailed, he added a postscript dated August 26:

> The weather has been calm for several days, and very warm, causing no doubt the generation of the peculiar poison which gives rise to the disease. Water and everything in the shape of vegetation rapidly undergoes decomposition here. The sea water suffered to stand in a bucket two or three hours becomes very offensive to the smell.[3]

The pestilence started gently, without terror or alarm. Suddenly it became a cataclysm, riding like the pale Fourth Horseman on a raging wind. One after another, men staggered to the prison hospital, throats inflamed, eyes weeping pus, limbs weak, intestines burning. There were five deaths in the next two days, and a score of new cases in the hospital.

To isolate the patients and supposedly prevent the spread of the disease, a new hospital was hastily constructed on Sand Key, and one company of the 5th Artillery was moved to an improvised camp on the adjacent Bird Key to escape infection. Perhaps it was only natural that this evacuation should arouse in Mudd some hope for his own removal to another prison, on the mainland, perhaps, even in the North. Anywhere that hope was not so totally abandoned.

"The outbreak of fever ought to furnish reasonable cause for our removal to a more healthy locality," he wrote to Frances on September 3. On Garden Key the disease would "most likely become epidemic" since there was no frost, no change of climate, and the woolen clothes and blankets the prisoners and guards were given "will serve as retentives of the poison or miasma." Since the War Department would quickly learn of the crisis, "You can advise with friends, and act as seems most fit. Humanity, apart from every other reason, ought to prompt our removal."[4]

But circumstances, as the rise of the disease became a tidal wave, cut off all hope of their removal. Fort Jefferson was quarantined, a plague ship in a pestilential sea. Supply ships from New Orleans and Key West would not approach the island; or if they arrived at all would send provisions, mostly medical supplies, ashore by tender. One by one, the garrison officers came down with the affliction, creating a state of panic and near anarchy on Garden Key.

Dr. Mudd was, of course, not working at the hospital since his escape attempt two years before. The current post physician, Brevet Major Joseph Sim Smith, was new to the job, having arrived some six weeks earlier. But the two doctors had had time to get acquainted—especially when they discovered they had Maryland friends in common. Smith had brought with him his wife and two small children, one a four-year-old son named Henry Prince, whom both Mudd and Grenfell had befriended, telling the youngster stories, teaching him sleight-of-hand tricks, making toys for his amusement in the carpentry shop.

On September 4 Dr. Smith himself came down with the fever, as did his wife, and almost two-thirds of the prison inmates. Except for ill-trained nurses and an ill-equipped, small hospital, the island was totally unqualified to cope with the disease. And now its only doctor was disabled. Samuel Mudd was faced with a soul-examining decision. He owed these people, who had been his captors and to some extent his persecutors, nothing. Nothing, perhaps, except retaliation or revenge.

Recording his thoughts at the time, he reviewed "the dread ordeal through which I had passed"—the military trial, the perjured testimony, the prejudiced commissioners who had robbed him of liberty, banished him to this island far from family and friends, subjected him to menial labor in chains and under guard—all for treating the injury "of a man for

whose insane act I had no sympathy, but which was in the
line of my professional calling."

His emotions revolved around "a horrid recollection of
the past." He considered his responsibility as a physician confronted by an epidemic. "Can I be a passive beholder? Shall
I withhold the little service I might be capable of rendering?...."
On the other hand, suppose he offered to the commandant
his services as doctor, and one or more of his patients died?
Was there not a likelihood that as a prisoner suspected of
the worst of crimes, he would be accused of murder, or at
best deliberate malfeasance? While pondering this question,
Mudd recalled:

> . . . a fellow prisoner remarked, "Doctor, the yellow fever
> is the fairest and squarest thing I have seen the past four
> or five years. It makes no distinction in regard to rank,
> color, or previous condition—every man has his chance,
> and I would advise you as a friend not to interfere." Another
> said it was only a little Southern opposition to Recon-
> struction, and thought the matter ought to be reported
> to Congress in order that a law might be passed lowering
> the temperature below zero, which would most effectually
> put an end to its disloyalty.[5]

Dr. Mudd ignored both the advice and the buffoonery.
He made up his mind, he recorded, on consideration of
the Christian precept, "Do ye good for evil." Actually one
wonders if the challenge to fulfill the role he had aspired
to throughout his adult life, that of applying his knowledge
of medicine to healing the sick, was not a stronger motive.
Feeling diffident about approaching Major Stone, now in
provisional command, he asked Arnold to carry his offer
of medical service to the major. Nearing the officers' quarters,
Arnold met the major, who was on his way to ask Dr. Mudd
to fill in as post physician for the ailing Smith until other
help could be obtained.

The arrangement was settled. Mudd was relieved of all
prison assignments and restrictions and given complete medical direction of the stricken Garden Key community. For
a man considered "timid," he was extraordinarily decisive.
Over Major Stone's objections he decreed that the Sand Key

Hospital be closed. The two-and-a-half-mile ride across open water, often in inclement weather, was disastrous for the ailing prisoners; virtually every man hospitalized on Sand Key died. Grudgingly, the major acquiesced. Four casemates in the fort and a section of the barracks were sealed off as hospital wards, and the patients' own beds and blankets were moved into these quarters.

The doctor also demanded and received a remarkable concession. The narrowness of the rifle slits, in the casemates and the bastions, helped, he believed, to contain the deadly miasma. Regardless of their importance to security, he ordered them blasted wide by dynamite and axe. A century later, the once-mightiest fortress on the continent, believed impervious to cannon fire, displayed the huge gaps wrought by a modest, rural doctor from Charles County, Maryland —the only damage the fort had ever suffered, or would ever suffer, from the hand of man.

Briefly, the drastic measures seemed effective. But Dr. Smith remained "delirious and unmanageable from the beginning," Mudd reported. "I could by no means induce him to take medicine." On September 7, four days after he was stricken, the post physician died. Even the acrimonious Arnold mourned his passing. During the army surgeon's short term on the island he had striven to correct "the abuse and reigning terrors which abounded" in the prison and, in Arnold's words, was "a man of humanity and kindness, a gentleman by birth and culture . . . good, noble, pure and upright." His was one of the few graves on the island over which a monument was raised.

On the southwest corner of Duval and Whitehead streets in Key West stood a house built of planks salvaged by wreckers in the early decades of the century. Silver-gray with weather and age, it was the home of Dr. Daniel W. Whitehurst, who, at sixty, was a quiet cultivated gentleman of education, travel and experience.

Whitehurst had in his lifetime, been a soldier, lawyer, editor, and doctor; had fought in the Seminole wars, then studied medicine, finally moved from his native Virginia to Florida to found the St. Augustine *News*. In 1842 he married Henrietta Weedon, dark-haired beauty of the oldest city in the South, only daughter of Dr. Frederick Weedon, who had served with Andrew Jackson in the Florida invasion. Weedon had attended Osceola during the Seminole leader's imprisonment in Fort Moultrie. When the Indian chieftain died, Weedon cut off his head and presented it to his son-in-law as a wedding gift.

Whitehurst brought both his bride and Osceola's head to Key West in 1845, shortly thereafter to serve for fourteen years as post physician at Fort Jefferson during the fort's unending construction. Came the war, and Henrietta's pro-Southern views were too outspoken. Whitehurst was expelled from the fort and forced into semiretirement at Key West.[6]

On September 7, 1867, he received a wire from the War Department. Army surgeon Joseph Smith had died; Fort Jefferson was paralyzed by yellow fever. In view of his previous experience, the Department requested that Whitehurst resume his post at Garden Key for the duration of the crisis. There was no time to settle details such as rank and salary. Whitehurst sailed immediately for the Dry Tortugas and arrived at Garden Key the following day.

He found conditions even worse than indicated by the War Department. Of the roughly 400 people on the island —soldiers, officers, and prisoners—270 had been stricken by the fever. Five of the six high-ranking officers were either dead or dying. All army discipline had given way to makeshift hospital routine. And the only person in command of this chaotic situation was an out-of-practice country doctor from south-county Maryland.

Whitehurst was impressed with Dr. Mudd's direction and accomplishments—so much that he later wrote with admiration of his "patient and noble conduct during the duration of my stay." Mudd was at first not equally impressed with Whitehurst, who automatically became his superior. He found him "very old and a little slow in his actions and treatment. The disease being quick, has to be treated vigorously from the start." But he commended Dr. Whitehurst's "Christian, constant, and unremitting attention" to his many patients "at all hours, even when duty seemed not to require."[7]

They worked well together. Though Mudd had expected to be relieved of authority with Whitehurst's arrival,

Whitehurst treated him as an equal, deferred to his decisions, was appreciative of his careful charting of the course of the disease. They divided their time unequally in a rotating schedule, Mudd on duty from seven in the morning until midnight, Whitehurst serving from midnight until noon. Volunteer nurses from the able-bodied prisoners and garrison, though generally without experience, accompanied the doctors on their rounds.

Among those volunteers was St. Leger Grenfell, who typically appointed himself to the post of "chief nurse." From his buccaneering days in South America he knew well the sights, signs, and smells of the disease and believed with the others that the fever was transmitted by proximity or contact. Hence, to his credit, he willingly faced a danger as great as he had formerly experienced in battle. Wrote his biographer, Stephen Starr:

> The same man who was capable of magnifying minor irritations and grievances to the point of outright falsehood, went about his self-imposed, loathsome duties of mercy at the risk of his life, without self-pity or heroics, or without ulterior motives. He expended on complete strangers, guards and prisoners alike—all the tenderness, pity, self-sacrifice, and even love, which for so many years had been without an outlet except for his devotion to his horses and dogs.[8]

By mid-September the epidemic raged beyond control, sweeping like a hurricane through every corner of the fort. On the sixteenth, Dr. Mudd recorded that "a small rain cloud arose to the south of the fort, accompanied rapidly by a heavy wind, which lasted about twenty minutes . . . and blew directly toward Company M, and the night following every man went to bed in his usual health, yet between eleven and one o'clock nearly one half of the company, or thirty men, were attacked with the most malignant form of the disease—beginning at the point nearest the hospitals and extending thirty beds without missing or skipping a single occupant."

Cut off from contact with the outside world, prisoners

and garrison were reduced to a diet of what they had left
of salt pork and salt beef. Those still able hunted for sea
turtles on the beach, slaughtered what they caught for meat,
or gathered up their eggs. Without fruit or vegetables, the
ravages of scurvy were added to the scourge of yellow fever;
those who escaped or recovered from one might well die
of the other.

Death was an assembly-line procedure. Coffins were placed
beside the cots of those expected to succumb so that they
might be quickly removed to make room for the waiting
patients. Morning, afternoon and evening, volunteer Cha-
rons would row across the Styx to Bird Key, fortified with
whiskey, to bury their loads and row back for the next contingent. "No more respect is shown to the dead," Mudd wrote
to Frances, "than to the putrid remains of a dead horse.
They are buried to get rid of the stench and infection."

Mrs. Smith, wife of the deceased physician, finally recovered, but her young son Henry Prince, whom Mudd favored
above all his patients ("He used to turn somersaults to amuse
me") caught and succumbed to the infection. Mrs. Stone,
wife of the commandant, died swiftly of the fever. Without
waiting to see his wife buried, Major Stone fled the island
with his only daughter, first promising Dr. Mudd that he
would say a good word for him in Washington and even
speak to General Grant about the doctor's self-sacrificing
service. He was never able to fulfill that promise. Before
reaching Key West, he died aboard the ship.

Major Stone's precipitous departure left the fort without
a commander, an extraordinary situation for an army post.
Of the six officers above the rank of sergeant, four were
dead and two were convalescent. Command as well as responsibility devolved upon Drs. Mudd and Whitehurst. Prison
discipline was no problem. Though restrictions and routine
had been abandoned, a sense of kinship had developed
between prisoners and garrison. A common terror seemed
to bind them in a common loyalty. Wrote Samuel Arnold:
"The island which before was more like a place peopled by
fiends, than anything else it could be compared with, suddenly became calm, quiet and peaceful. Fear stood out in
bold relief upon the face of every human soul."

Garden Key became in fact, an island of the dead, where those who walked trod softly and spoke in whispers. No vessels dared approach, and the mail from New Orleans and Key West was hung on a pole erected on Loggerhead Key, to be picked up by a rowboat from the fort. Only the black troops and prisoners seemed immune to the disease, but all shared a zombielike existence, thinking little, caring little, saying little. The wife of Lieutenant Elliott Gordon of Baltimore, one of the officers who later died, recorded her impressions in a letter to her parents:

> The whole island became one immense hospital. The silence was oppressive beyond description. There were no soldiers for drill or parade, and the gloom was indescribable. Five hundred at one time would scarcely cover the list of sick. . . . Those able to move about looked like ghosts. The mercury was 104 in the hospital. . . . We seemed in some horrible nightmare. It was terrible beyond description to be hemmed in by those high, literally red-hot brick walls, with so much suffering. I would see the beds brought out, hoping for a breath of air to fan the burning brow and fever-parched lips. There was nothing to brighten the cloud of despair that encompassed the island.[9]

Of the five state prisoners, Arnold was first to fall prey to the epidemic. Mudd kept him in their casemate quarters, separated from the others, and alone attended to his needs. Arnold was on his way toward recovery when O'Laughlin was stricken by the fever. He too remained in the cell and appeared to be recovering when, on September 21, he went into convulsions. By constant nursing and cold applications, Mudd and Ned Spangler kept him alive for thirty-six hours. Then, as if by appointment, O'Laughlin sat up, shook hands with his cellmates, said goodbye to each, and died.

Next to the loss of little "Harry" Stone, the doctor was most grievously affected by O'Laughlin's death. He had been closer to Mike than to any of the others, had found him more sympathetic, easier to talk to. He later wrote of O'Laughlin, "I never met with one more kind and forebearing, possessing a warm friendly disposition and a fine comprehensive intellect."

Apart from the human loss, he regarded O'Laughlin's
death as "a stain upon the country." The youth had been
murdered not by yellow fever but by Stanton, Baker, Johnson,
Holt, and all the rest who had sent him to this place. He
found wry amusement in the fact that the army had lost
dozens of its better soldiers, several of its finer officers, to
yellow fever—all for the principal purpose of keeping five
alleged conspirators (now reduced to four) in this inferno.
The government, he thought, had "paid too high a price
for the pleasures of vengeance."

Toward the end of that September there were scarcely
half a dozen on the island who had not been attacked by
the epidemic; the rest were either dead or convalescent, with
many suffering either from scurvy or a recurrence of the
fever. "But ten men appear at roll call," he wrote to Frances,
"and not more than twenty fit for duty in garrison." Mudd
himself was suffering from near exhaustion, dragging himself, bone-tired, from one improvised ward to another, up
at dawn and on his feet till after midnight. He wrote that
he was not sure whether his headaches and weariness were
symptoms of yellow fever, or simply the result of lack of
sleep and constant pressure.

Next on the sick list was St. Leger Grenfell. He had spent
twenty-three days and nights attending to the sick, catching
what little sleep he could, with only two nights spent in bed,
when the combination of fatigue and inadequate food caught
up with him. On September 24 he was stricken, and Dr.
Mudd gave him as much personal attention as he could spare.
In view of Grenfell's age, he thought the colonel's chances
doubtful. Grenfell himself later wrote that he had hoped
to die; he had had his fill of prison and looked to the grave
for his release.

Mudd never gave up on "St. Lege." A man who had fought
so many enemies, so gallantly, could not surrender now. And
surprisingly, though his life hung briefly in the balance, he
survived; he took, however, a full month of convalescence
to regain his strength.

Throughout the weeks of epidemic, when the whole fort
looked to them and them alone for courage and survival,

a strong bond developed between Mudd and Whitehurst. Mutual admiration, too. Normally diffident, the Maryland doctor recovered, under Whitehurst's fatherly aegis, the pride of profession he had first experienced working under Samuel Chew in Baltimore. He wrote glowingly to Jeremiah Dyer of Whitehurst's night-and-day devotion to his patients, "doing all that human judgment and skill can effect, without the hope of any other reward than that promised to those who do unto others as they wish to be done by."

The War Department, however, was less enthusiastic about Whitehurst; he and his wife were Virginians, and hence suspect. He had been useful as a stopgap in an emergency, but on September 25 he was replaced by a "contract physician" from New York, Dr. Edward Thomas. No doubt with some relief, Whitehurst packed up and sailed for Key West—back to Henrietta but not to Osceola's head. Taking advantage of her husband's absence, Henrietta had sent the grisly trophy to a medical-school museum in New York City.

Forty-seven days after the beginning of the epidemic, the fever appeared to have passed its peak. Three hundred had been stricken, yet, remarkably, only forty had died—a low mortality rate, which the garrison and prisoners attributed in large degree to Dr. Mudd's unflagging care and common-sense approach to the disease. The doctor himself was weary and depressed, as he recorded in his journal on October 4, "and after finishing my bowl of coffee and slice of bread, I fell upon my rude cot to spend a few minutes of repose."

An hour later he was tossing and mumbling in his sleep; and Ned Spangler, who had joked his way through the period of trial, amusing the sick with his "ready wit," became concerned. He positioned himself outside the cell and turned back all intruders, stating that "the doctor was feeling unwell," was taking a nap, and would return to the hospital within an hour.

Possibly the arrival of Dr. Thomas, sent to relieve him, permitted the doctor to yield to a weakness he might otherwise have struggled to resist. Fortunately, the epidemic had abated, and his was not a virulent attack. He was in bed for only two weeks, during which Dr. Thomas took over his now greatly diminished duties. Spangler and Arnold, the latter recovered, nursed him around the clock, following Mudd's own instructions. "I owe my life to the unremitting care which they bestowed," the doctor wrote to Frances.

Dr. Thomas, however, took no note whatever of his ailing partner, and, according to Arnold, never came to visit Mudd throughout his illness. With his usually low boiling point, Arnold flared with resentment at what he thought to be the reason. Thomas had been appointed by the War Department, with special instructions to let the "Lincoln assassins" die—especially Dr. Samuel Mudd. What other explanation could there be for Thomas' deliberate neglect? Arnold saw fit to add that throughout Mudd's illness Dr. Thomas "remained closeted in his room, constantly under the influence of liquor, and so continued, it may be truthfully stated, until his contract was annulled."

Whether or not the charge of drunkenness was warranted, Thomas himself was felled by yellow fever almost on the day that Mudd recovered. In fact, his was one of the last cases registered at the hospital. Mudd resumed his role of acting chief physician of the fort. He had only three patients besides Thomas; but he was weak from fever and found the job "unpleasant." He was not sorry to see Thomas leave the island as soon as he was well enough to travel.

He had been too busy to notice the change of attitude toward him among the troops and prisoners. He had never cultivated popularity or been a ready mixer; he had kept to himself and to the company of his cellmates. Yet among the garrison the political prisoners had aroused considerable sympathy. A corporal who signed himself only "A. O'D." sent an account of his experiences to a Northern journal, *The Galaxy Miscellany*, in which he wrote of "the skillful and self-sacrificing service" rendered by Dr. Mudd throughout the epidemic. "I may add that nothing can be more exemplary than the three political prisoners now on the island. They perform the work assigned to them without complaint, and with apparent cheerfulness; if the iron sometimes enters their souls, or the bitterness of their situation be felt, it is never exhibited."[10]

More substantial approbation came when several of the

garrison expressed to the doctor a wish to make his services known outside the fort. He wrote to Frances, "Many have come forward and pressed me to permit them to make some public manifestation of the esteem they hold toward me, but thus far I consider it a superfluous idea, and of no practical value. It could only serve to excite my vanity, which I am in no mood at this time to gratify."

Nevertheless, the entire garrison composed a testimonial to Dr. Mudd's conduct, signed by troops and officers alike, to be sent to the President in Washington. It closed with the paragraph:

> Many here who have experienced his kind and judicious treatment, can never repay him the debt of obligation they owe him. We do, therefore, in consideration of the invaluable services rendered by him during this calamitous and fatal epidemic, earnestly recommend him to the well-merited clemency of the Government, and solicit his immediate release from here, and the restoration to liberty and the bosom of his family.

It could not have been better conceived or better expressed if Mudd himself had written it. Former commander George P. Andrews, now returning to the fort in the wake of Major Stone's departure, took charge of the petition and agreed to send it on its way. The President never saw or heard about it.

20

RESURRECTION

THE siege had ended by the middle of October; the fever had subsided. Only five of the garrison and a few of the prisoners had escaped the epidemic. A number, like Samuel Arnold, still suffered from scurvy or dysentery. But the worst disaster in Fort Jefferson's grim history was over.

In the new atmosphere of camaraderie, old prejudices were discarded and replaced by mutual respect. Prison routine and discipline were reinstated but less rigidly enforced; the guards were more easygoing. The community had been challenged by a crisis, formed a united front, and won. All were entitled now to share the spoils in terms of relaxation and amusement.

Death took a holiday. So did the soldiers and officers according to the private who signed his memoirs only "A. O'D." They organized turtle-hunting expeditions and egg-collecting parties on adjacent keys. "Fat Charley," the prisoner who had deserted at Bull Run, fixed up the garrison boat *Rosetta* for nighttime cruises in the harbor, with Chinese lanterns hanging from the rigging. Devil's Island briefly acquired a different image in the eyes of its beholders, reflected in A. O'D.'s impressions of the period of convalescence and relief:

> In the calm evening it is pleasant from the ramparts to
> watch the golden sun sink to rest, and just as it touches
> the edge of the horizon to hear the bugles sound "Retreat",
> and before the last note of music has died away in space,
> the placid rest broken for a moment by the thunder of

the evening gun; the Stars and Stripes, that have all day
long flaunted their glory from the sallyport, are run down;
the toil of the day, with its petty cares, is over, and some
one, as he breaks ranks, indulges in the by no means original
exclamation, "Another day in for Uncle Sam." The beauty
of the setting sun in this climate surpasses anything I have
elsewhere seen.

A. O'D. added, however, a qualifying comment:

Whether it [the setting sun] is in reality more beautiful
than in other places, or whether being about the only beautiful thing we have here, and on that account liable to be
over-appreciated, I am unable to determine.[1]

A theatrical group, the Tortugas Amateurs, was organized,
with a section of the ground-floor casemates turned into an
auditorium. The regimental band gave concerts in the prison
yard. An orchestra was formed to play at dances in the barracks. If any of the prisoners evinced a talent, he was invited
to sing, dance, or otherwise perform at the impromptu social
gatherings.

In spite of his tendency to remain aloof, Mudd found himself involved in these diversions. He had not even thought
of music for the last three years; now he played almost any
instrument they handed him—to the amusement of St. Leger
Grenfell, who wrote tongue-in-cheek to Henry Stone: "From
a learned Physician, Dr. Mudd has descended to playing the
Fiddle for drunken soldiers to dance to or to form part of
a very miserable orchestra at a still more miserable theatrical
performance. Will wonders never cease? . . ."[2]

The doctor's attitude changed with the changing attitude
toward him. He was no longer a pariah but a hero; and
the guards and garrison seemed eager to do him favors in
return for his momentous service at the hospital.

"I have now all the liberty I could desire here," he wrote
to Frances. "I have plenty of books, papers, and pen and
ink, at my command. I have access to a very choice library
of over five hundred volumes. My fare is as good as the
island can afford, and I am pressed often to accept presents
in the shape of little luxuries from the soldiers. . . . I am

as well now as I ever was with the exception of weakness, and am still doing duty in the hospital."[3]

Though with the arrival of a permanent army surgeon, he was later relieved of his hospital chores, he returned to his work in the carpentry shop without regret. "I have gotten used to my present life, and do not feel much incommoded." His gnawing impatience with prolonged imprisonment had seemingly changed to philosophical acceptance. "When the apples are ripe they will fall without human intervention—so with my release."

The ships were coming in again, bringing such long-missed luxuries as oranges, pineapples, and bananas. The prison fare improved, though somewhat at the prisoners' expense. As Mudd wrote to Frances, "We have pretty constantly on hand Irish potatoes, yams, or sweet potatoes, onions, ham and butter, for which we pay the following prices, viz: ham, thirty cents; butter, seventy cents; Irish potatoes, seven dollars per barrel; yams, seven dollars per barrel; onions, eleven dollars per barrel."

In addition the prisoners received a flood of gifts from those who had read of their past ordeal. John Ford, the theater owner, sent a "very fine barrel of potatoes" to Mudd and his cellmates, who also received "a splendid ham from an unknown party." Varina Davis, wife of the ex-Confederate President, sent Grenfell a suit and a supply of underclothes and shirts.

Grenfell himself, like Dr. Mudd, was enjoying the respect and friendship of the garrison for his ministry to the yellow fever victims. He was back at work in his garden, this time proud of his success. By late winter he boasted of "Tomatoes, Peppers & Melons in full bloom, radishes, Peas & Beans at maturity." He even gloated in letters to England of the warm and pleasant climate of the Dry Tortugas, like a man enjoying a vacation in the sun.

Like Dr. Mudd, however, he was provoked that no clemency was offered in return for his services during the epidemic. Major Andrews had testified to his cooperation, as he had to Dr. Mudd's, Dr. Whitehurst had written of his "generous and invaluable aid." Supposedly, these testimonials had gone to Washington. The British minister, Sir

Frederick Bruce, had died that fall, and his post was now filled by Edward Thornton, whom Grenfell had known in South America.

Yet Thornton could offer no more encouragement than had his predecessor, no greater assurance than Mudd was receiving from Dyer, Frances, and the Washington attorneys. It was the same old story, growing stale with repetition. President Johnson was too deeply engaged in his war with Congress to act on the prisoners' behalf, and so long as Stanton and Holt remained in power, there was little hope for their release.

In December the four state prisoners, including Grenfell, had a visitor. William H. Gleason, an agent for Benjamin Butler's committee investigating Andrew Johnson's connection with Lincoln's murder, arrived at Fort Jefferson to interview the prisoners. Plainly he was looking for evidence, true or false, to implicate the President. Should the prisoners cooperate fully, giving the commission what it was after, they might be called to Washington to testify against the President, and, in reward, quite likely be released.

It was tempting bait. It was also an outrageous proposition, impugning the prisoners' honor and integrity. The prisoners discussed the matter in their cell. Mudd, for one, saw nothing wrong with talking to Gleason, provided that each revealed "nothing more than was known and acknowledged at our trial," with no invented evidence involving others.

Samuel Arnold was first to appear before Gleason. Instead of an interview, he was presented with a written affidavit, composed by Gleason, for the prisoner to sign. Arnold refused. He wrote his own statement and handed it to Gleason. Gleason edited it, amended it with concocted evidence of his own, and handed it back for Arnold's signature. The prisoner again refused.

Major Andrews was called to arbitrate the matter. He read Gleason's version of the affidavit and recommended that Arnold sign it. No, the prisoner said, if they handed it back to him, he'd tear it up. Then, according to Arnold:

"Sir, I will take you out in the Parade and shoot you," Andrews said.

"I am your prisoner, Major," Arnold replied. "If you feel

you have the right to shoot me, all that is left to me, I suppose, is to be shot."[4]

His bluff called, Andrews withdrew; and Arnold transcribed his own affidavit, as later did Mudd and Spangler. They offered Gleason nothing new—nothing to implicate President Johnson, Jefferson Davis, or anyone not already involved in the charges of conspiracy.

Gleason was "much disappointed," according to Sam Arnold. "After he had left the post, we were informed through reliable authority that he was armed with the power, in case we refused, to place us in solitary confinement and to be fed on bread and water . . . he was to obtain our voluntary statements. There was nothing voluntary on our parts, throughout the whole affair, but force in every instance used and threats made, beside inducements held out, to swear falsely in the premises."[5]

In a letter to his attorney, Frederick Stone, Mudd confirmed Arnold's charges. Gleason told him that "if we did not make statements"—presumably satisfactory statements—"it would result in our injury." His own contribution was a single paragraph, four sentences long, swearing to having had no knowledge whatever of John Wilkes Booth's conspiracy.

To what degree false testimony from the prisoners might have changed the course of history is hard to say. The following February, 1868, Thaddeus Stevens called on the House to impeach the President. Throughout succeeding weeks Benjamin Butler and his congressional committee did their best to collect the kind of evidence against the President that Gleason had been looking for on Garden Key. Yet the charges against Johnson, when finally presented, contained not even a suggestion that the President was in any way involved in Lincoln's murder.

Gleason's visit tended to revive old irritations and the atmosphere of prison gloom returned. Johnson's impeachment, if it came and ended in conviction, would remove all chances of a presidential pardon. More and more it seemed that Mudd was doomed to serve out his life sentence in the Dry Tortugas.

There had been no acknowledgment from Washington

of the petition signed in October by the officers and garrison, asking for clemency in Mudd's behalf. No recognition or reward for his heroic services throughout the yellow fever epidemic. "I have no doubt saved dozens of lives & thousands worth of property," he wrote to Frances, "yet you with me & the children are suffering for a crime which I am sure never entered our brains."

Worse was to come. General Hill was on his way back to Garden Key to replace the more kindly Major Andrews, whose tour of duty expired on the first of March. Hill's arrival would be delayed, however. In the interval, the post would be filled by Major C. C. MacConnell, 5th United States Artillery, who had been a first lieutenant at the fort when Grenfell had written his ill-fated letter to the New York *World*. Major Andrews' departure, wrote Grenfell, "was a great loss to us all, but to me in particular. His successors have a deadly hatred for me!"

MacConnell was accompanied by Lieutenant Frank Thorpe, now appointed provost marshal. "Between him and MacConnell," Arnold wrote, "the island became a hell again, they devising measures to make prisoners uncomfortable and imprisonment more galling. As soon as Major MacConnell assumed the reins of power, the tendency to persecute Grenfell became apparent. . . . Major MacConnell felt very bitter towards Grenfell, on account of the article published by him, it nearly being the means of his dismissal [from] the service." Further, regarding Lieutenant Thorpe:

> He picked as Provost Guards the most contemptible men of the garrison, who abused, cursed, struck and maltreated the prisoners under their charge in every conceivable manner. Col. Grenfell, finding, as he often expressed to me, that they had started upon him to kill him inch by inch determined to attempt escape at all hazards, preferring as he said, a watery grave in preference to the indignities such heartless and malicious men would impose upon him.[6]

Dr. Mudd, too, complained of the change in commanders, though he was not the target of MacConnell's persecution.

New orders prescribed that all correspondence be examined, and his letters were now subject to strict scrutiny. "I am restrained, in consequence of this," he wrote to Frances, "from saying many things that I wish to say." He considered the provost marshal prejudiced, "vengeful and unscrupulous." Oddly enough, the letter including these remarks went through the mails uncensored.

There are several versions of what happened next: the memoirs of Samuel Arnold, the report of Lieutenant Paul Roemer, who later arrived at Garden Key to investigate the incident, and the letters of Captain George Crabbe, the officer who had supposedly brought the yellow fever germ from Cuba to Fort Jefferson eight months before. Certainly MacConnell's and Thorpe's arrival, which resulted in Grenfell's being reinstated at hard labor, had some bearing on St. Leger's actions. But it was later discovered that the Englishman had for some time been making charts of the surrounding waters, showing principal channels and adjacent keys, with tables of compass bearings and distances from the Dry Tortugas to various landfalls in Florida, Cuba, and Louisiana. Discovered in his cell, too, was a revealing cable from Washington, which stated briefly:

YOUR APPLICATION FOR CLEMENCY HAS BEEN DENIED.

(signed) HOLT, JUDGE ADVOCATE GENERAL, ON ORDER OF THE PRESIDENT[7]

Whatever the immediate provocation, Grenfell's escape was well conceived. His cellmate, Johnny Adare, was an eager and experienced accomplice. Since his semisuccessful flight to Cuba, Adare had tried again to break away. Though still with a ball and chain around his ankle, he had managed to get outside the walls and paddle his way to Loggerhead Key with the aid of a piece of driftwood. This time, however, he failed to steal the lighthouse boat, was discovered hiding in the underbrush, and was ignominiously hustled back to Garden Key, blithely assuring his captors he would try again.

Two other prisoners made up the group: James Orr and Joseph Holroyd, the latter a cook in the prisoners' mess;

both occupied ground-floor cells, which made it possible to slip out through the gun embrasures. But with sentinels posted at the bastions and around the wharfs, they needed an accomplice in the garrison. Private William Noreil was induced to join them, either through bribery or because Noreil himself, according to Samuel Arnold, had received "harsh treatment at his [MacConnell's] hands and was anxious to desert." The escape was set for the night of March 6, a time when Noreil would be stationed on Wharf Number One, at which the fishing boats were tied.

It was close to the equinox, a time of tempests in the gulf. The night of March 6 was one of the stormiest that many could remember, with a wind of gale force blowing from the north and the island clouded by spray and rain. So much the better for Grenfell's plans. From his sailing days on the Barbary Coast, he had no fear of rough seas, and he welcomed the concealing darkness. It also happened that two companies from the garrison had temporarily left the island to quell a racial disturbance in New Orleans. All boded well.

An hour before midnight Private Noreil left his post, stole to Adare's and Grenfell's second-tier casemate, and released the prisoners. They lowered themselves through a gun embrasure and swam across the moat. On the wharf they joined Orr and Holroyd, who had followed the same procedure; Orr had carried the thirty-pound iron ball still chained to his ankle. All five crowded aboard the fishing vessel—Noreil had obtained the oars and rudders in advance —hoisted sail, and bore out across the harbor, hidden by almost total darkness.

As captain of the overloaded craft, Grenfell had two choices—to head north into the teeth of the storm or to head south with the wind astern. Either way, if his destination was Florida or Cuba, which seems likely, he sooner or later would have had to turn east, with his vessel broadside to the wind.

What tack he followed is, of course, impossible to say. But around the Dry Tortugas, especially beyond the Southeast Channel, lay treacherous shoals and reefs. The night was

pitch-black with all landmarks blotted out. The sea was a
churning maelstrom. It would have taken superhuman skill
and courage to have made it to Havana or the mainland.
Grenfell had both, especially the courage. . . .

Their disappearance was noticed at one A.M. with the
changing of the guard. At dawn Captain Scott of the garrison
schooner *Bibb* set out in dubious pursuit, criss-crossing for
seven hours the waters south and east of Garden Key. He
found no boat or wreckage, no oars or flotsam, and no bodies
of the missing men. Grenfell, it was concluded, had at last
found freedom in a deep-sea grave.

Not unexpectedly the prisoners, especially those who had
been close to Grenfell, suffered the consequences of the Englishman's escape. There was always the possibility, in Hill's
mind, that the "Lincoln assassins" might have had a part
in Grenfell's break for freedom or at least been privy to
it. As a result security was tightened throughout the fort.
According to Arnold, "No one after retreat was permitted
to place his head out of the aperture of his casemate under
the penalty of having a musket ball come crashing through
his brain."

Communication between guards and prisoners was once
again limited to giving and receiving orders. And again all
arriving packages were opened and inspected. All letters written or received were read and censored by the provost
marshal—a procedure Mudd found intolerable. He warned
Frances that they should correspond less frequently. What
he wrote to her and what she wrote to him was not for prying
eyes.

The departure of seven Southern prisoners from the island
enabled the doctor to send an uncensored letter by their
hands and to let off steam regarding the provost marshal:

> He is one of those officious individuals, fond of ruling,
> considering himself one of the elect, and adds daily new
> rules for the government of the prisoners, which tend to
> be more despotic than the laws of the ancient barbarians.

All letters are carefully perused by him, not as a duty of
his office, but because of his prying spirit and disposition
to meddle with matters that do not pertain to his office.
I have therefore concluded never to pass another letter
through his hands. I correspond with you only, and I would
sooner forego this satisfaction than again permit him to
pry into another letter, to gratify his mischievous curiosity.[8]

He was as good as his word. Throughout the rest of the
entire year he sent only a dozen letters to his wife (although
she begged him to write more often, "I am uneasy about
you"). All of his letters during this period were guarded
in tone, revealing less of what he thought and felt, leaving
a gap in his personal records for the last nine months of
1868.

He was able to follow the news from the papers in the
prison library. Andrew Johnson's impeachment trial ended
in mid-May with a Senate vote of 35 for conviction, 19 for
acquittal—one short of the two-thirds majority needed to
convict. As a consequence Secretary Stanton finally relinquished his post in the cabinet to General John M. Schofield,
who had served under Sherman at Atlanta. Schofield was
a man who looked like Socrates and wore red underwear
but overcame these stigmas by chewing plug tobacco.

In spite of his professorial manner Schofield was as rabid
a hater of the South, especially of the Southern planter aristocracy, as was his predecessor. The change meant no
improvement in Mudd's chances with the War Department.
Once again that summer attorneys for the three state prisoners tried to obtain a writ of *habeas corpus* through a lawyer
in Key West, at a cost of a hundred dollars to each with
a hundred more upon release.

Mudd believed, as he wrote to Frances, that Bennett Hill
had happened to be in Key West on the day his case was
brought before the judge, a coincidence that influenced the
magistrate's decision. True or not, the National Archives
retains a message from the Attorney General's office dated
September 5, 1868:

Hon: J. M. Schofield
Secretary of War.

Sir: I have the honor to inform you that I received a telegram
from the United States Marshal at Key West stating that Judge
Boynton refuses a writ of *habeas corpus* in the case of Mudd
and others.

Very Respectfully,
I. HUBLEY ASHTON
Acting Attorney General[9]

* * *

Down the long corridor of years the quiet closing, one
by one, of doors.

There was no further agency of recourse. "I have but little
hope," he wrote to Frances. "The good seem only to suffer
in this world as a general rule." Back came all the old anxieties:
Worry about Frances and the children. Worry about the
farm. Worry about his parents—his father was aging, his
mother still holding on. And of course about himself. Would
he ever get out of here? And if he did, would he have the
strength and spirit left to fulfill his duties as a father, husband,
self-supporting farmer? How about his interrupted medical
profession? Would he ever be able to take up where he had
left off on that April weekend, 1865?

Life was a little easier when Major MacConnell relinquished
command of the fort to General Hill. Discipline was slightly
less oppressive. Communications were restored. The mail
was generally unmolested. Mudd was able to report:

> We are in the midst of another warm and distressing
> summer. The atmosphere around the Fort, owing to the
> filthy condition of the moat outside, is terribly offensive
> at times and bids fair to breed another pestilence.

And later:

> Suffering again with a terrible cold and wearied with
> the apathy and indifference of those who call themselves
> my friends.

And later:

> Our sleeping quarters are the same miserable, damp
> casemates. My bed is made of moss gathered from the trees
> in the Floridas. It is very hard from long usage. I have
> shaved off my mustache and trimmed my goatee quite short,
> which has altered my appearance so much that I scarcely
> knew myself when I looked in the glass. . . . I believe my
> hair is much thinner than when I left home.[10]

Though he wrote that he was forced to return to sweeping
out the bastions, "in chains and under guard," this seems
to have been a figure of speech reflecting his malaise. He
was still often in the carpentry shop, he wrote to Frances
as winter approached:

> Tell Lilly that Pop has nearly completed her little work
> box. It is made of mahogany & inlaid with crab wood. Three
> little leaves representing a branch is inlaid in the corners
> of the top—a fancy piece in the centers with the initials
> of her name in German letters engraved & inlaid, which
> looks quite nice. I have the sides yet to finish. I have several
> little crosses made of crab wood which I will send to be
> distributed among you all.[11]

The year ended on a grim note. The rumor that had
plagued the prisoners three years before, that of a planned
rebellion of the convicts, rose again. No one knew how it
began or who was responsible for the rumor. According to
Samuel Arnold, "it was reported that some parties had been
overheard" saying how easy it would be—some night when
most of the garrison was at the theater—to break out of
the cells and into the prison arsenal, seize the guns, com-
mandeer the government schooner *Matchless*, and sail away
to freedom.

The rumor may have started, or at least gained credence,
when an ingenious prisoner named Gold Hall slipped from
his cell and broke into the ordnance depot. He opened a
canister of gunpowder and laid down a ropelike trail of the
explosive, leading from the magazine to the far side of the
yard. Caught on completion of this act, Hall confessed his

intent to set fire to the lengthy fuse and blow the fort to kingdom come. He was placed in solitary confinement, and thereafter in the daily Report of the Guard—a record of each prisoner present, the duration of his sentence, and the nature of his crime—the charge against Hall was listed as "insanity."

When the story of a projected mass escape reached the ears of the provost marshal, "the most stringent measures were adopted to frustrate the design." All privileges were suspended; double guards were placed at every cell, at the portcullis, and on the wharves. Once again the rifle slots were boarded up, so that no light and only a minimum of air came through. Thus sealed, the cells grew damp; green slime began to coat the walls—the same sort of miasma that had heralded the yellow fever almost exactly a year before—and creep out of the corners like an unseen foe.

Though not given to issuing formal complaints, Mudd sent a note to General Hill:

> Sir: The boarding up in front of our quarters and otherwise rendering our imprisonment more painful and odious, leads us to believe [it] was the result of secret information which you deemed reliable. We very respectfully ask an investigation in order that the truth be made known. If we are to be held responsible for every rumor or falsehood that may be trumped up by the evil disposed, we are liable at any moment to be called out and shot. I have the honor to be,
>
> Very respectfully, your obedient servant,
> SAMUEL A. MUDD[12]

No answer came from General Hill. The boards were not removed, the restrictions and the guards remained, the new regime had all the air of being permanent.

Shortly after this contumely, Mudd received another blow. On the last day of the year, Sarah Ann Reeves, the doctor's mother, died at the age of fifty-eight, of pleurisy compounded by the weight of unfamiliar sorrows. On receiving the news from Frances, Mudd could not contain his tears nor the righteous wrath he felt at having been driven from her side:

> Can I forgive those who have so inhumanly and mali-
> ciously caused our separation, and deprived me of affording
> all the consolation in my power—a debt of love and gratitude
> I owe—to the kindest and most loving of mothers? May
> the chastisement of Heaven fall upon and crush them to
> a sense of their wrong.[13]

In Bryantown Frances, too, had lost a much-beloved friend
in Sarah Ann. That winter her mother-in-law and Henry
Lowe Mudd had suggested that she and the children come
to live with them at Oak Hill until Sam returned, all knowing
that Sam might never return but refusing to acknowledge
it. She had been tempted and had written to the doctor of
this offer. "Try to remain where you are at present," he
had answered her. He added that if it were necessary, "Sell
off all stock except that which is actually needed for your
own use & which it costs to keep."[14]

Now Sarah was gone and Henry Lowe would be lonelier
than ever and perhaps more anxious for her company. But
Frances remained at home. If her husband returned, he
would want her there. Until then he would want to feel that
the farm had not been abandoned, but, however diminished,
was still waiting for him.

Only six weeks had passed after Sarah's death when, on
February 13, a courier arrived from Washington with a note
for Frances from Andrew Johnson. The President would
like to see her at the White House at her earliest convenience.

She started at once for the capital, stopped for the night
at her brother-in-law's, and the next day rode with Joseph
Blandford to the White House. While Blandford waited in
an outer chamber, she entered the executive office. The President rose politely, asked her to be seated, told her—as Frances
remembered:

"I imagine, Mrs. Mudd, you will think this is tardy justice
in carrying out my promise to you made two years ago. The
situation was such, however, that I could not act as I wanted
to do."

Then he handed her a four-page document bearing the
White House letterhead. The last page was signed by the
President and William H. Seward, Secretary of State. She

skipped the nine long paragraphs starting with "whereas" and came to the next-to-last sentence:

> Now, therefore, be it known that I, Andrew Johnson, President of the United States . . . do hereby grant to the said Dr. Samuel A. Mudd a full and unconditional pardon.[15]

All Frances could find to say, after three and a half years of hope and disappointment, took the form of haunting questions:

How would these papers be delivered?

Would they cut through hostile barriers, get past those who would go to any lengths to keep Sam in prison?

Would they, without a shadow of a doubt, actually reach her husband?

"They will if I put my seal on them," said Johnson, doing so. But he, too, had often been tricked by his subordinates and had his authority subverted in the past. Even now, despite the security of the presidential seal, he apparently had some misgivings, and told Frances bluntly:

"Mrs. Mudd, I have complied with my promise to release your husband before I left the White House. I no longer hold myself responsible. Should these papers go astray you may never hear from them again. They may be pigeon-holed or left forgotten in some corner."[16]

That was enough for Frances to make up her mind. She would take them herself to the Dry Tortugas. She left the President with her thanks and with the signed documents in hand went directly to Baltimore. She arrived at the Patapso River wharves only minutes late. The last steamer for the gulf had left; there would not be another for three weeks. She would arrive at a time when the man who had signed the pardon would have finished his term of supreme authority and left the White House.

Life had played her and the doctor too many tricks to warrant taking chances. She sent the papers by post express to her brother, Tom Dyer, in New Orleans, to be delivered to her husband at Fort Jefferson by special messenger.

Pardoning Dr. Samuel Mudd was not the President's last

act in office. Two days later, on Johnson's orders, four men worked secretly in darkness to remove a section of the flagstone flooring in the penitentiary. Gingerly they raised a rotted wooden coffin, buried four years earlier, which contained the remains of John Wilkes Booth. They pried open the coffin, removed the body—so decomposed that the head fell from the neck—and transferred it to an unmarked, white pine box.

A black teamster hauled the box to a funeral home behind Ford's Theater, passing the alley where John Wilkes Booth had fled the city for the last time. Waiting in anonymity to claim the load was Edwin Booth, who had achieved the fame John Wilkes had aspired to. Edwin refused to look at the body of his brother. He accompanied the box to Baltimore, to be buried in the family plot in Greenmount Cemetery.

It had not been a crowded week for Andrew Johnson, just a cleaning up of loose ends before leaving Washington. But he had disposed of two strangely related cases. He had freed the doctor and buried the devil. Thank God he, and the nation, could forget them both.

21

AVE ATQUE VALE

TWELVE days after passing through the prison gates on Garden Key, the doctor's ship reached Baltimore, and Samuel Mudd on March 20, 1869, arrived at home. His family, as his daughter Nettie wrote, found him "frail, weak and sick, never to be strong again. . . ."

> It is needless for me to try to picture the feelings and incidents of his home-coming. Pleasure and pain were intermingled—pleasure to him to be once more in his old home surrounded by his loved ones, and pleasure to them to have him back once more; pain to them to see him so broken in health and strength, and pain to him to find his savings all gone and his family destitute.[1]

Destitute was perhaps too strong a word. The farm had diminished in size, with land sharecropped or sold in parcels to his former slaves, a substantial plot having gone to Baptist Washington and his family. The barn destroyed in the freak tornado of 1865 still lay in a pile of rotting timber. The federal troops who had occupied the plantation after his arrest had torn up fences for firewood and made a shambles of the stables and tobacco sheds. The house itself was badly in need of repair, and it was true, he had no savings left. According to his grandson, Dr. Richard Mudd, he applied to the government for help and was offered a job touring the South to study the cause and prevalence of yellow fever. But because it would take him away from his family—and he had had enough of that—he turned it down.[2]

For weighted against his financial misfortunes was the fact that he was back with Frances and the children. And just as prison had taught him patience and acceptance, their lives without him had made them sturdy and resourceful. Frances' hair was tinged with gray, but the youthful lines of her features were as firm as ever. He hardly recognized the children: Andrew, eleven; Lillian, nine; Thomas, eight; and young Samuel Alexander, Jr., only five. The two oldest were attending public school in Bryantown; Frances was teaching the younger two at home.

John Best was still with them, now seventy and stooped with age, querulous, lovable, and not too able. Bettie Dyer, Jeremiah's unmarried sister, who had come to live with Frances during the latter years the doctor was in prison, stayed on to help around the house. But if the doctor were to support them all by putting the farm back on a paying basis, he would have to do it almost single handed. His older sons might help in time, but for now he was virtually on his own.

One might think that he would quickly put Fort Jefferson behind him. Yet one of his first acts on arriving home was to send a letter to the Adjutant General in Washington requesting clemency for William Bradley, a horse thief sentenced to the Dry Tortugas. Bradley had arrived, the doctor wrote, during the 1867 epidemic at the fort and had been so debilitated by fever that he was barely able to perform his prison duties. The doctor believed him sincere in his resolve to make amends "to those whom he has injured to the best of his ability"—if only the government would release him.

He also inquired of Frederick Stone as to the fate of Samuel Arnold and Edward Spangler, who had still been in prison when he left. He learned that pardons for both had arrived from the President while he himself was enroute for Baltimore, and they had quit the prison almost on the day that he, the doctor, had reached home.

The local census of 1870, which, along with names of members of the household, normally listed the net worth of the family, recorded no cash assets whatever after the name of

Samuel Mudd. He had much catching up to do. On top
of the burden of restoring Rock Hill Farm, he would need
to regain, if possible, some of his medical practice. No doubt
his cousin George, still one of the leading physicians in the
country, helped by referring cases to his former protégé. But
during Sam's absence many of his former patients had been
obliged to turn to other doctors, and as his daughter Nettie
wrote:

> Many of these families sought my father's services on
> his return, but some did not. Apart from this, the people
> of the neighborhood had become comparatively poor by
> reason of their losses occasioned by the war. A great deal
> of his attention and skill was therefore given gratuitously.[3]

He found south-county Maryland altered greatly by the
war. Gone were the days of clannish gatherings among the
planters; gone, in fact, was the planter aristocracy. No labor
to work the fields, no money, and twelve thousand of Maryland's youth lost on the peninsula or in the wilderness, at
Gettysburg or Shiloh. Even those in the professions, such
as Sam's cousin George, were struggling to make ends meet.

Among his friends and neighbors he encountered only
sympathy and kindness. There was no blot on the Mudd
escutcheon because of his imprisonment. In fact, the nation
as a whole was reacting with revulsion to the execution of
Mary Surratt and the manner in which the surviving suspects
had been tried and sentenced. Those who had testified against
the doctor at his trial, notably Daniel Thomas, were regarded
now as turncoats and pariahs.

On Garden Key he had eagerly searched the newspapers
in the prison library for items concerning his case. Now he
sought only anonymity. "Nothing was ever printed in connection with my name," he said, "that did not misrepresent me.
A burned child dreads the fire, and I have reason to be
suspicious of everyone." Yet shortly after his release he reluctantly granted an interview with a visiting reporter from the
New York *Herald*. The published story harked back to pre-
prison days and drew some hyperbolic contrasts:

The world went well and smoothly with him previous to that unhappy event. His house was furnished with all the comforts of a country gentleman's residence. He had his horses in town and in the sporting season was foremost in every foxhunt and at every manly outdoor sport. He had robust health and a vigorous athletic frame in those days.

The doctor could surely not have read and approved this popular conception of the Maryland tobacco planter. The reporter continued:

But it is very different now. Above the middle height with a reddish mustache and attenuated nose, his appearance indicates a man of calm and slow reflection, gentle in manner in a very domestic turn. . . . His whole desire now is to be allowed to spend the balance of his days quietly in the bosom of his family. In his sunken, lusterless eyes, pallid lips, and cold, ashy complexion, one can read the word Dry Tortugas with a terrible significance. In the prime of his years looking prematurely old and careworn, there are few indeed who could gaze on the wreck and ravage in the face of this man before them without feeling a sentiment of sympathy and commiseration.

The reporter concluded with an unlikely-sounding bit of dialogue. Before leaving, he remarked to the doctor:

"You must have felt seriously agitated after being arrested in connection with this matter."

"No, sir," Mudd allegedly replied, "I was just as self-possessed as I am now. They might have hanged me at the time and I should have faced death just as composedly as I smoke this pipe."[4]

In 1870, his first full year at home, a fourth son and his first post-prison child was born. Named Henry for the doctor's father, the baby died at eight months; by that time, however, a second daughter, to be christened Stella Marie, was on the way. Frances and Sam were losing no time in filling their expected quota of young Mudds. At the turn of the year there arrived another, wholly unexpected, addition to the household.

On a bright morning in the spring of 1871, a year and a half after Sam's release, Frances and her husband were seated at breakfast when a rapping on the window drew their eyes to a grinning gargoyle peering at them through the pane. To Frances the bearded face was unfamiliar, but to Sam the apparition was like Lazarus arising from the dead.

Ned Spangler!

There was none among his prison associates the doctor could have welcomed with more warmth. Grenfell he had found commendable and entertaining; O'Laughlin and Arnold he had felt a fatherly affection for. But this inarticulate, gritty little carpenter, more of his own age than the others, had been like an ever-devoted watchdog to him, guarding his cell when he was sick, nursing the doctor through his illness, and above all able to laugh and joke at prison adversities when Mudd himself was sometimes on the point of giving up.

Never one for lengthy explanations, Spangler wasted few words after their initial greetings.

"Mrs. Mudd, I came down last night and asked someone to tell me the way here. I followed the road, but when I arrived I was afraid of your dogs, and I roosted in a tree."

He had come, it was evident, to stay.

It seemed that when he and Arnold had left the fort, the government took them as far as Key West and dumped them on the town, without money or possessions or means of getting any farther. Arnold summoned his father down to pick him up and take him home, leaving Spangler stranded.

Using his carpentry skills to earn money when he needed it, Spangler drifted slowly north. He could not have relished returning to the shed behind Ford's Theater but it was the only home, aside from the Booth estate in Bel Air, he had ever known. And John Ford had done a lot for Spangler, sending him gifts and working for his freedom, while Ned had been in prison.

Arriving in Washington, he found Ford's Theater converted into an army warehouse, the stage piled high with filing cabinets, the orchestra pit awash with desks. And no sign of his benefactor, John T. Ford. When the government had confiscated the theater, Ford had demanded and received $100,000 for the building. With this he had left the capital and concerned himself with his other theaters between Baltimore and Richmond.

Ned headed south for Dr. Mudd's, the only other living person of importance in his microscopic life. Tuberculosis, the doctor guessed, was catching up with him; and Ned was no hand for farming. Mudd gave him five acres of land near the spring house on which to build a home—the wooded site where Dyer and his fellow rebels had hidden out in 1863. In return Spangler helped to rebuild the barn and repair other buildings on the farm and, as time allowed, earned money doing odd jobs in the village.

"He was a quiet, genial man," wrote Nettie about Spangler, "greatly respected by members of our family and the people of the neighborhood. His greatest pleasure seemed to be found in extending kindness to others, and particularly to children, of whom he was very fond." He never did build his home, however. With enough boards up to form a shelter from the elements, he let it go at that.[5]

The years have a way of slipping past with sly rapidity as one grows older, and for Samuel Mudd the decade between forty years of age and nearly fifty sped by so swiftly he felt cheated of it. After Stella Marie was born, a fourth son (not counting Henry) appeared in July of 1873, to be followed by another daughter, Rose de Lima, in 1875. The birth of Mary Eleanor or "Nettie" in January, 1878, rounded out the brood of eight surviving sons and daughters.

Certainly Dr. Mudd regretted not being able to give his children the kind of education he had had. Lillie attended her mother's alma mater, Visitation Academy, in Frederick, where she won high honors in her subjects. But Andrew failed to win a scholarship at Georgetown College, and the boys remained at home. Except for Thomas, who secretly yearned to be a doctor like his father—and after many years became one—all adapted well to farm life. Young Sam especially. But there was need for pocket money. And as they reached their late teens, Thomas taught at the

neighborhood school between Bryantown and Malcolm, while
young Sam took a clerk's job in a general store near Gallant
Green.

In the fall of 1877 the doctor's father died at Oak Hill
in his eightieth year. To his funeral flocked most of the Mudds
of Maryland and even many relatives and close friends from
the Western states—among the latter, ex-Governor John
Gately Downey of California, whom Henry Lowe had adopted
in John's early days in southern Maryland.

Henry's heirs, including Sam and Frances, sold most of
the farmland to cover outstanding debts. What to do with
the great white house that overlooked Zachia Swamp was
not a problem. The estate was barely settled before the manor
burned mysteriously to the ground; destroyed with it were
the peerless library and innumerable documents and records
that might have thrown more light on the family history
of the Mudds of Maryland.

It was not long before the doctor lost another friend in
Spangler. Never considerate of his health, often soaking wet
in his leaky shelter, Ned caught cold following exposure to
a heavy rain, developed a fever, and died of what Mudd
diagnosed as "rheumatism of the heart." He was buried not
at St. Mary's among his benefactors but in the tiny cemetery
of St. Peter's in the piney woods. For reasons Mudd never
explained, he left the grave unmarked.

Searching through the debris of the never-finished house
beside the spring, the doctor found an extraordinary document in Spangler's tool chest—handwritten and, for the
author, remarkably articulate. It appeared to be the secret
record of Ned's life and relations with John Wilkes Booth
up to the time of Lincoln's murder. Though he admitted
to having been present the night of the assassination, it would
seem that Spangler saw no evil, heard no evil, spoke no evil:

> I never heard Booth express himself in favor of the rebel-
> lion, or opposed to the government, or converse upon politi-
> cal subjects; and I have no recollection of his mentioning
> the name of President Lincoln in any connection whatever.
> I knew nothing of . . .[6]

And so it went, closing Ned's dreary life with a know-nothing innocence. And who could be certain, looking back on those days of frenzy and assassination, whether or not he wrote the truth?

In February of 1882, Mary Mudd Dyer, Jeremiah's wife, died at her home in Baltimore, the first to go among the younger generation. To Dr. Mudd Mary had been the closest of his sisters, a closeness further cemented when he nursed her through her serious illness in the spring of 1865. Only forty-two years of age, Mary had died young, in light of the clan's addiction to longevity.

Mudd himself was now in his fiftieth year, still in the prime of life by family criteria. He had never overcome the debilitating effects of life in prison. Yet he had outlived many who had been connected, one way or another, with events preceding his trial and with the trial itself. . . .

His archenemy Edwin Stanton was buried in December, 1869, ten months after Dr. Mudd's release. The attending physician certified the death as due to natural causes. But Mudd preferred to believe the prevalent rumor that Stanton had cut his throat with a razor (ex-Attorney General Caleb Cushing was certain of the fact), confessing at the end, "The Surratt woman haunts me."

Of the two stalwarts who had blocked poor Anna Surratt's attempt to see the President before her mother's execution, ex-senator Preston King, in the fall of 1865, tied a bag of shot around his neck and drowned himself in the Hudson River; Senator James Lane, six months later, put a bullet through his temple.

Of the three who shared the presidential box with Lincoln on the night of his assassination, Major Rathbone and Clara Harris were happily married until, one Christmas Eve, Rathbone shot his wife through the head and tried to stab himself to death. For these acts he was committed to a lunatic asylum.

Mary Todd Lincoln, after a suicide attempt, was also committed briefly to a hospital for the insane. Released, she shut herself up in a room of her sister's home in Springfield,

Illinois. There in the year 1882, seated in her widow's weeds with the shades drawn tight against the sun, she died in solitary darkness—almost on the day that another Mary, Mary Mudd Dyer, passed away.

John F. Parker, the scapegrace constable who had deserted his post outside the presidential box the night of the assassination, thereby leaving the way open for Lincoln's murderer, was soundly rebuked for his delinquency by Mrs. Lincoln but not by the Washington police. Parker was shortly back on duty at the White House, separated from the service only when he was caught for the heinous crime of sleeping in a streetcar.

Though out of the White House and partially vindicated in his fight against the Radicals, Andrew Johnson continued to battle for justice under the Constitution—justice especially for the South. The only ex-President to return to the Senate, he served briefly until his death in 1875. Almost his last words in a final speech before the Senate were, "Give me back the Constitution of my country!"—a cry that Mudd might have paraphrased in the Dry Tortugas.

Lafayette Baker had suffered a falling out with the authorities. Receiving only a fraction of the reward he thought due him for Booth's apprehension, he turned against his former bosses and accused Stanton of having torn the vital missing pages from Booth's diary. Baker retired, persona non grata in Washington, to write anew a history of the secret service; he died in Philadelphia in 1868 of causes no two doctors could agree on.

Thomas P. ("Boston") Corbett, the self-emasculated killer of John Wilkes Booth, basked briefly in a hero's limelight, then followed divine direction to become a "Glory to God" evangelist. Touring Kansas, he tried to kill a few more sinners with a shotgun—this time members of the Kansas legislature—and was thrown into an insane asylum. He escaped and vanished mystically into thin air.

John Lloyd, the tavern keeper whose malevolent testimony had reaped such a harvest of injustice at the trial of the conspirators, predictably drank himself to death. The name of Surrattsville was eventually changed to Clinton to erase dark memories; yet the tavern itself, once a den of iniquity in Northern annals, remained as a quiet travelers' refuge on the elm-lined crossway between peaceful Washington and peaceful Richmond.

John Surratt, released on bail in the fall of 1867, was again brought to trial in 1868, at which time Richard Merrick easily succeeded in having the case dismissed. Young Surratt took to the lecture circuit with tales of his life as a Confederate spy. Potential audiences stayed away in droves. Not only was John no speaker, but the image of one who had deserted his mother in her time of crisis was repellent to the public. John eventually turned to farming to survive.

But he kept his sights set for Louis Wiechmann, the man who had testified so devastatingly against his mother and himself. There is no evidence that his thirst for vengeance went beyond publicly castigating Louis, whenever and wherever he could get a hearing. But the apprehensive Wiechmann lived in sweating terror. Forced from his job in Washington, he fled to his native Philadelphia, where he was shot at twice by unidentified assailants. He fled again to his uncle's home in Indiana. There he taught school, forever glancing over his shoulder at unseen pursuers. When he finally died, protesting to the last that he had told the truth about the Lincoln assassins, the attending doctor diagnosed the cause of death as "extreme nervousness."

Among Dr. Mudd's prison associates, St. Leger Grenfell's name recurred from time to time. Like John Wilkes Booth, the Englishman died hard. He had reportedly been picked up the night of his escape by a yacht outside the Dry Tortugas and secreted by collaborators in New Orleans. His family in London believed he was hiding in Brazil or Paraguay. The United States government sent agents to investigate his reported presence in Havana.[7]

The last word came from one A. W. McMullen of Tampa, who, as a lad of twelve, had seen a man resembling Grenfell emerge from the waters of the gulf to seek refuge in McMullen's seaside home. The stranger regaled the family with tales of his picaresque life in Africa, India, and South America with details only Grenfell could have known. "He looked pretty well worn out," remembered young McMullen.[8]

However much Mudd had admired Grenfell in the Dry Tortugas days, the man he would miss most was Dr. Whitehurst. For the first and only time in Dr. Mudd's life, during Whitehurst's presence at the fort, he had risen to glory as a doctor and gained the unstinted admiration of his peers. He would cherish few memories of prison life, but he would cherish that one.

Whitehurst himself had retired to Key West where his only daughter became engaged to a visiting European count. The doctor raised passionate objections to this mismatch with "Count No-account." The daughter insisted on going ahead with the marriage even if it broke her father's heart. Whitehurst refused to attend the wedding ceremony. Instead he stayed home and killed himself by taking poison.[9]

There was one man, of course, whose haunting presence Dr. Mudd would never be rid of. "God help us, what a curse is on the Booths!" wrote Edwin after his brother's death. And one Booth had placed a curse on Dr. Mudd as well, and on his children and his children's children, which would plague them for decades to come—though the nation, let it be said, would come to recognize the truth and inscribe Mudd's name with honor on Fort Jefferson's surviving walls. Though no secret had been made of John Wilkes' burial in Baltimore, who could say for certain that the body buried had been Booth's? To some people, even in the year 1882, he was as alive as he had been in 1865.

The most persistent rumor of his survival was perpetuated by a Memphis lawyer named Finis L. Bates. Traveling through Granbury, Texas, Bates befriended a saloonkeeper who gave his name as John St. Helen. St. Helen confided to Bates that a doctor told him he was dying, and with nothing to lose, he wished to confess to being Lincoln's assassin, John Wilkes Booth. He gave Bates a tintype portrait of himself to submit to the authorities in Washington. Bates hurried to the capital with the tintype, which showed a remarkable likeness to official photographs of Booth. His story, however, was considered poppycock.[10]

Yet there were others who insisted the actor was alive. Booth's niece maintained that her uncle had visited her in Minneapolis after the assassination, but she had refused to let him in the house. John P. Simonton of the Judge Advocate's Office had peculiar access to official documents concerning the assassination and the capture of the culprits. After years of microscopic study of these documents he concluded, "Booth avoided justice and the War Department in 1865 killed an innocent man for the assassin."[11]

To Samuel Mudd these rumors were irrelevant. Booth would never be out of his life. He was still paying, and obliquely he would go on paying, for that morning of April, 1865, when out of charity he had opened his door to the stygian figure on the pale horse.

It was a cold and rainy winter as December blended into January, 1883. Out on the Great Plains, where a new America was burgeoning with the aid of westering Mudds, the cattle were dying by droves in unprecedented blizzards. In the Dry Tortugas, Fort Jefferson lay abandoned to a scorching sun, Spanish moss dripping from the battlements, spiked cactus growing from the cracked walls. And in Charles County, Maryland, the winter rain was more than usually persistent, promising receptive fields for the spring tobacco crop.

On New Year's Day, Dr. Mudd donned overshoes and muffler and went calling on his few remaining patients. Sometime that week he would need to visit E. D. R. Bean's store in Bryantown to buy some gifts, for Nettie's first birthday was on the tenth. That afternoon around dusk Father Edward Southgate, the new priest at St. Mary's, peered from his vestry window to see the doctor standing on the church veranda.

"He stood there for half an hour," remembered Southgate, "in the rain, without an overcoat." If he wondered about the reason for this vigil, he would never have an answer.

The next day Dr. Mudd was running a fever and remained in bed. The fever rose as the days progressed and his cousin George, called to the bedside, became worried about the possibility of complications. On January 10 the doctor was unable to attend Nettie's birthday party. That night he died, presumably of pleurisy.

He was buried in the family plot in St. Mary's cemetery— less than a hundred yards from the spot where he had first met John Wilkes Booth some nineteen years before—near the graves of his father and mother and surrounded by Mudds, Gardiners, and Dyers, so many of whom had been companions in his lifetime. On the stone above his grave was the simplest of legends:

SAMUEL A. MUDD

Died Jan. 10, 1883

One can leave Dr. Mudd to the generally kind, appreciative fate posterity was destined to accord him. But it is hard to take leave of Frances, just as it is hard to take leave of Anna Surratt, another who had suffered so direly for being in the wrong place at the wrong time. Anna attended her brother's trial. In fact, it was she who persuaded Joseph Bradley to accept John's case. "If you had seen her," said Bradley, "you would have known that I could not have done otherwise. She did not weep; not a tear fell from her eyes. . . . Two years of long continued suffering had wasted that fountain."

Anna survived only, believed Bradley, "in the hope that she might one day see again her blessed mother." She sold the H Street boarding house for less than half its purported worth (the purchaser and subsequent tenants complained of being disturbed by the night meanderings of Mary's ghost) and left Washington forever. But Frances carried on at Rock Hill Farm. It was expected of her. It was what her husband would have wanted.

And in the years to come she had the staunch support of young Sam, Jr., who on his father's death gave up his job at Gallant Green and returned to operate the farm. He was only twenty but strong and lithe, with his father's prudence and persistence. What he created on that hill above Zachia Swamp reads like a monument to the hopes and dreams of the first Samuel Alexander Mudd. Described by his daughter Cecilia Dyer (who became Sister Mary Samuela of the Order of the Holy Cross), the farm appears as a veritable eden in the heart of southern Maryland.

Sister Samuela's verbal picture is too long to quote in full, slowed by such opening sentences as her tribute to Sam, Jr.: "Mother nature early planted in his soul the bud of the profession which later developed into full bloom gradually unfolding its petals to the universe and yielding a special charm to many admirers." Yet we see the whole family, including Frances and two grandsons, working like a singing army in the fields, planting corn and tobacco in the early spring, wheat in the fall; tending a flock of sheep, a herd of Guernsey and Holstein cattle; feeding pigs, ducks, geese, turkeys. ("Sam was kind and gentle to his farm animals," wrote Sister Samuela.)

They ground the corn into flour, cut and cured the tobacco, churned their own butter, sheared the sheep for wool to sell; replaced the old orchard with new fruit trees, from which they made cider and preserved the peaches, pears and plums. Everything was done by hand, by themselves, and "joyfully" if we credit Sister Samuela. The money flowed in. Sam started a fish pond for his boys, bought croquet sets for his daughters, made them all sleds, and in the evening "he played the violin or told stories of fox-hunting days."[12]

And what of Frances in this comfortable world? At night or in the sleepless early-morning hours did she ever imagine she heard a pounding on the door? Or awake to see through the window, on the fringes of a nightmare, two mounted figures waiting on the driveway in the moonlight? One can only hope not. Every bad dream must have an ending.

NOTES

1. FROM STRANGEWAYS BY THE ARK AND DOVE

1. Biographical and genealogical details of the Mudds throughout this chapter derive from Dr. Richard D. Mudd's two-volume history, *The Mudd Family of the United States*, published in Saginaw, Michigan, in 1951. Dr. Mudd was kind enough to supply the author with additional facts as occasionally needed.
2. Like the elusive town of Strangeways, the villages of Bryn and Wigan do not appear on many English maps, though they appear in *The International Atlas* (Rand McNally), p. 252, some eighteen miles northeast of Liverpool.
3. Richard D. Mudd, *op. cit.*, p. 411. Though the Calverts came to America and ultimately to Maryland seeking religious freedom for their Catholic followers, uninhibited freedom was not immediately realized. Puritan influence in the colonies was strong. There were, moreover, many Protestant immigrants in Cecil Calvert's group, and the second Lord Baltimore wisely decreed that Catholic worship should be "done as privately as may be." In 1654 the Maryland Assembly repealed the Act of Toleration and substituted a law denying freedom of worship to adherents of "papacy or prelacy." There followed a systematic persecution of Catholics in which ten were condemned to death and many forced to seek sanctuary in Virginia. In time the religious breach was healed and Catholics, though not always numerically superior, became the ruling social class in southern Maryland. In the interval, however, the private chapel with a somewhat surreptitious service was common.
4. Richard D. Mudd, *op. cit.*, Vol. I, pp. 694-95. This strange coincidence, a relationship ironic in light of subsequent events, is discussed at some length by Dr. Mudd, with genealogical lines traced back through several generations.
5. Joseph C. Robert, *The Story of Tobacco in America* (Knopf, 1949), pp. 10-12, 48-50.
6. Calvert R. Posey, *A History of Charles County* (La Plata, Maryland, 1960), p. 2. Mr. Posey quotes family sources. His great-grandfather, Adam Posey, was personally acquainted with many of southern Maryland's leading citizens in the early and middle years of the nineteenth century.

7. *Ibid.*, p. 2.
8. Nettie Mudd, *The Life of Dr. Samuel A. Mudd* (Neale Publishing Co., New York and Washington, 1906), pp. 23-24. Nettie Mudd's biography of her father, all too abbreviated but given substance by a collection of letters written in the doctor's later years, was republished with additional material by Dr. Richard Mudd, in Saginaw, Michigan, in 1962.
9. Facts concerning the life-style and work methods of the Maryland tobacco planter of this period were provided by Dr. Claude McKee, Extension Tobacco Specialist, University of Maryland. Additional material from Robert, *op. cit.*, Chapters 2 and 3.
10. Port Tobacco *Times*, from notices appearing in issues of August and September, 1845.
11. Lloyd Lewis, *Myths After Lincoln* (Harcourt, Brace, 1929), pp. 163-64. Additional information on Booth's early years, appearing here and elsewhere, come principally from Asia Booth Clarke's *The Unlocked Door* (Faber & Faber Ltd., London, 1938).
12. Richard D. Mudd, *op. cit.*, Vol. I, p. 515.
13. Mobile, Alabama, *Advertiser & Register*, August 8, 1865, p. 1, col. 7.
14. Richard D. Mudd, *op. cit.*, Vol I., p. 2.

2. GENTLEMAN PLANTER, M. D.

1. Robert, *op. cit.*, pp. 17-26.
2. Nettie Mudd, *op. cit.*, p. 25, refers to her father attending "St. John's College" in Frederick during this period. The correct name was Frederick College. Judge Edward S. Delaplaine of Frederick believes the confusion may have arisen from the college's close association with St. John's Church in Frederick, which contributed to its establishment.
3. Constance M. Green, *Washington: Village and Capital, 1800-1878* (Princeton University Press, 1952) Vol. I., pp. 103, 214, 378.
4. Quoted by Nettie Mudd, *op. cit.*, p. 27.
5. George H. Callcott, *A History of the University of Maryland* (Maryland Historical Society, Baltimore, 1966). This and other items on the Medical School from pp. 54-82. Callcott presents a wide-screen picture of education in Maryland in the mid-century period.
6. *Ibid.*, pp. 114-115.
7. *Ibid.*, p. 86.
8. Asia Booth Clarke, *op. cit.*, p. 112.

9. Posey, *op. cit.*, p. 4.
10. Richard R. Duncan, *The Social and Economic Impact of the Civil War on Maryland* (doctoral thesis submitted to Ohio State University), p. 210.
11. Samuel Mudd to Orestes A. Brownson, January 13, 1862. Original letter in O. A. Brownson collection, University of Notre Dame Archives.

3. THE DESPOT'S HEEL

1. Samuel Mudd to Orestes A. Brownson, *loc. cit.*, quoted by Nettie Mudd, p. 343.
2. *Ibid.*, p. 343.
3. Posey, *op. cit.*, p. 3.
4. Duncan, *op. cit.*, p. 90
5. Port Tobacco *Times*, October 24, 1861.
6. *Ibid.*, May 20, 1862.
7. *Ibid.*, December 19, 1861.
8. L. C. Baker to Secretary of State William H. Seward, letter dated November 27, 1861, reprinted in Baker's *History of the United States Secret Service* (Philadelphia, 1867.)
9. Nettie Mudd, *op. cit.*, pp. 341-42.
10. *Ibid.*, pp. 342-43.
11. *Ibid.*, pp. 343-45.
12. Posey, *op. cit.*, p. 4. Also M. B. Klapthor and P. D. Brown, *History of Charles County, Maryland* (La Plata, Maryland, 1958), pp. 124-25.

4. MARYLAND UNDERGROUND

1. Osborn H. Oldroyd, *The Assassination of Abraham Lincoln* (Washington, 1901), p. 67. O'Bierne's description of the swamp has been attributed also to George Alfred Townsend, correspondent for the New York *World,* from whom the passage was allegedly appropriated. Also quoted in Baker, *op. cit.*, p. 492.
2. Baker, *op. cit.*, p. 490.
3. Posey, *op. cit.*, pp. 7-8.
4. In a lecture delivered at Rockville, Maryland, December 8, 1870, Surratt himself described his operation in the Maryland underground. His account is quoted in part in Oldroyd, pp. 238–39.

5. R. J. Kimball to William Seward, January 3, 1865. Original letter in National Archives. War Department Records, File K, Document 12, JAO.
6. Benn Pitman, *The Assassination of President Lincoln and the Trial of the Conspirators* (Cincinnati, 1865), p. 71.
7. Albert Henry Mudd, quoted by Richard D. Mudd, op. cit., Vol I, p. 463.
8. Pitman, *op. cit.*, p. 166.
9. Lewis, *op. cit.*, p. 191.
10. *Official Records of the Union and Confederate Armies* (Washington, 1880-1901), Vol. XIX, Part 2, pp. 601-02.
11. The Northwest Conspiracy is well outlined in *The Concise Dictionary of American History* (Scribner's, 1940), p. 252. It is presented in more detail in James D. Horan's *Confederate Agent* (Crown, 1954). But an idea of the skulduggery involved is best presented in Pitman, *op. cit.*, pp. 24-54. In reviewing Pitman's record of testimonies of those involved, one must remain aware that these are the words of professed conspirators and secret agents, and subject to the usual protective evasions and calculated fabrications. Which leaves the reader to judge who did what to whom. No writer of detective fiction could tie a more fascinating knot.

5. A STRANGER CALLS

1. Pitman, *op. cit.*, pp. 25, 28, 31, 35–36, 38–39. Also Theodore Roscoe, *The Web of Conspiracy* (Prentice-Hall, 1929), pp. 21-42.
2. Oldroyd, *op. cit.*, pp. 149–50.
3. Roscoe, *op. cit.*, pp. 58–59.
4. Pitman, *op. cit.*, p. 178.
5. Dr. Mudd's statement quoted by Nettie Mudd, *op. cit.*, p. 44.
6. Pitman, *op. cit.*, p. 71.
7. Quoted by Nettie Mudd, *op. cit.*, p. 30.
8. Booth's letter is reprinted in full in Roscoe, *op, cit.*, pp. 534-36. Also, Francis Wilson, *John Wilkes Booth* (Houghton Mifflin, 1939).
9. Speech of January 14, 1863, quoted in *Biographical Memoir of Clement L. Vallandigham, by His Brother* (New York, 1864), p. 60.
10. Grenfell's part in the Northwest Conspiracy and the Camp Douglas affair is presented in Stephen Z. Starr's *Colonel Grenfell's Wars* (Louisiana State University Press, 1971), pp. 133-92.
11. *Ibid.*, p. 214.
12. *Ibid.*, p. 205.

6. SPINNING OF THE WEB

1. Dr. Mudd's account of this meeting is given in Nettie Mudd, *op. cit.*, pp. 43-44.
2. Wiechmann's version of meeting, Pitman, *op. cit.*, p. 114.
3. Oldroyd, *op. cit.*, pp. 153-58.
4. Mudd's and Dyer's activities as recounted by Dyer, Pitman, *op. cit.*, p. 190.
5. David M. DeWitt, *The Assassination of Abraham Lincoln* (Macmillan, 1909), pp. 65-68.
6. Roscoe, *op. cit.*, pp. 65-68.
7. Booth's innocent and stationary presence at the inauguration was recently confirmed by a photograph in the Meserve Collection in New York, showing the actor in top hat seated in the stands. What the photograph also purports to show is that five of Booth's alleged accomplices, along with Dr. Mudd, were also present just below the stands. The poor quality of the photography makes accurate identification almost impossible, and the individual we are asked to consider as Samuel Mudd bears little resemblance to portraits of the doctor. The controversial pictures appear in D. M. and P. B. Kunhardt's *Twenty Days* (New York, 1965), pp. 33, 34-35, 197.
8. The aborted kidnap attempt is described by John Surratt in a statement made on May 6, 1870, reprinted in Philip Van Doren Stern's *The Man Who Killed Lincoln* (Random House, 1939), appendix, p. viii.
9. Gardiner's account of this visit in Washington appears in Pitman, *op. cit.*, pp. 196-97. Dr. Mudd does not mention the trip in any of his statements relative to this period; apparently he considered it irrelevant or unimportant.
10. Lewis, *op. cit.*, pp. 58-59.
11. The "Dear John" letter is reprinted in full in Jim Bishop's *The Day Lincoln Was Shot* (Harper, 1955), pp. 58-59.

7. NO DEED SO FOUL

1. Booth's actions throughout this critical day have been variously recounted, notably by Bishop, Roscoe, Oldroyd, Lewis, and DeWitt in previously cited works. These accounts are, of course, reconstructions based on such clues as the props discovered in Lincoln's box, the recollections of barbers, barkeeps, stablemen, and individuals encountered as the actor moved about the city. None would stand up in a court of law; no two people

serve as witnesses to an act save the assassination. But all accounts, confirming one another, seem eminently probable.

2. A facsimile of the 1869 script of *Our American Cousin* by Tom Taylor—from which these extracts were taken—is still available from the New York offices of Samuel French. In addition, the Government Printing Office in Washington offers, as part of its Historical Handbook Series, a booklet entitled *Ford's Theater and the House Where Lincoln Died*, which describes the stage arrangement and scenery and the President's box as arranged for this performance. Pitman offers, and Oldroyd reprints, a diagram of the stage end of the theater along with a map of the immediate environs. Both Bishop's book and Margaret Leech's *Reveille in Washington* (Harper, 1941) present excellent maps of the capital city at this period. With these as aids, one can draw one's own kinetic picture of the action at Ford's Theater and the probable movements of the various assassins on the night of April 14.

3. Roscoe, *op. cit.*, p. 24. "To this day," writes Roscoe, "nobody knows if Johnson ever saw the card."

4. Matthews put the letter in his pocket, to deliver when convenient. But after the assassination he panicked, raced from the theater to his hotel room, and tore open the envelope. The contents, Mathews said, "made him sick," and he forthwith burned the letter in the grate. Later, however, he professed to remember most of its wording and especially Booth's final paragraph: "The moment has at length arrived when my plans must be changed. The world may censure me for what I am about to do, but I am sure that posterity will justify me. [signed] John Wilkes Booth - Payne - Atzerodt and Herold." Quoted in Wilson, *op. cit.*, p. 107.

5. Pitman, *op. cit.*, pp. 84-85. Cobb later reported to the authorities that the first passing stranger had given his name as Booth. But Lafayette Baker, as well as others, thought that such blatant self-identification could be only a ruse. The real Booth would certainly not give his right name.

6. Johnson went first to the bedside of the dying President, stayed only briefly, returned for a moment to the Kirkwood House —then disappeared. His actions and whereabouts thereafter, until he finally returned to his hotel at daylight, remained a mystery. His enemies would make much of this peculiar gap in time.

8. AN ASSASSIN RETURNS

1. Mudd's full statement regarding the injured man's visit, dated April 21, 1865, is in the National Archives, War Department Records, File E, 315, JAO. The account given in this chapter, paraphrased largely from the doctor's words, is modified only by certain comments made by Frances, quoted by her daughter Nettie, *op. cit.*, which in general accord with Mudd's narration.
2. Nettie Mudd, *op. cit.*, p. 31.
3. *Ibid.*, p. 32.
4. *Ibid.*, p. 33.
5. As recounted by Bean. Pitman, *op. cit.*, p. 203.
6. *Ibid.*, p. 88, 176.
7. As related by Hardy and Farrell. Pitman, *op. cit.*, p. 218-19.
8. Quoted in Nettie Mudd, *op. cit.*, p. 33.

9. DRAGNET

1. As related by George Mudd. Pitman, *op. cit.,* pp. 206-208.
2. *Ibid.*, p. 208.
3. *Ibid.*, p. 88.
4. The copy of Booth's incriminating telegram to O'Laughlin was obtained from Edward C. Stewart, telegraph operator at the Metropolitan Hotel, which Booth was known to have frequented. It was sent apparently after Booth learned of Lincoln's likely appearance at Ford's Theater for the performance of *Our American Cousin*. Reprinted in Pitman, p. 223, the message reads:

> WASHINGTON, MARCH 27, 1864.
> TO M. O'LAUGHLIN, ESQ., 57 NORTH EXETER STREET, BALTIMORE, MD. GET WORD TO SAM. COME ON, WITH OR WITHOUT HIM, WEDNESDAY MORNING. WE SELL THAT DAY FOR SURE. DON'T FAIL.
> J. WILKES BOOTH.

Stewart told the authorities he did not recognize the man who wrote and handed the message to him. He explained the incorrect date, 1864, which should have been 1865, as due to his use of "last year's blanks."

The "Dear John" letter did more than link Sam Arnold to John Wilkes Booth's conspiracy. It tended to link the assassination plot to the Confederate government by questioning "how it will be taken in R———d," presumably meaning Richmond. Jim Bishop reprints the letter in *The Day Lincoln Was Shot*, pp. 90-91.

5. Klapthor and Brown, *op. cit.*, pp. 130-31. Also Posey, *op. cit.*, pp. 16-18. Posey particularly, because of his family's connection with the principals involved, gives a convincing account of Booth's and Herold's refuge and attempts to cross the Potomac. Oldroyd, *op. cit.*, in his final chapter also discusses at some length the hideout and crossing of the river, after having himself retraced the flight route and interviewed those who aided Booth in his escape.

6. Booth's diary is reprinted in full in Nettie Mudd's *Life of Dr. Samuel A. Mudd*, pp. 240-42. Though the assassin mentions riding sixty miles through southern Maryland with a broken leg, he does not mention Mudd's name or his visit to the doctor's house. The existence of the diary was not made known to the public until Lafayette Baker published his *History of the United States Secret Service* in 1867. By that time its usefulness as evidence had passed. By that time, too, several vital pages had been excised, presumably by the War Department, suggesting government suppression of the truth, something that would become disturbingly familiar to a future generation.

7. Posey, *op. cit.*, p. 17.

8. The critical business of the boot presents a minor puzzle in the riddle of Samuel Mudd. Why had not the doctor thought of it till now? Or had he? Mudd says in one statement (to Colonel Wells) that Booth had "left the boot behind" and that it was not brought to his attention until the four detectives arrived. Yet he tells Frances to bring it down before he says he was reminded of its presence.

In another statement the doctor says that "a day or two" after Booth's visit he found the boot and "thought of sending it to the authorities, but it escaped my memory." Frances agrees with her husband that he first mentioned the boot but that he, not she, went up to fetch it. According to Detective Williams it was Mrs. Mudd who mentioned the boot, while Joshua Lloyd declares that Mudd was not even present when Lloyd and his associates arrived, and that Frances voluntarily produced the boot when the detectives told her they would have to search the house.

None of this might seem to be important if the discovery of this piece of evidence were not so important to the pursuit and apprehension of the culprits. How could an article as obtrusive as a knee-length riding boot escape the household's attention for a week, with none thinking of looking for it or seeking to examine it? How Sam and Frances could remember its discovery so differently, just six days after the event, also seems peculiar.

9. Pitman, *op. cit.*, p. 169.
10. Roscoe, *op. cit.*, pp. 539-42.
11. Washington *National Intelligencer*, April 22, 1865. National Archives Microfilm Publications.
12. Nettie Mudd, *op. cit.*, p. 34.

10. THE SHAPE OF DESPAIR

1. Margaret Leech, *Reveille in Washington* (Harper, 1941), pp. 141-42.
2. James J. Williamson, *Prison Life in the Old Capitol* (West Orange, New Jersey, 1911), p. 42.
3. John A. Marshall, *American Bastille* (Hartley, Philadelphia, 1872), p. 330.
4. Williamson, *op. cit.*, p. 26.
5. Leech, *op. cit.*, p. 141.
6. *Ibid.*, pp. 432, 141.
7. "Old Capitol Prison," *Maryland Historical Magazine*, Vol. 64, No. 4, Winter 1970, p. 405.
8. Leech, *op. cit.*, p. 157.
9. *Ibid.*, pp. 432, 441.
10. Nettie Mudd, *op. cit.*, pp. 34-35.
11. *Ibid.*, pp. 35-36.
12. *Ibid.*, p. 36.
13. Washington *Evening Star*, April 29, 1865. National Archives Microfilm Publications.
14. Hal Higdon, *The Union Versus Dr. Mudd* (Chicago, 1964), p. 81
15. Samuel Arnold, "The Lincoln Conspiracy," *Baltimore American*, December, 1901.
16. Pitman, *op. cit.*, p. 403.
17. Lewis, *op. cit.*, p. 227.
18. Higdon, *op. cit.*, p. 93
19. Pitman, *op. cit.*, pp. 18-21.

11. COURT OF CONVICTION

1. Quoted in Leech, *op. cit.*, p. 412.
2. Among the newspaper correspondents present at the trial was Noah Brooks of the Sacramento *Union*, then one of the leading papers on the Pacific coast. A former resident of Illinois, Brooks knew President Lincoln well and, through the President, most of the leading lights of Washington in 1865. In his subsequent book, *Washington in Lincoln's Time* (Century, 1895), Brooks gives an intimate firsthand account of the trial and its procedure, with emphasis on personalities and atmosphere; see pp. 267-75.
3. Pitman, *op. cit.*, p. 23.
4. Quoted in Higdon, *op. cit.*, p. 99.
5. Noah Brooks, *op. cit.*, p. 271.
6. Putting aside historical accuracy, Reverdy Johnson's role in the defense of Mary Surratt was partly the subject of John Patrick's play, *The Story of Mary Surratt*, produced on Broadway in 1947. Though taking all the necessary license of the dramatist and rearranging chronology to suit his needs, Patrick manages to give a feeling of great authenticity to the trial, its abuses, distortions, and conflicts of emotions, along with Reverdy Johnson's eloquence expressed in his actual words in court. (Typescript of the play in possession of Samuel Carter.)
7. Pitman, *op. cit.*, p. 26.
8. *Ibid.*, p. 114. Pitman, in his transcript of the trial, did not always use the question-and-answer form presented here. He also resorted from time to time to convenient paraphrasing. This author has therefore used both Pitman's record and the word-by-word transcript published in Washington's *National Intelligencer*, checking one against the other and combining as necessary. The *Intelligencer's* daily transcript was obtained from National Archives Microfilm Publications, Microcopy 599, Roll 16.
9. Pitman, *op. cit.*, p. 175.
10. *Ibid.*, p. 177.
11. T. M. Harris, *Assassination of Lincoln; a History of the Great Conspiracy* (American Citizen Co., Boston, 1892), p. 77.
12. Pitman, *op. cit.*, p. 170
13. *Ibid.*, pp. 173-74.
14. *Ibid.*, p. 169.
15. *Ibid.*, p. 88.
16. Quoted by Nettie Mudd, *op. cit.*, p. 37. Frances' belief that Daniel Thomas had slanted his testimony with a view to collecting

a reward was supported by several witnesses during the trial and was also mentioned in General Ewing's summary for the defense. When the government posted its offers of reward for evidence against the suspects, Thomas approached several south-county residents, with the handbill in his hand, asking what they thought his testimony against Samuel Mudd might be worth in terms of dollars and requesting a certificate stating their belief in his right to that amount.

According to one of those consulted, William J. Watson of Prince Georges County: "He [Thomas] said he thought his portion of the reward ought to be $10,000, and he asked me if I would not, as the best loyal man in Prince Georges County, give him a certificate of how much I thought he ought to be entitled to."

None of the people thus approached complied with Thomas' request. Pitman, *op. cit.*, pp. 186, 188–189.

17. Nettie Mudd, *op. cit.*, p. 38. It is curious to find Mudd quoting the same phrase in later letters to his wife. He tells Frances of complaining of his prison sentence to a certain Judge Turner, who "remarked that somebody had to suffer, and it was just as well that I should as anybody else."

18. *Ibid.*, p. 38.

19. *Ibid.*, pp. 38–39.

20. Pitman, *op. cit.*, pp. 85–87. This was damning evidence against Mrs. Surratt. When grilled by the defense as to her alleged use of the term "shooting irons," Lloyd stuck to the words, though he was hazy about other circumstances of Mary's visit and confessed to the court, "I was right smart in liquor that afternoon."

21. The reporters' comments are noted in Higdon, *op. cit.*, p. 99.

12. THE WEIGHTED SCALES

1. Pitman, *op. cit.*, p. 179.

2. *Ibid.*, p. 183.

3. *Ibid.*, p. 179.

4. *Ibid.*, p. 183

5. *Ibid.*, p. 185.

6. *Ibid.*, pp. 184–185.

7. *Ibid.*, p. 175.

8. Leech, *op. cit.*, p. 149.

9. Pitman, *op. cit.*, pp. 206–208.
10. *Ibid.*, p. 209.
11. *Ibid.*, p. 324.
12. *Ibid.*, p. 332.
13. *Ibid.*, pp. 162–163.
14. *Ibid.*, p. 153.
15. *Ibid.*, pp. 107–108.
16. *Ibid.*, pp. 124–125.
17. Jenkins was a liability to his sister. In addition to his bullying beratement of all who spoke against her, he was throughout the war given to intemperate remarks against the Union, allegedly declaring that he would never serve "under such a God damned Government as the Government of the United States." Mary Surratt's defense is one of the saddest segments of the trial, because of the disappointing witnesses her attorneys were forced to rely on: Detective Cottingham, who reversed his testimony in court; brother "Zad," an outspoken secessionist; her friend and onetime boarder, Augustus Howell, about whom the generally imperturbable court reporter, Pitman, wrote in despair, "we can not present the contradictions and prevarications of this witness. . . ." Pitman, *op. cit.*, p. 135.

13. JOURNEY INTO DARKNESS

1. Pitman, *op. cit.*, pp. 246–47.
2. David DeWitt, one legal-minded student of the trial, believed that the commission and the jurists overreacted to the escape of John Surratt. He had been publicly proclaimed one of the principal conspirators and now apparently was off, scot-free. Mary would have to be punished in John's stead.

   The press had not helped Mary's cause, any more than some who testified in her defense. It was public knowledge that Augustus Howell, who appeared in her behalf, had been a notorious blockade runner during the war. In fact Mary's name was much more closely linked than Dr. Mudd's to rebel activists and to the actual assassins, Paine, Herold, Atzerodt, and Booth himself, who had been so often at the widow's house.

   But Theodore Roscoe (*Web of Conspiracy,* p. 487) advances one of the more likely reasons for the weighted verdict, namely, Secretary Stanton's interference. Stanton wanted Mrs. Surratt sentenced to be hanged "as an example." Judge Advocate Holt went along with Stanton. A deal was made. If the commission agreed to pass the death sentence, Stanton would then support a subsequent plea for clemency. The plea was entered, as here noted.

3. DeWitt, *op. cit.*, p. 284.
4. *Ibid.*, pp. 284–85.
5. Statement made to a correspondent for the New York *Tribune*, quoted by Higdon, *op. cit.*, p. 131.
6. *Ibid.*, pp. 128–29.
7. Nettie Mudd. *op. cit.*, p. 40.
8. Now, as throughout the trial, backyard gossip fed on the fact that Mary Surratt was a Roman Catholic, as were Mudd, Atzerodt, and Herold, John Surratt had studied for the priesthood, and it was rumored (without any evidence) that John Wilkes Booth had recently switched from the Episcopal to the Catholic Church. Lincoln was said to have been "a prominent heretic," offensive to the papal government. Hence, the assassination plot, although directed from Richmond, had originated in the Vatican or had at least been blessed with Vatican approval. This preposterous theory never gained voice above a whisper.
9. Lewis, *op. cit.*, p. 244. These side remarks from the condemned, presumably reported by their executioners, vary so much with each account that no one could be certain of them. In place of "Thank you, Captain," for example, Paine was quoted as having said, "Captain, you know best."
10. Samuel Arnold, *Defense and Prison Experiences of a Lincoln Conspirator,* p. 65. This little-known manuscript written by Arnold at various times during his imprisonment and after his release were discovered and published by Charles F. Heartman in Hattiesburg, Mississippi, in 1943. The volume is filed in the Library of Congress.
11. Nettie Mudd, *op. cit.*, pp. 110–11.
12. *Ibid.*, p. 112.

14. DEVIL'S ISLAND

1. A history and description of the fortress-prison is provided by the U. S. Department of the Interior in a National Parks pamphlet entitled *Fort Jefferson National Monument*, Government Printing Office, Washington, D.C., reprinted in 1971. Perhaps the most impressive ruin on the continent, the fort is in the process of being restored but as of this writing remains much as it was in Dr. Mudd's day.

2. George A. England, "Tortugas Tales," *Isles of Romance*, (Century, 1929), pp. 40–41.
3. Nettie Mudd, *op. cit.*, p. 135.
4. Arnold, *op. cit.*, pp. 68–69.
5. Nettie Mudd, *op. cit.*, p. 114.
6. *Ibid.*, p. 41.
7. *Ibid.*, pp. 346–47.
8. *Ibid.*, 117.
9. Dutton's sworn affidavit, dated August 23, 1865, is reprinted in Pitman, *op. cit.*, appendix, p. 421. Dutton is not, of course, quoting any written statement signed by Dr. Mudd. There seems no credible reason why Mudd should make such a verbal confession, there was nothing to gain and his attorneys were still working on the case. Theodore Roscoe *(Web of Conspiracy,* p. 492) advances one possible explanation: "The story smacks of invention in the Bureau of Military Justice, which seems to have become an industrious fiction factory. Soon after the four conspiracy trial survivors were banished to limbo, reports were leaked that all the hangees had 'confessed' on the eve of execution day. So far as is known, no one ever saw actual transcripts of these last minute confessions." Nor did anyone see any written confession supporting Dutton's affidavit.

Samuel Arnold, who does not claim to have overheard the interview, nevertheless recorded that Dutton "made affidavits of many things spoken" by the prisoners aboard the ship. Arnold concludes: "Capt. Dutton was as false to honor as to truth . . . and no doubt has received his paid reward for fidelity to his peers." Arnold, *op. cit.*, p. 64. Dutton is not listed, however, among those who received government money for information concerning the accused, although much of the reward money still remained unpaid.
10. Dispatch quoted by Nettie Mudd, *op. cit.*, pp. 113–14.
11. Nettie Mudd, *op. cit.*, pp. 42–48.
12. *Ibid.*, p. 120.
13. Arnold, *op. cit.*, p. 73. As a clerk in the provost marshal's office, Arnold apparently was able to see and copy all communications passing to and from the post. He includes a number of them in his written memoirs, careful to label each item "A True Copy."
14. *Ibid.*, p. 72.
15. Nettie Mudd, *op. cit.*, p. 119.

15. BREAK FOR FREEDOM

1. England, *op. cit.*, p. 43.
2. A. O'D., "Thirty Months in the Dry Tortugas," *Galaxy Miscellany*, February, 1869, pp. 286–87. A. O'D., who is not identified by more than his initials, appears to have been a New Hampshire private in the garrison whose term of duty, seemingly longer than the average, extended between 1865 and 1868.
3. Nettie Mudd, *op. cit.*, p. 120.
4. *Ibid.*, pp. 131–32.
5. *Ibid.*, p. 121.
6. Mudd to Jeremiah Dyer, October 21, 1865. Quoted in Nettie Mudd, *op. cit.*, pp. 350–51.
7. Original in the Illinois State Historical Library, Springfield.
8. Arnold, *op. cit.*, pp. 74–75.
9. Letter published in *Ohio Crisis*, October 11, 1865.
10. Nettie Mudd, *op. cit.*, p. 132.
11. *Ibid.*, p. 133.
12. DeWitt, *op. cit.*, pp. 184–85.

16. THE CHAIN GANG

1. Stephen Z. Starr, *Colonel Grenfell's Wars* (Louisiana State University Press, 1971), p. 10.
2. *Ibid.*, pp. 7–8.
3. T. P. McElrath, "Annals of the War . . . Story of a Soldier of Fortune," Philadelphia *Weekly Times*, May 3, 1879. McElrath was a captain of the 5th U. S. Artillery stationed at Fort Jefferson in Grenfell's time and (following events to be narrated) came in possession of Grenfell's diary—from which this extract is taken.
4. Quoted in Nettie Mudd, *op. cit.*, pp. 140–41.
5. Arnold, *op. cit.*, p. 78.
6. Nettie Mudd, *op. cit.*, p. 139.
7. Arnold, *op. cit.*, p. 77.
8. Jeremiah Dyer to Frances Mudd, November 6, 1865. Quoted in Nettie Mudd, *op. cit.*, pp. 137–38.
9. Arnold, *op. cit.*, p. 81.

10. Mudd to Jeremiah Dyer, December 25, 1865. Nettie Mudd, *op. cit.*, pp. 150–51.
11. *Ibid.*, p. 152.
12. *Ibid.*, pp. 148–50.

17. "I HAVE GROWN OLD IN MY YOUTH"

1. Nettie Mudd, *op. cit.*, p. 161.
2. *Ibid.*, p. 172.
3. Arnold, *op. cit.*, p. 85.
4. Starr, *op. cit.*, p. 289.
5. The speaker was Representative John Wentworth of Chicago, but he was quoting from a letter he had received from a Colonel Absalom B. Moore, who had "had the misfortune to fall into the hands of this infamous rebel [Grenfell] as a prisoner of war when he was adjutant general of John Morgan's brigands." The quotation is from Starr, *op. cit.*, pp. 293–94.
6. Dr. Richard D. Mudd, Samuel Mudd's grandson, makes much of this point in his *Petition to the President in the Case of Dr. Samuel A. Mudd*, first submitted to the Chief Executive in 1968, then revised and resubmitted in 1970—in a continuing family effort to clear the ancestral doctor's name. On the face of it, Salmon Chase's arbitrary dismissal of the writ of *habeas corpus* is contrary to judicial procedure if not downright unconstitutional. Dr. Richard Mudd observes that Chase gave little personal time to the case and, having been President Lincoln's appointee, might well have been biased against the alleged conspirators. That there is no written record of Chase's opinion in the matter is peculiar, and the family is still searching for more clarification.
7. Nettie Mudd, *op. cit.*, pp. 178–79.
8. *Ibid.*, p. 192.
9. *Ibid.*, p. 185.
10. *Ibid.*, p. 186.
11. *Ibid.*, p. 193.
12. Grenfell to H. L. Stone, January 15, 1866. Quoted in Starr, *op. cit.*, p. 285.
13. McElrath, "Annals of War . . . ," Philadelphia *Weekly Times,* May 3, 1879.
14. Nettie Mudd, *op. cit.*, p. 206.
15. *Ibid.*, p. 218.

18. WHEN ROGUES FALL OUT

1. Communications quoted by Oldroyd, *op. cit.,* pp. 230–31.
2. Nettie Mudd, *op. cit.,* p. 220.
3. *Ibid.,* p. 235.
4. *Ibid.,* p. 253.
5. Dyer to Frances Mudd, April 12, 1867. Nettie Mudd, *op. cit.,* p. 354.
6. *Ibid.,* p. 234. Turner is a murky figure in Mudd's life and trial. Though a member of the Bureau of Military Justice, he apparently took no part whatever in the trial proceedings, and his name appears nowhere in the records.
7. Nettie Mudd, *op. cit.,* pp. 231–32.
8. *Ibid.,* p. 230.
9. Arnold, *op. cit.,* p. 103.
10. Grenfell to Marie Pearce-Serocold, June 30, 1867. *Filson Club Historical Quarterly,* XXXIV, 1960, pp. 8–23.
11. Arnold, *op. cit.,* p. 105.
12. Nettie Mudd, *op. cit.,* pp. 246–47.
13. DeWitt, *op. cit.,* pp. 193–94.
14. Nettie Mudd, *op. cit.,* p. 250.
15. *Ibid.,* p. 239.
16. *Ibid.,* p. 252.

19. A TIME FOR DYING

1. Simon Harcourt-Smith, "Yellow Jack," *History Today* (London), Vol. XXIII, No. 9, September, 1973, pp. 618–21.
2. Nettie Mudd, *op. cit.,* p. 255.
3. *Ibid.,* p. 256.
4. *Ibid.,* p. 258.
5. Mudd kept a detailed journal of his day-to-day battle with yellow fever at the prison. His daughter quotes what she refers to as "a short extract" on pages 286–95 of her biography of the doctor. If only an extract, it still gives a comprehensive picture of his extraordinary work against such dreadful odds. He does not boast of his pleasant confidence-instilling manner at the bedsides of soldiers and prisoners alike—something they would acknowledge fully later—but he does admit to having discovered, "I could do more with nine cases out of ten by a few consoling and inspiring words, than with all the medicine known to me in the materia medica."

6. These biographical notes on Whitehurst were assembled from typescript material in the Dade County Public Library, Key West, Florida.
7. Nettie Mudd, *op. cit.,* pp. 262, 275.
8. Starr, *op. cit.,* p. 310.
9. England, *op. cit.,* p. 56.
10. A. O'D, *op. cit.,* p. 285. Although the writer mentions only "three political prisoners"—presumably Mudd, Arnold, and Spangler (after O'Laughlin's death)—Grenfell also fell into this category, leaving four remaining in the prison.

20. RESURRECTION

1. A. O'D., *op. cit.,* p. 284.
2. Grenfell to H. L. Stone, January 15, 1868, Stone Family Papers, Kentucky Historical Association, Frankfort, Kentucky.
3. Nettie Mudd, *op. cit.,* p. 279.
4. Arnold, *op. cit.,* pp. 116–19.
5. *Ibid.,* pp. 119–20.
6. *Ibid.,* p. 120.
7. James D. Horan, *Confederate Agent* (Crown, 1954), p. 283.
8. Nettie Mudd, *op. cit.,* pp. 309–10.
9. Dr. Richard Mudd cites this decision as another miscarriage of justice in his *Petition to the President in the Case of Dr. Samuel A. Mudd.* He notes that "Judge Thomas J. Boynton, who was appointed by President Lincoln as the youngest Federal Judge of record to that date, would be likely to follow the lead of the Chief Justice," who had ruled against the previous plea of *habeas corpus.* Presumably the attorney appearing for the prisoners in Key West was Anderson Peeler, although there is no record of the hearing. None of the prisoners was allowed to attend the hearing, though they were only seventy miles away.
10. Nettie Mudd, *op. cit.,* pp. 310–11, 315.
11. *Ibid.,* p. 358.
12. *Ibid.,* p. 316.
13. *Ibid.,* p. 316.
14. *Ibid.,* p. 355.
15. National Archives, Records of the War Department, Office of the Adjutant General, File P, Doc. 88, 1869.
16. Quoted in Nettie Mudd, *op. cit.,* p. 319.

21. AVE ATQUE VALE

1. Nettie Mudd, *op. cit.*, pp. 320–21.
2. Richard D. Mudd, *The Mudd Family of the United States,* Vol. I, p. 540.
3. Nettie Mudd, *op. cit.*, p. 321.
4. Quoted in Higdon, *op. cit.*, pp. 203–204. The reporter's name is not recorded, but the New York *Herald* had been one of the more militant Northern journals in demanding the "halter and the gallows" for the Lincoln conspirators, and in insisting that "justice should now take its course against treason and traitors wherever found." Apparently the relatively sympathetic picture portrayed in this instance did not include the doctor's name among among those "traitors."
5. Nettie Mudd, *op. cit.*, pp. 321–22.
6. Ned Spangler's manuscript, now in the possession of the Mudd family, is presented in full in Nettie's biography of her father, pp. 322–26. Spangler's sense of loyalty, to John Wilkes Booth among others, never left him. He describes his own innocent actions at the theater on the night of the assassination but never directly implicates the actor. "I heard a shot fired and saw a man run across the stage," he writes. "I did not recognize the man. . . ." He had of course been an old family retainer at the Booth plantation in Bel Air. Perhaps that explains his sole complaint regarding his late benefactor: "Bóoth promised to pay me for my trouble [tending his horse at the theater stable] but never did."
7. The New Hampshire private, A. O'D., stationed in the barracks at the time, wrote shortly after Grenfell's escape, "It seems . . . that Colonel Grenfel [sic] did actually reach Cuba, and at last accounts was about to sail for Europe." He does not quote his authority for the statement. *Galaxy,* p. 287.
8. A. W. McMullen, "Was It Colonel Grenfell?" *Confederate Veteran,* Vol. XXXVII, p. 25.
9. Whitehurst papers in Dade County Public Library, Key West.
10. Roscoe, *op. cit.*, pp. 517–23. The author reproduces the two photographs mentioned in this context as illustrating at least "the fantastic difficulties of body identification in the day before scientific necropsies and fingerprinting."
11. Quoted by Roscoe, p. 525, from a letter written by Lloyd Lewis to the Washington *Star*, May 18, 1929.
12. Sister M. Samuela, "Life of Samuel A. Mudd II," reprinted by Richard D. Mudd, *op. cit.*, pp. 554–56.

BIBLIOGRAPHY

ARNOLD, SAMUEL B., *Defense and Prison Experiences of a Lincoln Conspirator.* Hattiesburg, Mississippi, Book Farm, 1943.

BAARLAG, KARL, *Island of Adventure.* New York, Farrar & Rinehart, 1940.

BAINDER, HERMAN, *Maryland's Reaction to Andrew Johnson.* College Park, Maryland, University of Maryland, 1949.

BAKER, LAFAYETTE C., *History of the United States Secret Service.* Philadelphia, published by the author, 1867.

BATES, FINIS L., *The Escape and Suicide of John Wilkes Booth.* Memphis, Pilcher Printing Co., 1907.

BISHOP, JIM, *The Day Lincoln Was Shot.* New York, Harper, 1955.

BOWERS, CLAUDE G., *The Tragic Era.* New York, Literary Guild, 1929.

BROOKS, Noah, *Washington in Lincoln's Time.* New York, Century, 1896.

BROWNE, JEFFERSON, *Key West, The Old and the New.* St. Augustine, Florida, Record Co., 1912.

BRYAN, GEORGE S., *The Great American Myth.* New York, Carrick & Evans, 1940.

BURNETT, H. L., *Some Incidents in the Trial of President Lincoln's Assassins.* New York, Appleton, 1891.

CALLCOTT, GEORGE H., *A History of the University of Maryland.* Baltimore, Maryland Historical Society, 1966.

CAREY, GEORGE G., *Maryland Folklore and Folklife.* Cambridge, Maryland, Tidewater Publishers, 1970.

CARTER, HODDING, *The Angry Scar.* New York, Doubleday, 1959.

CLARKE, ASIA BOOTH, *The Unlocked Book.* New York, Putnam's, 1938.

CONRAD, THOMAS N., *The Rebel Scout.* Washington, D.C., National Publishing, 1904.

CORDELL, EUGENE F., *Historical Sketch of the University of Maryland School of Medicine.* Baltimore, Friedenwalk Press, 1891.

DEWITT, DAVID M., *The Assassination of Abraham Lincoln and Its Expiation.* New York, Macmillan, 1909.

DEWITT, DAVID M., *The Judicial Murder of Mary E. Surratt.* Baltimore, J. Murphy & Co., 1895.

DODD, WILLIAM E., *Statesmen of the Old South.* New York, Macmillan, 1911.

DOSTER, WILLIAM E., *Lincoln and Episodes of the Civil War.* New York, Putnam's, 1915.

DUNCAN, RICHARD R., *The Social and Economic Impact of the Civil War on Maryland.* Thesis submitted to Ohio State University, 1963.

EDWARDS, ELLEN, *Maryland During the Reconstruction Period.* Minneapolis, University of Minnesota Press, 1928.

EISENSCHIML, OTTO, *Why Was Lincoln Murdered?* Boston, Little, Brown, 1937.

————, *In the Shadow of Lincoln's Death*. New York, Wilfred Funk, 1940.

ELLIS, JOHN B., *The Sights and Secrets of the National Capital*. New York, U. S. Publishing Co., 1869.

ENGLAND, GEORGE A., *Isles of Romance*. New York, Century, 1929.

FLOWER, FRANK A., *Edwin McMasters Stanton*. Akron, Saafield Publishing Co., 1905.

FRANKLIN, JOHN H., *Reconstruction after the Civil War*. Chicago, University of Chicago Press, 1961.

FORT JEFFERSON PRISON BOOK. Selected pages, Report of Guards, 1867.

GOBRIGHT, LAWRENCE A., *Recollections of Men and Things at Washington during the Third of a Century*. Philadelphia, Claxton, Ramsen, 1869.

GREEN, CONSTANCE M., *Washington: Village and Capital, 1800–1878* (two vols.). Princeton, Princeton University Press, 1962.

GUTHEIM, FREDERICK A., *The Potomac*. New York, Rinehart, 1949.

HIGDON, HAL, *The Union vs. Dr. Mudd*. Chicago, Discoverers Press, 1964.

HOLDER, J. B., "The Dry Tortugas." New York, *Harper's* Magazine, July, 1868.

HOLLAND, CLAUDE V., *Tortugas Run*. Bonita Springs, Florida, Hol-land Books, 1972.

HORAN, JAMES D., *Confederate Agent*. New York, Crown. 1954.

HARRIS, T. M., *Assassination of Lincoln; a History of the Great Conspiracy*. Boston, American Citizen Co., 1892.

KIMMEL, STANLEY, *The Mad Booths of Maryland*. New York, Bobbs-Merrill, 1940.

KLAPTHOR, M. B. and BROWN, P. D., *The History of Charles County, Maryland*. La Plata, Maryland, Charles County Tercentenary, 1958.

KUNHARDT, D. M. and P.B., *Twenty Days*. New York, Castle Books, 1965.

LAUGHLIN, CLARA E., *The Death of Lincoln*. New York, Doubleday, Page, 1909.

LEECH, MARGARET, *Reveille in Washington*. New York, Harper, 1941.

LEWIS, LLOYD, *Myths After Lincoln*. New York, Harcourt, Brace, 1929.

LONG, E. B., *The Civil War Day by Day*. New York, Doubleday, 1971.

MANAKEE, HAROLD R., *Maryland in the Civil War*. Baltimore, Maryland Historical Society, 1961.

MARSHALL, JOHN A., *American Bastille*. Philadelphia, Hartley, 1883.

MANUCY,ALBERT, "The Gibraltar of the Gulf of Mexico." Gainesville, *Florida Historical Quarterly*, Vol. 21, No. 4, April, 1948.

McCARTHY, BURKE, *The Suppressed Truth about the Assassination of Abraham Lincoln*. Washington, published by the author, 1922.

McKEE, CLAUDE G., *Producing Maryland Tobacco*. College Park, Maryland, University of Maryland, 1963.

MUDD, NETTIE, *The Life of Dr. Samuel A. Mudd*. Washington, Neale Publishing Co., 1906.

MUDD, RICHARD D., *The Mudd Family of the United States* (two vols.). Saginaw, Michigan, published by the author, 1951.

O'D., A., "Thirty Months in the Dry Tortugas." New York, *Galaxy Miscellany*, February, 1869.

OLDROYD, OSBORN H., *The Assassination of Abraham Lincoln*. Washington, published by the author, 1901.

PITMAN, BENN, *The Assassination of President Lincoln and the Trial of the Conspirators*. Cincinnati, Moore, Wilstrach & Baldwin, 1865.

POORE, BEN P., *Perley's Reminiscences*. Philadelphia, Hubbard, 1886.

Port Tobacco *Times*. Selected news reports and notices from issues published 1845–1865.

POSEY, CALVERT R. and JUDITH L., *A History of the Role Charles County Played in the Civil War*. La Plata, Maryland, Times Crescent, 1960.

PRATT, FLETCHER, *Stanton, Lincoln's Secretary of War*. New York, Norton, 1953.

ROBERT, JOSEPH C., *The Story of Tobacco in America*. Chapel Hill, North Carolina, University of North Carolina Press, 1949.

ROBINSON, STUART, *Infamous Perjuries of the Bureau of Military Justice*. Louisville, published by the author, 1865.

ROSCOE, THEODORE, *The Web of Conspiracy*. Englewood Cliffs, New Jersey, Prentice-Hall, 1959.

ROSS, ISHBEL, *Crusades and Crinolines*. New York, Harper & Row, 1963.

STARR, JOHN W., *Lincoln's Last Day*. New York, Frederick A. Stokes, 1922.

STARR, STEPHEN Z., *Colonel Grenfell's Wars*. Baton Rouge, Louisiana State University Press, 1971.

STERN, PHILIP VAN DOREN, *The Man Who Killed Lincoln*. New York, Random House, 1939.

STRYKER, LLOYD P., *Andrew Johnson, a Study in Courage*. New York, Macmillan, 1929.

TODD, CHARLES B., *Story of the City of Washington*. New York, Putnam's, 1889.

TOWNSEND, GEORGE A., *The Life, Crime, and Capture of John Wilkes Booth*. New York, Dick & Fitzgerald, 1865.

U. S. DEPARTMENT OF THE INTERIOR, *Fort Jefferson National Monument*. Washington, Government Printing Office, reprinted 1971.

U. S. GOVERNMENT PRINTING OFFICE, *The Trial of John H. Surratt*. Washington, 1867.

Washington *Daily National Intelligencer*. Selected news reports from issues published during 1864 and 1865, from the files of the Library of Congress.

Washington *Evening Star*. Selected news reports from issues published during 1865, from the files of the Library of Congress.

WILSON, FRANCIS, *John Wilkes Booth*. Boston, Houghton Mifflin, 1939.

WINSTON, ROBERT W., *Andrew Johnson, Plebian and Patriot*. New York, Henry Holt, 1928.

Index

(Continued from front flap)

All that is definitively known is that he did indeed provide medical care for John Wilkes Booth as the wounded actor fled Washington after committing the crime, that the two men had met previously and that Mudd's viewpoints and attitudes were sympathetic to the Southern cause.

Around these facts the government, pushed and exhorted by its implacable and vindictive Secretary of War, Edward P. Stanton, constructed a case that may well have involved suborned witnesses and perjured testimony. Even more dubious was the legitimacy of the trial itself, in which nine civilians, including Mudd and Mary Surratt, the Washington boardinghouse keeper, were tried by a military tribunal in time of peace. THE RIDDLE OF DR. MUDD recreates the dramatic courtroom scenes and then continues to describe the gruesome fate that awaited the doctor in a lonely plague-filled prison on the aptly named chain of islands called Dry Tortugas. Here is readable and intriguing history focused on a neglected and puzzling personality who is finally receiving a well-overdue biography.

Upper Mar

RRATT'S
VERN
G E

T. B.

C O U

cataway

C H

C

IN 1865

0   2   4 Mi.

Showing Booth's
Probable Escape Route